SOFTWARE REUSE

WILEY SERIES IN SOFTWARE BASED SYSTEMS

WILEY

Series Editors **Colin Tully**
                 Ian Pyle

KRONLÖF (ed): Method Integration: Concepts and Case Studies

THOMÉ (ed): Systems Engineering: Principles and Practice of Computer-based Systems Engineering

SCHEFSTRÖM and VAN DEN BROEK (eds): Tool Integration: Environments and Frameworks

PYLE, HRUSCHKA, LISSANDRE and JACKSON: Real-Time Systems: Investigating Industrial Practice

KARLSSON (ed): Software Reuse: A Holistic Approach

SOFTWARE REUSE
A Holistic Approach

Edited by
Even-André Karlsson
Q-Labs, Sweden

JOHN WILEY & SONS
Chichester • New York • Brisbane • Toronto • Singapore

Copyright © 1995 by John Wiley & Sons Ltd.
Baffins Lane, Chichester
West Sussex PO19 1UD, England

National 01243 779777
International (+44) 1243 779777

Other Wiley Editorial Offices

John Wiley & Sons, Inc., 605 Third Avenue,
New York, NY 10158-0012, USA

Jacaranda Wiley Ltd, 33 Park Road, Milton,
Queensland 4064, Australia

John Wiley & Sons (Canada) Ltd, 22 Worcester Road,
Rexdale, Ontario M9W 1L1, Canada

John Wiley & Sons (SEA) Pte Ltd, 37 Jalan Pemimpin #05-04,
Block B, Union Industrial Building, Singapore 2057

British Library Cataloguing in Publication Data

A catalogue record for this book is available from the British Library

ISBN 0 471 95489 6; 0 471 95819 0 (pbk)
Produced from camera-ready copy supplied by the editor using
Framemaker
Printed and bound in Great Britain by Bookcraft (Bath) Ltd
This book is printed on acid-free paper responsibly manufactured from
sustainable forestation, for which at least two trees are planted for each
one used for paper production.

Contents

Preface

The goal of a software organization is to build useful working software systems in time and within given economic constraints. In such a situation, what would be better than to reuse parts of existing well-functioning systems to achieve these goals? Even if this sounds desirable, it is not easy to achieve.

The essence of software reuse is to use any information, artifact or product held in the software company's inventory. The reusable element can be code, requirement or design specifications, or knowledge of the domain. It can also includes processes, methods and templates which are known to be effective in specific cases.

The main purpose of this book is to present a sound holistic foundation to enable software reuse to succeed, covering both organizational and methodological aspects. We have tried to give the synthesis of our four years of reuse experience in the ESPRIT III project #7808 REBOOT ("REuse Based on Object-Oriented Techniques"), during which the methodology has been developed. This book has been a living document, with three releases during the life of the project, and the proposed methodology has been extensively tried out and debated in applications within and outside the project.

Many parts of the work have been presented in international journals and conferences. We have also paid a lot of attention to other published experiences which have helped us to consolidate our approach.

The book is accompanied by training material. We use this to present the methodology to the various participants (managers, project leaders, developers, librarians, etc.) in a company which decides to adapt to reuse, and to teach university students as well. We have also developed a *repository* and a complete set of tools supporting reuse which are now being incorporated in the REBOOT partner's commercial software development environment.

We like to illustrate the REBOOT holistic approach to reuse with the following figure:

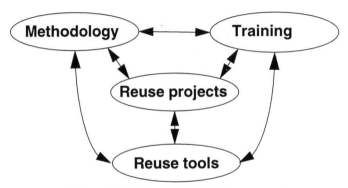

Figure 1 : The REBOOT holistic approach

We strongly emphasize that any organization wishing to sustain reuse must carefully consider all these four elements.

We are enthusiastic about reuse, and have found that it is applicable to almost any kind of application. We have found that reuse can greatly increase the quality of software and reduce the time required to bring a product to market. We hope this book can help to get that message across.

The purpose of the book

Reuse is concerned with improving efficiency, so the purpose of this book is the same as the purpose of the REBOOT project itself:

> 'To enhance productivity and quality in software development by promoting and assisting organized reuse'

What we mean by 'organized reuse' is summarized in the following figure, which inspired the design of the REBOOT logo.

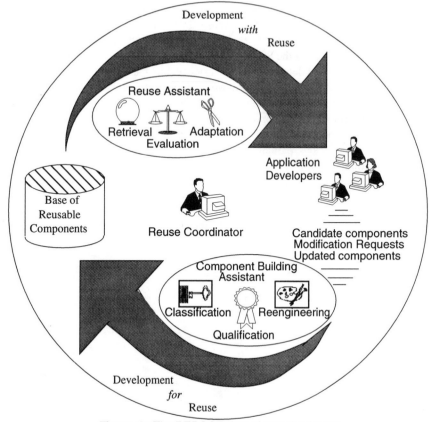

Figure 2 : The REBOOT view of organized reuse

The figure depicts the two main reuse activities, development *for* reuse and development *with* reuse.

Development *for* reuse

Development for reuse is the planned activity of preparing parts of a software system so that these parts can be reused in other contexts. We call these reusable parts *reusable components*. These reusable components can be any part of a software system, and are not restricted to any particular granularity or lifecycle phase. Development for reuse is supported by extending the ordinary development process with activities to:

- analyze the variability in requirements between different reusers of the components

- analyze the costs and benefits of incorporating these different requirements

- design the components with the appropriate level of generality for all reusers

In addition, development for reuse includes activities for re-engineering existing components, qualifying and classifying the components so that they are ready to be reused.

Development *with* reuse

Development with reuse, or application development, is the construction of new software products with the help of reusable components. This process includes the activities of:

- searching for a set of candidate components

- evaluating the set of retrieved candidate components to find the most suitable one

- if necessary, adapting the selected component to fit the specific requirements

Figure 2 also indicates the need for new roles and organizational changes to support reuse, for example the reuse coordinator, or the repository manager.

Our reuse goals

Our goal for promoting organized reuse can be broken down into the following specific subgoals:

- to provide a sound and complete understanding of the reuse problem, covering the range of issues from how to organize to take advantage of reuse to how to develop *for* and *with* reuse.

- to facilitate the mastery of the techniques needed to organize and develop *for* and *with* reuse. This includes being able to adapt reuse techniques to one's own organization, development process and methods.

- to show in detail how to apply the techniques in a specific software development.

- to provide a guide to the introduction, continuous measurement and improvement of the reuse capability of an organization.

Even if the view of organized reuse presented in the figure may seem focused on the development and tool aspects, we recognize that mature reuse cannot be achieved and sustained without full management understanding and commitment. For this reason, this book treats the managerial aspects of reuse thoroughly.

The scope of the REBOOT approach

We use object-oriented development as our chosen development paradigm. This reflects the aim of the REBOOT project, "Reuse based on object-oriented techniques", under whose auspices this book was written. However, we emphasize that most of the material described in the book is not restricted to object-oriented techniques. Our experience of presenting this material to software developers and managers is that users of many other types of programming language and development methodologies find the REBOOT approach highly relevant to them. In many cases, the techniques we present can be adapted with little effort to more traditional development environments.

This book focuses primarily on the compositional approach to reuse, that is, constructing a software product from reusable components, and only developing new components to implement application-specific functionality. It does not focus on the generative approach, for example the construction of an expert system from a set of rules and an inference engine. We consider the major benefit of reuse to industry will be found in the more traditional type of software development. Generative software development is a form of reuse, and can bring major savings (for example, the use of fourth-generation languages). However, it is only applicable in specific cases, and the development of specific compilers is complex and costly, requiring much use to reap the advantages.

We do not imply by the above that the generative approach is not appropriate, nor that reuse cannot be achieved without object-oriented development. In fact, much of the material in the book is also applicable to the generative approach, as well as to other development methods.

Intended readership

This book is written for a broad industrial readership, as reuse is a complex task which affects an entire company. We have tried to focus each chapter of the book on a specific type of reader:

- For the practising software engineer, we provide guidelines on how and when to develop *for* and *with* reuse, and how to search for and assess the reuse potential of components.

- For the project manager, we provide support for analyzing his project with regard to reuse, as well as managing and measuring reuse aspects to get the best results.

- At the executive level, we provide economic models to measure the cost and benefits of reuse; we outline how an ideal reuse company might operate, and we report on recent reuse experiences.

- For the *reuse agent* responsible for introducing and improving reuse in an organization, we provide the means to analyze how the work is currently organized, and a suggested plan for the incremental introduction of reuse.

- As methodologists responsible for adapting a given methodology to reuse, we provide generic reuse guidelines which permit such adaptation, including numerous examples.

To guide the different types of reader, the following table indicates the chapters of primary (P), secondary (S) and tertiary (T) interest. Particularly relevant chapters are shown with an asterisk:

Table 1 : Readership guide

Chapter	Practitioner	Project manager	Executive	Reuse agent	Method-ologist
1	T	P	P	P	S
2	S	P	S	P	S
3	S	T	T	P	S
4	S	P	T	P	P
5	T	S	P	P	S
6	P	S	T	S	P
7	P	S	T	S	P*
8	P	S	T	S	P
9	P*	S	T	S	P
10	P*	S	T	S	P
11	P*	S	T	S	P
12	P	S	T	S	P

The book is not intended primarily as an introductory text for students. Nevertheless, with accompanying course material, it can easily be used in:

- a course in practical development for reuse for a specific development methodology, with emphasis on project work. Here one could let different groups use different development methods for the same example and compare the results;

- a more advanced course where the students adapt a given development process to development for reuse; or

- an introductory course on the different aspects of reuse.

The structure of the book

The book is divided into twelve chapters and two parts, each with its specific focus and intended readership.

Part A, *Managing Reuse*, is intended primarily for executives, project managers and reuse agents, and describes the organizational changes, techniques and roles that are involved in implementing reuse within a company. It is organized as follows:

- Chapter 1, *Organizing reuse*, is mainly intended for managers. It gives an insight into candidates for reuse by providing a picture of a well-functioning reuse organization, and emphasizes the necessity of full management support for reuse. It also gives examples of some of the pitfalls encountered when introducing reuse, and how they can be avoided.

- Chapter 2, *Managing a reuse project*, is mainly intended for project managers and team leaders. They have the task of organizing the development of a project *for* and/or *with* reuse. The chapter proposes how best to organize the project to achieve these goals.

- Chapter 3, *Managing a repository*, is about repository organization. It covers all topics from insertion and retrieval of components to repository maintenance. This chapter also contains a section on the information needed to classify components.

- Chapter 4, *Measuring the effect of reuse*, covers reuse-specific product and process measurements and cost models. It uses product measurements to assess the reusability and quality of the components, and process metrics to measure costs and savings. It presents cost models to estimate the extra effort involved in development *for* reuse, and the savings and costs in development *with* reuse. The material in Chapter 4 is aimed at component producers and consumers who want to assess the quality and reusability of components, as well as project managers who need to estimate the costs and benefits of different reuse strategies. It requires some familiarity with discrete mathematics to make full use of the material.

- Chapter 5, *Introducing reuse*, is aimed at those responsible for introducing reuse into an organization. It discusses how to introduce the methods, procedures, techniques and roles described in the first four chapters of Part A and Part B. A step-by-step introduction programme is proposed, tailored according to the organization's current level of reuse maturity and its products and markets.

Part B, *Practising Reuse*, covers specific methods and techniques to guide practitioners in systematic reuse throughout the software development life-cycle, from analysis to maintenance. Since the techniques for development *for* and *with* reuse are largely independent, we treat them separately. We also provide a section on re-engineering techniques for those companies that have a large legacy of existing software, and want to benefit from the knowledge incorporated in it to build future systems. It is organized as follows:

- Chapter 6, *Development for and with reuse*, giving a short overview of Part B.

- Chapter 7, *Generic reuse development processes*. Here we discuss what is different when we incorporate development *for* and *with* reuse into the development process.

- Chapter 8, *Object-oriented components, techniques and life cycles*. This chapter gives a short overview of the major object-oriented techniques and how they support reuse.

- Chapter 9, *Object-oriented development for reuse*. This chapter is dedicated to technical aspects of development *for* reuse.

- Chapter 10, *Development with reuse*. This chapter is dedicated to technical aspects of development *with* reuse.

- Chapter 11, *Re-engineering for reuse*. Here we discuss how to re-engineer reusable components from existing systems.

- Chapter 12, *Cleanroom adaptation*. This chapter provides an example of how reuse activities and object-oriented concepts can be integrated in an existing development process.

Appendices A to E describe the Fire Alarm example used in various places in the book, how to document the introduction of reuse, questionnaires for the reuse maturity assessment, a Glossary of terms used throughout the book, and a list of References.

The REBOOT consortium

This book is the result of a successful teamwork within the REBOOT consortium:

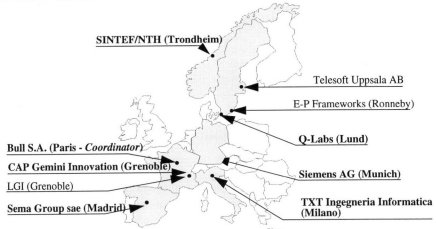

Figure 3 : The REBOOT consortium

The REBOOT project team consisted of the following people and organizations:

- Bull S.A. (prime): Jean-Marc Morel (Project Manager), Jean Faget (Technical Manager 1990-1992), Brian Brown (Technical Manager 1992-1994), Pascal Graffion.

- CAP Gemini Innovation: Claude Villermain, Danielle Ribot, Bjorn Gronquist, Blandine Bongard, Fabrice Mrugala, Olivier Lagneau.

- Frameworks (1992-1994)/Electronikcentrum (1990-1992): Tomas Althen, Roger Hedenäng, Johan Larsson, Magnus Nilsson, Lars Sandberg, Michael Mattsson, Peter Jansson, Grace Bosson.

- Q-Labs (1992-1994): Geir Fagerhus, Even-André Karlsson, Johan Brantestam, Magnus Ahlgren, Anders Sixtensson, Erik Johansson, Anders Gustavsson, Charlie Yeh, Claes Wohlin, Per Runeson.

- LGI: Jacky Estublier, Christophe Gadonna.

- Sema Group sae: Gabriel Sanchez, Alejandro de Mora, Susana González, Alfredo Cosculluela, Ana-Isabel Hernandez, Carmen Alvarez.

- Siemens AG: Claus Jäkel, Hans-Günter Tempel, Thomas Keller, Frank Buschmann, Anne-Hilde Veastad, Arno Semmelroth, Patricia Paul and Wolfgang Steinke.

- SINTEF/NTH: Reidar Conradi, Svein O. Hallsteinsen, Erik Odberg, Tor Egge, Guttorm Sindre, Sigurd Thunem, Sivert Sørumgård, Joe Goeman, Eldfrid Øvstedal, Tor Stålhane, Asgeir Langen, Tor Didriksen.

- Telesoft Uppsala AB (1990-1992): Lars Ponten, Carl-Magnus Ekermann.

- TXT Ingegneria Informatica S.p.A.: Andrea di Maio, Stefano Genolini, Maddali Paci, Marco de Michele.

Acknowledgments

This book is primarily the output of the REBOOT Methodology team, and we wish to thank the many members who contributed their particular knowledge and personality to create the working atmosphere that produced this book.

Different partners have focused their contribution to specific parts of this handbook:

- Chapter 1 was the responsibility of CAP (Blandine Bongard, Danielle Ribot and Bjorn Gronquist) and Q-Labs (Even-André Karlsson and Geir Fagerhus).

- Chapter 2 was divided between Q-Labs (Even-André Karlsson), SINTEF/NTH (Sigurd Thunem) and Sema (Gabriel Sánchez Gutiérrez).

- Chapter 3 was the responsibility of SINTEF/NTH (Guttorm Sindre and Sivert Sørumgård) and Q-Labs (Even-André Karlsson).

- Chapter 4 was divided between Q-Labs (Magnus Ahlgren and Even-André Karlsson) and SINTEF (Tor Stålhane).

- Q-Labs (Even-André Karlsson), CAP (Blandine Bongard and Danielle Ribot) and Bull (Jean-Marc Morel) were responsible for Chapter 5.

- Frameworks (Roger Hedenäng, Magnus Nilsson, Johan Larsson and Grace Bosson) had the overall responsibility for Part B, and wrote Chapter 6, Chapter 9 and Appendix A. Q-Labs (Even-André Karlsson and Johan Brantestam) were responsible for Chapter 7 and Chapter 12. CAP (Blandine Bongard, Danielle Ribot and Claude Villermain) did most of the work in Chapter 10. Chapter 8 was produced in collaboration between CAP and Frameworks. Siemens (Hans-Günter Tempel and Frank Buschmann) provided Chapter 11.

We are also in debt to the numerous practitioners involved in reuse applications for their willingness to try out the REBOOT ideas and their valuable feedback. The following table lists the main companies that contributed:

Table 2 : REBOOT applications

Partner	Application	Focus
Bull	Workflow	Development *with* reuse in the large
CAP	Resource allocation	Development of reusable components
	Telecommunication	General introduction of reuse
Q-Labs	Telecommunication	Adaptation of existing methodology to reuse
E-P Frame-works	Real-time inspection	Development *for* reuse
	Fire alarm system	Development *for* reuse: OO framework
	Gateway system for telecommunication	Development *for* reuse: OO framework
Siemens	Material flow control	Development of reusable components
	Telecommunication	Re-engineering *for* reuse
	Defence electronics	Reuse for communication servers
TXT	Factory planning	Development *for* and *with* reuse
	Embedded systems for aeronautics	Introduction of reuse in Ada real-time applications
SINTEF	Voice communication systems	Reuse of role model (OORAM) and finite state machine components

Special thanks to the REBOOT's project manager Jean-Marc Morel, who always worked to establish and maintain common goals and successful cooperation within the project. He also significantly contributed to the quality and consistency of this book by thorough reviews of several versions and by providing excellent feedback.

Special thanks should also be given to Brian Brown, Reidar Conradi, Frank Buschmann and Claus Jäkel for reviewing the different versions of this handbook, and for providing innumerable suggestions for improvement.

Many external individuals also helped in the review of the V1.5 version. In particular we wish to thank Patrick de Bondeli, Sadie Legard, Stefano Longano, Jacques Printz, Gael Renault, Guy Tassart, and Robert Troy for their thorough reviews and comments.

We also would like to give special thanks to Steve Rickaby from Syntagma who helped us with the final version, and Dick Thomas who worked with us to help us provide marketing material for REBOOT.

Finally we acknowledge the support of the European Commission, NUTEK and NTNF, which have funded the REBOOT ESPRIT project, and especially thank the Project Officer Patrick Corsi and the EC reviewers (Professor Patrick Hall, Gilles Pitette and Gerry Johansson) for good feedback and for keeping the project focused.

Part A
Managing Reuse

1 Organizing Reuse

1.1 Introduction

The main intention of this chapter is to serve as an introduction to software reuse for managers of companies developing software. It is also intended for anyone else who wants an overview of the potential and challenges of reuse. Once you have read this chapter, you will have an overview of the elements that enable you to:

- understand the fundamental principles of reuse, and how it affects software development

- decide if it is appropriate to investigate the consequences of reuse for your company

- understand what is involved in implementing reuse in your company

- create and spread a vision of how your company will work as a mature reuse company

It is important to define software reuse and introduce the related concepts. *Software reuse* is the process of creating software systems from existing software assets, rather than building software systems from scratch [Krueger92]. Software assets that constitute building blocks are also called *software reusable components*. In the remainder of the book, we refer just to *reuse* and *reusable components*. By development *for* reuse, we refer to the development of reusable components. By development *with* reuse, we refer to the development of systems from existing components.

Reuse is not an end in itself, but a means of achieving the general objectives of the company. Companies today are faced with new and more challenging market pressures. In response, companies have to reduce the time-to-market with new or enhanced products, increase the diversity of products available to the customers, and enhance the standardization and inter-operability of the products. Reuse is a means to achieve such objectives.

For example, software reuse can be a solution in the following scenarios:

- you (plan to) develop a family of products and want to optimize their development, evolution and maintenance to make them as consistent as possible,

- you develop similar applications (or parts of applications) for many different customers, and you want to avoid developing the "same" solutions over and over again,

- you have several old systems that contain important embedded knowledge, and you wish to capitalize on this to built a new generation of similar systems,

- you have potentially reusable components and would like to take advantage of them in the development of new systems.

The introduction of reuse in the strategies of major companies such as AT&T, Hewlett Packard, IBM, NEC, CAP and Ericsson, as well as the existence of significant corporate reuse programmes, show that reuse is a reality today.

Even if the advantages of reuse are obvious, it is far from trivial to make it work in practice. Establishing a mature level of reuse in a company requires more drastic changes than most other changes in technology. Many aspects of the company are affected: organization, responsibilities, planning, communication, development, etc. That is why the implementation programme requires a strong commitment from senior management.

The time span for the maximal return on investment in reuse is relatively long. Experience indicates a period of one to five years, depending on the size of the organization and on the variety of its products. Reuse differs from other technology investments in that it requires two phases of investment before the full pay-offs appear. The first phase is to adapt the company's processes to incorporate reuse, and the second is to produce reusable components. The full pay-off comes only when the reusable components are actually reused. Therefore a company must start by analyzing its current situation and establishing how it can benefit from reuse over a suitable time scale. Focusing on business segments that are strategic for the company decreases the pay-off period and is a key factor for success. Focusing on development for reuse and enhancing the company's processes to prepare for reuse will, however, also give more immediate pay-offs in better designed and maintainable products.

We have chosen to start with words of caution, but the bottom line is that reuse provides a considerable competitive advantage for managers who know how to adapt reuse technology to their company and products. To remain competitive, now is the time to implement reuse. This book is intended to enable your company to reach its reuse potential, but remember:

> If you as a manager do not talk to people about something (such as reuse) each week, you are not serious about it!

The rest of this chapter is organized as follows:

- Section 1.2 presents the motivations for reuse, the potential benefits and main consequences of reuse,

- Section 1.3 is a survey of existing reuse practices,

- Section 1.4 draws up a profile of a mature reuse company and presents organization models supporting reuse practice,

- Section 1.5.6 addresses how to proceed with the introduction of reuse. This is a preview of Chapter 5, which gives detailed guidelines for the introduction of reuse in a company.

1.2 The motivation for reuse

What would you gain by introducing reuse into your company?

This section presents the motivations for reuse by first painting a picture of reuse practice in an average software development company faced with a complex evolving market. We then analyze, through ISO 9126 quality factors, the impact of reuse on overall software quality, and show the economic impact of reuse. From a very basic return-on-investment model, we finally illustrate the main benefits you can expect from reuse.

1.2.1 Today's picture

What is your current situation, and what do you expect will be your main obstacles to introduce organized reuse?

Today, in most software development projects, we are able to perceive only opportunistic and informal reuse. Generally there is little exchange of information between departments relative to on-going work and production, and when shared requirements are discovered it is too late to take advantage of them. Poor coordination between project teams developing similar products causes them to choose their architectures independently, which makes later reuse impossible.

The failure to build a few reusable products instead of many specialized products also results in a growing proportion of effort dedicated to maintenance instead of development of new products. This is aggravated by monolithic systems in which it is difficult to isolate and replace specific functionalities. Continuously maintaining software by *ad hoc* patching is also inferior to replacing larger units. Nevertheless, company internal budgeting policies frequently discourage the production, marketing and support of reusable components. Managers believe that reuse is good, but think it can happen by itself, and do little to encourage it. The role of management is frequently reactive, trying to meet deadlines and minimizing over-runs, rather than visionary, forecasting opportunities and threats.

Insufficient time is spent in the earlier phases of the development process such as analysis and design, in which the possibility for reusing existing components and defining new reusable components is greatest. Software development is not considered as an investment over the whole life span of the product line, but more as a one-shot development ending when the first release is out of the door. This is quite natural, as it is still very difficult—even in retrospect—to estimate the impact of immature analysis and design on the implementation, testing and maintenance of a software system.

A widespread and dangerous misconception is that since it is so easy to fix software, we can start to implement now, and adjust the system later. It helps to examine the experience of traditional manufacturing industries, where a mistake in design is very costly to correct in later phases. Quality is lowered by bug fixes and patches in the final product, and the software no longer corresponds to the specification. The result is that potential reusers are suspicious of each other's components, the "not-invented-here syndrome". All these factors detract from reuse.

However, most organizations have some limited reuse:

1. most good designers reuse their own components from earlier projects, in the form of either problem solutions, templates or code,

2. there are always individuals who have a talent for generalizing and reusing solutions picked up from other developers,

3. standard libraries are becoming widespread,

4. commercial database systems, user interface systems, operating systems and even compilers may be considered as reuse,

5. layered architectures favour reuse by providing a common platform for several applications.

If we investigate these five reuse practices, we can see that they fall into two different categories. The first two cases constitute informal reuse on an individual basis, requiring little extra effort, but giving only relatively small and local benefits. The last three cases require major initiatives, and here most organizations only use off-the-shelf products. The aim of this book is to help bridge the gap between these extremes, building on the good practices from both groups, and proposing a range of reuse strategies.

1.2.2 The impact of reuse on software quality

Quality is usually defined as the ability of software to meet its requirements. We distinguish here the different factors which are incorporated in the concept of quality according to the ISO 9126 definition [ISO 9126], and for each of these we analyze the consequences of reuse. The observed factors are shown in Figure 4.

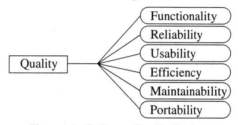

Figure 4 : Software Quality Factors

The following paragraphs define these factors, and discuss how they are impacted by reuse:

- **Functionality** is the existence of a set of functions and their specified properties. The functions are those that satisfy stated or implied needs. Functionality is relative to the customer requirements, but as most customers have unclear expectations in the initial phases of software development, reuse can affect these requirements in several beneficial ways:

  — Reuse provides an opportunity to reuse similar systems as prototypes to capture the functional requirements.

  — In development *with* reuse, we can uncover hidden requirements during the evaluation of potential reusable components. The evaluated components can also help the customer revise the requirements, a similar effect to that achieved with fast prototyping.

  — In reusing a component there is a risk that we sacrifice the "right" functionality in favour of reuse, but there may also be an opportunity to provide additional functionality which was not possible without reuse.

  — If we have an opportunity to reuse a system covering for example 95% of the customer requirements without modification, the additional 5% of the functionality is in most cases negotiable, provided the customer can share some of the benefits of reuse.

  — In developing a system *for* reuse there are usually several customers involved. They can influence each other and elucidate latent requirements which might not have emerged until later in a traditional development process, causing considerable problems.

  — In development *for* reuse there is always a compromise between different customers for the component. Thus some conflicting functionality might have to be sacrificed, but additional functionalities provided for other customers may be gained.

  The process of developing *for* and *with* reuse, and its consequences, are discussed in more detail in Part B of the handbook.

- **Reliability** is the software's ability to maintain its performance level under stated conditions for a given period of time. Reuse can influence reliability both in a positive and negative fashion:

  — The correct reuse of a well-tested component increases the reliability of the system (positive).

  — Several uses of the same component increase the confidence in the component (positive).

  — Incorrect reuse or reuse outside the intended scope of a component, however well-tested, constitutes a risk (negative).

  The importance of proper documentation and evaluation of components is further discussed in Part B of the handbook.

- **Usability** is the effort needed to use the system by the total set of users. Reuse also has impacts on this aspect of quality, both positive and negative:

— A reused component usually has more effort put into its development than a one-off component (a positive effect on the usability of the component and the system).

— Components with slightly different characteristics might be unacceptable from a usability point of view (negative). The evidence of this can be found in the market for administrative systems, where even with an abundance of cheap commercial standard packages, companies opt for custom development instead of changing their procedures to fit the available products.

- **Efficiency** is the relationship between the performance level of the software and the amount of resources used. This is also affected by reuse:

— More effort can be justified to make a reusable component efficient than for a specific component which will only be used once.

— Specific components can be tailored for specific needs, and thus be more efficient than a more general reusable component. The reuse of a component tailored for specific needs might downgrade the efficiency in other environments.

- **Maintainability** represents the effort needed to make specific modifications. For a reusable component, many of these modifications are already incorporated or planned in the extended requirements of development *for* reuse. Modifications outside the intended plan are more difficult, as the functionality of the component is more complex than a specialized component, but the cost of modifications of a reusable component can be divided between the various reusers.

- **Portability** is the ability to be transferred from one environment to another. This aspect of quality is directly correlated with the reusability of the component, and portability analysis is an important aspect of development *for* reuse. We can compromise the portability of the system by reusing components which are not portable.

Quality factors are discussed further in Chapter 4, *Measuring the effect of reuse*, in which we estimate their costs and outline how they relate to the reusability of a component. We should always bear in mind that as for any quality improvement, the development of reusable components is not without cost. Perhaps the most important lesson to be learned in connection with reuse is that the development of reusable components should be treated as an investment, the profits from which are reaped by using them outside the product for which they were developed.

1.2.3 The impact of reuse on costs, productivity and lead time

What should your most important goals be, and what are the benefits of reuse?

Software development costs

Reuse is expected to be one of the major sources of costs savings in the software industry in the next few decades [Griss93] [Hall92a] [Poulin93] [Tracz92] [Isoda92]. Figure 5 (presented by Barry Boehm at the STARS conference in 1991) illustrates the relative importance of the three major sources of cost saving in software development:

- working faster (through a better tool set)

- working smarter (through a better process for software development and better control over the process by estimation, planning, assessment and improvement)

- work avoidance (through reuse)

The baseline total is the expected expenditure without any improvement in software development technology.

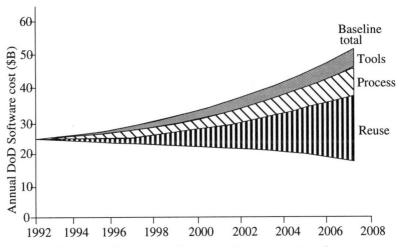

Figure 5 : Projected software development costs savings

This simple figure also demonstrates the general view of state-of-the-art companies and research communities—the focus is on reuse and process: tools are there to support improvements in the first two areas, and not as an end in themselves. This approach is promoted in the REBOOT project and is reflected in this book.

Productivity

The overwhelming part of software cost comes from labour. Productivity is a major factor in the cost of the product. We define productivity as the amount of functionality produced per person-month. Note that we have replaced the more usual *lines of code* with *amount of functionality* in the measure of productivity. This is because reuse fundamentally alters the way we can measure productivity. Neither the number of new lines of code nor the number of reused lines of code give a good picture of what a developer has produced. The number of new lines is an inadequate measure when a lot of effort has been put into reusing and combining a number of carefully chosen, large components. Conversely, the number of reused lines is inadequate when large components, of which only a fraction of the functionality is needed, are included.

Independently of how we measure productivity, reuse has the potential of increasing it—if the right functionality is reused and the component fits! It should also be mentioned that the extra resources invested when developing *for* reuse appear as a productivity *decrease*, as with any kind of long term investment. We discuss how to measure productivity with reuse in more depth in Chapter 4, but it should be kept in mind that this type of measurement is still in its infancy.

Lead time

Lead time, or time-to-market, is possibly the single most important factor in today's rapidly changing technological environment. The marketing lifetime for a single generation of a product is steadily decreasing, and requests for rapid changes and extensions to products are increasing. Developing new products by combining readily available components---development *with* reuse---is a way of reducing time to market.

Experience data from NASA/GSFC

The previous paragraphs contained some predictions of what impact reuse will have in the future. There is unfortunately very little concrete evidence for these predictions. There are mainly two reasons for this:

- The lack of good baseline data for comparison, i.e. the metrics collected in industry today on productivity and quality are not adequate.

- The difficulty of determining what is reuse and what is just use, as discussed in more detail in Chapter 4.

Thus much of the data which is collected and presented on the impact of reuse is of limited value. There are fortunately exceptions to this; one of them is NASA/GSFC where metrics are collected systematically for a long period of time in a relatively stable environment. Data showing the trend in quality, cost and reuse from NSAS/GSFC were presented by Frank McGarry at a seminar at the European Software Institute in October 1994 (Figure 6).

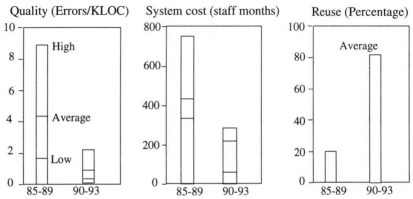

Figure 6 : NASA/GSFC quality, cost and reuse data

Figure 6 shows that there is an improvement in quality (4 times) and productivity or cost (2 times) in connection with an increase in reuse. The data are collected from 7-8 similar systems in each period. This does not give any proof that reuse was the major contributor to these improvements, but other improvements, e.g. changes in tools (CASE) and process (Cleanroom), were introduced and measured in the same period, and neither gave more than limited improvements.

1.2.4 A simple reuse return on investment model

How can you estimate the initial cost, extra effort and saved effort of reuse?

The benefit of multiple reuse is well known in more mature industries like car manufacturing, where it is common to use the same parts for many different models. We believe it is just a matter of time before it becomes a matter of survival in the software industry as well.

Figure 7 illustrates some simple technical and economic arguments that can be made for reuse. It represents the costs of developing software, excluding both the initial cost for introducing reuse and the maintenance cost. Similar models for lead time and maintenance costs can also be made, for example that the reused components have a better quality, and the maintenance costs are divided between all products reusing the components. It is also acknowledged that the extra effort spent making components reusable enforces good design, and thus contributes to the quality of the entire product. The total amount of saved effort for the company can be significant if the appropriate reuse strategy is chosen.

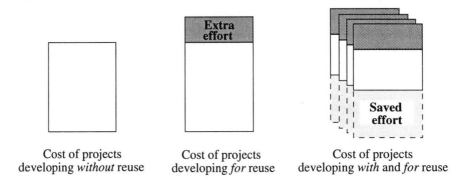

| Cost of projects developing *without* reuse | Cost of projects developing *for* reuse | Cost of projects developing *with* and *for* reuse |

Figure 7 : A simple reuse cost model

It is clear from the figure that management commitment is vital to the success of reuse. Since there are initial costs involved in the implementation of a reuse programme, pressure from software practitioners alone is not sufficient. A more detailed model of return on investment is presented in [Gaffney92].

Even this simple model needs a word of caution about the difficulty of acquiring supporting data. As described in more detail in Chapter 4, isolating and measuring the effects of reuse is complex. Even a supposedly simple measurement such as the amount of code reused in a new product is not trivial [Bieman91]. This should be kept in mind when comparing numbers from different organizations, and when reading the more concrete experiences in Section 1.3.

Within some of the applications in REBOOT we have collected experience data based on this simple cost model. This model is particularly useful to serve as a basis for decisions to invest in development for reuse and to measure the overall effect. An example is shown in Table 3.

Table 3 : Costs and benefits associated with produced/reused components

Component	Cost to develop	Extra cost for reuse	Times reused	Cost to reuse	Effort saved each time
ContentPATH	10 PY	0	1	0.5 PM	6 PM
IODA	2 PY	+30%	2	4 PM	2 PY
Communication layer	4 PY	0	5	1 PM	4 PY
ImageEditor	4 PY	+20%	3	1 PM	2 PY
Installation facilities	9 PM	+20%	5	0	4.5 PM

We emphasize the importance of quantitative goals for the effect of reuse, and in Chapter 4 we discuss how to set up and measure specific goals on productivity, lead time and quality in more detail. It is important to remember that the estimated impact of reuse for a given company cannot be given without a thorough analysis of its reuse opportunities, and this estimate cannot be validated until data from the actual reuse of components are available, which might take some time.

1.3 Some reuse approaches and experiences

What kind of reusable components have the largest reuse potential in your company?

Should you develop reusable components for internal reuse or for external clients?

This section gives an overview of reuse approaches as well as existing experiences. It starts with a classification of reuse approaches, and then presents the results of some reuse approach experiments.

1.3.1 A classification of reuse approaches

Reuse experiences can be classified using three criteria: the *scope of reuse*, the *target reuser*, and the *granularity* of the components involved:

1. The *scope of reuse* includes three categories: general, domain and product-line reuse. This defines the area of potential reuse for a component. Product-line and domain reuse describe components that are specific to a particular context, while general reuse means components that can be reused whatever the context of the application.

2. The *target reuser* is either internal (in-house) or external (market).

3. The *granularity* of manipulated components, where we distinguish mainly fine-grain and coarse-grain components.

Figure 8 represents these three criteria as orthogonal axes of a graph.

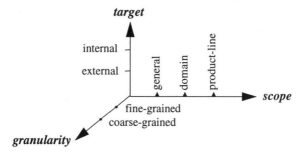

Figure 8 : Three-axes classification for reuse approaches

The next sections describe the three criteria in more detail.

1.3.1.1 The scope of reuse

The scope of reuse axis has three different values, as illustrated in Figure 8:

*   **General reuse** means domain-independent reuse, for example general-purpose components such as list managers, mathematical functions, user-interface toolkits and database management systems. The term *horizontal reuse* is also commonly used. Components of this type are almost entirely abstract data types with common behaviour throughout various domains. Libraries with abstract data type classes are examples from this category.

*   **Domain reuse** means reuse within a specific application domain, that is, a specific product area such as a financial application. In this case, the semantics of the components are domain-dependent. The term *vertical reuse* is also commonly used. In the telecommunications domain, a subsystem of performance management is a good example, because it is standardized inside the domain. Such a component is potentially reusable in any telecommunication application.

*   **Product-line reuse** means reuse within a specific application family such as a product line. In this case, the semantics of the components are bound to a specific application type. A product line may dictate a generic architecture, and component roles will be

developed to fit it. Here the reusable components are entire architectures, either specific or generalized. Examples are a common code generator used for a series of compilers, the Fire Alarm framework [Larsson93] described in Appendix A, and similar systems for which a complete end user system can be derived from the reusable system.

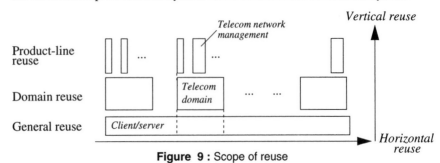

Figure 9 : Scope of reuse

Note that the same techniques for developing the reusable components can be used for different approaches, e.g. the framework technology is used both in domain reuse (MacApp [Schmucker86]) and in product-line reuse (Fire Alarm, Appendix A). A company can focus on one or several of these reuse scopes at the same time.

1.3.1.2 The reuse target

The reuse target axis has two values:

• The **internal approach** or **in-house approach** means that the company is developing *for* reuse and providing services internally (to the company itself). This approach does not have a company barrier between service providers and customers.

• The **external approach** means that the company is developing *for* reuse and providing its services on the external market (for another company). This approach introduces a company barrier between service producers and consumers, which complicates communication.

1.3.1.3 The granularity of components

Granularity of components can be classified into fine-grained and coarse-grained categories. The terms *small-scale* and *large-scale* are also commonly used to name the same concepts. Fine-grained components are generally generic and domain independent. Components such as I/O functions, file and database-access functions, data-structure manipulation functions and individual object classes are in this category. Coarse-grained components can be application subsystems such as order-processing subsystems, database servers, user-interface packages and so on.

1.3.2 Current practice

This section describes how various companies have made use of reuse, in terms of the three criteria described above: general reuse, domain reuse and product-line reuse.

1.3.2.1 General reuse

The general reuse approach is an ambitious one that promotes reuse at the most general scope. At present, the external approach has been driven by the development of general purpose libraries, while movement towards in-house reuse has concerned the introduction of appropriate reuse organizations.

Several companies have developed general purpose components for sale on the market. Well-known recent examples are the libraries of Grady Booch in Ada and ICpack in Objective-C. In general, those libraries provide *abstract data type* components and are limited to fine-grained components. Currently, selling general purpose components is a difficult business where it is hard to make a profit. These types of components are often available free of charge from universities or non-profit-making organizations. This probably contributed to the lack of commercial success of ICpack. In addition, many of the basic components are becoming standardized within a given programming language.

Companies such as Toshiba in Japan have applied reuse strategies on a large scale within their company over long periods. They have considered general reuse and also domain-specific components, and they have undertaken major efforts to introduce the necessary support for reuse. A specific team is in charge of the development and maintenance of general reusable components. The most important aspect of success is the explicit introduction of reuse procedures in the software development process. The reuse process is supported by appropriate tools (adapted design tools, central repository, standardized coding techniques) and appropriate management techniques (clear and measurable reuse targets, follow-up procedures).

IBM's experience with a corporate reusable software library [Poulin94] mentions limited benefits when reusing domain-independent components (about 20% reuse), although benefits can range from 70%–90% reuse for domain-specific reuse.

1.3.2.2 Domain reuse

Domain reuse refers to the sharing of components within a specific application domain such as a product area. Up to now, efforts have concentrated on domain analysis [Arango92] and identification of common components. Major companies have invested heavily in modifying existing application components to make them reusable. Some software houses have tried to market such components, but most examples are generally in-house oriented.

Software houses have also developed domain-specific components for sale. In general, they have started by providing a specific client with reusable domain components. Later, efforts have been made to generalize such components to sell them to other clients working in the same field. Well-known experiences are the CAMP (Common Ada Missile Packages) project in the US and the Swedish Telesoft company trial, both dealing with Ada components. The CAMP project developed a library of reusable components for the use in missile control systems [McNicholl85]. The Telesoft trial [Pontén91] concerned the development and sale of complex components for real-time applications.

These experiences are not recent, and were not convincing. A problem was that the component providers did not have direct access to the functional and non-functional requirements of potential customers. During the specification of components, detailed input from clients is needed. The client is only willing to invest the time required to express his specific needs when being provided with custom software. An explicit communication channel between component providers and component users is needed. In addition, the users require follow-up support in the use and adaptation of components. The benefits of reuse are only ensured if modifications are integrated into the supplier's reference component, and if standard test programs are used.

Several companies have attempted to develop domain-specific components for internal delivery. The best known are NEC, Toshiba [Matsumoto89] in Japan and GTE in the United States. These companies made major efforts to analyze specific domains and develop reusable components.

Not all domains are appropriate for this type of reuse. For example, efficient reuse is difficult to obtain for application domains with significant time and space constraints. Before investigating domain reuse, an evaluation of the return on investment should be carried out. Domain reuse—especially with a market approach—can be successful only when standards are available. Depending of the maturity of the domain, existing standards will be useful to a greater or lesser extent. Standards can define functionalities, methods to use when working in the domain, communication protocol and so on. An example is STEP (Standard Exchange of Product Model Data, ISO 1033) [EXPRESS92], a design language to use in the CAD domain.

1.3.2.3 Product-line reuse

Product-line reuse involves the analysis of a product family and its variability. Major efforts gave been made to define generic architectures and to assess common programming standards. The product-line reuse approach has only been applied in-house, since it is strongly linked to a specific product.

Companies that focus on a specific product line have applied this reuse approach. They have usually started by making a detailed study of existing and future requirements. Variant and invariant structures can be determined, and a generic application architecture fixed. This leads to the specification of standard building blocks. This approach is currently applied by Hewlett Packard, where they are called "domain-specific kits". Hewlett Packard define this approach as a complete and coherent packaging and delivery of (several different) reusable work products to simplify application building [WISR93]. A kit is comprised of domain-specific frameworks, components and a glue language.

This reuse approach has been successfully applied to application families, even within small companies. An overall analysis of a product family makes it possible to determine a common architecture, and to identify reusable components. It imposes significant constraints on the developers, since they have to follow common rules for development. It can therefore require a major education effort for developers. However, the introduction of an appropriate development methodology is of primary interest. The reuse approach makes it necessary to manage a reference product line and specific products in parallel, often a missing feature in organizations. Strong technical leadership is a key factor for this approach to work.

1.3.3 Some existing reuse experiences

Several successful implementations of reuse have been based on *ad hoc* approaches—a technical breakthrough is not absolutely necessary to achieve success in software reuse. This section describes the specific reuse experiences of several companies.

- At **Schlumberger**, reuse has been improved throughout the Schlumberger group via the "Design programme", supported by senior management. This consists of reuse introduction by an incremental, natural approach:

  — capitalizing on reusable design knowledge by setting up volunteer pilot sites for well-defined domains, either for a given technology or for a given class of application,

  — capturing critical design knowledge into "technology books" with the help of a *reuse champion*.

  The reuse champion controls on-going reuse initiatives, launches new ones in other areas, promotes the use of the technology books, and generally acts as a consultant in the design of new systems. Technology books assume vertical (domain) reuse, but also describe horizontal (general) reuse when it concerns common technologies.

- The **Fuchu Software Factory** established by **Toshiba** is an environment that allows software manufacturing organizations to design, program, test, ship, install and maintain commercial software products in a unified manner. The program was launched in the domains of process-control software for electric power networks, nuclear-thermal power generation, and the steel industry. Their experiment focused more specifically on the reuse of code, and not on high-level information such as design. Code reuse has been the most important contribution to productivity improvements over a period of eight years. The other major improvements due to reuse are better quality (2-3 defects per 1000 lines of source code compared with 7-20 defects per 1000 lines previously) and shorter development times [Matsumoto89].

- The Command and Control Systems Division of **Hughes Aircraft Company** created a Common Air Defence Ground Environment (CADGE) and reported a 37% saving over projected development costs while building two systems with reuse [Benson91].

- The Analytical Product Group of **Hewlett-Packard** [Martin91] set up a multi-site reuse initiative to develop assets for reuse without modification, amounting to 10% of the lines of code making up the Group's software products.

- **IBM** launched reuse programmes around the development of domain specific reuse libraries. These programmes address all reuse considerations: organizational, methodological and tool support [Poulin94], [Poulin93].

- The **U.S. Navy** Fleet Combat Direction System Support Activity [STARS92a,b] restructured the maintenance activity for its shipboard tactical data systems to provide a high degree of reuse of common components, and automated the production of system builds from a reusable component repository.

- The **Swedish Defence** built the TOR (Terminal Oriented Accounting and Logistics) system in the early 1980s, relying heavily on reuse of code written in Cobol. It now consists of about two million lines of code, distributed over fifty communicating sites all over Sweden. It will be used and be maintained until 1996.

These organizations have all reported successes in various reuse situations. The reuse was mainly in-house, with a domain or product-line scope. A quantitative forecast of success was possible through the use of reuse economics models. However, economic benefits can also be identified on a non-quantitative basis, such as meeting an organization's overall objectives.

1.4 Reuse-driven organizations

What difficulties do you expect to experience with reuse?

What is your vision for your company as a mature reuse organization?

This section describes the operation of different types of mature reuse organizations, and their competitive advantages. It also shows the various ways reuse can be organized within your company. Its purpose is to help you decide how to organize reuse in your company.

1.4.1 Optimizing reuse

What can be the maximum return from your reuse efforts?

The reuse capability refers to the results a company can expect from reuse. Every company can be described by two aspects:

- a *reuse potential*, which is the maximum it can achieve by reuse in its current market niche, and

- a *reuse effort*, which reflects the effort specifically targeted towards reuse.

The *reuse success* is the overlap between the potential and the effort, as illustrated in figure 10.

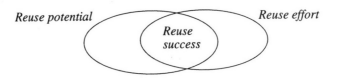

Figure 10 : Reuse potential, effort and success

From figure 10 we can define the *proficiency* and *efficiency* of the reuse programme, as:

• Reuse proficiency = Reuse success / Reuse potential

• Reuse efficiency = Reuse success / Reuse effort

The aim of this handbook is to help you maximize reuse efficiency, and achieve a reuse proficiency which maximizes your company's profits. It is important to be aware of the fact that not all reuse opportunities are profitable!

This aim can only be achieved through a thorough analysis of your company's products, markets, and internal capabilities. This analysis must be followed by a reuse introduction plan to achieve the reuse objectives. This process is described in detail in Chapter 5.

The reuse potential must be continuously monitored by your management, particularly by those responsible for long-term market and product planning, i.e. product management. In a mature reuse company the reuse potential of different products and markets should be assessed periodically, and long-term plans should exist.

Reuse effort and reuse success can only be quantified through measurements of the factors important to your company, e.g. lead time, productivity and quality. Detailed measurements can also give feedback to your product managers on how well they have assessed the reuse potential and the reuse efficiency. Detailed measurement methods are suggested in Chapter 4.

1.4.2 An example of an advanced reuse company

The small Norwegian software company Taskon bases its entire product development on the reuse philosophy. Taskon develops tailored management information systems. These systems build on the existing information systems in a client organization, extracting and presenting information tailored for managers at different levels.

The applications are constructed in Smalltalk from a reuse repository of about 1500 Smalltalk classes. There is a strong management commitment to, and knowledge of, software reuse, and reuse penetrates the entire company. Smalltalk is a reuse-friendly environment and facilitates reuse. Taskon have their own object-oriented development method/process, OORAM [Reenskaug92], that supports reuse.

At the end of application projects with short lead times, effort is allocated to a "back-room" activity to extract and build reusable components from the developed applications.

Experienced developers are used as "kernel makers", maintaining and improving the repository of reusable components. One particular activity is the re-engineering of class hierarchies. This is done regularly as a class hierarchy grows and its mechanisms mature. This leads to an incremental development of reusable components through continuous application coupled with explicit maintenance of the components in the repository.

Here are the results of an interview about their experiences of reuse with members of the management and development staff from Taskon.

What are the main advantages of reuse for Taskon?

"It gives us the capability to create high quality customized software with a minimum of effort. In more commercial terms, we can produce and sell as many customized software solutions as possible, while minimizing costs relating to details of particular system instances".

Do you measure the cost and benefits of reuse at Taskon? Could you give us some figures?

"No. We have been searching for meaningful reuse metrics without success, and have still no idea how to measure reuse. We know that of the total number of classes or source lines in a delivery, between 95% and 99% are typically reusable components from our library. But we like to know how much effort we save and by how much the quality is improved".

Did you evolve your organization to improve reuse?

"Yes, most definitely. We organizationally distinguish between forward engineering (creating customer products) and reverse engineering (creating reusable components). Our software experts migrate between the two activities for learning purposes, but they are always organizationally distinct".

Did you evolve your development process to favour and support reuse? Do you apply reuse throughout the life cycle?

"Yes. We have a layered, two-dimensional software life cycle which we call a *value chain*. Software development processes run horizontally in each layer. The process builds on reusable components created on the layer below, and delivers valuable results to the layer above. The roles in each layer are *end user*, *toolmaker*, *module-maker* and *kernel-maker*".

Are all your staff reuse minded (for example managers, developers, maintainers)?

"Yes, it is and has always been a fundamental part of our business philosophy".

How do you train new people?

"'On the job' training is most important; documentation is only supplementary".

Is it necessary to remind people about reuse?

"In principle, no. In practice, yes, because it is always tempting to management to give priority to activities that yield quick results and postpone long-term investment. So there is a tendency for management to push the forward engineering activities while the technologists defend the reverse engineering activities".

Did you meet problems with reuse, and what decisions did you make to overcome them?

"Reusable components are assets. They do not arise by accident, they are discovered by studying existing software and created by hard work. The investment which goes into their creation can only be written off against their successful applications. This implies repeat business, which is in conflict with a natural desire to make the most of available market opportunities. It also takes some hard decisions when a promising market dries up and we have to search for other markets where we can recover some of the investments".

How many Smalltalk classes do you have in your library?

"About 1500".

Do you have reusable components of a different type (e.g. specifications, designs, C++, tests, O-O frameworks, etc...)?

"We use the term *mechanisms* to denote reusable models, and *frameworks* to denote reusable ensembles of classes designed for subclassing".

Are your components well documented, and how?

"We have a standard for documentation of reusable components which include step-by-step instructions for their use and documentation of their general logic. The *OOram* (Object-Oriented Role Analysis and Modelling) method with tools supports this. In addition, we have quality assurance programmes which analyze applications of reusable frameworks and check various constraints".

Do you certify components, and how?

"We check concepts, architecture and design by peer review. Implementations of reusable components are checked by retrofitting them into operational applications and repeating the standard tests for those applications".

Do you have fine and/or coarse grained components?

"Both. But the tendency is towards large components to reduce the learning burden on the application programmers".

How your library managed? Do you classify components, and how?

"Our complete library of reusable components is in a Smalltalk-80 image. From time to time we extract the source code and recreate the library image from scratch to make sure we have full control. We do not classify the reusable components, but maintain documents according to the *OOram* method, which give us an overview of available components".

Do you reuse components from external producers (for example freeware or commercial libraries)?

"We have done so in the past, but found that they clashed with the transactions, persistent objects and MVC (model view controller—a Smalltalk framework for building a user interface) of our basic architecture and caused more trouble than benefit".

Do you expect to market your library of reusable components?

"We have looked into the economy of packaging our components for a general market, but have not been able to find a profitable solution. We are marketing much of our experience through the non-proprietary OOram-method (a new text book, *The Object Industry*, presents the method thoroughly) and the object-oriented software engineering product TASKON/OOram".

Do you plan actions to increase your reuse level further?

"We have a continuous investment effort to improve and extend our reusable components. The value of reusable components diminishes over time because the needs of application programmers change and because the technology becomes obsolete. A steady investment is therefore needed to maintain the value of our reusable assets. In addition, it is the policy of Taskon to increase the value of these assets over time".

What would be your main recommendations about reuse for another software organization that has not yet started to reuse?

"You must use before you can reuse. Successful reuse requires repeat business, management dedication and perseverance, programmer willingness to build on other people's results, and a willingness for all to see beyond the current project".

1.4.3 Reuse-driven projects and product life cycles

How should you relate the degree of reuse to product life cycles?

The dynamic properties of a company in which reuse is mature are illustrated in the following figure:

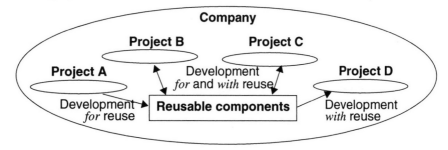

Figure 11 : Dynamic properties of a reuse company

Here we have four projects A, B, C and D, interacting with a central component repository, developing new reusable components (development *for* reuse), and reusing existing components (development *with* reuse).

There are, however, some differences between the projects:

- Project A only develops for reuse in a domain in which the company has made a strategic decision to work. Therefore project A accumulates reusable components for products in this domain. It does not necessarily develop a specific product, but rather builds the basis for a family of future products. This project can also reuse existing components as building blocks of new and larger reusable components.

- Projects B and C both use and produce components. They produce products the company sells, some parts of which are made from existing components. Some of the components being developed for these projects have a potential for future use, and are therefore developed for reuse.

- Project D does not produce any reusable components; it constructs a product from reusable components taken from the repository. This is often the case for products with very high demands on time-to-market, or products at the end of the life cycle of a product line.

Let us consider these different project types in the light of their product life cycle.

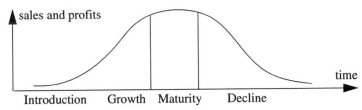

Figure 12 : Typical product life cycle

The life cycle of a product is typically composed of four stages:

- The *introduction* stage corresponds to the period where the product is introduced into the market.

- The *growth* period corresponds to a rapid market acceptance and substantial profit improvement.

- The *maturity* period corresponds to a slowdown in sales growth, because the product has achieved acceptance by most potential buyers.

- The *decline* stage is when sales show a strong downward trend.

For the different types of project shown in Figure 11, we can draw the following conclusions:

- Projects developing mainly *for* reuse (A) are justified for products in the introduction phase of their life cycle.

- Developments mixing *for* and *with* reuse (B and C) are justified during the growth and maturity phases.

- In the declining phase of a product, development resources are less justified for development *for* reuse. Projects should be of type D.

Once reuse is established in a company, strategic decisions to develop product families can be taken, and controlled projects can be started. This requires a greater degree of inter-project coordination than without reuse, but the advantages are that software can be brought under the same managerial control as other types of investment, and a proper return on investments analysis can be performed.

1.4.4 Different reuse organization models

How is your company's software development organized?

This section presents three models for organizations supporting reuse, and their impact on existing development practices. The changes they imply at project and company level are discussed. The models all rely on a common repository where reusable components are stored. Techniques to manage such a repository are discussed in Chapter 3. These organizational models show three basic possible organizations suitable for reuse from which real cases can be derived; they are simplified, and should be treated with caution. In practice, a typical organization is likely to be some combination of the three models.

1.4.4.1 The project-oriented company

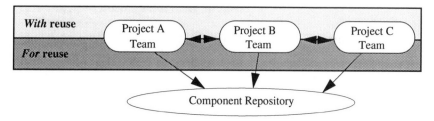

Figure 13 : Project-oriented company

The organization of a company around projects may sometimes be sufficient to support reuse. In projects, people with different roles work together to produce an application. In most companies, people belong to projects and not to technical groups. Within the project, however, work is organized according to the technical skills of individuals. Applications are often decomposed into modules covering specific parts of the application, for example a graphical user interface, communication layers or a database management system. In this sense, the internal project organization does not differ much from that of a domain-oriented company. A project organization encourages efficient reuse of the developer's technical experience, but it requires strong technical management to get reuse to work at the project level, and to coordinate with other projects. There is no formal responsibility for the repository management, which can lead to problems if not addressed.

1.4.4.2 The component production-oriented company

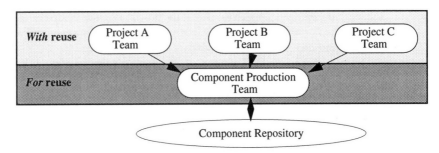

Figure 14 : Centralized component production-oriented company

The component production-oriented company is based on centralized production of reusable components. This approach separates the project teams from the component production team. The component production team acts as a kind of subcontractor to each project.

1.4.4.3 The domain-oriented company

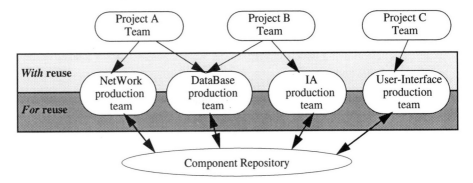

Figure 15 : Domain-oriented company

A domain-oriented company consists of specialized component production teams, and of project teams that build applications by acting as integrators of components. Exchanges between production teams and project teams are important and need good support. The company is built on knowledge of specific software domains. The main advantages are the acquisition of specific skills, and a secure way of developing reusable components. Good knowledge about components is ensured, and reuse needs are correctly identified. The major drawback is the high communication overhead between production teams and project teams.

1.4.4.4 A comparison of the reuse organization models

The most immediate approach to reuse is the project-oriented company, as this allows reuse to be applied on a small scale within individual projects. However, this approach requires good support and changes to a company's working methods.

The component production-oriented company requires a minimal investment in the development of shared components. It can be applied to domain reuse where components are shared among projects in a common domain. It requires:

- efficient domain analysis,

- generic component development,

- strong management of components.

The domain-oriented company implies the most fundamental change in organization. The company must be of a sufficient size to create and maintain specialized teams working on specific software areas. Such an investment is possible only in the case of *general reuse* where components are shared over a range of domains based on common software areas. It requires:

- reorganization of development around specialities,

- efficient inter-team communication,

- group planning of work between projects.

The following table summarizes the advantages and disadvantages of the proposed reuse organizations.

Table 4 : Advantages/disadvantages of the proposed reuse organizations

	Project-oriented company	Centralized component production-oriented company	Domain-oriented company
For	•no direct over-head •permits pilot ap-plication	•simple links between teams •explicit cost management of components	•knowledge of components •good control over "*for* and *with* reuse" development
Against	•limited approach	•communication overhead	•complex planning

1.4.5 Roles in a reuse organization

What new roles and changed roles do you need to support reuse?

A company in which mature reuse is established requires changes to current roles, and the creation of new roles.

In this section we describe the changes to management roles in some detail. The roles connected to projects are discussed in more detail in Chapter 2. Roles needed in the transition to reuse are described in Chapter 5.

Changed roles

Some of the most important changes to current roles are:

- Senior managers direct the company through reuse strategies. Investments in reuse are an important topic at every management level. To ensure that reuse strategies are achieved, the reuse processes must be monitored closely.

- Marketing managers analyze variability in current and future customer requirements, which are used as inputs to strategic reuse decisions.

- Product-line managers carry out strategic planning to organize reuse throughout the product-line life cycle as described in Section 1.4.3.

- Quality managers should consider reuse as a means of contributing to the improvement of quality in the company.

- Project managers coordinate between related projects, and are thus faced with a more complex environment. Planning a reuse project is also more challenging, because reuse opportunities are discovered as the project progresses. The changed role of the project manager is discussed further in Chapter 2.

- Designers, developers and testers have their roles expanded from "programmers" to "integrators", and the ability to evaluate, understand, adapt and integrate larger components will complement their skills. A stronger emphasis on quality is placed on the reusable components that are produced. Effort is also shifted from implementation and test to analysis, design and integration.

New roles

The new or largely modified roles involved in a mature reuse organization are:

- Domain experts. These are specialists in using the company's domain knowledge to work with customers and projects to achieve the maximum reuse potential, in both development *for* and *with* reuse. They actively participate in the domain analysis activity.

- Component coordinators. These are responsible for coordinating reuse development within a domain. This role will overlap with the product manager when the domain is the product line. They are an important resource for projects using and enhancing components.

- Component experts. These are specialists in adapting a set of components for different needs. They will typically work with a project in the development phase.

- Development *for* reuse experts. These are specialists in techniques for increasing the reusability of components. This includes the best methods of representing, documenting and testing reusable components. This role is further described in Chapter 2.

- Repository managers. These are responsible for the repository, and for helping less experienced users locate suitable candidate components. They do not require deep knowledge about specific components, but are specialists in the repository structure, i.e. the classification and *term space*, and have a general overview of the available components. The role of the repository manager is discussed further in Chapter 3.

- The reuse coordinator. He is in charge of coordinating the chosen reuse strategy for the whole company.

Some of these roles may be performed by the same person. This is dependent on the company involved, its size and organization. In general, more cooperation and communication is required in a reuse organization.

1.4.6 Incentives for reuse

What kind of incentives could you use when introducing reuse?

Incentives provide a means of stimulating immediate organizational and individual interest in reuse.

We can divide incentives into two factors:

- the incentive receiver, such as an individual, group, project or line organization.

- the incentive timing: immediate or delayed.

For each factor, we can provide incentives to promote both development *for* and *with* reuse. This section briefly discusses some of the most common incentives and their applicability in different contexts.

The incentives discussed here are equally applicable within an accounting unit or between accounting units. They are also applicable for commercial reuse libraries, i.e. for companies acting as component brokers.

Funding component development

Paying for development of reusable components is an effective incentive, but has several drawbacks:

- Immediate payment for components delivered to the repository can result in a number of components which are never reused. This can be avoided by ensuring that the component producer must reimburse the reuse incentive for "bad" components.

- Delayed payment until the component is reused is difficult to administer on projects for which temporary organizations have been set up. Unrestricted use of this type of incentive can result in a "cheating" relationship between producers and consumers. It may also be difficult to get the consumer to pay for reused components.

- Payments to a group may be better than to an individual, as the opportunity to create reusable components depends on the job allocation. Reward for producing reusable components should not take the focus off the project, i.e. it should not be more profitable to produce reusable components than components for the project.

- It might be difficult to distinguish between extra effort which should be rewarded, and effort which is already paid for, for example, in a project already devoted to development for reuse.

Funding component reuse

When a component is reused we can provide funds to the reuser, effectively rewarding the reuser for using a reusable component. Such funds should not be connected to the reuse *per se*, but rather to the resources saved through reuse. This payment should be divided between the provider and the consumer of the component. There is an obvious possibility for abuse of this incentive by overestimation of the amount of resources needed to develop the functionality without reuse.

Recommendation

If financial incentives are to be used to encourage reuse, we recommend the following approach:

- Immediate payment of (part of) the extra cost involved in development *for* reuse on completion of the component. The development for reuse should not be started before approval by the reuse coordinator. The payment should be allocated to the project, but distributed internally to those responsible, i.e. the extra cost can be refunded at a project, group or individual level.

- Establishing a bonus system to be awarded when components are reused, where the bonus depends on the resources saved or additional functionality provided. For this, some part of the reduction in project budget should be divided:

  — One part for the component consumer. This can be a financial bonus at an appropriate level, otherwise the reduction in project budget may discourage reuse.

  — One part for the component producer, to reward the reuse of his component.

  The remainder of the savings brought about by reuse will cover the initial bonus for the component and administration of the reuse repository and constitute reuse profit. Any bonus should not be paid before the successful completion of the project that is reusing the component, as the decision to reuse may change.

Recognition programmes and promotions

The recognition of expert reusers, both producers and consumers, is an effective means of gaining publicity and recognition for the reuse programme, as is the promotion of expert developers for reuse. The risk in the use of promotion is that a new position might not make maximum use of the developers' reuse skills (the Peter Principle). This can be avoided by providing a separate career path for reuse experts and reuse coordinators.

1.5 What should you do next?

A company which focuses only on the technical issues without addressing non-technical ones, or which treats reuse as an independent collection of tools and techniques, is likely to get disappointing results.

Implementing reuse in a company is a matter of adopting new ways of thinking and new habits at all levels in the hierarchy: designers, testers, middle and senior management. Because of the human tendency to resist change—at least initially—the implementation of reuse is difficult and time-consuming.

A company employing planned reuse requires a more mature infrastructure. Better communication and coordination is required from employees at all levels of the company. The adoption of reuse within a company implies a certain maturity. Accordingly, a *reuse maturity model* has been developed to support the evaluation of a company's reuse status and stepwise improvements that may be used to progress towards reuse. To be successful we need a properly defined reuse strategy, a well defined action plan, a reuse implementation process and the right resources. Both these issues are discussed in detail in Chapter 5.

In summary, the definition of a reuse introduction programme implies:

- Defining and understanding the critical issues for reuse: technical, economical, organizational and cultural.

- Defining your reuse objectives, and assessing the reuse potential of your organization, preferably by using a reuse maturity model.

- Assessing the business potential for reuse.

- Defining possible strategies for the introduction of reuse that address product and contractual issues, the development process itself, the development environment, the organization and the organizational change process.

- Choosing a reuse introduction strategy based upon prevailing priorities and risks, and adopting a suitably progressive and iterative process.

Defining a reuse introduction programme suitable for your company depends on the extent to which it already implements reuse. You can establish this by carrying out a *reuse maturity assessment* of the company. This assessment is based on a number of key factors internal to the company that must be taken into account when devising its reuse strategy and defining the appropriate actions programme. These factors belong to five categories, presented below.

1.5.1 The organization

Successful reuse introduction requires a new way of working for your organization, all the way from management commitment to a new way of doing business. The following factors are relevant:

- **Reuse strategy**: Reuse introduction has to be built upon a long-term strategy of planning and coordination for reuse among projects.

- **Reuse assessment**: Reuse introduction is a costly process, and the company must continuously monitor its ability to achieve its reuse goals.

- **Legal issues**: It is important for a company to be aware of any relevant legal or contractual constraints on reuse, and to comply with them. This is discussed in Chapter 5.

- **Cost and pricing**: The company must invest in reuse to increase its reuse capability. The investment should be based upon a product pricing and funding approach which supports the company's reuse strategy.

- **Product line**: The way a company presents its product line has a strong impact on its ability to implement reuse. Consolidating the product line relies on two sub-factors: the ability of the company to meet its customer's requirements, and its commitment to provide a long-term, consistent and adequate product line.

1.5.2 Project management

Project management is more challenging in a reuse environment, with new objectives, new processes, and new relations outside the project to consider. The following factors are relevant:

- **External coordination**: Project managers have to manage relationships external to the project, as reuse increases dependencies with other projects.

- **Project planning**: Classical planning of time, costs and resources is harder when introducing reuse.

- **Project tracking**: Tracking and accounting procedures have to be applied on newly introduced specific reuse activities.

- **Staffing**: The ability of staff to develop and exploit reusable components must be taken into account—not all programmers are capable of developing reusable components, and not all designers are able to build generic reusable architectures. In reuse, the management of individual competence is a key factor for success.

Chapter 2 discusses techniques to manage reuse projects in more detail.

1.5.3 The component repository

The key factors for a component repository cover the storage and retrieval of the reusable components. These are:

- **Component information**: The component is an aggregate of different pieces of information. Some constitute the information which will actually be reused; the remainder is present to assist in its reuse.

- **Component classification**: Classification support is necessary to be able to store and retrieve reusable components in an efficient manner.

- **Change management**: Change management includes the activities performed when components in the repository are updated due to enhancements or bug fixes.

- **Repository maintenance**: Repository maintenance is the continuous management of the components to assure that they satisfy the current needs of the company's cost effectiveness, and are actively used to meet the business objectives of the company.

Chapter 3 presents the techniques necessary to set up and maintain a reuse repository which fits the needs of your company in detail.

1.5.4 Reuse metrics

An effective measurement programme is essential to quantify the benefits gained from reuse. This is especially important, as development *for* and *with* reuse is very much a cost-benefit question, and without good quantitative data it is difficult to make objective decisions. The key factors are:

- **Process metrics**: these are used to estimate the effect of reuse on the lead-time and productivity of products and components.

- **Product metrics**: these are used to measure the reusability and quality of a component. Product metrics are mainly used by producers and consumers of reusable components to evaluate the components.

Chapter 4 covers reuse-specific product and process measurements and cost models.

1.5.5 The development process

In order to support reuse, the development process must integrate all technical activities needed to produce and reuse software components. The level of integration of reuse specific activities within the current development process, as well as the type of reused information, are key indicators of a company's reuse maturity.

- **Development process integration**: Development *for* and *with* reuse processes have to be fully integrated into the fundamental procedures of the company. This is a key point for successful reuse introduction.

- **Type of produced and reused information**: Reusable information is not limited to development—it appears also upstream of development. Reuse of commercial proposals is a means to respond more rapidly to market demands and to increase the competitiveness of the company. The sooner reuse components can be used in a product life cycle, the more impact reuse will have on the subsequent stages.

Development *for* reuse

Development *for* reuse deals with making reusable components that match a set of reusability and quality constraints. Emphasis in developing reusable components is placed on quality criteria, to the detriment of the production costs of the component. The capacity to develop *for* reuse raises three main factors:

- **Analyzing variability**: Different reusers will have slightly varying requirements for a reusable component. To make an optimum component, we must analyze variability in the requirements for the reusable component. At each phase of the development, variability has to be analyzed and represented in the output models of the relevant phase.

- **Expressing generality**: To satisfy reusers with varying requirements, a reusable component is constructed as a general component. This means that the component can be specialized by each reuser to fit their specific requirements. At each phase of the development, generality has to be expressed in the output models of the relevant phase.

- **Cost/benefit analysis**: A cost/benefit analysis has to be done for each of the development *for* reuse alternatives.

Development *with* reuse

The techniques used in the development *with* reuse process depend greatly on the components which we have prepared in development *for* reuse, i.e. components where a lot of effort has been invested in ease of reuse require less effort when reused. The capacity to develop *with* reuse raises three main factors:

- **Functionality evaluation**: The effort required to understand a component and evaluate its functionality is one of the most costly aspects of reuse. This cost has been estimated for the maintenance activity at 40-70% of the total maintenance cost of a component. It is therefore necessary to offer extensive support to reusers, in the form of tools, methods, organizational infrastructure and so on.

- **Reuse cost evaluation**: Before deciding to reuse a component, a reuse cost evaluation must be done to assess the cost of the adaptations needed to make the components fit the requirements.

- **Adaptation/integration**: Specific techniques can be used to adapt a component. This depends on how the component has been prepared for reuse. Some of these techniques are discussed in Chapter 10.

Part B of the handbook covers the techniques that can be employed in development *for* and *with* reuse in great detail.

1.5.6 What should you read next?

This chapter has provided an introduction to the key areas of software reuse and given an insight into possible candidates for reuse. The remainder of the book goes into more detail about these key areas, and is structured as follows:

Chapter 2, *Managing a reuse project*, proposes how best to organize a project to achieve reuse goals. It will be principally of interest to project managers.

Chapter 3, *Managing a repository*, is about repository organization, and contains advice on how to classify components in the repository.

Chapter 4, *Measuring the effect of reuse*, describes reuse-specific product and process measurements and cost models. It is aimed at component producers and consumers who want to assess the quality and reusability of components, as well as project managers who need to estimate the costs and benefits of different reuse strategies.

Chapter 5, *Introducing reuse*, discusses how to introduce the methods, procedures, techniques and roles. It is aimed at those responsible for introducing reuse into an organization.

Part B, *Practising reuse*, describes specific methods and techniques for reuse using object-oriented development methods. It will be mainly of interest to engineers considering, or actively engaged on, development *for* and *with* reuse.

2 Managing a Reuse Project

2.1 Introduction

How should project managers manage reuse projects?

Managing a project involving reuse is a challenging opportunity, requiring increased communication and planning skills from the project manager.

The intention of this chapter is to serve as the project manager's guide to reuse, with emphasis on how to run a project involving an appropriate mix of development *for* as well as development *with* reuse.

The major differences in managing a project incorporating reuse are:

- an increased number of external stakeholders, leading to more negotiation and complex trade-offs,

- increased complexity in planning, because decisions concerning development *for* and *with* reuse must be taken during the project, influencing the cost and lead time.

This chapter is intended to prepare project managers for these challenges.

After having read this chapter the project manager should understand how reuse affects the traditional responsibilities of the project manager in his company:

- Committing to project goals under given constraints.
  Development *for* reuse of specific components can be part of the goals, and reusing specific components can be considered as constraints.

- Interfacing with the environment external to the project.
  Future reusers of components produced, producers of reused components, and reuse support roles will all interact with the project.

- Planning, executing and monitoring the project:

— Using a development model. This model will be developed in the sections covering development *for* or *with* reuse. A sample model is described in Section 2.4.

— Organizing and planning the project. Activities to investigate opportunities for reuse must be explicitly planned.

— Estimating resources and lead time. These estimates must continuously be updated to allow for new reuse opportunities that have been discovered.

— Staffing and scheduling. This includes planning of reuse expertise, both general and specifically for reused components.

— Defining deliverables and milestones. Reuse activities must have clear deliverables and decision points: to reuse or not to reuse a component, and which reusers should be considered as clients for the reusable components to be developed by the project.

— Monitoring the progress and review of deliverables. Suitable staff must be allocated for the development and review of reusable and reused components.

— Ensuring software quality. A project developing *for* reuse not only delivers a product, but also a set of reusable components whose quality is at least as important as the quality of the product.

The rest of this chapter is organized as follows:

Section 2.2 characterizes different types of reuse projects to help you understand and control how reuse influences software development projects, and the risks involved in each type of project.

Section 2.3 provides an overview of the roles involved in a reuse project, and some problems that can arise due to conflicting requirements. This section is intended to help a project manager staff the generic roles with actual people from his own project, and to anticipate and be prepared for any conflicts.

Section 2.4 outlines how to plan and monitor a reuse project.

Section 2.5 gives advice on appropriate reuse tool support and scenarios, with examples from the REBOOT tools.

2.2 The characteristics of reuse projects

A project manager can only achieve his reuse goals if he fully understands the reuse characteristics of the project he is managing. This section gives a project manager some guidance on how the project's reuse goals and constraints should influence his planning.

We will characterize the different types of project incorporating reuse. For each project type we will indicate its advantages and disadvantages, giving guidance on when it is appropriate to initiate a specific reuse project type. This is followed by a discussion on the maintenance and support of reusable components. The section concludes with a list of the major differences compared with "traditional" projects.

2.2.1 Development *for* reuse

What approach to development for reuse is appropriate for your organization?

Development *for* reuse consists of producing reusable components. It is appropriate early in the life cycle of a product line. We can distinguish three types of *development for reuse* project illustrated in Figure 16 (shaded area represents *development for reuse* effort):

A priori development for reuse

A posteriori development for reuse

Integrated development for reuse

Figure 16 : Development for reuse timing

- *A priori* development for reuse
  In this type of reuse project we set up a *software factory*, a specific group for designing and manufacturing reusable components for later reuse. The advantage of *a priori* development for reuse is the clear separation roles. The disadvantage is the increase in lead time for reusers of the components, and the lack of a method of ensuring their reuse. The software factory may be organized in any of the ways described in Section 1.4.4, for example, by using a permanent software factory (the *component production-oriented* company) or by using a project task force (the *project-oriented* company). The former carries the advantage of a build-up of reuse competence over time, whilst the advantage of specialized project teams in *a priori* is a build-up of domain expertise.

- *A posteriori* development for reuse
  In this method a project is initiated to extract reusable components from one or more specific applications developed within a domain. As for *a priori* development for reuse, this can be organized either as a permanent reusable software factory, or as a project task force. A permanent reusable software factory can build up a large expertise in specific techniques like reverse engineering, and people from the application domain are useful for their specialized knowledge.

  The disadvantage of the *a posteriori* approach is that the reuse potential of specific applications is limited by design decisions made during their development. It may also be difficult to involve key project members after the project is finished, as they will have been reallocated to other projects.

- Integrated development for reuse
  In this type of project the reusable components are developed in parallel with development of a specific application. This is perhaps the most mature type of reuse project. Development for reuse can be incorporated into any application development where a potential for separating out generalized components has been discovered. The

generalized components can be specialized and reused immediately in the same project, thus the lead time of the first application developing with reuse is not seriously increased.

It has also been found that this provides a good way of managing the additional costs inherent in reuse, because they are absorbed as soon as the first two applications incorporating the reusable components are delivered. It provides advantages from the management point of view, as it is only necessary to set up three teams, one to develop the reusable components and one each for the applications being developed. The disadvantages of this approach are the complexity of separating the development *for* reuse activities and the additional lead time.

Many reuse projects are a mix of all three types above. What is important is to identify which characteristics are represented in each project, and to try to avoid the disadvantages.

2.2.2 Development *with* reuse

How might development with reuse be organized in your projects?

Development *with* reuse consists of reusing existing components to build new applications. These reusable components can be sought:

- in concurrent projects if the company recently started development in this domain (as for integrated development *for* reuse),

- in a base of reusable components if we are working in a mature application domain where a considerable investment has been made in developing reusable components (as with *a priori* development *for* reuse), or

- in previously developed applications in the same domain (as with *a posteriori* development *for* reuse).

In the first case, close cooperation is needed between the product line manager and the project managers. In the last case, a significant re-engineering effort is generally needed because the selected components have probably not been developed for reuse and may be highly specialized. Nevertheless, components which encapsulate complex core functionality are usually worthwhile and can yield substantial savings.

For all cases of development with reuse, domain and component experts are key people to help identify, evaluate and adapt components. When a reuse repository is available, the repository expert also plays an important role. Section 2.3.3 describes these roles in more detail.

Another important factor is at which stage the project should start searching for the reusable components to incorporate into the product. Investigation of candidate reusable components must start early in the life cycle of the project, to allow adequate time to adapt the requirements, the specification or the design to make the best use of the components. As Ralph Johnson has said:

> If you reuse code,
> You'll save a load,
> But if you reuse design,
> Your future will shine.

There is no watertight separation between development *for* and *with* reuse. For example, people developing reusable components quite often make extensive reuse of components at lower levels. Similarly, people working on projects developing *with* reuse are inclined to identify new components within their application which have reuse potential.

2.2.3 Maintenance and support of reusable components

How should the maintenance and support of components be organized?

The maintenance and support of reusable components involves assisting reusers, correcting errors and distributing information about new versions. The maintenance and support organization deserves explicit consideration, because reusable components by their nature will be reused in different applications. There are several alternatives:

- A permanent reuse organization.
  A reusable component is taken over by a separate team. The disadvantage of this approach is that the new team generally has less knowledge about the component and the domain than the developers. The advantage is that continuity is guaranteed independent of the project.

- The project or organization developing the component.
  Here the component is supported by those that developed it. The advantage of this approach is that project members have knowledge of the domain and the component, but the continuity of the support will depend on the specific development project, e.g. if it is an *a priori* task force, it will be dissolved after the reusable components are made. It is also a heavy burden to require development projects to support their components forever.

- The most prominent reuser.
  This is an alternative for components developed within an *a priori* task force or from an application which is no longer supported as a product, but which contains reused components.

The maintenance and support of components forms an intrinsic part of reuse which must be formally organized.

2.2.4 Comparison with traditional software projects

What differences will you experience when managing a reuse project?

A project manager familiar with non-reuse software projects needs to be aware of the changes required when moving to a reuse project:

- More time may be required in earlier phases of the project.
  The analysis phase of a reuse project tends to be longer than for a traditional project without reuse, because we need both to evaluate the potential components to be reused, and to capture requirements from potential reusers. This extra effort is counterbalanced in the development phase, where we reuse some or all of the evaluated components. This is discussed in Section 2.4 and in Part B.

- Planning can be critical.
  Scheduling has to be more flexible, because decisions to reuse or develop for reuse sometimes cannot be taken at the start of the project, but rather as opportunities appear. If we find a component that can be reused and will save a lot of development time and effort, the planning of the project must be adjusted to allow for it. This also holds true (in the opposite sense) for extra time and effort allocated to developing reusable components. This is discussed in Section 2.4 and Part B.

- More dependencies on other on-going and future projects.
  The need for inter-project planning and coordination is increased, because we are dependent on other projects for the components we reuse, and other projects are dependent on us for the components we develop for reuse. This is discussed in Section 2.3.

- New roles are defined.
  The task of managing people on the project can increase, because there are more people to coordinate. The different roles in a reuse project are discussed in Section 2.3.

- Documentation is more important.
  The decision to reuse is based on the documentation quality of the reuse candidates. A component cannot be reused unless it is well documented. We must document a component to fit the development *with* reuse process, allowing for the processes of search, evaluation, reuse "as is" and possible adaptation. Documentation is discussed in Part B.

2.3 Roles in a reuse project

What new roles will you interface with on a reuse project?

How will existing roles be impacted by reuse in a project?

Good project management implies that different roles in the project are clearly identified and filled by suitable people.

Many misunderstandings can be avoided if project members are allocated clearly defined roles. A project manager needs to analyze the abilities and interests of each potential member to determine his or her role. It is particularly important to establish whether conflicting roles have been assigned to a single person. Assigning conflicting roles to the same person can avoid the potential conflict if the person is able to handle the conflicting roles. If, however, the person does not handle the conflicting roles appropriate, one of the roles will dominate, leading to biased decisions.

In this section we analyze the different roles involved in reuse projects. We have split the discussion of the roles into three points of view:

- Development.
  This covers those directly involved in stating and satisfying requirements for the component or product. We analyze this view separately for development *for* and *with* reuse.

- Management.
  This includes project and line management of resources, products, and components.

- Support.
  This includes domain experts, repository managers and so on.

We analyze each of these views in detail, and summarize the conflicts that can occur and how they may be resolved.

Note that the roles described here can be represented by one individual or a group of individuals, e.g. a component consumer can be a specific customer for a custom-made application, or a customer for an off-the-shelf application.

The following sections present the various roles we have identified from each point of view.

2.3.1 The development view

Who will be the reusers of your development effort?

2.3.1.1 Development with reuse

In development *with* reuse, the reuser must satisfy a set of requirements and he has a collection of reusable components at his disposal to achieve this. He will continuously search for and evaluate components which he may reuse to satisfy these requirement. If he wants to reuse a component, and it does not exactly match his requirements, he has two options:

- Either he adapts the component to fit the requirements (the *adaptor* role), or

- He changes the requirements so that the component can be integrated "as is" (the *integrator* role).

It may be that a combination of these alternatives is possible; this requires a cost-benefit analysis. The reuser has the opportunity to act as either integrator or adapter; he can have two different roles. Alternatively, the integrator and the adapter can be two different people, possibly not even from the same company. Note that if a component can be reused without adaptations, "as is", the reuser has only an integrator role.

If the adapted reusable component is a complete system, the reuser is only performing adaptation and the customer replaces the integrator, and any changes in the requirements must be negotiated with the customer. We can say that the customer integrates the product in the operation his business.

In earlier phases of development with reuse, for example search and evaluation, the distinction between adaptor and integrator is not important—in many cases they may be the same person. In the following sections, these roles are not distinguished unless they differ, and are just referred to as *reuser*.

2.3.1.2 Development for reuse

Can you identify all actual and potential reusers for your development effort?

Will the integrators and adapters be the same for all reuses of your development effort?

The developer *for* reuse develops components that meets the reusers' requirements. Thus the developer is responsible for:

- developing generalized solutions that satisfy all the differing requirements (both functional and non-functional) of actual and potential reusers,

- documenting both for reuse *as is* and for reuse *with adaptations*,

- testing and qualifying the components,

- delivering all the items that compose the reusable component: analysis, architectural and detailed design, code, test, test data and user documentation.

Developers for reuse should be assisted by the cost-benefit analyzer in making decisions about which functionality to incorporate in reusable components. The requirements the developer has to take into account during development for reuse come from both actual and potential reusers:

- *Actual reusers* are those waiting for the reusable components under development. They are able to express their requirements and ensure that they are taken into account.

- *Potential reusers* are those who in the future might need the functionality provided by the component. Their requirements are much harder to predict, and are thus difficult to take into account.

It is useful to divide the reuser into the integrator and adapter roles during development for reuse. This is because they have different interests to protect:

- The integrator is interested in the functionality, performance and quality of the component, as either an actual or potential customer, or as an internal customer interested in integrating the component in a subsystem or product. Different integrators will have different requirements of the component.

- The adapter imposes requirements on the reusability of the component, i.e. how easy it is to adapt. Different adapters may also have different requirements, as their domain knowledge, geographical distribution, development skills or external constraints might be different. Their requirements must also be taken into account when we develop the component for reuse, e.g.:
  — Adequate documentation is needed to allow easy adaptation of the component.
  — The developer should try to predict the types of adaptations users may require, and prepare for them.
  — The developer should predict the lead time and effort required to reuse the component.
  — Support for the component should be planned.

In development for reuse we have possibly five different roles involved: the potential and actual integrator, the potential and actual adapter and the developer. The first four are the reuser roles during development for reuse; there may be several instances of each.

2.3.1.3 Connection between development roles

An example of the rather complex connections between the different development roles is depicted in Figure 17 below.

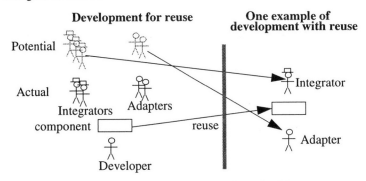

Figure 17 : Roles in development *for* and *with* reuse

This example shows a component developed *for* and *with* reuse. In the left of the figure the component is developed *for* reuse. The component must satisfy five integrators (instances of reuse), two actually waiting for the component and three potential users. The component will be adapted by four different adapters, i.e. one of the potential adapters is supposed to adapt the component for two potential integrators. There need not be a one-to-one correspondence between the integrators and the adapters.

The right of the figure shows an example of development *with* reuse, where the adapter is adapting the component for the integrator. Thus there may be a possible five cases of reuse, two for the actual integrators and three for the potential integrators.

As an example of what we mean by integrator, adapter and developer, take the fire alarm framework (described in Appendix A). The framework itself is the reusable component:

- The integrators are customers for the fire alarm systems, i.e. the adapted fire alarm framework is not integrated in any other product, but instead sold. We can say that the customer is integrating the system for his building or site.

- The adapters are those adapting the framework to provide fire alarm systems for different buyers of the fire alarm system framework.

- The developers are those developing the framework for reuse.

Suppose that the manufacturers of the fire alarm system have several product lines, each with its own framework, and that fire detectors are common subsystems for many of these product lines. The detectors are then the reusable components:

- The integrators are the developers of the different product lines, i.e. the users or buyers of fire detectors.

- The adapters are those adapting the detectors to fit the different product lines.

- The developers are those developing the fire detectors for reuse.

In this last case the integrator and the adapter might be the same person, for example in a component production-oriented company (Section 1.4.4.2), but we could also envisage that the adapter and the developer might be the same, i.e. a production-line oriented organization (Section 1.4.4.3). They could equally well be three different people.

2.3.2 The management view

Who will take the decisions concerning reuse on a project?

Who will be responsible for long-term product planning, and how is it related to reuse?

How will the division or resourcing between line and project affect reuse?

The management consists of:

- The project manager, who has the short-term goal of delivering a specific product within given resources.

- The product line manager, who has long-term responsibility for the entire product line. He has to define the product strategy, coordinate the projects developing for the product line, and allocate resources among them.

We can distinguish between technical and resource responsibilities for both project and product line. At project management level:

- The *project manager* is responsible for the project. He has a finite set of resources, primarily time and manpower, and a set of goals. He has to plan the project and allocate the resources to achieve his goals.

- The *technical manager* is responsible for the technical coordination of the project. His role includes providing the time estimates for the project manager, ensuring that the requirements are satisfied and assuring the technical quality of the product.

At product-line management level:

- The *resource manager* allocates resources to projects. This is a continuous task, initial allocations being adjusted during the course of the project. These adjustments may be necessitated by a change in goals, or due to over- or under-estimation. For example, it is not easy to predict the exact amount of work needed to adapt a component for reuse. It is important to take account of this when estimates are made.

  The resource manager is also responsible for assessing the actual usage of resources compared to planned usage throughout the lifetime of the project, and when it is completed.

- The *product line manager* determines the overall strategy and planning for the set of projects which makes up the product line, and the technical content of each project.

  He is also responsible for setting up and monitoring the reuse goals of the projects. In this task he is assisted by the quality manager and the reuse manager, for continuous assessment of the product quality and reuse goals respectively.

2.3.3 The support view

How will development for and with reuse be supported?

How will you fill the following roles: reuse development expert, cost-benefit analyzer, application domain expert, repository manager?

Reuse needs specific support at the product-line level. This support is provided by experts whose knowledge and expertise can be shared by all projects in the product line. These roles were introduced in Section 1.4.5. This section details the roles and their responsibilities within reuse projects.

- *Domain experts* support projects with their specialized knowledge of a specific domain:
  — In development *for* reuse, they support projects with their knowledge of the domain, and help analyze the *variability* and find general abstractions.
  — In development *with* reuse, they help in the analysis of the specific reuser's requirements in the context of the company's knowledge of the domain.

- *Development for reuse* experts help to represent the generality and assure the reusability of components during analysis and development for reuse. They can be experts in development for reuse:

    — in general,

    — for a specific domain or

    — with a specific development process.

    Their expertise also includes how to prepare the component for reuse, for example the preparation of documentation and test information.

- *Component experts* support the project in the reuse of specific components. This includes evaluating, adapting, integrating and testing the components. Adaptation of a component should be done so that as little as possible needs to be changed in the subsequent development phases and in the documentation.

- *Maintainers* are responsible for correcting errors, providing functional enhancements and supporting reusable components.

- The *cost-benefit analyzer* examines costs and potential earnings and is proficient in reuse cost/benefit trade-offs:

    — In development *for* reuse we must weigh the potential benefits of adding additional functionality against additional development costs. These benefits are hard to estimate as they depend on future reuse of the components.

    — In development *with* reuse, unless the component matches the requirements exactly, we must weigh the cost of adapting the component or its environment against developing the functionality from scratch. This is a difficult decision in which the main problem is evaluating the degree of change required.

    Both estimated and actual costs and benefits should be recorded with the relevant components, so that future reusers can make more precise forecasts. Such a reuse history also helps in making decisions when developing new components.

- The *repository manager* is responsible for the reuse repository and for helping the developers insert and retrieve components:

    — In development *for* reuse, the repository manager ensures that the components are inserted correctly into the repository so that they can be retrieved by potential reusers. He is also responsible for extending the classification system if it is found to be necessary. Different classification systems are described in more detail in Chapter 3.

    — In development *with* reuse, the repository manager assists the reusers to retrieve a set of candidate components which can be evaluated for possible reuse.

2.3.4 Some possible conflicts

What role conflicts might you experience?

The roles described in Sections 2.3.1-2.3.3 represent different and sometimes conflicting interests. If these differences are not understood and properly handled, problems may arise and undermine the benefits of reuse. Most of these problems appear in all software development, but they become even more important in reuse projects.

Problems occur when there are insufficient time or resources to satisfy all requirements. To analyze the possible solutions objectively, we must determine where the conflict has arisen, and the long and short term costs and benefits of different solutions.

For example, it is often the case that one person will have more than one role. This can arise when a person both develops and reuses a component in an application. In this case they may be biased towards their own requirements and tend to disregard others' requirements for the component. In this situation we should consider appointing another person to represent the interests of the other reusers.

In the following sections, we analyze the role conflicts that can arise in development *for* and *with* reuse.

2.3.4.1 Conflicts in development for reuse

The main challenge in development *for* reuse is to find the right level of generalization for a component; a component that is too general is difficult to adapt, but a highly specialized component may not fit the requirements of many reusers. As we collect the requirements from potential reusers we must always keep this trade-off in mind, because each reuser will try to maximize their benefit from the component.

This is a classical problem which occurs when analysing and specifying a product to be used by different users. It can only be solved by following a well-defined process which includes:

- holding meetings of all parties to explain and discuss their respective requirements,

- preparing detailed requirements and system specifications,

- holding formal reviews and gaining approval from all parties, i.e. reusers, developers and management.

The potential reusers in the project should follow the project after the initial requirements are agreed. They should continuously monitor the project and review intermediate development results to ensure that their requirements are satisfied. This is because new problems appear, and latent problems tend to be pushed forward in the hope that they will disappear. Unfortunately they tend to resurface just when resources are becoming exhausted. This can lead to conflict at a stage when it is difficult to find any satisfactory solution.

We strongly recommend the use of change control in reuse projects. This is best achieved by setting up a *change control board* that meets regularly to vet requests for modification throughout the development and maintenance phases.

The rest of this section discusses specific conflicts between the roles involved in development *for* reuse.

Integrator–integrator conflicts

Different integrators have differing requirements. This often leads to conflicts over the functionality of a component. The aim of development *for* reuse is to identify common requirements which are invariant for many integrators, then design components which reflect these requirements, preparing the components for specialization to meet the particular needs of each actual and potential integrator.

These conflicts are particularly dangerous when an unbalanced relationship exists between the different integrators, for example between actual and potential integrators. It can also occur in reuse development within an application project in which the application developers have most influence. In such cases it is important to find someone who can represent the minority interest, such as an application domain expert.

Adapter–adapter conflicts

The various adapters of a component may have quite different requirements for the adaptability of the component. For example, an adapter with advanced expertise who serves integrators with wide requirements will require a very general and flexible component, compared to an adapter with limited expertise who serves integrators with similar requirements. In such situations it might be advantageous to build two components, or to provide a semi-adapted version of a more general one.

Normally all reusers will want reusable components to be as close to their overall requirements as possible, minimizing the effort required to specialize the component.

Reuser–developer conflicts

Reusers and developers may conflict over the architectural design of a reusable component. Typically, reusers like components to be as specific as possible to minimize specialization effort, whereas developers prefer coarse-grained components which are easier to develop and maintain.

To avoid this conflict, the reusers and maintainers of components should participate in reviews and approve the design of components. Development for reuse experts should also be used to resolve such conflicts.

Another source of conflict concerns the combination of different functionalities which were not designed to work together. This problem is similar to "feature interaction" in telecommunication systems, and multiple inheritance problems in object-oriented programming. For every combination of functionalities required, we should perform an analysis to see if it is really necessary, and study its impact on the design.

Developer–management conflicts

Developers and potential reusers who have identified a reuse opportunity are usually interested in developing it *a priori* or within the project, as this is more practical from an engineering viewpoint. This leads to the consumption of more time and resources than planned, and can also affect the lead time of the actual reuser due to the extra effort required to make the component reusable.

On the other hand, the resource manager wants to keep the project to its cost and time schedules, and may be unwilling to allocate further resources without guaranteed benefits. He will usually suggest an *a posteriori* development for reuse to reduce the risk to the project.

This conflict can be resolved with a cost-benefit analysis of the different alternatives, examining alternative strategies of developing *for* reuse at different times, and weighing them against possible added functionality.

Product-line management–project management conflicts

The product-line manager, responsible for the long-term evolution of a product line, and a project manager, responsible for a specific product, may conflict over how much development for reuse effort a project should provide for the benefit of subsequent reusers. This may happen when additional development for reuse opportunities are discovered after the project has settled its goals and resources. These opportunities allow the product-line management to enhance the possibilities for development *with* reuse in future projects, but constitute a risk to the current project.

It is important to re-evaluate the original goals of the project when additional development for reuse becomes a possibility, so that the project can maintain realistic goals. We can also consider a change to the timing of the project to take the new opportunities into account. The assistance of the application domain expert is useful here, to evaluate potential reuse, and a cost-benefit analysis will also help in making a decision.

2.3.4.2 Conflicts in development with reuse

The main problem in development *with* reuse is to know when to reuse. Is the effort to search for, evaluate, understand and possibly adapt a reusable component less than the effort used to develop it from scratch? When we have decided to reuse a component that does not fit our requirements completely, we must decide what change is required to the component and who will do the work.

Integrator–adapter conflicts

Integrators and adapters may conflict if the adapter has found a component which fits some but not all of the integrator's requirements. The adapter will save considerably by reusing the component, but the component will not meet all the integrator's requirements. A change in the requirements must then be negotiated between the integrator and the adapter.

During the requirement analysis this should not be considered as a conflict, as such negotiation is part of the requirement process. It can offer mutual benefits if the adapter can reduce costs by reuse and by negotiating a relaxation in the unfulfilled requirements. It may also be that the reused components offer additional functionalities that were not part of the original requirements, but enhance the end-product.

Later in the development (for example during the design phase), new reuse opportunities may occur. These should not lead to a reconsideration of the agreed specification unless this also appears to have unqualified advantages.

Reuser–maintainer conflicts

Reusers adapt and use reusable components, whereas maintainers are responsible for correcting bugs and, when necessary, enhancing components. There is a grey zone between *enhancement* and *adaptation*. If a reuser can persuade the maintainer to enhance the component so that he can reuse it afterwards without modification, the reuser saves in both the development and maintenance of the adaptation. It may even be cost effective, because the maintainer may understand the component better than the reuser.

Developer–reuser conflicts

There is always a tendency to regard any code one has not written oneself as a risk—the "not invented here" syndrome. This is why reusable components should be developed and documented according to a well-defined procedure, to ensure a specific quality level and thus increase the confidence of the reusers.

Nevertheless, a reuser will be disappointed if a component proves difficult to adapt to his needs, and he may blame the developer. The best way to avoid this conflict is to maintain and provide full quality documentation, development history and reuse documentation with reusable components.

The domain expert and repository manager are roles which help the reuser select a relevant set of components, and the component expert is a role which helps him to evaluate, adapt and integrate the component. They provide a bridge between the developer and the reuser.

Reuser–management conflicts

Development *with* reuse requires time to be spent on investigation of potential reusable components early in the life cycle of the project. Many components investigated will turn out not to be usable, so allocating resources to this activity is a risk. The optimum amount of time to allocate to this activity is difficult to estimate. Reusers must have enough time to be sure that a component can be reused before they commit to reusing it, whereas management will require a decision as soon as possible. The evaluation of potential components can run in parallel with the system analysis stage of the project. Synchronization between component search and analysis is necessary when good candidates are found which have to be incorporated in the architectural design. Domain experts and component experts can provide support in these activities.

Where reuse is possible, it is more difficult to plan early phases of the development (analysis and architectural design). However, once reusable components have been identified and evaluated, it becomes easier to plan subsequent phases than in classical software development, where the time required to design and implement complex objects is subject to frequent re-evaluation.

2.3.5 Summary

From the detailed discussion in this section, each company and project must determine how the existing organization and personnel can satisfy the new roles required for reuse, and whether any new skills or expertise are required.

2.4 Adapting a project to reuse

How will you adapt your project planning to incorporate reuse?

How will planning be different from a project not involving reuse?

To successfully execute a reuse project, you need to know how reuse affects the planning, activities and documentation of a project.

This section discusses how a project manager's work is affected by reuse. We do this by showing where reuse manifests itself in the various tasks of a project manager. To make this discussion more realistic, we use as an example an incremental development process influenced by [SEL-84-101] and the ideas behind the "Cleanroom" software development process. The Cleanroom process is described in detail in Chapter 12. Incremental development is only one possible development model; for example, it is possible to consider the traditional "waterfall" model as an incremental development with only a single increment. The adaptations to incorporate reuse are equally applicable to other development models.

This section is organized as follows:

- Section 2.4.1 gives an overview of a possible project life cycle, and its activities. For each stage we identify additional activities that can arise due to reuse. The technical content of these activities is explained in more detail in Part B.

- Section 2.4.2 analyzes the project plan, and suggests how reuse should be taken into account and made visible in the plan.

- Section 2.4.3 discusses cost estimation, scheduling and planning in a reuse environment. Specific cost models are described in Chapter 4.

- Section 2.4.4 examines the deliverables of the project, and how they are influenced by reuse. The documentation of reusable components is discussed in more detail in Part B.

- Section 2.4.5 considers the impact of reuse on quality assurance. Part B treats testing of reusable components in more detail.

- Section 2.4.6 discusses measurements. The particular product and process metrics suggested for reuse are discussed in more detail in Chapter 4.

2.4.1 The impact of reuse on the phases of a project

How will you adapt your project life cycle for reuse?

Figure 18 illustrates a sample development life cycle with activities and corresponding document reviews. The development life cycle uses incremental development under the control of a construction plan. How incremental development can be used to achieve the reuse goals is explained later. We have expanded the specification phase in some detail.

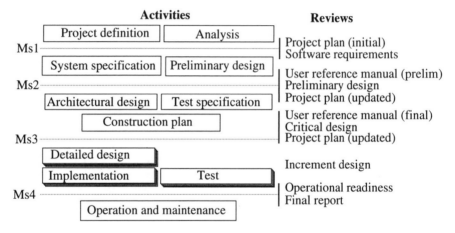

Figure 18 : A general development life cycle

This figure shows critical milestones (Ms) where we make formal decisions about the content and direction of the project, for example whether a project should be continued. The decisions made at the various milestones are:

- *Milestone 1*: We decide which requirements to analyze

- *Milestone 2*: We decide which requirements to implement

- *Milestone 3*: We review the feasibility of the project and its resourcing

- *Milestone 4*: We check that the product is complete and ready for use.

These milestones (in particular Milestone 1 and Milestone 2) should also be extended with reuse decisions, such as which customers we should give priority to, which development *for* reuse approach (Section 2.2.1) we should use, and so on. We will discuss in more detail the appropriate reuse decisions to prepare for at each milestone in connection with the discussion of the corresponding phase.

In the rest of this section we briefly describe each activity and the impact of reuse. For each adaptation for reuse, the goals, resources and deliverables of the corresponding activity must be clearly defined and monitored by the project manager.

2.4.1.1 Project definition and reuse

How will reuse affect the project definition phase?

The intention of the project definition is to establish the project and the project plan. The project plan includes the purpose of the project. A project definition contains the following additional reuse activities:

- *(for)* Identify product potential within the company, i.e. find out if this is a possible product line for the company, or whether it is likely to be a one-off product.

- *(for)* Identify potential generality in the software requirements. Add these proposals (clearly marked as proposals!) to the software requirements, and list them in the project plan as potential reuse opportunities.

During the definition of a project incorporating reuse, the project manager must ensure that the appropriate reuse roles are available to carry out the initial phases of the project (see Section 2.3 and Chapter 1). He should also compile a list of experts he may need, including their expertise and availability.

Initial reuse activities in the analysis phase should be clearly defined with resources and deliverables.

2.4.1.2 Requirements analysis and reuse

How will reuse affect the analysis phase?

Analysis is the establishment of the user requirements, i.e. what the software system is required to do. This results in a software requirements document. Reuse activities that should occur in parallel to requirements analysis are:

- *(with)* Study potential reusable components. Evaluated components should be recorded as potential reuse opportunities. If we find components which cover large parts of the customer requirements, we should investigate the possibility of negotiating the customer's requirements so that the components can be reused without adaptation. There is also a possibility that components with additional functionality will be discovered, that can be offered to the customer.

- *(for)* Identify potential reusers (reuse customers), and collect and analyze their requirements. A list of all potential reusers should be included in the project plan.

The output of this phase is the software requirements document which is presented to all customers, both end-users and potential reusers. To analyze the requirements it is helpful to map them into an analysis model. In Part B we illustrate this with an object-oriented model. The analysis model will then be an important input to the preliminary design.

The milestone 1 decision (deciding which requirements to analyze) will then be extended with overall reuse decisions such as:

- Which reusers are worthy of further investigation, and how much resource should be allocated to this activity?

- Which large components should be reused, and how should resources be allocated for further investigation of potential components?

The decisions at this stage will be on a strategic level, e.g. reuse of platform, development for market segments. It can also involve decisions to allocate further resources for investigation of more operative reuse opportunities, e.g. the reuse of a specific subsystem or the requirements of some potential customers.

2.4.1.3 System specification and reuse

How will reuse affect the system specification phase?

System specification is an implementation-independent specification of what the system should do. In our example it takes the form of a user reference manual, or can be an application programmer's interface for internal components. The following activities are added to this phase due to reuse:

- (*for*) Prepare documentation describing how reusability in the system can be exploited by reusers, including their required knowledge, and any constraints on the system.

2.4.1.4 Preliminary design and reuse

How will reuse affect the preliminary design phase?

Preliminary design consists of a draft of the design, prepared to estimate the feasibility of implementing the requirements. The preliminary design should capture the invariant parts of the design, and prepare for variability in the reusable components. The preliminary design should also investigate the incorporation of any existing reusable components that have been evaluated. Since we still have not taken a final decision on which potential reusers to satisfy, the preliminary design can have alternatives. Additional activities at the stage due to reuse are:

- (*with*) Analyze identified reusable components for the required functionality. Evaluate their reusability and adaptability.

- (*for*) Analyze reuse requirements from different potential reusers to discover common, specific and conflicting requirements. Collect benefit figures and probabilities for actual reuse from all reusers for all requirements.

- (*for* and *with*) Propose alternative solutions and make an estimate of their costs, lead times and risks.

- (*with*) Identify subsystems that can be reused.

- (*for*) Identify subsystems that can be made reusable.

We should also analyze the effort needed by the different support roles (see Section 2.3) for each alternative design, and estimate the need for different experts and personnel to fill the roles of the potential customers. Some roles will already be involved in the project by this time, such as the domain expert and cost-benefit analyzer.

An example of this activity is illustrated in Figure 19. Here we have developed both *for* and *with* reuse when making a new reusable system. There were in total of eleven possible requirements for the system, and we evaluated five potential reusable components.

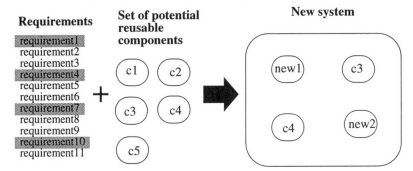

Figure 19 : Reusing components and satisfying reuse requirements

The particular design alternative shown in Figure 19 incorporates the seven non-shaded requirements, and reuses two of the potential components (*c3* and *c4*). We need two new components (*new1* and *new2*). Note that the two new components can themselves have reuse potential, i.e. be candidates for development *for* reuse. A more thorough search might show that there are further components we can reuse.

The selected preliminary design, updated software requirements and user reference manual should be reviewed by all potential customers. At the milestone 2 meeting, a decision should be made in favour of one of the design alternatives, including both components to be reused and requirements to be fulfilled. This decision should also include a strategy for development *for* reuse (see Section 2.2.1). Plans and resources for the investigation of additional reuse opportunities with components at lower levels should be allocated.

2.4.1.5 Architectural design and reuse

How will reuse affect the architectural design phase?

Architectural design extends the preliminary design to enable a construction plan to be defined. There are no additional activities due to reuse other than to ensure the reusability of the architecture (when developing *for* reuse), and to ensure that the identified components are properly integrated in development *with* reuse.

2.4.1.6 The test specification and reuse

How will reuse affect the test specification phase?

The test specification is the basis for testing and certifying the system. Testing must also incorporate the variability, so that reusers can reuse as much as possible of the test effort. The testing of reused and reusable components is discussed in more detail in Part B.

2.4.1.7 The construction plan and reuse

How will reuse affect the construction plan phase?

In incremental development, the construction plan provides a basis for starting with a small system and incrementally adding functionality. The construction plan can incorporate invariant requirements in the initial increments, and add specific requirements for particular reusers in later increments. This will ensure that a reuser takes his component from the most suitable increment, and adds his additional functionality. We can also choose not to do the detailed design and implementation of the increments only needed by potential customers, allowing them to add their own increments. It is also advisable to include reused components in early increments, to reduce the risk that they are found unsuitable. Deliveries from subprojects set up to develop larger subsystems must be included in the construction plan. The development of a construction plan is treated in more detail in Chapter 12.

   After the completion of the architectural design, test specification and construction plan, a final decision about the content of the project is taken. This may include minor reuse decisions, similar to those at milestone 2.

2.4.1.8 The detailed design and reuse

How will reuse affect the detailed design phase?

This is the detailed design of a specific increment. The project manager must ensure that the detailed design preserves the variability and invariance in the architectural design, and monitor the reuse of components for required effort and resultant quality.

   Further reuse opportunities, regarding development both *for* and *with* reuse, can be discovered as development proceeds, and these must be handled by making the required changes to the project. It may be found that the reuse of selected components is more difficult than initially expected. The project manager must then decide on suitable action.

2.4.1.9 Implementation and reuse

The project manager must ensure that components intended (or declared) to be reused *as is* are not modified, otherwise problems may arise with maintenance.

2.4.1.10 Testing and reuse

The project manager must assure that the components developed for reuse are of an appropriate quality. Milestone 4 after final testing ensures that the product is ready to be delivered and put into operation. The product includes any components developed for reuse.

2.4.1.11 Operation and maintenance and reuse

How will reuse affect the operation and maintenance phase?

This stage consists of the handover of the developed system to the operation and maintenance organization. This handover includes any components developed for reuse.

The project is concluded with a final report. This should summarize the reuse experiences, including the reuse cost data. The project plan discussed in the next section details the reuse aspects that should be summarized in the final report.

2.4.2 The impact of reuse on project planning and reporting

How will reuse affect the project plan?

In this section we discuss the activities of project planning and reporting, and how they are affected by reuse. We first discuss the impact of reuse on project planning activities, then discuss how an example project plan will be affected by reuse. Finally we discuss how reuse affects progress reporting.

2.4.2.1 Project planning and reuse

Project planning consists of the following activities:

- Determining the goals of the project. When reuse is involved, this will include specific reuse goals, for example, how does the project fit into the reuse strategy for the product family?

- Planning the technical work of the project in terms of resources and scheduling. Here we must allocate time and resources for the necessary reuse activities, for example, allowing specific time to investigate reusable components and possibilities for development for reuse.

- Organizing the project with respect to project and external personnel. Here we must ensure that we have sufficient manpower and competence to perform the reuse activities and to fill the reuse roles described in Section 2.3.

- Analysing the risks of the project. The risks associated with reuse, for example specific components or customers, must be explicitly considered.

The results of these activities are documented in the project plan.

2.4.2.2 The project plan and reuse

The intention of the project plan is to serve as a living record of the plans, status and history of the project. The project plan is usually updated and reviewed three times, once after the project definition, again after the preliminary design, and finally after construction planning. The construction plan is the detailed project plan for the development phase. The relationship between the different versions of the project plan and the construction plan is illustrated in Figure 20.

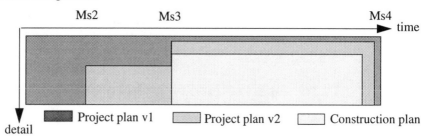

Figure 20 : Project plan and construction plan

The initial project plan (v1) prepared at the beginning of the project only contains a detailed plan for the requirements analysis, and only rough estimates for the project beyond milestone 2. This is represented by the darkest area in the figure. The project plan (v2) updated after the preliminary design contains everything except the construction plan.

We can choose to split the project plan into several documents covering different phases of the development process. We can also decompose the project plan in a hierarchy if the project is divided into subprojects.

To show how reuse affects a project plan, we have used as an example a project plan structure adapted from [SEL-84-101]. The areas specifically concerned with the impact of reuse on the project are italicized:

Title page. Document number, project name, report title, revision, report date (initial and revision data), customer name, contract identifier.
Table of contents

1. Functional overview

   1.1 Purpose. The "mission statement". Here we should state *the major reuse purposes of the system*, i.e. how it fits into *the reuse strategy of the product line*. Actual and *potential reuse customers* are listed here.

   1.2 Background. A brief description that shows where the software fits into any overall system or product line. How any current system is improved, how the new system will operate, and the expected benefits. *A summary of any components to be reused.*

   1.3 A list of functions and estimated resources. This is a summary, and refers to more detailed technical documents.

   1.4 Items required from customers (including schedules). Here we should analyze the different customers independently, and also *take into account reusers*. This is also the place to state *dependencies on reusable components under production*.

   1.5 Customer deliverables (including schedules, delivery location, medium and quantity). If the structure of the deliverable is known it should be stated, otherwise a more detailed structure should be provided on a specified date. *In development for reuse, the deliverables for different customers and reusers should be stated separately when they differ.*

2. Organization

   2.1 Internal organization. An organization diagram of the project organization, roles and relationships, and a list of assigned personnel with expertise and period on the project. For critical members, other responsibilities should be recorded. *For a project involving reuse, we must identify and document reuse roles, responsibilities and tasks.*

   2.2 Subprojects. References to subprojects which are part of the project. These subprojects will appear in resources, milestones and schedules, but will have their own detailed project plans. *For development of larger components for reuse, it is helpful to establish a separate subproject so that we can plan this effort independently, and so that the current project only becomes one among several customers.*

   2.3 Management and support organization. The project steering committee, with product and resource interfaces between line management and the project, are *extended with reuse tasks and responsibilities*. Project support organizations are *extended with reuse support* and *their reuse interface with the project is defined here*.

   2.4 External organization. Customers, *reusers*, interfacing groups and projects (and their schedules) etc. *In a project incorporating reuse, actual people representing all potential customers and reusers can be found here.*

3. Technical approach

   3.1 Development process. A reference to the chosen development process, and documentation of deviations. *Additional reuse approaches, activities and changes done to incorporate reuse development are documented here.*

   3.2 Development environment. The target, development, hardware, software etc. This is a summary of data from the software requirements, and *can contain relevant reuse information, such as different platforms to be supported etc.*

   3.3 Project repositories and configuration management. This section details information such as change control, configuration control, communication methods and the organization of a change control board. *In a project incorporating reuse, this includes the treatment of reusable components, both reused and produced.*

   3.4 Technical assumptions and constraints. For a large or complex project, these could be defined in a separate technical plan.

4. Management approach

   4.1 Project goals and priorities. *Here we include the reuse goals of the project and their priorities relative to the other goals.*

   4.2 Milestones, schedules and costs. Here we must specify *what to check regarding reuse at key milestones*, the *scheduling* and *costs of the reuse activities*. Frequency and mechanisms of reporting should *incorporate reporting on reuse activities and results*. Deliverables and sign-offs should *specify reusable components*. Project initiation and termination with *regard to the reuse goals*. These topics are further discussed in Section 2.4.3.

   4.3 Resource requirements. This section lists personnel, hardware, office accommodation, conference facilities, team structures, training and team formation. Here we should specifically *consider team structure with respect to the reuse goals of each team*, and the *need for additional reuse training or support.*

   4.4 Risk management. This section details both technical and managerial risks, such as contractual risks, technology, size, complexity, personnel, the customers and external factors. For each risk, a probability of occurrence and severity analysis should be estimated. The responsibility for each managing risk should be allocated. *When reuse is involved, we should analyze the risks involved with each additional customer and with the larger potentially reusable components.*

   4.5 Quality assurance. This section describes the project's approach to quality assurance, i.e. external and internal, process and product, project and team. Quality assurance is discussed in Section 2.4.5. For a large project, or one with stringent quality requirements, a separate quality plan may be necessary.

   4.6 Metrics. This section describes how the project will collect data on its progress and products. This is described in Section 2.4.6 and Chapter 4.

5. Plan update history

   Plans for updating the project plan.

How much of the information we must document in the project plan, and how much we can refer to standard company procedures and structures, will vary from company to company. As experience of reuse matures, it is possible to standardize much of the project plan, including how to handle reuse.

2.4.2.3 Progress reporting and reuse

The status of the project is reported regularly to monitor the project. This progress report usually contains major recent and planned events, schedules and resource changes and consequences, problems, risks and status. Reuse events should be recorded explicitly:

- *For* reuse decisions. This section contains all open (under investigation) and closed (accepted or rejected) *for reuse* opportunities, such as potential generalizations, customers and reusable subcomponents. Each opportunity should be closed with an explanation.

- *With* reuse decisions. This section contains all open and closed *with reuse* opportunities, i.e. evaluated components. Each opportunity should be closed with an explanation, which should also be included in the reuse history of the component.

In addition to this, the resources used and work completed should be reported explicitly for the reuse activities.

2.4.3 The impact of reuse on cost estimation

How will reuse affect cost estimation?

Estimating and monitoring the time and effort used on the project, and allocating the right people to different activities are key tasks of a project manager.

Making good estimates is still an art in software engineering, and the pressure on the project manager to change his estimates due to market forces may be considerable. This situation can be compared to a cook promising an omelette in ten minutes, and the customer becoming impatient after six minutes and asking for it to be finished in nine. The cook can either say that this is impossible, or turn up the heat. The result will be an omelette nothing can save—burned in one part and raw in another [Brooks75]. The same is true of software development!

Costs estimation in projects incorporating reuse, for example resulting from lead time and staff, needs more incremental treatment. This is mainly for two reasons:

- Development for reuse requires extra resources and time. It is not possible to estimate at the start of the project which components should be developed for reuse, and the number of additional requirements we may want to incorporate.

- Using reusable components represents potential savings, but also requires investment in investigating components, not all of which can be reused.

Wherever possible you should start from a cost estimation based on no reuse. From this you can estimate how the different reuse decisions will affect staffing and lead time, and weight the benefits and costs against the risks for the entire project. The calculation of the overall saving due to reuse must take into account cases where reuse is abandoned and all candidate components are discarded. The effort saved in reusing components that were easily found and reused partly pays for more complex retrievals and evaluations that do not lead to reuse.

The following is an example of distribution of time and effort on an average project without reuse. You should compile a similar table based on your company's development process and experience with similar projects, and use it to evaluate the effect of reuse. The

Table 5 : Time and effort distribution in average project

Phase	% time	% effort
Project definition	5	2
Requirements analysis	10	8
System specification	5	5
Preliminary design(s)	8	5
Architect design	6	6
Test specification	6	6
Construction plan	10	8
Detailed design	20	20
Implementation	20	30
Testing	10	10

numbers we have used as examples are partly based on [SEL-84-101] and experience with Cleanroom methods (see Chapter 12). A lot of emphasis is put on requirements capture and specification. The numbers for testing refer to acceptance testing only, and assume that unit and subsystem tests have been replaced with inspections during design.

This table can be used to prepare estimates at the following key project stages:

- After analysis. This should be an initial estimate without taking reuse into account. The estimate will of course be very uncertain, and minimum-average-maximum values should be used to indicate a probable spread. At this stage we should be able to estimate the reuse potential for the system, both *for* and *with* reuse. The estimate is used to allocate time and effort for the system specification and preliminary design. The investigation of reusable components is quite independent of the analysis, and can be carried out by extra staff. The possibility of including a reuse expert where the reuse potential is large should be considered.

- After system specification. At this stage we have a better idea of the total size of the project. This should be used to re-estimate the entire project without reuse, and to prepare an initial estimate for each requirement.

- For alternative preliminary designs. We may wish to construct alternative designs to incorporate both *for* and *with* reuse possibilities, and the estimates should now reflect this. The risk of each alternative should also be evaluated. This estimate might be very different from the original estimate, as we might discover that we can build 90% of the system from reuse-as-is components. Alternatively, we may discover that we should build 50% of the system *for* reuse, developing all the reusable components from scratch. Detailed estimation models for reuse can be found in Chapter 4.

- After architectural design review. This is an update of the estimate for the selected preliminary design. It also contains an estimate for each of the increments in the development.

- After completion of each increment (see Section 2.4.1.7). Here we update the estimates for the remaining increments.

Generally we can say that both development *for* and *with* reuse will increase the time and effort expended on the first third of the project (up to the end of preliminary design). Depending on how much we can reuse, this can be saved in later phases, with most effort being saved in detailed design, implementation, and testing.

Development *for* reuse will increase the time and effort of all phases; the benefits are to future projects. Not, however, that time spent analyzing different reuse requirements in the earlier phases, even if we decide to not implement them, will often be valuable in stabilizing the requirements of the original customer.

2.4.4 The impact of reuse on key documents and deliverables

Here we discuss briefly the key documents produced during the project, and how they are affected by reuse. The documentation for reuse is discussed in more detail in Part B. For a discussion of the effect of reuse on the project plan, see Section 2.4.2.

2.4.4.1 Software requirements and reuse

How will reuse affect the software requirements document?

The detailed software requirements (the requirement specification) is a textual representation of all the requirements to the system. When reuse is considered, it should contain:

- A list of users. The list includes actual as well as potential customers and reusers. The different categories of users (end user, operator, etc.) for the system should be detailed. We list all customers, and the decisions, with rationales, for including or excluding their requirements in the product.

- The system context, which includes:

    — a description of any current system to be improved,

    — how the new system will operate,

    — the expected benefits,

    — any hardware and software platform and limitations, and

    — the relationship to other projects.

- A list of numbered requirements, each followed by

    — a justification of how it contributes to the requirements,

    — a classification of the requirement, including customer and importance (for example, mandatory, derived, "wish list", information only, "to be decided"),

    — a rationale for any quantitative constraints, values with limits, or a rationale for lack of specific values,

    — how the requirement is seen by the user.

- A list of components evaluated for reuse, each followed by:

    — a rationale for why it was considered, i.e. which requirements it was supposed to satisfy,

    — the evaluation criteria,

    — the result of the evaluation.

In development for reuse we identify the importance of each requirement to each potential and actual reuser. Variable requirements, i.e. requirements specific to a subset of customers, are recorded as "Special for user x". We must identify conflicting requirements. Customers are also listed in the project plan, and the decisions to include them in the reuse analysis are reported in the progress report (Section 2.4.2.3).

In development with reuse, we record all the components evaluated, as well as plans and actual resources used in the activities related to their evaluation. This information is saved both within the project and with the evaluated component.

The software requirements document and user reference manual include the requirements for the entire system, including subprojects, but for larger systems it can be split into several documents.

2.4.4.2 The user reference manual and reuse

How will reuse affect the user reference manual?

The user reference manual helps to establish a validation of the system's functionality with the customer early in the project. The advantages of drafting a user reference manual at this stage are that it:

- improves the developer's understanding of the functionality of the system,

- establishes and enforces a design-independent description of the system,

- provides a vehicle for collecting feedback from end-users.

When we develop for reuse, we have two types of customers: the customers for the final applications, and the reusers of the reusable components who build the applications. Thus when developing for reuse, we must prepare two documents:

- the *customer reference manual*, for the end-users of the components or entire system,

- the *reuser reference manual*, to help potential reusers use and adapt components.

The customer reference manual

The variability in components developed for reuse must also be reflected in any documentation for the customer. This can be provided by a partially completed document template, for example using blank space with guidelines, conditional text etc.

The reuser reference manual

The reuser reference manual helps the reuser adapt the component to his specific needs. It can be structured similarly to the customer reference manual, but in this case it can explain in each section how the component can be adapted to specific needs.

Both the customer and reuser reference manuals should be checked against the test specification (Section 2.4.4.4) to assure that all features are testable, and that tests allow for adaptations.

2.4.4.3 The architectural design and reuse

How will reuse affect the architectural design?

The architectural design exists in two versions: first there may be several alternative preliminary designs, then one is chosen and finalized. It shows the decomposition of the system into subsystems, highlighting the reused and new components, the allocation of functionality to each subsystem, and their internal interfaces.

Part B of this handbook discusses how to represent invariance and variability in the architectural design. The aim of reviews of this document is to ensure that the requirements for all customers are covered in development *for* reuse, that the integration of the reused components is feasible, and that all customer requirements are satisfied in development *with* reuse.

The architecture can be broken down into subsystems. A subsystem might be a component which we will develop *for* reuse, and can be treated as a separate subproject if necessary. Once the subsystem has been accepted as a candidate for development *for* reuse, the reuse requirements are treated with the same priority as the original customer's requirements. Components developed *for* reuse will themselves need a software requirements document, user reference manual and test specification.

In development *with* reuse, the subsystem description for a reused component in the preliminary design describes the planned adaptation and integration needed for the component.

2.4.4.4 The test specification and reuse

How will reuse affect the test specification?

The test specification models how the users will use the system—the *usage model*. This model is used to select test cases. By testing the system according to its total range of use (*usage testing*) we can make predictions of its reliability, i.e. mean time to failure estimates, and we can certify the system to a given degree of reliability. Usage testing is also most efficient in finding faults that will otherwise lead to failures in operation. The test specification will be affected by reuse in several ways:

- In development *for* reuse, we need to prepare the usage model so that potential reusers can reuse as much as possible of the test effort.

- In development *with* reuse, we must evaluate how much retesting each reused component needs based on its existing test history, and determine how that affects the selection of test cases (the *usage profile*) in the new system.

The usage model is part of the critical design review that is held before development starts. Usage modelling is treated in more detail in Part B.

2.4.4.5 The construction plan and reuse

How will reuse affect the construction plan?

The construction plan defines the incremental development of the system. Incremental development, producing working system increments that demonstrate increasing levels of end user functionality, is an effective approach to achieving better control over the quality and progress of the project, and avoiding integration problems late in the project. The construction plan is a detailed plan for the development and testing of the system; this is illustrated in the description of the project plan in Section 2.4.2.

A construction plan consists of:

- An overview in which each increment is briefly described and scheduled in time.

- For each increment:
  - Timescale and effort, giving a rough plan for each increment. These will be updated before the detailed design of each new increment. This plan is also used to estimate the cost of completing the project.
  - Implemented functionality, describing the end-user functionality that the increment implements, by reference to the user reference manual.

— Increment architecture, i.e. what part of the architecture is involved in the increment. Several increments may affect one subsystem. This situation requires additional planning.

— Increment usage profile, needed to test the functionality of the increment and its interaction with the previous increments.

— Individual reuse potential of the increment, which describes whether the increment (or part of it) implements a stand-alone functionality, and with which previous increments it can be reused.

• For each subsystem affected by several increments:

It is preferable to organize subsystems so that each increment only affects one subsystem. Sometimes this is not feasible, in which case we need to plan the implementation of the subsystem in more detail. We can then let each increment development team add their functionality to the subsystem. Alternatively, we can allow the subsystem be handled by a team or subproject that delivers the functionality required for the subsystem in increments, to fit in with the construction plan. The definition of a separate team or subproject to implement a subsystem should also be considered when the subsystem is independently reusable. For each conflicting component (i.e. affected by several increments) we must describe:

— which increments are involved,

— the functionality added by each increment,

— the development schedule, including time for fault rectification.

Reuse does not affect the structure or outline of the construction plan, but the actual selection of increments is influenced by reuse, as described in Section 2.4.1.7. This is further discussed in Part B.

2.4.4.6 The detailed increment design and reuse

How will reuse affect the detailed increment design?

The detailed increment design is the final design of each increment. This is documented in two parts, one detailing the increment's place in the construction plan, and the other updating the architectural design document for the subsystems affected. The latter part will add one new subsection for each subsystem in the architectural design document. This subsection should be updated for each increment affecting this subsystem.

2.4.5 The impact of reuse on quality control and assurance

How will reuse affect quality processes?

Quality control in projects involves walk-throughs, regular reviews, end of work inspections, testing and so on. Quality assurance consists of ensuring that these activities are carried out, usually by collecting metrics and auditing. The quality activities must ensure that we are achieving our reuse goals.

A good way to ensure that the whole project is following its plans and will reach its goals is to appoint a steering committee. This provides a forum for discussion of any change in constraints on the project, such as resources, requirements and effort. When problems or conflicts arise, the project manager can propose several solutions, which are then discussed and decided within the committee. This committee should also have a mandate to decide on issues concerning development *with* or *for* reuse which have a major impact on the project schedule and goals. Responsibility for project quality assurance to monitor the day-to-day project work should also be assigned. This is an important role for projects developing reusable components, as they should follow extended standards for documentation and testing.

For each quality control activity, we should evaluate the following reuse-specific questions:

- Are there any undiscovered potential reusers of our reusable components?

- Has all generality in the specification been taken into account? This should be checked against the list of potential reusers and their requirements.

- Is the generality appropriately documented? Part B of this handbook gives guidance on how to do this.

- Can this component or any subcomponent be generalized further? A list of components and subcomponents should be checked and a rationale be provided for each.

- Are there further opportunities for reuse of components? Each component we intend to develop from scratch should have a rationale justifying our choice. A search for reusable components should have been performed, and any decisions to reject any of the retrieved components recorded.

- Are the reuse activities planned, documented and monitored?

- Are the reuse processes appropriate?

2.4.6 Measuring the effectiveness of reuse

Should you collect any additional reuse metrics, and if so, what?

Measurements are used for two reasons on the project:

- to assess the progress of the project compared to similar projects in the past

- to provide data for improving estimation models for future projects.

Reuse can have a dramatic effect on common metrics used in quantitative project management; if we do not use models that take reuse into account, the measurements will not be very useful. Some examples of the effect of reuse are:

- *Source code growth rate* will be increased by reused components. Additional time used in development for reuse, as well as time spent on the evaluation phase prior to including a component in the system, will decrease it.

- *Effort estimated and used* will be affected by reuse: successful reuse will decrease the effort estimate, whereas unsuccessful attempts to reuse will increase used effort without any benefits.

- *System size estimates* are unreliable if we include large reused components of which we only reuse parts. Size estimates become misleading if we do not distinguish between new and reused code.

- *Error and remark rate* represents the number of errors found in the different phases by quality assurance activities. Error rates tend to drop when we use reusable components.

Collecting measurements increases the overhead of the project, and only measurements which are useful should be collected. The following four fundamental measurements are collected in most projects and should be adapted to reuse:

- time, e.g. planned versus actual start and completion date for activities,

- effort, e.g. planned versus actual effort data for activities,

- functionality (or size), e.g. function points, lines of code, documentation,

- quality, e.g. defects found in reviews, testing and operation.

For each of these measurements, we should record the estimates that we use and the final results. We must also decide on the measurement granularity we want, or that is feasible. They should be collected at the same granularity as that at which the planning has been carried out. The following gives some indications of how to adjust these measurements for reuse:

- make an estimate of development effort, time, functionality and quality without reuse,

- collect time and effort used in development *for* and *with* reuse activities in each phase and for each component,

- calculate the percentage of functionality added by incorporating reuse requirements (in the preliminary design and critical design estimates),

- calculate the percentage of functionality reused by incorporating reusable components (in the preliminary design and critical design estimates).

For all these measurements, we must be careful to distinguish between discrepancies that arise from to reuse, and those from other sources.

Chapter 4 discusses reuse measurements in detail.

2.5 Reuse tools

What tool support will you need?

Reuse projects require special tools to support the reuse process. Some of your existing tools may help, but new tools are usually required to obtain successful reuse.

This section examines these reuse requirements, and describes how these can be fulfilled by appropriate tools. We have also included a tool scenario based on the REBOOT environment, and described how REBOOT can be integrated into a CASE tool.

2.5.1 The requirements for tool support in reuse

We have already described typical reuse activities. These include the activities of the project manager and the software developers. Their tool support is described separately below.

2.5.1.1 Tool support for project management

The project manager is active before, during and after the project is finished. His activities include the planning of the project, the monitoring of the project and (often) the evaluation of the project. The project manager has special needs in the project evaluation phase of a project incorporating reuse. The important issues are:

- the number of components reused

- the number of reusable components developed

- their quality

- the productivity of the developers

- the development time required

The data for the first two can be obtained from a reuse development environment by logging the insertion and extraction of reusable components from the repository. The data for quality can be obtained using a tool to collect quality metrics for components, and by user experience when reusing them. By quality, we mean the robustness, bug-count and portability of the component, as well as the accuracy of its classification in the repository. In all these cases we need an integrated reuse environment where we can store and prepare information about the reusable components.

The last two issues (productivity and time) cannot be supported by data extraction from the development environment—the project manager must use his usual techniques for obtaining the necessary data. As an alternative, the tool support can include a set of questionnaires to gather this information and automatically process the answers to obtain approximate measures of productivity and development time.

2.5.1.2 Tool support for system developers

System developers need tools that support them in the development process. Currently CASE tools are considered as the "state of the art" in tool support for systems development.

These CASE environments are typically organized around a central database (repository) and an integrated toolset that normally includes a graphical editor. The philosophy of such CASE environments is appropriate also for reuse projects. However, the actual toolset is slightly different because of the differing requirements of these projects. The development process of a reuse project is described in detail in Part B. From this description we can identify a list of activities that should be supported by appropriate tools. These include:

- the storage of reusable components

- system decomposition

- search for reusable components

- evaluation of reusable components

- adaptation of reusable components

- development of new components

The *storage* of reusable components is solved by a repository. The repository is a database where you can store complex objects, i.e. objects with complex relationships both internally and externally. In this repository we store the actual components (usually design or code), together with their supporting documentation. The storage requirement includes tools for inserting and extracting components from the repository.

The *system decomposition* task is central to all systems development. It makes it possible to break down the system into manageable parts. Where a defined methodology has been used for the design process, a graphical editor that specifically supports the methodology is the usual solution.

When developing *with* reuse, we must be able to find the reusable components we require in the repository. A classification mechanism is important when *searching for components*, because it allows us to describe the components more precisely. We therefore need tools for classifying the components to be inserted into the repository, and tools for searching the repository for components according to their classification.

The *evaluation* of reusable components allows us to decide whether to reuse a component or not. A tool for examining the metrics of a component is useful in this situation, as well as tools for testing the components. The evaluation is preceded by a *qualification* phase, where information needed to assess the quality of the component is obtained, using either automatic tools to extract the information, or questionnaires.

Classification and qualification must be done before the insertion of the components in the repository. This avoids a huge database containing components that cannot be retrieved because they are not classified, and cannot be evaluated because they are not qualified.

The *adaptation* of reusable components is used to fit reused components into the developed system. Support for adaptation of both design and code should be provided.

In a project *developing* reusable components, we need specific tool support. For example, a reverse engineering support tool can extract reusable components from earlier systems that were not specifically developed for reuse. Support for reverse engineering is discussed in detail in Chapter 11.

If a reuse toolset is integrated into a CASE environment, the activities described above can be performed either in the reuse toolset or in the CASE environment.

2.5.1.3 Tool integration

The integration of new tools into the existing environment is a risk for the project manager and the systems developers. A reuse project has special requirements, resulting in a demand for new tools. All companies have an existing tool set, and are usually unwilling to throw any of it away. The problem is therefore to make the old and the new tools act together as one integrated environment.

There are three main topics to cover during the integration of a reuse toolset in a CASE environment. These are:

- communication integration

- data integration

- process/control integration

Both the old and the new environments have to be able to exchange information—they must have some way to interact. A typical element in the architecture of a CASE tool is a *software bus*. This provides a common channel to all services present in the CASE tool, allowing them to send messages and execute remote commands in a transparent way. The process of integrating new tools is made much easier if this bus has been designed according to a specified standard.

Data integration is another serious problem. The reuse library and toolset should be able to access data in the existing toolset, and vice versa. This might require modification of existing tools and databases, which might be impossible or impractical. Control integration is a further problem. If we want the environment to act as one, it should be possible to activate tools from both the new and the old toolset interactively. This will require modifications to one or both toolsets. This problem should be taken seriously, and the necessary amount of time allocated to this task.

During the integration of the REBOOT toolset into Concerto we have found appropriate solutions for these problems. Section 2.5.3 describes how we did this.

2.5.2 Some possible tool support for reuse

This section describes a toolset suitable for a reuse project. In the previous section we identified some tools that would be useful in such a setting; this section will describe how these tools should act together as a whole, and the support currently offered by the REBOOT toolset.

2.5.2.1 Tools for supporting reuse

The repository

The repository is implemented as a database storing complex objects. A reusable component is typically a cluster of objects, including code, documentation, design, classification and description files. The database also stores any internal tool data associated with the component, to avoid unnecessary regeneration of this data. In addition the database stores all administrative information like users, access rights and so on.

The repository acts as an integrator of the environment in the sense that all tools access the data of the database. This makes data integration easy, as all tools have complete access to all necessary data.

The coordinator tool

The coordinator tool integrates the control flow within the toolset, and manages the status information of the tool environment.

The developer accesses the toolset by means of sessions. A session has a local status, with a set of working tools, and a set of components the developer is working with. The component can be depicted on a *workbench*, and the tools are then accessed by selecting from menus. The workbench also offers structural decomposition, by allowing relationships between components, expressing different levels of abstraction. Thus the coordinator tool with the workbench acts as the central tool of the environment, and the remainder of the tools are services allowing operations to be executed on components.

A system is developed by creating new empty components on the workbench, and then substituting reusable components from the repository or newly developed components for them. The components are then manipulated by tools accessible through the coordinator tool. The coordinator tool acts as a data integrator by supplying the database reference for the component data.

The search and retrieval service

This service allows a developer to search the database using the classification of the required reusable components. The developer enters the requirements for a component, and the database is accessed to see whether a component with this or similar functionality exists. If any components are found, they are transferred to the workbench, where the developer can further manipulate them.

The evaluation service

To see if the components found by the search service are useful, the developer accesses the evaluation service. This provides a display of the component's metrics, and services for testing the component in a realistic setting. Based on the results of this activity, the developer can then decide whether to reuse the component. Each component can be evaluated in this way by selecting it on the workbench and then activating the service.

The adaptation service

When reusing a component, it is usually necessary to modify it to fit the requirements. This is done by selecting the component on the workbench and then activating the adaptation service. This tool includes both a graphical editor, and display functions showing the dependencies and functionality of the component. After the component has been changed it is transferred back to the workbench.

The re-engineering service

The re-engineering service allows old code to be decomposed into potentially reusable components. These components can then be inserted into the repository using the insertion service.

The browser

As a support for adaptation and re-engineering, the user needs access to a graphical display of the internal structure of the component being adapted or re-engineered. The browser provides information about parts of the component and the relations between those parts.

The repository services

The repository services are used by the project manager and the repository manager. The project manager can also use this service to access statistical information about reuse on previous projects and the history of components. The repository manager uses the services for maintaining the repository; this includes expanding the classification schema and maintaining the integrity of the database after failures, keeping the contents of the database up to date and so on.

2.5.2.2 The REBOOT toolset

The REBOOT project has developed a toolset, consisting of a repository and a complete set of tools to support reuse. This is being incorporated in the REBOOT partner's commercial software development environments. The current version is known as the REBOOT V2 Environment. The toolset currently provides support for the following aspects of reuse that were detailed in the preceding section:

Repository structure

The repository integrates the toolset; all tools have complete access to all necessary data from the database. The REBOOT database has all the functionality necessary to allow it to function as a repository. The REBOOT environment also provides an important additional feature: it is independent of the database platform. This architecture has been achieved using an intermediate layer between the database and the tools that isolates tools from possible changes in the database.

Reuse coordination

The REBOOT environment offers a coordinator tool fulfilling this function. It also coordinates the running of the rest of the REBOOT toolset, including starting and terminating tools. The potential for integration with existing toolsets is only weakly supported, as the coordinator tool has no knowledge of tools outside the REBOOT toolset. The environment is prepared for extensions in this direction, but this must be done locally.

The REBOOT toolset is, however, provided as a set of services with a clear interface, the REBOOT API (application programmatic interface). The reuse coordinator tool can be seen as a client of the REBOOT API; it provides a clear separation between the reuse services and the way they are managed and controlled.

The existence of this REBOOT API makes integration between the REBOOT core services and external environments easier.

Search and retrieval

The REBOOT environment offers a search and retrieval service with a classification scheme based on faceted classification. Faceted classification is described in detail in Chapter 3. Retrieval mechanisms are enhanced by using Boolean operators and parentheses, which permits the building of complex queries using a user-friendly graphical interface.

Evaluation

The REBOOT environment offers a service for entering and displaying component metrics. The display functions include Kiviat diagrams (explained in Chapter 4) and textual listing to represent the complex results of quality assessment based on Factor-Criteria-Metric models. It is also possible to access comments from previous users of a component; this *reuse history* is invaluable when the component is evaluated. A further service provides support for testing, gathering information about use cases, stubs, input and output files for testing and so on.

Adaptation

The REBOOT adaptation service offers adaptation for components coded in C++. Design components or components developed in other languages are not yet supported.

Re-engineering

The REBOOT environment supports re-engineering of C and C++ components, and the insertion service assures that all necessary classification and metrics data are supplied with the component. It also provides support for other languages such as Assembler, with services to find objects in non-object-oriented code. This enables a developer to obtain more information about the internal structure of a component. Re-engineering is described in Chapter 11.

Browsing

The REBOOT environment provides a browser that works with an internal representation of a component. This representation is independent of the language and is generated automatically by a collection of parsers. The REBOOT browser is able to display the internal structure of components written in different languages such as C++, C and Assembler.

Repository management

The REBOOT V2 environment provides a set of utilities to support the activities involved in repository management. These activities include:

- customizing of the classification tree: adding or deleting concepts, facets, synonyms and so on,

- customizing quality and reusability models, to adapt them to each site where REBOOT is installed,

- customizing the development history template,

- direct browsing of the database.

2.5.3 The integration of the REBOOT toolset into Concerto

During recent years, several CASE tools have appeared on the software market. These tools support project managers and developers in reaching their objectives with the given constraints. Some of the characteristics of these tools are:

- a complete coverage of the software life cycle

- a smooth transition between the various phases

- integrated general management services

Reuse can be seen as an activity totally integrated in the normal life cycle. Users require the same kind of support in their CASE tools. This was the rationale behind the integration of REBOOT into Concerto.

Concerto is a "software factory" designed for the development of large technical applications, and now it is recommended by the European Space Agency (ESA/ESTEC) for space projects. It is produced and marketed by Sema Group. The Concerto tool catalogue includes:

- general tools for software development control:

    — *Organizer*, for process modelling

> — *Configurator*, for configuration management
>
> — *TRACE*, for traceability support

- specific environments to support different languages and methods:

  > — HOOD
  >
  > — Ada
  >
  > — REVE (reverse engineering from Ada to HOOD)
  >
  > — SDL
  >
  > — C++, and others.

The goal of the integration exercise was to provide reuse facilities to the HOOD/Ada/DOC environment in Concerto. The integration was carried out at three different levels:

- communication between two environments using RPC

- sharing of data between databases

- integration of the reuse process in Concerto.

Figure 21 shows a block diagram of the architectural features involved in the integration exercise.

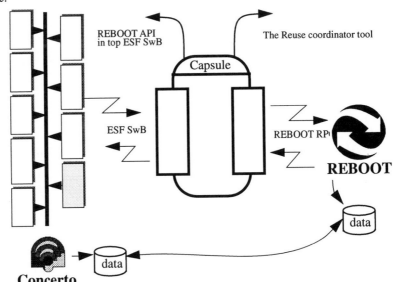

Figure 21 : Architectural blocks involved in the integration of REBOOT into Concerto

Following the Concerto architectural guidelines for integration of external tools, we built a *capsule* for the REBOOT toolset, software that encapsulates all the REBOOT services that provide the required interfaces to the Concerto environment.

For Concerto, this capsule provides access to all the REBOOT services. The REBOOT toolset is also attached to the capsule; the capsule provides all the services provided by the reuse coordinator tool in the REBOOT V2 Environment. The capsule also provides conversion functions between both of the software buses involved in the integration, the REBOOT RPC, and Concerto's ESF SwBus.

The solution to the data integration problem (see Section 2.5.1.3) is based on pointers to information in the corresponding remote database. This prevents information from being duplicated between the two environments.

The main conclusions we obtained from the integration of the REBOOT toolset into Concerto are:

- The integration of a reuse support into a CASE tool gives added value to the CASE tool, providing support for a software production life cycle that incorporates reuse.

- There are several aspects the integrator must deal with when the REBOOT toolset is integrated in a CASE tool:

  — Communication integration
    This can be achieved if the same mechanisms for data transmission through the network are used. If not, translators are needed to convert between the mechanisms involved. These have to support the running of services by means of remote procedure calls.

  — Data integration
    This can be achieved using different approaches. A cheap and easy solution for data integration is to use pointers to remote information.

  — Process integration
    This has to be considered a key aspect for a successful integration.

- Tools managing users, roles and tasks, such as the Concerto Organizer, provide a perfect background to carry out the integration process.

3 Managing a Repository

3.1 Introduction

How can you analyze the current and future needs for reusable components in your company? How can you use the analysis to determine your repository management requirements?

Effective management of a large set of reusable components for a company requires well-defined structures and processes. Without these, the reuse repository effectively becomes a write-only storage medium. The repository of reusable components is the link between development *for* reuse, where the components are produced, and development *with* reuse, where the components are reused.

This chapter presents the techniques necessary to set up and maintain a reuse repository that fits the needs of the company. It is important to emphasize that the reuse repository is not an end in itself, but must be carefully tailored to the reuse needs of the company. A large multi-site company experienced in reuse between different sites needs a different repository from a company that is focusing on single-site reuse of a small set of large components. The need for more advanced repository management also increases as reuse spreads throughout the company, and the company adapts more advanced reuse techniques in other areas.

This chapter is written mainly for repository managers, i.e. those responsible for setting up and managing the repository for the company's reusable components. Based on the repository structure chosen, the user documentation for insertion, search and configuration management of components should be provided by the repository manager.

The repository structure we describe in this chapter is concerned with component-based reuse. It is intended for the situation in which the set of components is so large that it is not possible or practical to be familiar with all of them. The function of the repository in object-oriented component development *for* and *with* reuse is illustrated in Figure 22.

The numbers in Figure 22 refer to the steps that can occur in the reuse process:

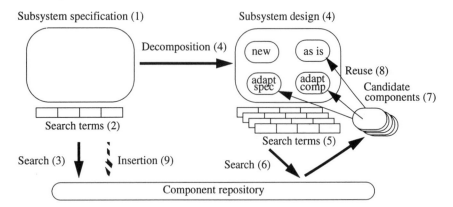

Figure 22 : Component-based reuse

1. The subsystem specification is established.

2. The specification is formalized into a search condition.

3. A search in the component library is performed, but no suitable component is found.

4. A decomposition of the subsystem is performed, leading to a subsystem design.

5. The specification of each of the subsystem's components are formalized into search conditions.

6. A search for the subsystem's components is performed.

7. A set of candidate components is retrieved.

8. Three of the candidate components are found to be suitable for reuse. One can be reused *as is*, the second requires adaptation, and the third can be reused *as is* by adapting the specification, i.e. changing the subsystem design. The fourth component is developed from scratch (or from lower-level reusable components).

9. The newly developed subsystem (and possibly the adapted component) is inserted into the component repository.

The focus of this chapter is on object-oriented components, but the principles are applicable in other circumstances, such as:

• object-oriented frameworks where we have a large set of specialized components for the abstract components in the framework,

• generative reuse where we can reuse fragments of programs in the generative language.

These two approaches are illustrated in Figure 23. With frameworks and generative languages, we are generally moving the component-based reuse one layer higher in the

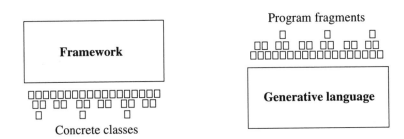

Figure 23 : Framework and generative language components

system organization. The specific components will only be useful with the framework or generative language.

When we talk about a reuse repository, we most often think of a set of components separate from development or product repositories. This need not be the case, however, as it is perfectly feasible to use one repository for all the components of a company—the reusable components are then just distinguished by specific attributes. This chapter does not discriminate between these approaches.

The rest of this chapter is organized as follows:

• Section 3.2 describes the *component model*—the information we need to store in the repository in connection with a reusable component.

• Section 3.3 discusses theoretical and technical aspects of classification in general, and presents our recommendation for a facet-based search and classification scheme for a object-oriented components.

• Section 3.4 is devoted to configuration management and discusses how this may be accomplished in the reuse repository.

• Section 3.5 discusses the organization and maintenance of the repository.

• Section 3.6 discusses the relation between computer supported cooperative work (CSCW) and reuse.

3.2 The REBOOT component model

How should you analyze the packaging and additional information necessary to support the reuse and the maintenance of reusable components?

A reusable component is a part of a product at some level of development (requirements, design, code and so on), together with information about the component to make reuse feasible. For reuse to be feasible, the reusable component must be self-contained. Thus when a company has decided which components they want to reuse, they must decide how these components are packaged for reuse. The component model describes the information needed for a packaged reusable component.

In this section we describe the suggested component model, and give an example of its use (Section 3.2.10). For smaller libraries or libraries in a start-up phase, simplification of this model is possible. In one application of reuse in the REBOOT project, we used a data sheet for each component containing text or references to Unix file names. The information in the data sheet was a subset of that described in this section. If you already have a CASE or configuration management tool where your products are stored, this will also influence your choice of component model. Each company has to adapt the model based on how it wants to store information about reusable components.

The component model we suggest is shown in Figure 24, which uses *entity-relationship notation*. The reusable component is the white box; its various contents are represented by the grey boxes connected to it. Note that the reusable component (the entity) itself does not contain anything except relationships to other data. The following sections explain the contents and relationships of the reusable component in more detail.

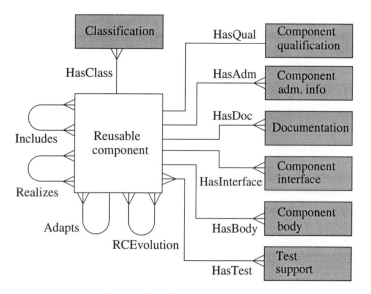

Figure 24 : The component model

Note that the granularity of the information related to the reusable component is not fixed. You can choose to subdivide any of the information represented by grey boxes into smaller pieces with independent relations to the reusable component. The advantage of having a finer-grained component model is that sharing of information becomes easier, i.e. we do not have to duplicate invariant information. If we have a more coarsely-grained model, it will be easier to understand and maintain, but there will be more duplication of information.

3.2.1 Classification information

The *classification* of a component is the information specifically intended to aid identification and retrieval. We discuss different approaches to classification in more detail in Section 3.3.

3.2.2 Component qualification information

This information describes the quality and reusability of the component in terms of the factor-criteria metrics models discussed in Chapter 4. This information is used when you want to decide whether a candidate component fulfils your quality and reusability requirements. There is a 1:1 relationship between a reusable component and its qualification information.

The qualification information also contains the reuse history of the component. A reuser can record any critical or positive comments about the component, any problems that occurred when reusing it, and how these problems were solved. This will help future reusers to avoid the same problems—or to avoid the component. Note that this information should not only be recorded when the component is reused, but also when it is retrieved and evaluated, even if it is subsequently rejected. The information will also be valuable to the repository manager; Section 3.5 describes repository management in more detail.

3.2.3 Component administrative information

It is useful to save the following administrative information for a component:

- general component information

- authorization

- pricing

General component information consists of attributes, such as the name, address, phone number, and e-mail of the component's developer and current maintainer, the time the component was developed, inserted into the repository, last modified and so on.

An authorization scheme is usually required for a repository; for example, only some users should be able to perform repository administration tasks. It may also be necessary to distinguish between different groups of reusers—not all reusers may be allowed to reuse all the components in the repository. This is particularly true if the repository is used for inter-company reuse, or if some components contain sensitive information. In such cases, it might be necessary to equip components with attributes indicating any restrictions on their use.

For inter-company reuse, or even reuse between different departments or projects, it may be useful to have some method of payment for components that are reused, especially as this encourages development for reuse. The component model can allow for the storage of contain information about a component's price.

The relationship between administrative information and the reusable component is N:1; several reusable components can be connected to the same administrative information, but one component only has one set of administrative information.

3.2.4 Documentation

Documentation is essential if a component is to be reused. Two different kinds of documentation are required:

- reuse documentation supporting the reuse of the component,

- component information intended for the documentation of the product in which the component will be included.

Documentation supporting reuse is needed on three levels:

1. documentation to enable the evaluation of each component in a set of candidates retrieved from the repository,

2. documentation to enable the understanding of the functionality of the component,

3. documentation to enable the adaptation of the component for specific needs.

The difference between the first and second levels is that the first answers questions like "Which of these five candidate components is most appropriate for my purpose?" and "To reuse or not to reuse?". This decision may partly be taken on the basis of quality information, which is treated separately in the component model. However, the reuser will also have to consider functional differences between candidates. The reuser needs information about *what* the component does, rather than how its behaviour is achieved internally. The component's classification is complemented by more detailed textual documentation.

For adaptation, the reuser needs details about the internals of a component. This level of documentation is more detailed than the second level, for example explaining internal data structures of components.

The relationship between documentation and reusable components is N:1. The rationale for this is that one item of documentation can apply to several components (for example components which are functionally identical but written in different programming languages).

A component can have alternative documentation (for instance written in alternative natural languages: English, French, etc.) or be written to different documentation standards. It is better to represent these as different versions of the component.

3.2.5 Component interface and component body

The distinction between the interface (the specification) and the body (the implementation) of a component plays an important part in the modularization of software, not only in object-oriented development, but also in more traditional paradigms. In object-oriented programming, these are often called *type* and *class*. The interface describes the boundary of the component, i.e. what operations it offers, what parameters it takes, and what it demands from its environment. The body is the description of the internal workings of the component, i.e. how things are done.

Reusable components can be found at many different specification levels. The distinction between interface and body may be similar at all these levels (at least when a structurally uniform approach like object-oriented development is chosen), but the contents will vary. For an analysis component, for example, the component may consist of diagrams in some object-oriented analysis technique, and similarly for design, in some object-oriented design technique. For code such as C++, the interface would contain the header (the.*h* file), and the body would contain the C++ code itself (the.*c* file).

As is shown in Figure 24, both interface and body have an N:1 relationship with the reusable component. This means that several reusable components can have the same interface or body. We do not allow the same reusable component to have different interfaces or bodies. If we change the interface or body of a component, it will be a new reusable component—possibly a version of the existing one.

3.2.6 Test support

Although components should be tested prior to their insertion in the reuse repository, it will probably be necessary to test them again when they are reused. The need for testing is greater if the context in which the component is reused is different from the one for which it was originally intended and tested.

Since the construction of good test suites is a costly process, it is useful to have the test suites available in the reusable component. This part of the component should contain test fixtures (programs written specifically to test the component), test data on which to run the them, and information about expected results. When the component is used in a way that differs from its original purpose, or modified, it may of course be necessary to develop new tests.

Note that the relationship between the test support and the reusable component is N:N, as one component may have many alternative test suites, and one test suite may also apply to several components.

It may be possible to reuse test suites independently of the component for which they were originally intended, to test similar components. This is achieved by searching for components which are similar to those you want to test, and reusing the test suites of the components you find.

3.2.7 The *realizes* relationship

The *realizes* relationship relates analysis, design and the resulting code. It reflects the fact that reusable components may exist at many different levels of abstraction. If you have reused an analysis component, you are likely to be interested in design and code components corresponding to the component you have just reused, to save you work in subsequent phases of the development.

A requirement at a higher level can have many different solutions at a lower level, and vice versa. Hence the *realizes* relationship is N:N. This means that it is not advisable to aggregate specifications of several phases (e.g., analysis, design, implementation) into a single component, as this could lead to a combinatorial explosion in cases where there are many alternatives. For example, if there were three versions of a design, each if which had three versions of code, this could potentially represent nine possibilities. Keeping the phases separate also prevents users recovering design components, for example, when they are only interested in analysis. Each component in the repository should be either an analysis component, a design component, or a code component. However, you can easily use the *realizes* relationship to navigate the repository, for example to find all alternative designs for an analysis component, or all alternative requirements related for a design component.

3.2.8 The *includes* relationship

The *includes* relationship relates one or more code components to form a composite object. It represents the fact that large reusable components will be composed from several smaller ones. These smaller components may also be reusable on their own, and thus separately classified in the repository. For efficiency and flexibility, it is better to represent a composite component as a set of pointers to other components than to duplicate the contents of the components involved.

The *includes* relationship is also N:N—one component may consist of several smaller ones, and one component may be part of several larger ones.

At the level of the composite component it is not necessary to describe the contents of the parts, only the way they are related (i.e., their interaction). Design frameworks are particularly interesting for reuse; these contain a set of abstract and concrete classes working together. Design frameworks are discussed in Part B.

3.2.9 The *RCEvolution* relationship

The *RCEvolution* relationship links different versions of the same component to show their version history. It is possible to represent different versions of a component as different components. However, if many components exist in several versions, this would lead to an explosion of the component space, especially for composite components with a possible choice between several versions of their parts. It is better to represent a versioned component as a single component, and hide the fact that there are several versions until a choice between alternatives has to be made: this is an application of *information hiding*. The use of the *RCEvolution* relationship is further discussed in Section 3.5.

3.2.10 An example of the use of the component model

To illustrate the use of the different relationships, we will use a subset of potential components from the Fire Alarm System (FAS) described in Appendix A:

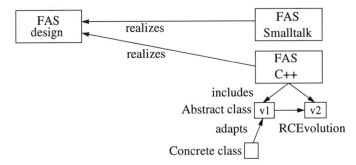

Figure 25 : FAS example reusable component

This diagram shows two realizations of the FAS design, one in Smalltalk and one in C++. The C++ implementation includes an abstract class of which there are two versions, *v1* and *v2*. The version *v1* of the abstract class is adapted to a concrete class. The adapt relationship (inheritance) is not included in the component model, as it is explicitly stated in the concrete class.

3.3 Classification

How should you organize your repository so that reusers can easily find the most suitable component?

3.3.1 Introduction

Classification is the primary feature of the repository that the reuser utilizes to search for specific components. The word *classification* refers to the search information attached to components, allowing components with the same information to belong to the same class or group. The search information divides the components into equivalence classes. (Note that this is not the same class as in object-oriented class hierarchies.)

Classification is the primary means to search for components, but it does not preclude other means of searching the repository, such as browsing, searching by attribute (author, date of creation etc.) or direct access by identity.

In common with most other aspects of reuse, the needs for classification will evolve as reuse matures in a company. Initially, most reuse will be local to small groups, with limited needs for classification. This state is characterized by a repository with a small—up to a few hundred—and relatively constant set of components. As reuse spreads through the company, with reuse occurring between projects or departments, the number of components in the repository increases and more advanced classification is needed. The company should prepare for this natural evolution in its reuse strategy, planning a migration from a simple classification local to a department to a more advanced company-wide classification.

This section assumes a development process with a large and evolving repository of reusable components available throughout the entire software development process. We do, however, provide recommendations for a simplified classification.

Independent of the kind of classification employed, the search for components can be divided into three activities, as shown by Figure 26:

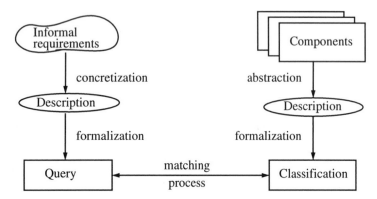

Figure 26 : Retrieval and classification (adapted from [Albrechtsen92])

- the classification of components

- the formalization of requirements into a query

- the matching of components with the query

The left half of Figure 26 illustrates the formalization of a query (part of development *with* reuse). This process has three steps:

- The reuser collects the requirements to form an idea about the component he wants.

- He makes the idea more concrete to allow it to be used as the basis of a search for components, starting by making an informal description of key aspects (the *concretization* step in the figure).

- From this informal description, a query is formalized (the *formalization* step in the figure), and is then matched against the classification information of existing components.

The right half of the figure shows the corresponding process for classification of components in the repository (part of the development *for* reuse process). This process also has three steps:

- The component developer has a reusable component.

- He abstracts a description from the component (the *abstraction* step in the figure).

- This description is formalized into a classification (the *formalization* step in the figure) so that it can be matched against the formalized requirements.

In principle the same process is performed when both classifying a component and formulating a query. In both processes there is room for subjective decisions; for this reason the matching should be relaxed to compensate for the effect of subjectivity, i.e., a *fuzzy retrieval* method should be available when searching the repository.

The intermediate step in both these processes, producing the description, is not always necessary, but it helps to split the process into smaller, more manageable steps. The intermediate description also helps to understand and evaluate a small set of candidate components after retrieval.

The rest of this section is organized as follows:

- Section 3.3.2 deals with the requirements for classification.

- Section 3.3.3 discusses different general approaches to classification.

- Section 3.3.4 presents our recommendation of a faceted classification for object-oriented components.

- Section 3.3.5 discusses the construction of a classification scheme.

3.3.2 The requirements for classification

This section discusses the general requirements for classification. The key requirement is to enable the reuser to identify a set of candidate components that match his requirements. This can be broken down into the following more detailed requirements:

1. The classification must be meaningful to the reusers. As shown in Figure 26, we need to match the reuser's informal requirements to components. A good classification scheme can help us achieve this.

2. The classification must be applicable to components of different granularities, and taken from different phases in the software development life cycle. The same classification should be applicable to systems, subsystems, frameworks, classes, analysis, design, code and any other components we want to reuse.

3. The classification must be easy to use, for both classification of components and formalization of requirements.

4. The classification must be easy to develop and extend.

5. Fuzzy retrieval should be available, to enable recovery of components similar to the query. This is necessary because:

— it can be cost-effective to reuse a component even if some modifications are necessary,

— the formalization of classification and queries for components involve subjective judgement. The effect of this subjectivity can be compensated by fuzzy retrieval. For example, if a component is classified using a term unfamiliar to a developer, he may still be able to find the component using a term more familiar to him, if the two terms are close in meaning.

6. The classification must not be too complex. High complexity decreases the benefits of reuse, as more work is required to understand and use the classification.

Some of these requirements relate to the classification method, in particular 3 to 6; requirements 1 and 2 have more to do with how we apply the chosen classification.

3.3.3 Classification methods

3.3.3.1 Introduction

There are several classification methods that are applicable to software components. This section discusses the following methods:

* Free text

* Keywords and terms

* Facets

* Term spaces and fuzzy retrieval

All these methods have advantages and are appropriate in specific circumstances. The following sections discuss each in more detail. Other methods are also possible, for example that described in [Wood 88], in which components are characterized by component descriptor frames.

3.3.3.2 Free text search

Free text search relies on the existence of a textual description for each component [Salton 89]. This description can be any information connected with the component, such as source code, existing documentation, or descriptions written specifically for free text searching.

Free text search is based on recognition of specific patterns in the text. These patterns can be single words or combinations of words, for example *noun + verb* or *function(parameters)*. When using natural language searching, the patterns can be made arbitrarily complex, limited only by advances in natural language research.

Free text search can be applied to both the classification and the retrieval processes shown in Figure 26. The reuser and the component producer can provide free text descriptions from which patterns for matching are extracted. Free text matching directly between the components and the requirements is more difficult, as these representations are not on the same level of abstraction. The matching process must therefore handle the difference in level of detail between the description of the component and the requirement. This is achieved by the steps of *concretization* and *abstraction* shown in Figure 26.

The advantage of free text search is that it can be fully automated, in contrast to the formalization process. The problems are that it is quite inaccurate, resulting in a risk that garbage will be retrieved. Its reliance on textual descriptions, which may require a substantial amount of work unless they already exist, in also a disadvantage.

3.3.3.3 Keywords and terms

Keyword-based methods are based on attaching keywords to each component that describe its properties. In the simplest form of keyword search, keywords are entered arbitrarily by the component producer. The keywords are not checked, and no standard terminology is enforced. At the other extreme, the method requires that each keyword is chosen from a common vocabulary, enforcing a standardized labelling method.

In this method, reuse is based on a retrieval mechanism in which the user enters keywords that describe the component he needs; these keywords are then compared to the keywords of the components in the repository. Components with keywords matching the search criteria are presented to the user.

Keyword methods may be refined by enforcing a standardized vocabulary, and further by defining a structure that quantitatively relates keywords to denote the differences between them. We refer to such keywords as *terms*. The remainder of this section discusses the use of terms. When we refer to keywords, we assume that they are uncontrolled and unstructured.

The term classification method can be refined in several ways:

- By applying *weights* to terms

- By adjusting for missing and superfluous terms

- By adding composite terms

The following sections describe these refinements in detail.

Term weights

If we use several terms to classify the same component, we can give each term a weight indicating its relative importance. For software reuse it is natural to relate importance to the functionality represented by the term. We therefore define the term weight as an estimate of the effort needed to develop the functionality represented by the term, relative to the entire component. The number of lines of code is one possible basis for this weight. We denote term weights for component c and term t by w_c^t. The weights of all terms used to classify an aspect of a component need not add up to 1.0. This only indicates that the terms do not fully describe the component, or that they overlap.

For example, consider a stack with the operations *push*, *pop*, and *top*. Usually the operation *top* is easier to write than *push* and *pop*—an estimate for the effort required might be the number of lines of code, as mentioned above. For example, it may be that *push* and *pop* should have weights 0.35 each, and *top* 0.2, indicating the greater effort required to write these operations. With a stack that provides more operations, for example *push*, *pop*, *top*, *swap*, *dup*, *empty*, *full*, and *count*, the weights of each operation would again be smaller —not because each of them is smaller, but because each of them is smaller relative to the total number of operations available from the component. The more complex stack component itself will of course be bigger.

Term weights become valuable when a reuser is specifying search criteria. The search terms do not describe an actual component, but rather the ideal component which the user is looking for. The weights given in a query will describe the relative importance of the various terms specified. For example, he might definitely want a bounded stack, and force the selection of this by giving the term for the operation *full* a weight of 10.0. (1.0 is the default weight indicating that all terms are equally important.) Weights associated with search terms therefore have a different meaning from weights associated with terms used to classify a component. We denote the weight for term t in query q as w_q^t .

Unmatched and superfluous terms

When we search for a component there will seldom be a complete match between the query and the component's term: some terms in the query will be missing from the component, and some terms in the component will be superfluous. The set of terms will therefore be divided into three categories: *matching*, *superfluous* and *unmatched*. These three sets of terms are defined in Figure 27.

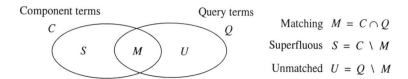

Figure 27 : Matching, superfluous and unmatched terms

The implication of unmatched and superfluous terms will differ depending on the meaning of the term. There are two main cases:

- terms representing functionality—the more of such terms a component possesses, the greater its functionality

- terms representing limitations, typically of a non-functional kind (such as platform requirements). These are the opposite of functional terms, in that more terms imply a reduced potential for reusing the component.

For terms representing functionality, superfluous and unmatched terms represent superfluous and missing functionality, and will both detract from the reusability of the component. To compare a query and several components, each with matching, superfluous and unmatched terms, we must take into account the impact on reusability of the non-matching terms. The following provides a recommendation for this:

- Superfluous terms contribute with:

where u is a constant representing how much extra it costs to understand unnecessary functionality, and $size_c$ is the size of the component. We recommend a value of 0.03–0.10 for u. This value can be adjusted based on feedback from the reuse of components.

- Unmatched terms are more difficult to estimate, as the component does not give any indication of how much it costs to add the functionality represented by the unmatched terms. One solution is to base an estimate on the average of other components with the unmatched term. We define the set of all components with a specific term t as C_t. This gives the following expression for the average size of the other components with the unmatched terms:

$$w^t_q \cdot \frac{\sum\limits_{x \in C_t} size_x \cdot w^t_x}{num(C_t)}$$

Based on the estimates represented by the above two equations, we can provide an estimate for the mismatch between the query conditions and each component in a set of candidate components, based on the superfluous and unmatched terms. In the example of simple and complex stacks used earlier in this section, both stacks will match a query for a simple stack, but the complex stack will be penalized because of its superfluous terms.

For terms representing limitations, the situation is different. Here, an unmatched term in a retrieved component does not necessarily have negative implications. If a reuser wants a component with functionality F to run on platform P, he might be just as happy with a component which has no platform restrictions, and would also be perfectly happy with a component which, in addition to running on platform P, also runs on Q and R. Additional terms need not be a problem either, provided that they are of the same category as terms already matched.

However, if the reuser has a blank search criterion for a platform category, restrictions in a recovered component may or may not be a disadvantage. For example, requesting functionality F might mean that you want a component for F which runs on as many platforms as possible. Alternatively, it might mean that you are interested in finding out what components are available for F, and are not interested in platform restrictions. For this reason, to provide sensible retrieval support for terms representing limitations, the following should be supported:

- AND and OR relationships between terms, indicating whether restriction terms apply together or apply alternatively

- the predefined terms *anything* and *nothing*, for use in the specification of search criteria, so that a reuser can indicate whether unrequested restrictions should be considered a demerit.

Composite terms

For many components, the most appropriate term to use will be a composite term, for example *bounded stack, last access and delete* (if *dequeue* did not exist), *first access and delete* (for *pop*). There are two ways of implementing this:

- Treating composite terms as primitive terms. This is a simple solution if the number of composite terms is limited. The disadvantage of this approach is that it introduces many different terms, and makes it difficult to know which terms are related.

- Using term composition operations. We can then keep the number of terms small and can compare parts of terms. However, we need to define how to perform term matching. The number of possible composition operations is also large.

If composition operations are preferred, we recommend starting with:

- qualification terms, e.g. *bounded, first, last, random* etc.

- addition of terms, e.g. *access and delete* for destructive get (stack *pop*).

Note that both the qualified terms and the qualification terms can be added together, for example (*last AND first*) (*access AND delete*), to characterize an operation which removes and returns the last and first element of a list.

In the same way that we provide weights for the primitive terms, we can also provide weights for each part of a composite term. A weight between 0.0 and 1.0 for a qualifying term indicates how much the qualification represents. When terms are added (ANDed), the sum of added terms should be 1.0. This is because addition splits a concept into parts, which must sum to the whole. If we cannot find composite terms that fully represent a specific functionality, the sum may be less than 1.0.

Combined and partial matching of composite terms can now be done by finding components with parts of the composite term, e.g. the four composite terms *last access, last delete, first delete* and *first access* can be matched with (*last AND first*) (*access AND delete*). If fewer than the four primitive terms are present for a component, we will only have a partial match. Based on the weights for the parts of the composite term, we can determine how much of the functionality represented by the term a component possesses. Each part of the composite term will therefore belong to one of the three sets, *matched*, *superfluous* or *unmatched*.

3.3.3.4 Faceted classification

Faceted classification is classifying something along several dimensions. The dimensions are called *facets*. Each facet can be represented by a set of terms with any kind of structure. Faceted classification is suitable for software components, allowing them to be classified from several viewpoints. However, it is not trivial to determine which viewpoints should be represented by facets. Section 3.3.4 discusses faceted classification for object-oriented components in more detail.

As we group terms into facets, the difference between terms and attribute values decreases. In principle a facet is just a multivalued attribute, where there can be some control or structure on the attribute values (terms).

Faceted classification was proposed by the Indian mathematician S. R. Ranghanathan [Ranghanathan57]. Rubén Prieto-Díaz [Prieto-Díaz85, Prieto-Díaz87] described a faceted classification scheme for the reuse of function-oriented software.

3.3.3.5 Term spaces and fuzzy retrieval

Both keyword and free text classification methods are based on the matching of terms: keywords are matched directly, and in free text classification the extracted words are matched. If a classification method is based only on isolated terms, these can only be matched exactly, and the fact that one term may be nearly the same as another term is hidden. Introducing structure into the set of terms by relating similar terms enables us to relax the search, by matching terms that are similar.

Structuring terms also eases the selection of suitable terms for classification and retrieval, because the structure helps us navigate in the set of terms. Without any structure, we can only look for appropriate terms alphabetically.

We call a set of terms with structure a *term space* or *thesaurus*. This section discusses different relations between terms, weights on relations and relaxed search methods using weighted relations.

Term relations

The most common relations to introduce in a set of terms are:

- the specialization/generalization relation

- the synonym relation

An example of a term space is shown in Figure 28.

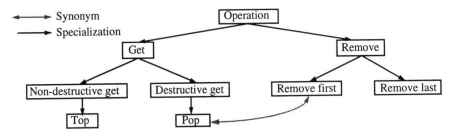

Figure 28 : An example term space

The well-known enumerated classification (e.g. Universal Decimal Classification, see [UDC 79] for details) is a special case of this classification. It has one facet common for all books, one term for the facet and a 1:N specialization relation between the terms. It represents a breakdown of knowledge in one dimension (for example, the subject of a book), providing a linear ordering of components. For books, the classification is usually by subject, and books on the same subject are alphabetically ordered by title or author. Note that as soon as we use alphabetic or any other non-semantic enumeration, we only have limited support for searching based on the contents of components.

Enumerated classification is often used for software documentation, for example Unix documentation, which is organized into eight subjects, with alphabetic ordering of topics within each subject.

The advantages of enumerated classification are simplicity and a stable frame of reference for classification. The problems are that it is difficult to define a good enumeration scheme, and the classification only reflects one viewpoint.

We recommend enumerated classification for smaller sets of components, where it is possible to collect the data sheets of components under appropriate headings. It is possible to dynamically extend the headings with sub-headings when the number of components under a heading becomes too large. This scheme should be sufficient for a repository with up to a thousand components (i.e. two to three binders or volumes).

In the fire alarm system described in Appendix A, we used a binder with labels for each of the component types: detectors, actuators, control units, panels and connection components.

Weights on relations

Even if we establish relations between terms, we still do not know how close a term is to a related term. *Edge weights* allow us to represent the distance between the related terms in the term space. For software reuse, the weight between two terms should represent some aspect that will influence the decision of whether we should reuse a component with a related term. One possibility is the effort to adapt the functionality. Thus edge weight $w_{t,u}$ between two terms t and u in the term space estimates the effort (E_C) needed to change the functionality denoted by the term t into the functionality denoted by the term u, relative to the effort (E_S) needed to provide the functionality denoted by the term u from scratch, i.e.

$$w_{t,u} = E_C/E_S.$$

Weights are not symmetric—the effort of changing t to u may not be the same as changing u to t. Not all terms are directly connected, but we still use $w_{t,u}$ to denote the total weight of the shortest path connecting t and u. A weight $w_{t,u}$ exceeding 1.0 means that there is no point in modifying the part of the component covered by the term, since it will take more effort than developing the functionality from scratch.

Note that adding relations between the terms increases the number of matched terms. In Figure 27, the set of matching terms M, i.e. the intersection between the set of component terms C and the set of query terms Q, increases. Unlike term weights, edge weights are a property of the term space. The weight on the relation represents an average of the relative effort needed to change all components classified with one term into similar components classified with the other term. Initially these weights will be subjective estimates, but after some experience of searching, modification and reuse of components, we can get a more empirical basis for the weights. This feedback can be provided in the same way as for term weights: manually by the reuser, for each term that differed in the search condition and reused component, or semi-automatically based on lines of code changed.

Fuzzy retrieval

Based on the weighted relations between terms, we can extend the definition of fuzzy retrieval to take related terms into account. Here we will discuss different methods of achieving this when we estimate the distance between a query and the resultant components.

An initial estimate of this distance is

$$size_c \cdot w_c^t \cdot w_{t,u} \cdot w_q^u$$

Here $size_c \cdot w_c^t$ represents the size of the matched functionality, $w_{t,u}$ the effort to change it into the required functionality and w_q^u the importance of the required functionality.

There is a problem with this initial estimate, as it favours matching of terms with small weights. Fuzzy retrieval should favour terms that represent about the same effort ($size_c \cdot w_c^t$) as the required term. As an example, assume a query with term A and two components, C1 with term B where

$$size_{C1} \cdot w_{C1}^B = 5$$

and

$$w_{B,A} = 0.3$$

and C2 with term D where

$$size_{C2} \cdot w_{C2}^D = 10$$

and

$$w_{D,A} = 0.2$$

Component C1 with the "smaller" functionality will always be preferred, irrespective of the expected size of the functionality required by term A. If this was closer to 10 (the product of the component and the weight), component C2 would be a better choice. To take this factor into account, we use part of the expression for effort of unmatched terms from Section 3.3.3.3:

$$size^t = \frac{\sum_{x \in C_t} size_x \cdot w_x^t}{num(C_t)}$$

Here $size^t$ is the average effort required to implement the functionality represented by the term t. Based on this we can add the absolute difference between the expected and actual size, thus we have the following equation:

$$(size_c \cdot w_c^t + \left| size_c \cdot w_c^t - size^u \right|) \cdot w_{t,u} \cdot w_q^u$$

Continuing the example above, we suppose that the average size of A $(size^A)$ is 9. The distance for the two components C1 and C2 are then 2.7 and 2.2 without taking w_q^u into account. This will result in C2 with the "larger" functionality being shown as the better choice.

There are problems with this method as well, as it treats too "big" and too "small" terms equally. In practice it is generally easier to remove or ignore code than to add new code. Taking this into account, we derive a final expression for the distance between the two terms:

$$((size_c \cdot w_c^t - size^u) \cdot r + size^u \cdot w_{t,u}) \cdot w_q^u \quad \text{for} \quad size_c \cdot w_c^t > size^u$$

$$((size^u - size_c \cdot w_c^t) \cdot a + size_c \cdot w_c^t \cdot w_{t,u}) \cdot w_q^u \quad \text{for} \quad size_c \cdot w_c^t \leq size^u$$

Here r is a reduction factor, representing how much it costs to remove or ignore superfluous code, and a is the addition factor, representing how much it costs to add code. If we use $r = 0.5$ and $a = 1.0$ in the example above, we get $4 + 1.5 = 5.5$ for C1 and $0.5 + 1.8 = 2.3$ for C2, again without taking w_q into account.

Further discussions on fuzzy retrieval can be found in [Karlsson92] and [Ostertag92].

3.3.4 Facets for object-oriented components

This section discusses our suggestions for using facets when classifying object-oriented components. To choose suitable facets for classifying a set of components, the following steps must be performed:

- Construct an overview of the components of interest.

- Determine which aspects of a component are most important for retrieval.

The general requirements for facets are as follows:

- Each facet must say something about the component that is interesting to the person wanting to retrieve it.

- There must not be more facets than we can cope with simultaneously. Three to six seems appropriate.

- Each facet should be well defined: there should be no ambiguity about which facet covers which aspect of the component, and the facets should be as orthogonal to each other as possible.

- All facets should be relevant for most components, regardless of their size, form, internal structure or contents.

- It should be as easy as possible to construct a term space for the selected facets.

Each facet can have an arbitrary number of terms in its restricted vocabulary, and an arbitrary number of these terms can be selected for classification of a component.

From the above requirements it follows that the facets should be relatively stable; the introduction of new facets should be undertaken only after careful consideration.

For object-oriented software components we recommend the following four facets:

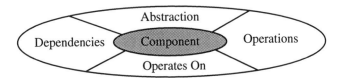

Figure 29 : The four REBOOT facets

- **Abstraction**—what the component *is*. Usually an object-oriented component can be characterized by a noun that can encompass high or low levels of abstraction, e.g. stack, flight manager.

- **Operations**—what the component *does*. Components perform operations, characterized by the *operations* facet.

- **Operates On**—what the component *does it to*. This facet describes what kind of components this component is able to act upon or cooperate with, e.g. integer, set, list, resource.

- **Dependencies**—what the component *is constrained by*. This facet lists dependencies (platform and other) which constrain potential reuse of the component, for example C++-based, Unix-based, HOOD-based.

These facets seem to be the most interesting for reuse and applicable to the majority of (object-oriented) software components, regardless of size and whether they are design or code components. However, they are not completely orthogonal, since abstraction and operations clearly overlap—a stack is very likely to have the operations *push* and *pop*, whereas a queue is equally likely to have *enqueue* and *dequeue*.

Some companies might find it useful to divide the repository into different domains. For example, a company may develop software products for totally different vertical markets (e.g. chemical engineering, university administration, local authority tax collection and so on). Having all components in the same repository might be confusing. There are several solutions to this problem:

- Add a facet for *domain*. This will enable us to retrieve only software relevant to the domain of interest. The disadvantage of this approach is that components relevant to all domains may be difficult to find. It also hinders inter-domain reuse.

- Have separate repositories for each domain. This solution gives complete separation, but suffers the same disadvantages as the previous one.

- Include the domain as part of the term space in the *dependency* facet. This method enables us to mark only domain-specific components, and allows inter-domain searching by simply not specifying a domain term.

All these methods provide the same functionality in principle. We recommend the last one, because of its advantages in supporting inter-domain search and reuse.

3.3.5 Constructing a classification scheme

This section gives guidance on methods used to define and maintain a classification scheme for object-oriented components.

3.3.5.1 Guidelines for term space development

The possibility of reuse should be considered, of course, in the development of a repository, including the development of the term space. However, if no term space exists, it must be developed from scratch.

If this is the case, it may be achieved in two different ways, which we may call the *top-down* and *bottom-up* approaches:

- The top-down approach starts with a domain analysis [Shlaer89], concentrating on the required functionality in the domain rather than the functionality of existing components. From this, terms can be identified and connected in a term space.

- The bottom-up approach starts with a set of reusable components and tries to classify these with appropriate terms. The set of components is then investigated to find common and related terms.

In both cases, the following guidelines apply:

- Work in the following order:

    — Identify terms
    — Connect them into a generalization hierarchy (which will also give hints about unmatched terms)

— Connect terms that are felt to be closer than the generalization hierarchy indicates using a synonym relation

— Classify a number of reusable components to test the applicability of the term space

— Try to assign weights to the edges

- Use standard terminology, for both domain functionality and platform dependencies. In situations where several terms relate to the same concept, preference should be given to terms that:

  — have a precise meaning within the domain

  — are understood by as many as possible of the potential repository users

  — are not used for something completely different in another domain (since reuse between domains may also be profitable, and confusion in this case should be avoided)

- Although class names naturally correspond to abstraction terms, and method names to operations terms, do not assume that class and method names of components are appropriate as terms. Developers may differ in their use of terminology. Restricting the developer's use of terminology when naming may be necessary if automatic classification of components is to be supported.

- The assignment of weights to terms is difficult, and if you have no initial estimates to work from, you can consider initially omitting weights from your term space. You can get an estimate about weights by measuring the difference between various example components, or estimating the work needed to change one into the other.

- It is hard to get a term space perfectly right the first time. It is best to avoid becoming immersed in discussions about terminology and weights. The term space can be gradually improved when more experience is gained. This point is enlarged in the following section.

3.3.5.2 Feedback and maintenance of the term space

The weights of terms will be initially *ad hoc* since the relevant efforts are not known. One of the tasks of the repository manager is to maintain the term space. In addition to introducing and removing terms, this requires tuning the term weights to make them as consistent with actual modification efforts as possible. In a large repository, this is a complicated task which requires feedback from the reusers and tool support.

To help with providing such support, all activity in the repository should be logged. This will provide accumulated averages for the following:

- what users search for

- what is retrieved

- which component is chosen among a set of retrieved ones

- how well the actual modification effort corresponded to the estimated one determined from the term space

The last statistic, which is important for the maintenance of term weights, must be entered by the retriever after he has modified the component to fit his needs. For a single component, a discrepancy between the actual modification effort and the estimated one may not tell us anything about the term space and weights—it might just be that the query or the component are wrongly classified. When such discrepancies are averaged for a large number of retrievals, however, we get a better indication of whether weights between various terms are wrong. A more detailed discussion about heuristics for term weight calculation can be found in [Sindre92a].

Most of the feedback can be provided automatically from the statistics described in the list above, but some of it must be provided by the reuser. It is also possible to establish a crude measure of the degree of modification of an adapted component, and compare it with the distance between original query and the component's classification in the term space. Feedback must be as easy to enter as possible, and should be an integrated part of the evaluation and adaptation process. One example where automatic feedback can be acquired in a reuse repository is to use the number of changed lines as a measure of the modification effort.

3.4 Configuration management of the repository

How should you manage the use and evolution of components?

3.4.1 Introduction

The repository of reusable components will not be frozen, but will evolve as reuse in a company evolves. Components will be used and adapted in different products, and new and enhanced versions of existing components will be inserted into the repository. This requires that we keep the components in the repository under configuration management.

This section focuses on the connection between the reuse repository and the structure of the application under development. We do not give a survey of concepts and methods in configuration management, which can be found elsewhere, e.g. [Tichy88]. We do, however, describe the terminology we use in some detail.

Large software applications are usually structured as a set of smaller pieces, i.e. components, where relationships exist between the components, such as *realizes*, *includes* and *uses*. Note that we use the term *component* here to denote any part of the application, regardless of whether it is a reusable component or not. The only difference between a reusable component and a non-reusable component in the context of configuration management is that the reusable component is used in many more places.

Consider a simplified version of the fire alarm system (FAS) (see Appendix A) consisting of four components: actuator (A), detector (D), control unit (CU) and panel (P) as shown in Figure 30.

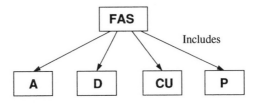

Figure 30 : An example fire alarm system

The components can also be internally dependent, indicating that a change in one component may require a change in the dependent components. These dependencies are introduced if one component is the realization of, or uses, another component. An example of a possible structure representing the *uses* relationship between the four components is shown in Figure 31. This structure indicates that a change in the actuator may necessitate changes in all other components, as they are all directly or indirectly dependent on the actuator. The panel, on the other hand, may be changed without affecting the other components.

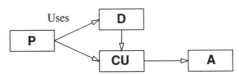

Figure 31 : Uses structure

As long as the application only exists in one version, there is no need for configuration management. But when the application starts to evolve, through bug fixes, extensions or special adaptations for new customers, we get different application versions. These versions will be represented as specific selections of different versions of the components. When bound into a composite component that represents a version of the whole application, it becomes a *configuration*. The application configuration is therefore dependent on the versions of its components.

Changes to the application will be changes either to the individual components or to the composition of components, i.e., the relationships. An example of the first type of change is the introduction of a new version of the actuator. An example of the second kind of change is the inclusion of a new component, e.g., a dual dependency unit (DD). We must also distinguish if the change gives rise to a new version of the application which is alternative to or a replacement for the current version. An alternative version exists in parallel with the original version, and is usually called a *variant*, whereas a replacement version replaces the previous version, and is usually called a *revision*.

How much we choose to split the application into separate components influences how we propagate changes between variants. Representing the application as one atomic component means that changes have to be propagated manually (by copying). Splitting it into separate components means that we can incorporate changes by changing the relationships.

The example illustrated in Figure 30 should make this clear. Here we have built the

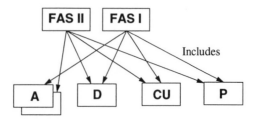

Figure 32 : Two configurations of the system

systems FAS I and FAS II for two different customers, each with a different version of the actuator. If we now find a fault in any of the common components, such as the control unit, we can build a new version of the control unit, and include this in both systems. If we had not split the system into components, we would have had to implement the change separately in all systems—an error-prone activity. The disadvantage of a fine-grained system decomposition such as this is that there are more entities and relationships to keep track of.

An alternative to representing the relationships of the specific versions explicitly is to keep a list of the versions of components which are involved in a configuration of a composite component, for example as a text document.

3.4.2 Managing classification and evolution of components

When a component is changed and re-entered in the repository, it represents a new and unique component. The developer should be able to indicate that the component is a new version of an existing one. An instance of the relation *RCEvolution*, as mentioned in Section 3.2, should connect the two components. This relationship may then be used for various purposes, such as making a later retriever aware of the existence of alternative components, and supporting configuration management generally.

To increase the visibility of new versions of components, the nature of the change and the corresponding description in the classification will determine whether the new version appears different from the original. If the change to the component represents an extension, deletion or alteration of the component's major functionality, then the classification of the new version should be different as well.

In other cases, the change need not be directly visible as a functional change. Such changes are bug fixes, efficiency improvements, code restructuring and so on. In these cases, the original component and its new version may be indistinguishable via the classification. In this case, the change should be expressed through the documentation of the component. The documentation should of course be changed appropriately for all modifications to a component, but in these cases it will be the only source of information about the change.

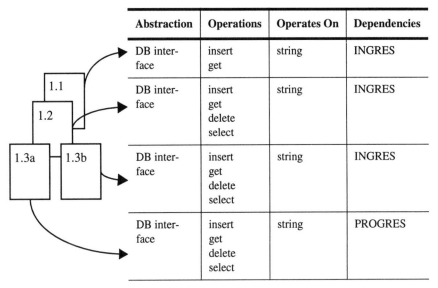

Abstraction	Operations	Operates On	Dependencies
DB inter-face	insert get	string	INGRES
DB inter-face	insert get delete select	string	INGRES
DB inter-face	insert get delete select	string	INGRES
DB inter-face	insert get delete select	string	PROGRES

Figure 33 : Classification of different component versions

Figure 33 illustrates these different kinds of change, and how they may be reflected in the component classification. The figure shows a component which is a database interface. The component is functionally enhanced from version 1.1 to 1.2, where its functionality is extended to include operations for deletion and selection. Then the component, previously used exclusively with an INGRES database server, is extended for use with PROGRES as well. This necessitates the introduction of a variant labelled 1.3a in the figure, while the INGRES variant is labelled 1.3b.

The number of available components will increase rapidly as new versions are developed. Since different versions of the same component have similar functionality, their classification will be accordingly similar. The probability is therefore high that several versions will match the search criteria of a reuser, who will be confused by the apparent number of potentially reusable components. To alleviate this problem, versions of a component can be presented to the user as one component, or as a component family. This allows the reuser to make the choice of one particular version later.

In this way, the repository can support evolution of the components. Support for more advanced configuration management mechanisms, such as product descriptions using dependency structures, system building using configuration descriptions, and so on, could be constructed on top of these basic mechanisms, but this is beyond the scope of this book.

3.5 Managing the repository

How should you allocate responsibility for management of the repository?

3.5.1 Introduction

Repository management consists of several tasks, which we describe in this section independently of the actual people involved. At the end of the section we propose a mapping from responsibilities to people, to suggest how different people may interact to carry out the necessary tasks.

This section discusses *repository services*. A service in this context represents some functionality intended used for a particular purpose in connection with the repository. This it is not necessarily a single tool, and may well be a combination of several tools. We assume that users can be assigned different access rights to the different services.

3.5.2 Overall definition of responsibility

This section clarifies the relation of the repository management role to other roles in reuse.

The focus of reuse services and inherent knowledge characterizes the different roles. All activities that have maintenance of the services as their main goal can be considered a part of the responsibility for repository management. Other roles in a reuse scenario are characterized by their view of the services as a part of a development process, where the goal is to develop a software product, the services only providing support for this process.

The role of repository management is therefore not only restricted to the actual repository, but also concerns maintenance of the repository services, database administration and so on. According to this definition, the repository management role is complex and wide-ranging. For the purpose of structuring this section, we will divide this role into three sub-responsibilities:

- *Term space management* consists of maintaining and extending the term space, facets and other aspects of component classification. This concerns the classification information and knowledge which is *not* a part of the components—maintenance of the classification for each component is not a part of this activity.

- *Component management* consists of maintaining all information regarding the components in the repository, *including* their classification.

- *System administration and user support* consists of carrying out the day-to-day administration of the repository. This includes database maintenance and control, user guidance, maintenance and checking of access rights and privileges, and so on.

From this decomposition of repository management, we can see that there is a difference in focus between the sub-roles. The first two deal with two different kinds of knowledge and information stored in the database. The last sub-role deals with the services operating on the database. We do not consider initial development of a preliminary term space as part of repository management.

The next subsections discusses each sub-role in more detail. Finally we suggest how these roles may be mapped onto people in an organization.

3.5.3 Managing the term space

3.5.3.1 Introduction

Term space management consists of maintaining the classification information used in the repository. This consists of:

- Maintaining information based on requests from users of the repository.

- Continuously evaluating the term space, and changing it according to new terminology and knowledge independently of the users of the repository.

Even though the responsibility may logically be divided like this, the resulting actions will be the same, consisting of adding or deleting terms, relations, facets and domains, and adjusting the weights of the relations in the term space.

3.5.3.2 Managing terms and relations

This activity is part of the continuous evaluation and refinement of the term space. When the term space has been used for a while, it will become relatively stable. At this stage, term and relation changes will be mainly triggered by users. A typical example is when a component developer has built a new component and wishes to classify it. If he has problems finding terms that express what he wants, he may need to request a new term. The same situation may occur when a search is performed and the need for a new term is identified.

A request for a new term might be automatically supported by the classification and retrieval service, for example by selecting a menu choice *Request Modification*. In this request, the user could enter information such as the domain, facet and position of the new term in the term space. The term space manager may respond to such requests in two ways. Either he adds a new term corresponding to the user's request, or he can reply stating which existing term should be used instead of the requested one.

When adding a new term, the term space manager might use the display and maintenance part of the classification and retrieval service. The maintenance could be done interactively by navigating in the term space to find the correct place to add the new term. The term might be connected to the remainder of the term space by explicitly drawing a relationship. Finally, this relationship can be weighted according to the predicted modification effort associated with the functionality represented by the term.

Adding new terms implies adding new relations, since the new terms must be connected to the existing term space. However, new relations may also be added on their own. For example, if two unrelated terms are used as synonyms, a synonym relationship should be inserted between them.

Managing the weights of relations is another important aspect of relation management. These may be adjusted corresponding to term space heuristics based on statistics from classification and retrieval. Automatic logging of all classification and searching should be used as a basis for these statistics; this may enable a suggested change to be issued automatically.

Terms and relations may also need to be removed. If a term is never used for classification or searching, it should be removed from the term space. Terms should be replaced as terminology evolves, although sometimes it will be necessary to keep old terms to ensure backward compatibility with components that use them in their classification. Replacing and deleting terms that are in use introduces a problem. The best solution is probably to generate a list of the affected components, and then notify the respective component responsible about the change. The component responsible can then decide how the component should be re-classified.

User requests for modification of the term space are handled in the same way as described for addition of terms. If this is supported by the classification and retrieval service, the user can select an operation (for example *Request Modification*) from the service, and provide all the information required. The type of modification (*add term*, *delete term*, *add relation* etc.), as well as the suggested modification could be provided. The collected information is then sent to the term space manager, for example by electronic mail.

3.5.3.3 Managing facets and domains

The management of facets and domains is similar to the management of terms and relations, except that maintenance is at a higher level of abstraction. Identifying the characteristic set of facets for one domain should be done only once, when the domain is first taken into consideration. Changing the set of facets should be avoided as far as possible, since such changes will require spending a substantial amount of work on reclassifying every component to bring it in line with the change.

Domains should also be relatively stable, and a domain should not be removed after it is introduced. Care should therefore be taken when introducing a domain, and an existing one should be applied whenever possible.

Changes to facets and domains should thus occur much less frequently than changes to terms and relations. The cause of a change will also be somewhat different—user requests will rarely result in a change to facets or domains. Such changes are more likely to occur as a result of policy decisions, for example if a company has decided to include all their user interface components in their reuse repository, and must therefore consider adding a new domain and new facets. User requests affecting facets and domains may of course occur, entered in the same way as the requests for terms and relations.

3.5.4 Managing components

3.5.4.1 Introduction

This activity has many similarities to term space management. It also has two aspects:

- Maintaining components based on requests from users of the repository.

- Continuously maintaining the repository.

3.5.4.2 Inserting and deleting components

Inserting new components is usually the responsibility of the component developer. If suitable terms for classification cannot be found, a request is issued to the term space manager. In this situation, the repository manager will only act as an evaluator of the component—he may reject insertion of the component due to low quality, low reusability or some other factor. The classification and insertion of a component should automatically generate a message to the repository manager describing what was inserted and by whom.

Inserting components not developed in-house, such as public domain software, or software bought from other vendors, should be the responsibility of the component manager. The component manager acts as the developer in this case, and interacts with the term space manager to establish a classification.

Deleting a component can be done when the component is faulty, or has very limited reusability. Two problems arise when deleting a component:

- a component used or inherited by other components must not be removed,

- developers who have reused it must be notified that the component is about to be removed.

3.5.4.3 Configuration support

The component manager must provide support for configuration management, providing the ability to store several versions of a component, and recording where a version of a component is reused. This will allow reusers to be notified about new versions of components they are using. He is not responsible for the actual configuration management himself, but acts as a notifier, broadcasting information about changes to the users of the repository.

Configuration support must be provided when there is a change in the state of a component in the repository (for example, removal, new versions and so on). Such changes will often be a result of a user request, for example if a user has discovered a serious error in a component necessitating its removal, or if he has developed a new version.

Information about changes to a component must be propagated to the reusers of the component—the component manager sends them a message that a new version of the component is available. To enable this, the component manager must be able to obtain the names of everyone who has reused the affected component.

3.5.4.4 Changing the existing classification

This action may be caused by two events:

- The classification of a component is incomplete, or wrong.

- A change in the term space necessitates a reclassification of the component.

The first event arises when a component is frequently rejected after fuzzy retrieval. This may lead to the conclusion that the component should be reclassified, as its properties are not correctly reflected by its classification. Statistics based on search and retrieval may be applied here, but users could also point out weaknesses and errors in the classification.

The second event is a result of a change in the term space. Here, the relevant component developer and the component manager are notified by the term space manager about the change.

For both these events, the component developer has the primary responsibility for the reclassification, because he possesses the greatest knowledge about it. However, the component manager should have the overall responsibility of ensuring that the reclassification is carried out, if necessary by doing it himself.

This task is done in two stages:

- The invalid component is first deleted from the database.

- The component is classified in the same way as a new component.

Thus, the component manager is responsible for removing the component, and the component developer is responsible for classifying it again by using the classification service.

3.5.5 Suggestions for mapping roles to people

We have identified three main roles within the responsibility of repository management:

1. Term space management

2. Component management

3. System administration and user support

How can these three roles may be mapped onto people? The responsibility for term space management is concerned with domain specific knowledge, and therefore people with a deep understanding of the domains concerned are best for this role. This responsibility should be given to a relatively small group of people consisting of one expert in each major domain.

The component manager should also be a member of this group, since the responsibilities for term space and component management are strongly related to tasks such as reclassification. The component manager should be someone with a good knowledge of class libraries and general data structures. He does not need to be a domain expert.

The responsibility of system administration and user support for reuse is not different from any other type of system administration. A company's existing system administration personnel could be used in this role.

3.6 Computer-supported cooperative working

Classification, retrieval, and repository management may involve cooperation between people possibly in different locations, and therefore it may be useful to consider support for computer-supported cooperative working (CSCW). This is certainly worthwhile for large-scale inter-company reuse, where the possibility for face-to-face contact between the various participants is lost. This means that rather than having users (providers, reusers, repository managers) working separately towards a passive repository facility, reuse activity becomes a group activity.

Three aspects are crucial for the support of any group activity: communication, collaboration, and coordination [Ellis91]. There are a number of ways to assist group interaction. Groupware applications may be divided into:

- message systems

- multi-user editors

- group decision support systems

- electronic meeting-rooms

- computer conferencing

- intelligent agents

- coordination systems

In particular, multi-user editors together with advanced computer conferencing facilities and intelligent agents provide great advantages for inter-group reuse. If the people involved are geographically distributed, a problem such as deciding on the classification of a component can be solved by discussions between component developers and repository managers. Using a desktop conferencing facility, for example, those involved could see each other and discuss the component together.

A starting point for CSCW support is a multi-user facility supporting both synchronous and asynchronous contact, in which sessions can be initiated by anyone involved in reuse. Some scenarios for the use of such a facility are:

- A repository manager discovers from logged information that a particular company which is a reuse client of the repository has problems with understanding the term space, since an unusually large number of their component requests fail.

  The repository manager can initiate a discussion session with relevant staff in the company to discover the problem. For example, by examining the term space, it may turn out that the company has a different terminology than the one used in the term space. In this case, the repository manager can explain the terminology used. It might be that the components in the repository do not match company's needs, providing valuable ideas for new components.

- A reuser does not find any component matching his requirements.

  He may contact the repository manager, to ensure he has not overlooked anything. If it turns out that the requirement is not covered, the reuser can contact groups or companies known to make components of the type he needs. The reuser can explain his needs to the developers, to check whether a component covering his requirements exists already, or whether the developer can build a component at short notice. The reuser can also broadcast his needs, or the identity of any component he has found, to involve other prospective reusers with similar requirements, or other developers who may have partial solutions to the problem.

- A reuser retrieves a component which looks promising for reuse, but has problems adapting it.

  He can start a communication session with the developer of the component. They can examine the component together, as well as the context of the reuser's application. This may enable the developer to suggest how the component could be adapted, or conclude that the component should not be reused in the application, possibly suggesting an alternative.

- A developer has built a component and tries to classify it, but cannot make it match the term space.

  He can contact the repository manager, and they can discuss the component and the term space together to see whether a solution can be found. If the component necessitates an extension to the term space, this may indicate that it represents new functionality that has not been anticipated. It will be useful to notify potential reusers of the component that it is available.

CSCW support is not limited to repository management, and can be used directly between providers and reusers, for example to issue advertisements for new components or to broadcast requests for new components. An advanced multi-user reuse repository can thus become a bustling marketplace for software components, with a great potential for sharing, leading to substantial saving of effort.

4 Measuring the Effect of Reuse

4.1 Introduction

How can you measure the effect of reuse?

"You do not have to do this—survival is not compulsory". This is a quotation from Dr. W. E. Deming, referring to the concepts of statistical control, which he helped the Japanese to apply to many of their industries. The basic principle behind statistical control is measurement.

Measurements have been widely applied in many engineering disciplines, but in the software industry there has been—and unfortunately still is—some scepticism about their use. Lack of proper measurements is one of the prime reasons for software engineering being a craft rather than a discipline. During recent years, interest in metrics has grown in the software community. This is shown by several ESPRIT initiatives in Europe, the focus on measurements in software capability assessment models (such as the Capability Maturity Model) and an increasing number of reports from industry referring to the use of measurements for managing business.

To be successful when performing measurement activities, their objectives must be clear. The objective of the metrics activities suggested in this chapter is to capture aspects of software development that are important in reuse. It does this by defining attributes and metrics relevant to reuse, and by showing how they can be applied and used. The chapter deals with reuse-specific product and process measurements and cost models. It shows how to use product and process measurements to assess the reusability and quality of components, and cost models to estimate the extra effort involved in development *for* reuse, and the savings in development *with* reuse.

The chapter is aimed at component producers and consumers who want to assess the quality and reusability of components, as well as project managers who need to estimate the costs and benefits of different reuse strategies. Some familiarity with discrete mathematics will be helpful in making full use of the material.

The chapter is organized into the following sections:

- Section 4.2 discusses how to set up quantitative goals for reuse, and how to measure whether they have been reached. It deals with how to measure the amount of reuse, and how to account for the effort used in the reuse activities, process metrics.

- Section 4.3 contains models, metrics and methods suitable for the evaluation of a product developed by a reuse organization, with an emphasis on object-oriented development. The attributes that are considered to be of greatest importance for reuse are *quality* and *reusability*. Both of them are modelled according to a Factor-Criteria-Metrics model. The products (entities) considered are code (traditional software, Ada and C++), design and requirements. The influence of the type of reuse (*as is*, *small change* and *large change*) on the model is also considered.

- Section 4.4 covers cost estimations. It describes a model for estimating the cost of projects developing components *for* and *with* reuse, based on the COCOMO approach with explicit cost-drivers *for* and *with* reuse. It also describes a model for estimating the costs and the benefits for developing a component *for* reuse. The purpose of this model is to evaluate the economics of developing a component *for* reuse rather than developing it for one-off use only.

Product and process metrics can be seen from two viewpoints:

- the measurement view—the objects we measure

- the evaluation view—the objects we want to evaluate by the objects we measure

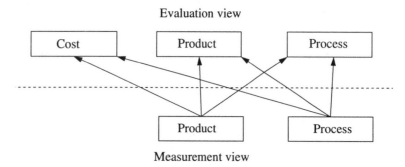

Figure 34 : Measurement view and evaluation view of software metrics

Figure 34 shows that measurement performed on a product can be used to evaluate either the product, the process or the cost. The same is true for measurements performed on a process, for example the number of faults found during testing. From the measurement viewpoint, it is the number of faults in a product that is being measured, but this can be used to evaluate the process, the product or the cost.

4.2 Process metrics for reuse

How can you determine the effect of reuse on productivity, quality and lead time?

4.2.1 Introduction

4.2.1.1 The purpose of reuse measurements

The purpose of any measurement programme is to set quantitative goals and determine whether they are reached. A measurement programme should therefore be goal-driven, defining the quantitative goals we want to achieve and how we determine whether we have reached them. Measurements are also a prerequisite for any kind of quantitative improvement programme.

When we implement a reuse programme, we want to understand the effects of reuse on our goals, and we want to find out if our reuse programme is cost effective. To do this we need to know:

- The improvements due to reuse (savings)

- The effort used in reuse activities (costs)

The goals of a reuse programme can in most cases be connected to improvements in:

- productivity

- quality

- lead time

For this discussion, we will use simple definitions of these measurements:

- productivity = functionality / cost,

- lead time = development calendar time / functionality

We will use number of lines of code as a measure of functionality. This is not a perfect measure of functionality, but it is still an accepted approach to compare the functionality of different products. We will then discuss how counting lines of code will be affected by reuse. Any other measure of functionality, such as function points, can be used instead. For cost we will use effort (person-days), since the major part of software development cost is labour cost.

In Section 4.2.2 we describe how to measure the lines of code (or functionality) and faults in a product when we have reused components when building it. In Section 4.2.3 we describe how effort should be measured when reuse is involved. The measurement of calendar time will not be influenced by reuse.

Our hypothesis is that productivity, quality and lead time can be improved with reuse. Some examples of more detailed hypotheses which we can propose and test with reuse measurements are that reuse will:

- save work (by improving productivity and lead time) by reusing existing components;

- reduce number of errors (through improved quality) by reusing tested components;

- reduce maintenance costs (therefore improving productivity) since we have several users of the same code, and errors only need to be corrected once. It is a separate hypothesis that errors really are corrected only once for reused components, which can be tested;

- reduce rework, since development *for* and *with* reuse places more emphasis on analysis and design. This reduces the amount of rework due to incomplete or unclear requirements.

We will show how each of these hypotheses can be tested with the proposed measurements.

Measurements such as the amount of reuse in a product are also easy to derive, based on the estimated number of lines of code reused, and the total number of lines of code. They are of less importance, however, as reuse is not a goal in itself. They could be used to determine the correlation between the amount of reuse and productivity, quality and lead time for different projects, if all other effects are factored out.

4.2.1.2 Objects for measurement

What should you measure to determine the effect of reuse?

What can you learn from these measurements?

The main objects for measurement will be the project, the support organization, the product and the reusable components, as described in the figure below:

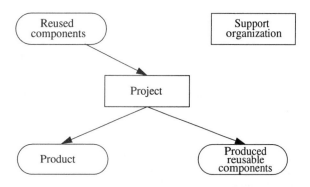

Figure 35 : Objects for measurement

In the figure:

- Reused components are components the project has tried to reuse.

- The product is what is delivered by the project.

- Produced reusable components are any components on which the project has performed development for reuse activities.

- The project carries out all activities performed in connection with producing and maintaining the product and components (i.e. life cycle costs).

- The reuse support organization carries out all reuse activities which are not allocated to any particular project.

Note that in a specific project, reused components, product or produced reusable components may be absent.

In common with any other measurements of the software process and product, reuse measurements are influenced by many external factors that make it difficult to compare two instances of the same activity. Reuse measurements should therefore be thoroughly analyzed before they are used in any form. More complex models such as Boehm's COCOMO model [Boehm81] attempt to quantify the factors influencing projects.

It is also important to ensure that we collect all relevant data if we want to test any hypotheses on reuse. For example, if we do not include all activities influenced by reuse, we will not get an accurate picture of the effect of reuse. However, since organized reuse influences so many of a company's processes, this is difficult to achieve in practice. We must carefully evaluate all relevant data (activities), and provide rationales for their inclusion or exclusion from our models.

The introduction of reuse in a company will also have indirect, long-term benefits, including:

- Improved understanding of a product, through the consideration of more requirements and discussion of alternative reuse solutions.

- Improved design capabilities when development for reuse is employed.

- Improved knowledge of standard solutions when development for reuse is employed.

- Increased standardization of components, because reusable components are collected in one repository, and evaluated during development with reuse.

These benefits are, however, difficult to quantify, and will not be further discussed here.

4.2.1.3 Objects for evaluation

What should you evaluate to assess the effectiveness of your reuse effort?

We want to evaluate both the products (the reusable components) and the reuse processes.

Product evaluation

Productivity and quality can be evaluated on a component, project and organizational basis, whereas lead time is only meaningful on project and component basis. At the component level, we can use productivity, quality and lead time measurements to get a quantitative understanding of what is a good or bad reusable component. This can be used to improve the processes producing and reusing the components. Some examples of indicators of good or bad processes are components where:

- only parts of the functionality are reused, which may mean that the component should be split;

- productivity, quality or lead time in development with reuse is different from what is expected: the reuse of the component leads to a very high or low value;

- the degree of modification during reuse differs from that expected for similar components;

- reuse of the component throughout an organization differs from that for similar components: the component may be adopted for reuse much more quickly or more slowly than expected.

Process evaluation

Evaluation of the reuse processes can be used on an organization, project and component level to:

- Understand the reuse processes.
  By measuring process values during an activity, we can start to understand what is normal for the activity, and what constitute indicators of problems. Typical variables can be effort, size, number of open questions, change activity, faults and so on.

- Estimate and plan new activities.
  Based on previous experience, preferably collected in a database, we can estimate the time and effort needed to perform similar activities in new projects. These can be general reuse activities, or activities connected with specific components.

- Control the progress.
  Based on measurements of the current activity, we can detect indications of problems in the progress of the activity.

- Improve the processes.
  Based on an analysis of the measurements and results of the activities, we can attempt to improve the processes so that the activities become more cost-effective.

The remainder of this section is organized as follows:

- Section 4.2.2 describes how to measure the consequences of reuse on the size and fault-rate of a product.

- Section 4.2.3 suggests how to measure effort in reuse activities.

- Section 4.2.4 discusses possible uses and presentations of reuse metrics.

- Section 4.2.5 discusses continuous reuse process improvements.

4.2.2 Measuring the effect of reuse on software size and fault-rate

How might you measure the size of a system when you have reused parts of it?

What is reuse and what is use?

In this section we discuss how to measure system size and fault-rate when we have incorporated reusable components.

4.2.2.1 Measuring software size

Size in some form is a fundamental measurement for most computed metrics. In this section we discuss the non-trivial question of how to count the lines of codes in a product when it has been constructed partly with reused components.

Figure 36 illustrates the different types of code which are involved when we reuse a component in a system we are building. The definition of size taking reuse into account has to address this.

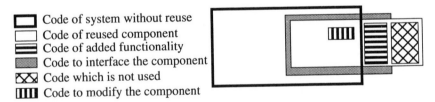

- Code of system without reuse
- Code of reused component
- Code of added functionality
- Code to interface the component
- Code which is not used
- Code to modify the component

Figure 36 : Code involved in development with reuse

The following list also demonstrates some of the problems that need to be addressed when defining how much of a reused component should be included in the product size:

1. If we do not count the reused code in lines of codes produced, we will not be able to see any benefits from reuse.

2. How can we distinguish between use and reuse? Using an operating system, database server and so on is hardly reuse, whereas reusing a component from another product is. For use, we can only count lines of code interfacing to the used component, whereas for reuse we count all or part of the reused component.

3. What is the distinction between reuse and maintenance or enhancement? In maintenance, how much of the previous version of the product must we redesign before

we can say that we are starting to reuse components?

4. Where is the borderline between reuse and customization? For example, telephone systems undergo major customizations before they are delivered to a specific customer. Is this use or reuse?

5. What is reuse within a project? For example, two subprojects discover that they need a similar general component and decide to develop one in common. Another example is a project within which a subproject provides common functionality to other subprojects.

6. How should we estimate lines of code if we reuse only parts of a component's functionality?

7. How should we count lines of code that are included because they can be reused, but would have been left out if reuse was not possible—the case in which reuse has provided additional functionality?

8. How should we treat code generators, that is, application-specific languages? Where is the borderline between the configuration of reusable components and application generators?

9. How should we count reuse of a large component in which we modify or replace some of its subcomponents?

10. How should we count a component in which we only reuse the results from earlier life cycle phases, for example, reusing the analysis and design, but redoing the implementation and testing? How should we count a component if we only reuse the implementation?

11. How many times shall we count reuse of the same component within one product family, one project or one department?

To get any reliable measurements of the effect of reuse, we need to define a measurement method for the amount of reuse which can treat these questions uniformly.

A proposed definition of the size of a reused component

We base our definition of the size contribution of a reused component to a system on an estimation of the equivalent number of lines of code necessary to provide the same functionality if the component was not reused (EQLOC). Note that the EQLOC estimate is only one of two estimates needed to determine whether one should reuse a candidate component or develop from scratch—the other is how much it costs to reuse the candidate component.

The following provides guidelines for how to determine the EQLOC estimate. The numbers in parentheses correspond to the questions in the list above.

1. Reuse is any case in which we have a real choice between using one or several components, or of developing from scratch. (2, 3, 4, 5, 8, 11)

2. For any reused component, the number of lines of code reused is estimated as the

number lines of code needed to provide the used functionality if the component had not been reused. This estimate should be made both when the component is considered for reuse, and when the work is finished. (1, 6, 8, 9)

3. The lines of code needed to adapt, modify or extend the reused component are not added to EQLOC, as that would count them twice. (8, 9, 10)

4. Additional functionality provided by reuse is valued as a percentage of the EQLOC for the functionality. The percentage is based on the expected profit or benefit from the added functionality. (7)

These guidelines are rather vague; we have used terms like "real choice", "valued" and "estimated". You may need to determine more specific guidelines based on your own product structure and components.

It is possible to compare the estimated number of lines of code needed to provide the reused functionality, EQLOC, with:

- the actual number of lines of code in the reused component, either *as is* or minus the extra lines of code added to make the component reusable (for example to increase robustness, or generalize data structures),

- the estimated cost of producing the non-reusable component used when the reusable component was developed originally, and/or

- estimates from other reusers of the component.

These three estimates must be adjusted by the percentage of the component that is actually reused. This percentage can be estimated from the percentage of code, interface functions, documentation or test cases reused.

Even if we do not include the lines of code required to integrate, adapt, modify or replace parts of a reused component in the size of the product, these measurements are important for determining the productivity and quality for the individual component. Some interesting properties of a component are:

- how easy it is to use or modify (productivity)

- how many errors we introduce when reusing it (quality)

To determine these and other properties, we need to know the degree of modification. For each component we reuse, the number of lines of code needed to use, adapt, modify or replace parts of the component should be recorded.

The following section provides two examples to illustrate these ideas:

Example 1

We use a windowing system in a product. Not using the windowing system would have required us to write 6 KLOC (thousand lines of code). The use of the windowing system meant that we could provide several features in our system that were otherwise not planned. To implement these features from scratch would have required 2500 LOC, and we expect to have a benefit (a larger market) corresponding to the cost of developing 1500 LOC. To reuse the windowing system, we write 2 KLOC, 0.5 KLOC of which provided the additional functionality.

This is only reuse if we have a real choice between using the windowing system and providing the functionality from scratch. The equivalent number of lines of code is 6 KLOC and the additional functionality is 1.5 KLOC, a total of 7.5 KLOC. The 2 KLOC written to use the windowing system are not included in our total. The size of our reusable component is therefore 7.5 KLOC.

The productivity increase gained by reusing the windowing system is therefore 7.5/2 = 3.75. This does not take into account the effort needed to understand the reused component. We assume that the productivity in writing the 2 KLOC to use the windowing system is the same as we would have achieved if we wrote the 7.5 KLOC from scratch.

Example 2

We find an architectural component that we intend to reuse, but it is written in the wrong language, so that we can reuse the earlier lifecycle products (analysis, design) but not the later. The estimated EQLOC for writing the component from scratch is 5 KLOC. This means that we include 5 KLOC in the size of our product, but we do not count the lines produced when writing the new code for the component.

4.2.2.2 Measuring faults

The number of faults should be collected at a component, project and company level. This is common practice in most organizations.

Faults are not only failures during execution, but all kind of corrections required to finished products to make them conform to customer specifications. These might result from errors in requirements, design, or code, as well as documentation. Faults can be discovered during any kind of quality assurance or development activity. Faults can be traced back to errors in the code. Three types of errors in the reused code can be identified:

1. Errors in the original component.

2. Errors in the code written to modify the component.

3. Errors in the code using the component, caused by the use of the reusable component.

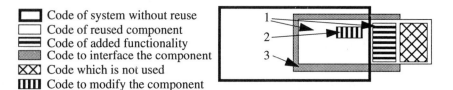

☐ Code of system without reuse
☐ Code of reused component
▤ Code of added functionality
▨ Code to interface the component
☒ Code which is not used
▥ Code to modify the component

Figure 37 : Faults in code involved in development with reuse

These three types of code where faults can occur are shown in Figure 37—we do not distinguish whether the reused code was needed, included or not used. The stage in the process at which faults are detected should also be recorded.

Faults in the code written to modify the component and faults in the code using the component are used to evaluate the reuse quality of the component. Based on these faults it should be easy to suggest improvements to the component or its documentation, and thus to the process producing or reusing such components, so that they can be avoided in future.

Since we use an estimate of the equivalent number of lines of code, measured quality will be relative to the functionality that we reuse. This gives a good picture of the total quality of the component if we assume that faults are evenly distributed. If some reusers experience a different quality than others, it may be that they have estimated the amount of functionality that they reuse in a wrong way, or that they are reusing the component in a different way to other reusers.

4.2.3 Measuring reuse effort

How could you measure how much time and effort you spent on reuse?

Reuse has associated costs. These costs can be measured as effort, for example:

• the effort to develop the reusable component

• the effort to maintain the repository

• the effort to reuse the component

Incorporating systematic reuse in a development process introduces several new activities in the development process, as well as new support processes. To quantify the effects of the reuse programme, we need to measure the effort used on these activities.

This section provides an initial list of activities for which we should collect effort data. The activities are arranged to correspond with the structure of this book:

• organization (Chapter 1)

• project management (Chapter 2)

• repository management (Chapter 3)

• development *for* and *with* reuse (Part B)

To track the effort and effectiveness of reuse activities we need a plan for each activity and measurement of:

• the completion of milestones for the activity compared to the plan

• the work completed and effort used compared to the plan

To get indirect measurements of the stability of the product, project or component we can use measurements that include:

- the number and severity of defects found and changes made to the software requirements

- the number and severity of defects found during development and test

- the total number and change rate of new, open and closed fault management items

All these measurements should be recorded for each reuse customer and component. A suggestion for collecting measurements from reuse projects is provided in the cost forms presented as part of the reuse implementation plan in Appendix B.

4.2.3.1 Collecting data from the organization

The organization of a company provides reuse services to individual projects. We have to collect data from the following activities:

- reuse strategy planning, including legal and contractual issues and cost pricing

- continuous reuse assessment and reuse process improvements

- product strategy

- senior management motivation and review of reuse plans, policies and activities

- training and tool support

We can do this by collecting information about effort used, the number of people involved, and the efficacy of planning, perhaps by the use of questionnaires. These mainly constitute overhead costs, which may be partly spread across product families, but not to individual components (perhaps with the exceptions of larger components).

Effort used by reuse experts associated with the organization should be allocated wherever possible to the actual project or component where they assist.

4.2.3.2 Collecting data from project management

Project management manages the reuse activities in the project. This involves planning, resolving reuse conflicts, and re-planning as reuse opportunities appear. It is difficult to distinguish between project management of reuse activities and other project management, but it should be attempted. Alternatively, we can assume that the project manager's proportion of effort on reuse activities compared to his total effort will correspond to the ratio of reuse effort to total effort in the development work.

The use of external reuse experts should be allocated to the project and component, even if these resources are not directly funded by the project.

An indirect measure of the impact of reuse on project planning can be gained by tracking change activity for the software development plan by both cause and effect. Reuse *causes* are reused components or reuse customers.

4.2.3.3 Collecting data from repository management

There are no special considerations to take into account when recording the effort used on repository organization. The effort should be recorded for the different activities, and allocated to specific components or products where possible. The effort used to insert and retrieve components from the repository by the developers or the repository is recorded against the projects concerned. It may be helpful to establish a separate project for repository maintenance, to make collecting the cost information easier.

4.2.3.4 Collecting data from development for reuse

Development *for* reuse is the process of making a component reusable. This section is focused on development *for* reuse from scratch. Re-engineering can be treated as a combination of development *with* and *for* reuse.

In development *for* reuse we will use additional effort to construct a reusable component, compared to a non-reusable one. Usually, this extra cost can be divided in two:

- extra functionality required to satisfy more customers,

- extra reusability and quality to make the component acceptable as reusable.

These two costs should be kept separate. For the second, we can expect to find some fixed overhead based on the size of the components and the acceptance criteria we have for reusable components. These can vary if we accept components with different scopes of reuse, that is, a component intended for use within the same organization or development process will need a lower overhead than one intended for wider reuse. Section 4.3 presents an approach to measuring the reusability and quality, and to estimating their cost.

The extra functionality required depends on how many potential customers we intend to satisfy. The span of functionality is large, from none at all when all customers will use the component *as is*, to several magnitudes greater when the component is for widespread use, such as an application generator or a database management system.

The decision of the amount of extra functionality to incorporate into a component is an investment decision, based on estimated effort and the likelihood of reuse by potential customers. The original estimate for making the component non-reusable should be included, as well as a cost estimate for the increase in functionality. The actual cost of the component needs to be recorded, to assess if the reuse investment was profitable. The estimated and actual cost of reusing the component can also be used to improve the estimation models.

To enable reusers to estimate how much of the component they actually reuse, an estimate of how much each separate functionality provides towards the total should be provided. This estimate can be based on:

- the cost estimates for the various functional requirements that were used in the cost-benefit analysis for development for reuse

- the number of lines of code or effort actually used to implement these requirements.

Reasonable estimates can be provided by a requirements traceability tool that allows us to trace and count the number of lines of code needed to implement each requirement.

It may be decided not develop a component for reuse. In this case the effort used to reach this decision should be reported separately, as reuse overhead. This information is valuable if we later want to make a similar reusable component. The effort need not be wasted, as it may uncover hidden or unclear end-user requirements that will lead to less rework and a better product.

Development *for* reuse can therefore be profitable early in the project developing the reusable component, since:

- a reusable component is usually more flexible, and therefore better adapted for later changes in the requirements,

- we can uncover hidden or implied requirements from the original customer which would otherwise lead to rework.

The extra cost spent "up front" in providing the extra functionality may therefore be recovered in the same project. However, these savings are hard to quantify. One possible approach for the first type of savings is to record historical data on the cost and size of changes in requirements for non-reusable components, and when in the development process they are introduced. When we get a change in the requirement for a reusable component, we can compare its size and cost to the average for non-reusable components. A requirements traceability tool that can trace changes from requirements to code can provide some assistance with determining the size of the change.

The second source of saving can be estimated by recording when changes are usually introduced, their cost, and how much new functionality (in terms of new or changed requirements) is detected during the analysis of variability.

It is important to split the measured effort both over the different phases of the development life cycle (analysis, design, code and testing) as well as between the different activities of development *for* reuse (analysis of variability in requirements, cost-benefit analysis and representation of generality). This requires a well-defined development process.

4.2.3.5 Collecting data from development with reuse

Development *with* reuse is the process of searching for, evaluating, understanding, adapting and integrating a reusable component, instead of developing the component from scratch. Effort on each of these activities should be recorded separately, and saved with all the components involved in the evaluation. The result of evaluating each component should be recorded with the evaluated component, so that each component carries a record of its rejections, as well as its acceptances.

The effort needed to understand, adapt and integrate the selected component should be treated in the same way as any other development activity, with a plan and monitoring of the plan. If possible, the measurements of effort for the different activities of analysis (understanding), (re)designing, coding and testing should be kept separate. The plan and experiences are recorded with the reusable component so that they can be reused later. It is important to do this even if the component was abandoned at any stage.

Measuring the effort needed to evaluate and adapt the component is necessary to determine:

- the profitability of reusing the component

- the total profitability of the reusable component

- the reusability of the component, that is, the productivity increase or decrease achieved when understanding and modifying it

The phase of development in which the decision to reuse the component was taken should also be recorded. This is used to measure the impact of reuse on the different phases. Our hypothesis is that productivity will increase the earlier we reuse components—the size is the same but the effort will be reduced.

We also recommend that the following are recorded for each component:

- how many times the component has been reused previously by this reuser or his group (two values)

- who developed the component (self, others in group, others in the company or external to the company)

- how the component was found (searching the repository, browsing the repository, informal search in other sources, recommendation from others or own experience)

In the same way as analyzing variability in development *for* reuse, the activity of searching for and evaluating candidate components in development *with* reuse leads to a clearer understanding of the requirements and possible solutions. Candidate reusable components can be used as prototypes for demonstration to the customer, and so help to clarify the requirements. This is a beneficial effect even if the component is not reused. These effects are difficult to quantify. However, as for development *for* reuse, we can estimate the size of changes to the requirements, and estimate the total effect based on historical data.

Later changes in the requirements when we have reused a component should be tracked for both size and effort. These can be compared to the historical data for how much similar changes would cost for non-reusable components. These data can be used to assess the reusability of the individual components.

4.2.4 Use and presentation of reuse measurements

How could you use reuse metrics to increase motivation for reuse?

We can set up and measure quantitative goals for reuse based on company-specific customization of the guidelines for lines of code reused and measurements of effort and faults described in the previous sections. We can make measurements for productivity, lead time and quality including reuse. These measurements should be collected and used at the following levels:

- Measurements of individual components will tell us how profitable each reusable component is, both for each reuse and for all reuses. Component measurements can also be used to evaluate the effect of any new component, such as a new or replacement database system, by estimating the number of lines needed, EQLOC, and monitoring the effort needed to use the new system.

- Project measurements tell us if the project satisfies its reuse goals.

- Organization-level measurements tell us if the organization's reuse programme is profitable.

The historical data collected for each component should be actively used when new reuses of the components are considered.

To present the effect of reuse in the company, we should publish data for:

- Productivity, lead time and quality plotted against the amount of reuse for the organization and different projects. These data should also be compared to the company's goals.

- The profitability (in terms of average number of reuses, average resources saved per reuse) of the entire reuse effort, at the company, project, product families and specific component level. The profitability for each project and component should be presented both in total and relative to the size and effort needed to develop and use the component.

- Both "component of the month"—the component which has brought most profit per line of code—and reuse which saved most effort for the month could be presented.

These are only three suggestions for presentation methods, and it is up to your company to choose which to use. Popular components will tend to migrate from reuse to use over time, until eventually it becomes a matter of course to use the component in standard development processes. These events should also be recorded, perhaps leading to a component "hall of fame". The achievement of reuse goals can be marked with small celebrations, for example when a component developed for reuse becomes profitable, or when a component enters the "top ten" of the hall of fame.

4.2.5 Improving the reuse process

How could you use metrics to determine the strengths and weaknesses of your reuse efforts?

Reuse measurements collected from the reuse processes and components can be used for the continuous improvement of processes. This section provides a list of examples showing how to detect opportunities for such improvements. Most of these require detailed measurements of the development and reuse of specific components:

- Low or high productivity or quality for a component might mean that the reusability or quality of the component needs to be examined. The productivity of a component should be measured as the productivity when reusing the component (see Section 4.2.2.1); it is defined as the size of the component divided by the total cost of reusing it. Note that a difference in productivity can arise either as a result of a really good or bad component, or from wrong estimates for the effort needed to provide the equivalent functionality, EQLOC.

- Incorrect estimates of how much effort is required to reuse a component could indicate inadequate documentation or training in development for reuse.

- Data on the component's ability to accommodate changes in requirements indicate how general it is. This can be measured as the percentage of changes in system requirements that lead to changes in the reused component. A generalized component should not need to be changed even if the surrounding system is changed.

These are only examples of quantitative warning signs that should trigger further action. For each of these cases we can discover the cause of the warning, and from that we can learn something that can be used to improve the process. A simple suggestion is to create checklists for each component, product or process activity. In these we should—for each error we discover—draft a question which, if asked, would have helped us to avoid the error.

4.3 Product metrics

How could you determine the reusability and quality of a component?

4.3.1 Introduction

This section discusses product metrics. By product metrics we mean numerical values used to evaluate one or several characteristics of a product. The characteristics most interesting for reuse are the reusability and quality of the component.

This section uses the terms *a priori* and *a posteriori* metrics. *A priori* metrics are collected during development of the component based on check-lists and static measurements. They provide an estimate of the reusability and quality of the component. *A posteriori* metrics are calculated when a component is reused based on data collected from the reuser. One of the major aims of this section is to relate *a priori* and *a posteriori* metrics, so that we can improve the model for *a priori* metrics and better forecast the quality and reusability of the component. The *a priori* metrics also provide guidelines for how to develop reusable and high quality components.

This section is organized as follows:

- Section 4.3.2 presents a discussion of why we should use product metrics.

- Section 4.3.3 provides a general description of the Factor-Criteria-Metrics (FCM) model and its calibration. The metrics described are for object-oriented development, but other aspects of the model apply equally to other development methodologies.

- Section 4.3.4 provides a description of how we arrived at our present metrics model.

- Section 4.3.5 describes how the factors and criteria are defined, and how the model is applied to the assessment of quality and reusability.

- Section 4.3.6 shows how to apply the FCM model to design and code components.

- Section 4.3.7 describes how an analysis of the metrics can be presented to the user, and how he can use them to improve the reusability and quality of his components.

- Section 4.3.8 describes *a posteriori* factors and how FCM models can be calibrated.

4.3.2 Why product metrics?

Product metrics are used to assess the quality and reusability of components in the repository objectively. The main reason for introducing product metrics is the need for objective control over the reusable components in the repository—it may be desirable to include only highly-reusable high-quality components into the repository. We need a way to assess a component based on the information from acceptance testing or initial field experience, for example.

If we find that the component is good enough to be included in the repository, we need to inform potential reusers of its reusability and quality. This assessment must be stored with the component. It can then be retrieved with the rest of the information relating to any selected component.

To assess the reusability and quality of a software component, we need to be able to rank components. The ranking must be done so that it meets the following requirements:

- The ranking must be public. This implies that it is clear how an assessor has arrived at his result. This must hold even if the assessment is done subjectively, for example as a result of a subjective ranking based on one or more component attributes. Note that "public" does not necessarily mean "objective"; the important thing is that it must be possible to explain *why* the component has acquired its ranking.

- It must be possible to use the ranking rules as guidelines during design and coding of a component. An example of a good rule is "No member functions in classes should have more than twenty lines of code", while a corresponding bad rule is "All member functions should be small".

- The ranking must be improvement-oriented. This implies that when a component is rejected, it must be possible to deduce a set of improvement steps from the assessment that guarantees to improve the ranking of the component, providing that the same ranking method is used.

- The ranking must be fair. This implies that any competent software engineer must be able to recognize that the reasons for ranking a component as highly reusable, for example, really are relevant to reusability as he understands it.

It is highly unlikely that any single software metric will be able to explore all relevant attributes of a software component. For this reason we decided at an early stage that we needed a set of software metrics, where each metric should take into consideration one of the characteristics that make a software component reusable. The component's reusability and quality can then be estimated as a weighted sum of these metrics.

4.3.3 Introduction to the Factor-Criteria-Metrics model

How could you determine what reusability and quality is?

The Factor-Criteria-Metrics (FCM) model is generally accepted as a basis for software assessment, and is used by IEEE and ISO amongst others. To stay close to international standards, we have also used the FCM model as a basis for all assessment of quality and reusability. The basic principle behind this model is that each attribute can be decomposed into a set of factors which themselves can be decomposed into a set of criteria. The criteria values are assessed from a set of software-related measurements, *software metrics*. The following diagram shows how attributes, factors, criteria and metrics are related:

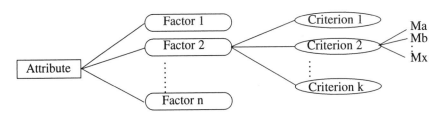

Figure 38 : The main characteristics of the Factor-Criteria-Metrics model

The three terms *factor*, *criterion* and *metric* are organized in an evaluation and assessment hierarchy as follows:

1. Factors are used at the customer and management level. All non-functional requirements for the software are stated at this level. A typical example is "The software should be highly maintainable".

2. Criteria are used at the software designer and project manager level. At this level we decide how we should realize the set of requirements for each factor. For example, "To make the software highly maintainable we must make the software consistent, self-descriptive etc.".

3. Metrics are used at the software and document level. For example, "To make the software self-descriptive we must provide it with a header that describes its functionality, parameters etc.". The metrics used for reusable components are computed

from two sources:

— answers to checklist questions

— counting software characteristics, such as number of decisions (that is, predicates) in the code, the number of inheritance levels and so on.

The factors and criteria we use for reusable components are defined in Section 4.3.5. We have adopted the IEEE definitions of software terms, later referred to as [IEEE83] wherever possible. If the term is missing from the IEEE glossary, we have used other sources.

To understand the discussion of product metrics for software, it is important to keep the following points separate:

• The factor definitions.

These are used to explain what the terms used mean. For example, *portability* is a measure of the ease with which the software can be ported to another computer or operating system.

• Each factor's decomposition into criteria.

This is used to show which software characteristics affect each factor. For example, portability is affected by the software's degree of environmental dependency.

We have chosen to use criteria as a concept to bridge the gap between high-level customer-related factors and low-level measurements from the software as it is implemented. The criteria are not really needed for the factor assessment, but they are of great help as a stepping stone when moving from user requirements to the software itself.

In this section we will use the Factor-Criteria-Metrics model in the following ways:

• The *a priori* use of the model

In the *a priori* use of the model, we collect values for different metrics at development time and compute the values of the criteria, factors and attributes according to the weights in the model.

• The *a posteriori* use of the model

In the *a posteriori* use of the model we define estimates or measurements for either the factor or criteria level which can be collected from the reusers of the components. In our model we have defined these *a posteriori* estimates on the factor level. We can then combine the *a priori* values and several *a posteriori* values to get a better value for the factors.

• The calibration of the model

The *a posteriori* and the *a priori* values for the factors can be compared, and if they consistently differ or are very different for some components this information can be used to improve the model to give better *a priori* values.

4.3.4 How we arrived at our product model

To obtain a reasonable quantification of quality and reusability, we carried out the following:

1. We decided to use the Factor-Criteria-Metrics model as a vehicle for describing a software component's reusability and quality.

2. We distributed a questionnaire to software engineers in five European countries. In this questionnaire, we asked how several attributes related to the software, its development and user experience would influence their decision to reuse or not to reuse a software component.

3. From the answers to these questions, we obtained a set of requirements that software engineers considered important for a component if they were to reuse it. These requirements are used as the factors in our FCM model.

4. The factors used in our model were found to fit into one of the following categories:

   — Cost-related. An example is *portability*, which is concerned with the cost of porting the component.

   — Productivity-related. An example here is *adaptability*, which is concerned with the programmer productivity during adaptation of a component.

   — Event or probability-related. An example here is *reliability*, which is related to the probability of fault-free operation.

5. Each factor or requirement has an activity as its counterpart. An obvious example is that when the software has high portability it means it is easy to port. Each factor-related activity can be decomposed into a subset of activities needed to achieve the goal stated by the factor. With this as our starting point, we were able to define a set of criteria. As an example, consider the factor *understandability*, with its corresponding activity of understanding a software component. If we want to understand a software component, this can be done by:

   — getting a general understanding of the component. This activity depends on the quality of the documentation

   — identifying each part of the component and how they are related to each other and to the component as a whole. This activity depends on the component's structural complexity

   — getting an understanding of each part of the component. This activity depends on the component's self-descriptiveness

6. To decompose each criterion into metrics, we had to find out which software characteristics influenced each step in the activity model described above. The metrics we use are obtained from the literature, the questionnaires and through discussions with application projects. As an example, consider the criterion *documentation level*. We decided that the quality of the documentation depends on:

— the amount of documentation in relation to the size of the component

— the scores from a set of checklist questions concerning the quality of the documentation

4.3.5 The factors and criteria for reusability and quality

The following sections describe the definitions of factors and criteria suggested for the reusability and quality of components. Section 4.3.5.1 describes the factors for reusability and quality, and Section 4.3.5.2 describes the criteria. The criteria used are defined in Section 4.3.5.3.

4.3.5.1 The factors for reusability and quality

Which factors are relevant for the reusability and quality of reusable components?

This section describes our choice of factors for quality and reusability attributes.
    We decomposed the reusability and quality attributes into the following factors:

Figure 39 : The quality and reusability factors

The reasoning behind the two models is as follows:

* Reusability.
  When we reuse a software component we perform a mixture of the following activities:

  — porting the component to a new environment. To do this successfully we need high portability

  — adapting the component to the specific functional requirements of the new system. To do this successfully we need high adaptability

  — understanding the functionality of the component, to decide whether it meets our functional requirements. To do so we need high understandability

  — ensuring that the reused component does not introduce any extra, uncontrolled risks to the system's environment. To do this, we need high confidence

* Quality.
  Many of the non-functional requirements that are usually placed on a software

component are included in reusability. However, the following requirements are not covered:

— we need a low failure rate. To meet this requirement, the component must have high reliability

— we need to change the component when the functional requirements change, for example because the operational environment has changed. To do this, we need high maintainability

We must therefore extend our previous definition of quality. We use the following definition for the factors involved in quality and reusability:

• Confidence: The (subjective) probability that a module, program or system performs its defined purpose satisfactorily (without failure) over a specified time in another environment than that for which it was originally constructed and/or certified.

• Adaptability: The ease with which a component can be adapted to fulfil a requirement that differs from that for which it was originally constructed. Adaptability is sometimes referred to as *flexibility*.

— Adaptation: Modification of existing software in order that it may be used as a module in program development, as opposed to developing another module for that same purpose [DACS79]

• Maintainability: The ease with which maintenance of a functional unit can be performed in accordance with prescribed requirements [IEEE83]

— Maintenance: Modification of a software product after delivery to correct faults, to improve performance or other attributes, or to adapt the product to a changed environment [IEEE83]

• Portability: The ease with which software can be transferred from one computer system or environment to another [IEEE83]

• Reliability: The probability that an item will perform a required function under stated conditions for a stated period of time [IEEE83]

• Understandability: Attributes of software that bear on the user's effort of recognizing the logical concept and its applicability [ISO9126]

Adaptation is different from maintenance in that maintenance concerns the system, while adaptation concerns a part of the system used in a new setting or environment. Table 6 connects software project-related activities to one or more of the factors of *maintainability*, *portability* and *adaptability*.

Table 6 : Relation between factors and activities

Software-related activity	Adaptability	Maintainability	Portability
Correct reported error		X	
Move a component to a new operating system or hardware			X
Enhance a component in the system to include new or changed functionality		X	
Change a component so that it can be used for a new purpose	X		

4.3.5.2 The criteria for reusability and quality

How can you refine the factors for reusability and quality into criteria?

This section defines the criteria used for the factors in the quality and reusability models. It starts by describing the criteria for quality and reusability, and concludes with a definition of the criteria. These criteria are applied when the models are used to give an *a priori* estimate of the factors.

The quality model

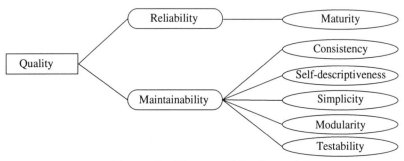

Figure 40 : The general Quality model

The rationales for the decomposition of factors into the given criteria are as follows:

• Reliability. This is directly related to:

— Maturity, i.e. the failure rate

- Maintainability. From the activity-based model decomposition described in Section 4.3.4, we can arrive at the following criteria:

  — Consistency, i.e. adherence to standards for notation

  — Self-descriptiveness, i.e. explanation of how the functionality is implemented

  — Simplicity, i.e. the degree to which we have managed to find the simplest possible implementation solution

  — Modularity, i.e. how well we have managed to split our solution up into disjoint sub-functions

  — Testability, i.e. how easy it is to check that we have implemented the stated requirements

The reusability model

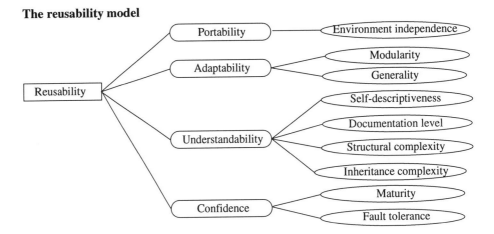

Figure 41 : The general Reusability model for code

The rationales for the decomposition of factors into the given criteria are as follows:

- Portability. This is directly related to

  — Environmental independence, i.e. to which degree the software depends on environment-specific features

- Adaptability. This can be decomposed into:

  — Modularity, i.e. how well we have managed to split our solution up into disjoint sub-functions

  — Generality, i.e. the component's degree of independence from the rest of software, for instance other functions, global variables and so on

- Understandability. This can be decomposed into:

  — Self-descriptiveness, i.e. explanation of how the functionality is implemented

— Documentation level, i.e. the accessibility, level of detail and quality of the supplied reuse documentation

— Structure complexity, i.e. how easy it is to understand the relationships between the component's parts

— Inheritance complexity, i.e. how easy it is to understand the relationships between a class and its superclass

- Confidence. This can be decomposed into:

  — Maturity, i.e. how often does the component fail

  — Fault tolerance, i.e. how well does the component handle these failures when they occur

4.3.5.3 Definition of the criteria

The requirements expressed by each management-related factor (see Section 4.3.3) are realized by a set of software-related criteria. While the factors are "outer" requirements, the criteria are "inner"—software-related—requirements.

The criteria in the model are defined as follows:

- Consistency. The strict and uniform adherence to prescribed symbols, notation, terminology, and conventions which tends to foster a quality software product.

- Documentation level. A description of required documentation indicating its scope, content, format and quality. Selection of level may be based on project cost, intended usage, extent of effort or other factors [IEEE83].

- Environment independence. The degree to which the software is constructed in such a way that it is independent of hardware and system-dependent software.

- Fault tolerance. The built-in capacity of a system to provide continued correct execution in the presence of a limited number of hardware and software faults [IEEE83].

  — Note that fault tolerance does not imply that the system gives correct results when a fault occurs. It implies that the system does not crash, but gives a reasonable error message and then works correctly for other inputs, i.e. inputs that do not activate the errors.

- Generality. The degree to which a software system or software component is applicable in different software environments [DACS79].

  — Environment. The combination of all external or extrinsic conditions that affect the operation of an entity.
  Note that the definition of an environment is relative to the level where the entity, in this case a component, is operating.

- Inheritance complexity. A measure of the degree of simplicity of the relationship between a class and its superclasses.

- Maturity. Attributes of software that bear on the frequency of failure through faults in the software [ISO - 9126].

- Modularity. The extent to which software is composed of discrete components such that a change to one component has a minimal impact on other components [IEEE-83].

- Self-descriptiveness. Those attributes of the software that provide explanation of the implementation of a function.

- Simplicity. Those attributes of the software that provide implementation of functions in the most understandable manner. Usually avoidance of practices which increase complexity [MCCA80].

- Structure complexity. A measure of the degree of simplicity of relationships between subsystems [DACS79].

  — Complexity: The degree of complication of a system or system component, determined by such factors as the number and intricacy of interfaces, the number and intricacy of conditional branches, the degree of nesting, the types of data structures and other system characteristics [IEEE83].

- Testability: The extent to which software facilitates both the establishment of test criteria and the evaluation of the software with respect to those criteria [IEEE83].

4.3.6 Metrics for reusable components

What metrics should you collect for reusable components?

This section discusses the detailed metrics that allow you to determine the criteria described in the previous section. Section 4.3.6.1 discusses the type of metrics, then Section 4.3.6.2 presents the way in which the criteria are decomposed into metrics. Section 4.3.6.3 gives an overview of the metrics. Section 4.3.6.4 shows check-lists we used. In Section 4.3.7 an example of the estimation of quality is included.

4.3.6.1 Types of metrics

We have made two important decisions concerning metrics:

- We should not use a linear dependency between one or more software measurements and a software factor. Instead we decided to use metrics values as trouble or success indicators. For example, we say that if a certain measure is increased above a specific limit, it will probably lead to problems in meeting one or more quality or reusability requirements.

• All measurements should be normalized so that they yield a value between zero and one, where a value close to zero indicates that the measured characteristic may cause problems, and a value close to one indicates that the corresponding characteristic is kept inside its limits.

From these two assumptions, we decided that all metrics should be of one of the following types:

1. *Upper limit metric*, characterized by a break-off value *a* (the point at which the value of the metric starts to decrease) and a 50% limit *b*. An example is the number of predicates used in a member function. The formula for this type of metric is:

$$M(m) = \frac{1}{1 + e^{(x \times (m-y))}}$$

The parameters *x* and *y* are defined from the following relations: $M(a) = 0.99$, $M(a+b) = 0.5$. The relationship between the computed metric *M* and the observed software measurements *m* can be illustrated by the following graph:

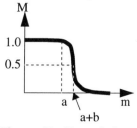

Figure 42 : Upper limit metric

2. *Optimum value metric*, characterized by centre value *a* and 50% limits at *a+b* and *a–b*. An example here is the relative number of in-line comments in a member function. The formula for this type of metric is:

$$M(m) = e^{-x \times (m-a)^z}$$

The parameter *z*, an even positive integer, determines the "squareness" of the graph. The parameter *x* is defined by $M(a+b) = M(a-b) = 0.5$. The relationship between the computed metric *M* and the observed software measurements *m* is illustrated by the graph in figure 43:

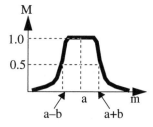

Figure 43 : Optimum value metric

3. *Linear dependency metric.* A typical example is the relative number of system-dependent code lines. The relationship between the computed metric *M* and the observed software measurements *m* can be illustrated by the following graph:

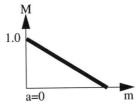

Figure 44 : Linear dependency metric

4.3.6.2 Metrics for the quality and reusability models

Figures 45 and 46 define the metrics used to define the criteria in the quality and reusability models. The specific metrics are defined in the following sections. Note also that the models presented here also apply to C++ code reused with small modifications. Simplified models for design and *as is* reuse are described in Section 4.3.7.

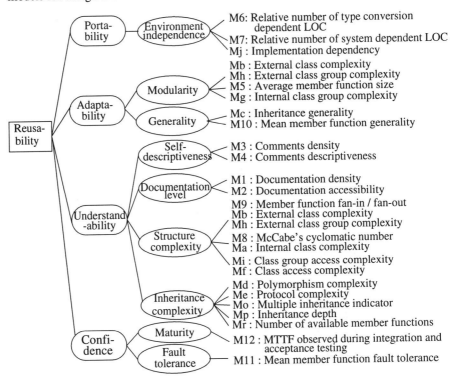

Figure 45 : The model for Reusability of C++ code

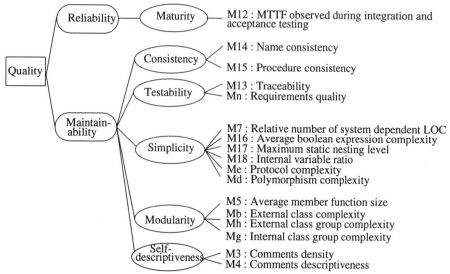

Figure 46 : The model for Quality of C++ code

4.3.6.3 Overview of the metrics

The models use a total of 35 metrics. They are given in Table 7 with information on identifier (Id), short name, type (T) and parameters (a, a–b, a+b) for the quantitative metrics and the questions (QcX and QmX, see Section 4.3.6.4) for the check-list metrics. There are two groups of metrics, namely general software metrics, denoted by M*integer*, and object-oriented metrics, denoted by M*letter*. In the table, '#' indicates 'number of'.

Table 7 : Overview of reusability and quality metrics

Id	Short name	T	a	a –b	a + b
M1	Documentation density (product and user) - pages per KLOC	2	105	30	180
M2	Documentation accessibility	3	$\dfrac{Qc1 + Qc2 + Qc3a + Qc3b + Qc3c + Qc3d}{6}$		
M3	Comments density - lines of comments per LOC	2	0.20	0.15	0.25
M4	Comments descriptiveness	3	$\dfrac{Qc4 + (\sum Qm1_i + Qm2_i) / \# \text{ member functions}}{3}$		

Table 7 : Overview of reusability and quality metrics

Id	Short name	T	a	a −b	a + b
M5	Average member function size - LOC per member function	2	12.5	5	20
M6	Relative number of type conversion dependent LOC	3	$1 - \dfrac{\text{\# type-conversion dependent code lines} \times 10}{LOC}$		
M7	Relative number of system dependent LOC	3	$1 - \dfrac{\text{\# system dependent code lines} \times 10}{LOC}$		
M8	McCabe's cyclomatic number	1	9	-	11
M9	Member function fan-in / fan-out	1	5	-	7
M10	Mean member function generality	3	$\dfrac{\sum (Qm3_i + Qm4_i + Qm5_i)\,/3}{\text{number of member functions}}$		
M11	Mean member function fault tolerance	3	$\dfrac{\sum (Qm6_i + Qm7_i)\,/2}{\text{number of member functions}}$		
M12	MTTF observed during integration and acceptance testing	3	$\dfrac{\text{number of person-hours used for testing}}{\text{number of errors found} + 0.5}$		
M13	Traceability	3	Qc9		
M14	Name consistency	3	(Qc5 + Qc6)/4		
M15	Procedure consistency	3	(Qc7+Qc8)/4		
M16	Average boolean expression complexity	3	$1 - \dfrac{\text{number of IFs} + \text{number of WHILEs}}{LOC}$		
M17	Maximum static nesting level	1	3	-	5
M18	Class internal variable ratio	3	$\dfrac{\text{number of declared variables}}{\text{total number of different variables used}}$		
Ma	Internal class complexity	1	9	-	11
Mb	External class complexity - potential class fan-in / fan-out	1	30	-	50

Table 7 : Overview of reusability and quality metrics

Id	Short name	T	a	a −b	a + b
Mc	Inheritance generality	3	TBD		
Md	Polymorphism complexity	3	Qc10		
Me	Protocol complexity	1	1	-	3
Mf	Class access complexity (W is a weight, suggested value 3)	3	$\dfrac{\text{\# parameters} + \text{\# global variables}}{\text{\# parameters} + \text{\# global variables} \times W}$		
Mg	Internal class group complexity	1	9	-	11
Mh	External class group complexity - potential class group fan-in / fan-out	1	30	-	50
Mi	Class group access complexity (Mf_j is the Mf metric for each class)	3	$\dfrac{\sum Mf_j}{\text{number of classes}}$		
Mj	Implementation dependency	3	(Qc12+Qc13+Qc14+Qc15)/4		
Mk	Exception handling - Ada only	-	TBD		
Mm	Template generality - Ada only	-	TBD		
Mn	Requirements quality	3	(Qc16+Qc17+Qc18+Qc19+Qc20)/10		
Mo	Multiple inheritance indicator	1	1	-	2
Mp	Inheritance depth of class	1	4	-	6
Mq	Design maturity	3	$1 - \dfrac{w \times \text{number of signals}^{1.5}}{ELOC}$		
Mr	The number of available (public) member functions (also inherited)	1	20	-	30

The following paragraphs contain short explanations of some of the metrics, assuming some knowledge of standard product metrics. They use the notation $n = \|x\|$ to indicate n is equal to the number of items in the set x.

M6: Relative number of type conversion dependent LOC

A type conversion dependent code line is defined as a line that contains:

- a *char* declaration that is not specified as *signed* or *unsigned*

- an implicit or explicit type conversion

M8: McCabe's cyclomatic number

Cyclomatic complexity $v(G)$ is defined as:
    (# edges − # processes + (2 (# functions))) or (# predicates + 1)
where:
    number of predicates = number of IF + number of ? + number of WHILE + number of FOR + number of CASE − 1 + number of AND + number of OR + number of GOTO − (number of GOTO's inside IF statements)
Note that the '?'s are counted to include the C++ and C equivalent of an IF expression.

M9: Member function fan-in / fan-out

The number of parameters to the member function plus the number of external variables (other objects or global) accessed (read from and/or written to).

M12: MTTF observed during integration and acceptance testing

The present estimator for the maturity (mean time to failure, or MTTF) is defined so that if no errors are observed, the MTTF estimate will be twice as long as the experienced testing period. Since testing usually gives a much more error-prone behaviour than operation in the field, we use a test compression factor—introduced by John D. Musa—to get a reasonable estimate for operational MTTF. This compression factor is currently set to 12.5 based on Musa's data, but should be adjusted based on operational experience from actual reuse. When operational experience is available, we compute M12 as follows:

$$M12 = \frac{12.5 \times \text{Time (Test)} + \text{Time (Operation)}}{\text{Errors (Test)} + \text{Errors (Operation)} + 0.5}$$

Ma: Internal class complexity

The following diagrams are used to explain how we compute the complexity ($v(G)$) for a class (m are methods, D data (instance variables in general), the outer ellipses are classes, large arrows method calls and small arrow data access):

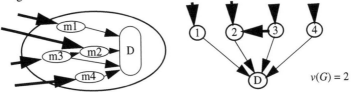

$$v(G) = e - n + 2$$

$$n = \| \{i | m_i \text{ uses data in D}\} \cup \{j | m_j \text{ calls } m_k, \forall j, k \neq j\} \| + 1$$
$$e = \| \{i | m_i \text{ uses data in D}\} \| + \| \{j | m_j \text{ calls } m_k, \forall j, k \neq j\} \|$$

Figure 47 : Class complexity metric

Here n is the number of nodes plus 1, i.e. all methods using data or calling other methods, and e is the number of edges, i.e. all uses of data by a method plus all calls of other methods.

Mb: External class complexity - potential class fan-in / fan-out

The suggested limit value for the number of member functions is 10-15 and the suggested limit value for the number of parameters per member function is 3-5. 10*3 = 30 is the limit value and (10+15)/2*(3+5)/2 = 50 the 80% value. The following figure shows how to compute Fan-in / Fan-out for a class:

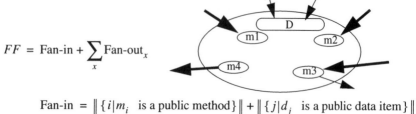

$$FF = \text{Fan-in} + \sum_{x} \text{Fan-out}_{x}$$

$$\text{Fan-in} = \| \{ i | m_i \text{ is a public method} \} \| + \| \{ j | d_j \text{ is a public data item} \} \|$$
$$\text{Fan-out}_x = \| \{ x | m_x \text{ calls } m_y, x \in S, y \notin S \} \cup \{ x | m_x \text{ uses } D_y, x \in S, y \notin S \} \|$$

Figure 48 : Class fan-in / fan-out metric

Me: Protocol complexity

The purpose of this metric is to measure whether the functionality is evenly distributed through the inheritance chain. The value of m is determined by:

$$\frac{\text{Largest protocol in inheritance chain}}{\text{Average \# of member functions for classes in chain}}$$

Mg: Internal class group complexity

The complexity $v(G)$ for a class group is the cyclomatic complexity of the graph described by the calls/references between the classes in the group. The following figure explains the computation of the complexity $v(G)$ of a class group (the definition of edges and nodes are similar to those for Mb):

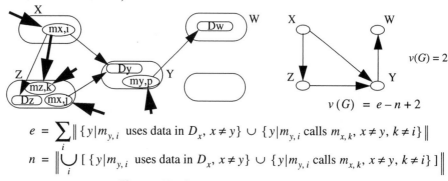

$$e = \sum_{i} \| \{ y | m_{y,i} \text{ uses data in } D_x, x \neq y \} \cup \{ y | m_{y,i} \text{ calls } m_{x,k}, x \neq y, k \neq i \} \|$$
$$n = \left\| \bigcup_{i} [\{ y | m_{y,i} \text{ uses data in } D_x, x \neq y \} \cup \{ y | m_{y,i} \text{ calls } m_{x,k}, x \neq y, k \neq i \}] \right\|$$

Figure 49 : Class group complexity metric

Mh: External class group complexity

The external class group complexity (also called potential fan-in / fan-out) is the number of externally accessible member functions and data inside the class group. This is illustrated in the following figure, showing a class group (the outer ellipse) that contains classes W, X, Y and Z:

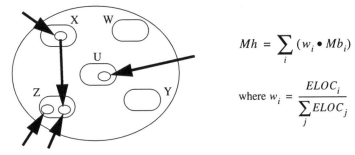

$$Mh = \sum_i (w_i \bullet Mb_i)$$

$$\text{where } w_i = \frac{ELOC_i}{\sum_j ELOC_j}$$

Figure 50 : External class group complexity metric

Mq: Design maturity

Design maturity is a measure of the potential reliability of the design. Investigation has indicated that the two variables that control this are the number of signals exchanged between classes and the final size of the resulting implementation.

4.3.6.4 Check-list metrics

Check-lists are used to evaluate some of the metrics in the Factor-Criteria-Metrics model. There are two set of questions, one for member functions and one for classes. All questions are prefixed with the codes that are used in the metrics forms field denoting the metric. The check-list questions that are marked with an asterisk can have one of the three following answers:

- *All*, with the score equal to 2

- *Some*, with the score equal to 1

- *None*, with the score equal to 0

The normalization factor must therefore be 2*n, instead of n, when n is the number of check-list questions used to compute the metric.

Class-related questions

- Qc1: Is all documentation clear and sufficient?

- Qc2: Is the documentation adequately indexed?
- Are the following documents available:
  - Qc3a: Functional specification?
  - Qc3b: Design specification?
  - Qc3c: Implementation description?
  - Qc3d: Test procedures?
- Qc4: Is a standard format defined for the organization of the member functions?
- Qc5*: To what extent do all identifiers comply with a specified standard?
- Qc6*: Are public names semantically consistent?
- Qc7*: Are all parameter lists in function definitions consistent?
- Qc8*: Does the handling of detected error conditions comply with standards specified for the project?
- Qc9: Is there a direct mapping between specification and implementation or is the correspondence easily traceable?
- Qc10: Will all versions of a virtual function perform corresponding operations?
- Qc11: (not used)
- Qc12: Is the result of the execution independent of the order of the static allocation?
- Qc13: Is the result of the execution independent of whether new allocated areas are initialized or not?
- Qc14: Have you checked that all "#include" statements will work as intended?
- Qc15: Is the result of the execution independent of whether *long* is longer than *int* or other such relations?
- Qc16*: Are the original requirements for the implementation of the component unambiguous and precise?
- Qc17*: Is it possible to verify that each requirement is met in an objective manner?
- Qc18*: Is it possible to trace each requirement back to the set of problems that the component is supposed to solve?
- Qc19*: Can we change each requirement without large changes to any of the other requirements?
- Qc20 *: Are the requirements organized such that they can be used in a simple manner during component development?

Member function-related questions

- Qm1: Is comment set off from the code in a unified manner?

- Qm2: Are the comments meaningful?

- Qm3: Are input processing, output processing and pure processing mixed in a member function? (A well-structured component will input data, carry out the required processing and then output the data, as separate operations.)

- Qm4: Are system or machine-dependent functionality mixed in the member function?

- Qm5: Is data, value or volume-limited processing avoided? (An example of a data-limited component is a component with an array declaration of the form "REAL ARRAY (1:100)", instead of "INTEGER N = 100, REAL ARRAY (1:N)".)

- Qm6: Does the program operate on the basis of mutual suspicion (for example validating input parameters passed between procedures)?

- Qm7: Does the member function use fault containment (trapping faults without bringing the program to an uncontrolled halt)?

4.3.7 The FCM models for design and small change of code

How could you determine the reusability of a design?

This section discusses adaptations of the general models for quality and reusability presented in the last sections. The adaptations are for design and reuse *as is* and *small change* reuse.

4.3.7.1 The FCM model for design

The models shown in the previous section are the complete models. We support reuse of both design components and code components; the reuse repository will thus contain both types. It will often be convenient to store both the design and the finished, coded version of a component. We must therefore be able to assess the quality and reusability of design and code separately.

If we want to assess the quality or reusability of a design component, we can make some simplifications to the reusability model. The reason for this is that many decisions are left open during design and only resolved during implementation. The simplified reusability model is shown in Figure 51.

The following simplifications have been done:

- Portability is removed; this is not required, as system and hardware dependencies are introduced during coding.

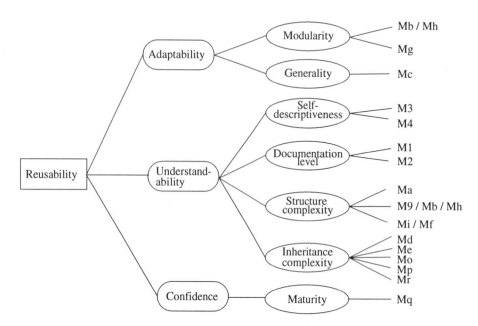

Figure 51 : The FCM Reusability model for Design

- Confidence is simplified by removing the fault-tolerance, since this is included during implementation.

Note that *maturity* used here refers to design maturity. This is a measure of how often the design "failed" during reviews, and thus gives an indication of the expected amount of trouble during reuse of the design component.

4.3.7.2 The Factor-Criteria-Metrics model for code

A reusable component can be reused in several ways, called *reuse modes*. These are referred to as *as is* ("black box"), *small change* ("grey box") and *large change* ("white box") respectively. These modes are described in more detail in Chapter 10. Since the economy of *large change* reuse of code is rather dubious, we will not discuss it any further. In addition, *large change* reuse of code in reality tends to be *as is* or *small change* reuse of a component's design structure.

Reuse *as is* implies that one or more components are reused without any changes. If possible, this type of reuse is the most profitable. The reason for this is that when no changes are made, we need only concern ourselves with the external characteristics of the component. The factor criteria models mirror this fact.

If we want to make small changes to the component, we need information concerning the internal working of the component, for example information on the component's self-descriptiveness, its internal complexity and how modular it is. It is thus possible for a component to have a high level of reusability and quality for the *as is* case, while its *small change* reusability and quality can be quite low.

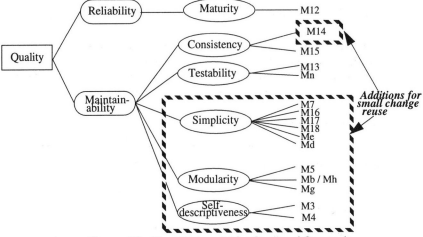

Figure 52 : The FCM model for Quality of C++ code

The *as is* model for component quality is simplified by removing the criteria *simplicity*, *modularity* and *self-descriptiveness*, since these are all concerned with the internal characteristics of a component.

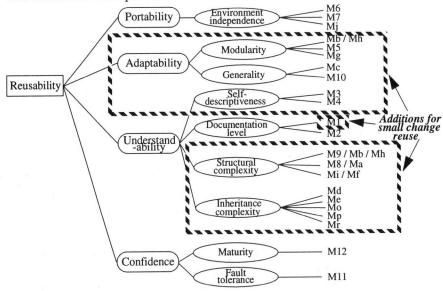

Figure 53 : The FCM model for Reusability of C++ code

The *as is* model for reusability is simplified by removing:

• the criteria concerned with the inner characteristics of understandability

- the factor *adaptability*, since adaptability is only decided during implementation

4.3.7.3 Quality estimation for "as is" reuse – an example

In this example we will show how reuse *as is* quality is estimated, here based on software metrics, an *a priori* estimate. Section 4.3.9 shows how it can be calculated from field data, an *a posteriori* estimate. Since we want to use the same example to illustrate model calibration, the two estimates are made to differ markedly.

A priori maturity

Maturity = M12 = Test effort / number of errors found. Total test effort is measured in person-hours. Dividing this by the number of errors found in that time gives a value in hours.

A priori consistency

Consistency = M15

- M15 = (Qc7+Qc8)/2. The two check-list questions used for consistency are the following:
  - — Qc7: Are all parameter lists in function definitions consistent?
  - — Qc8: Does the handling of detected error conditions comply with a specified standard?

A priori testability

Testability = (M13+Mn)/2

- M13 = Qc9. The check-list question for M13 is the following:
  - — Qc9: Is there either a direct mapping between specification and implementation or is the correspondence easily traceable?
- Mn = (Qc16+Qc17+Qc18+Qc19+Qc20)/10. The five check-list questions used for requirements quality are the following:
  - — Qc16: Are all requirements unambiguous and precise?
  - — Qc17: Is it possible to verify that each requirement is met in an objective manner?
  - — Qc18: Is it possible to trace each requirement back to the set of problems that the component is supposed to solve?
  - — Qc19: Can we change each requirement without large changes to any of the other requirements?
  - — Qc20: Are the requirements organized in such a manner that they can be used in a simple manner during component development?

Example data

The reported data and answers to the check-list questions give the following metric values:

- M12 = 100/30 = 3.3

- M13 = 1.0

- M15 = 0.5

- Mn = 0.6

From these values, we find the following *a priori as is* component quality criteria and factors:

- Maturity = 3.3 operation hour $^{-1}$

- Consistency = 0.5

- Testability = 0.8

If we assign the same weights to consistency and testability, we get the values:

- reliability = 0.00 for the next 100 hours of operation (a failure is almost certain in this time),

- maintainability = 0.65.

With equal weights, this gives us a quality assessment of 0.32, which indicates a low quality component. This example is treated further in Section 4.3.9.

4.3.8 The use of measurements

This section is concerned with three problems, namely:

- How do we compute the criteria and factors based on information from the software component itself and the answers to check-list questions?

- How do we display this information to users?

- How can the user use this information to obtain a better, more reusable software component?

4.3.8.1 How to compute the factors and criteria?

The factors are computed as weighted sums of the criteria, which again are computed as weighted sums of the software metrics. The weights are assigned as described in Section 4.3.10.2. We need two sets of weights, one set for *as is* reuse and one set for *small change* reuse.

The *as is* reusability model needs only two weights to assess the factors based on the criteria, and three more weights to assess the criteria based on the metrics. The *as is* quality model needs two criteria weights and two metrics weights. The remaining metrics and criteria need no weights since they are used alone. A typical example is the assessment of portability, based on the *environment independence* criterion.

The number of weights needed for *small change* reuse is much larger. For the reusability model for *small change* reuse we must assess eight criteria weights and twenty metrics weights. For the quality model we need five more criteria weights and fifteen more metrics weights. However, when all the weights are assessed, it is straightforward to compute both the criteria and the factors from the model.

To find the reusability and quality scores, we must decide which weights to use when combining factors into the final attribute scores. The problem here is that these weights will be company or project-dependent. The reason for this is that the importance of each factor involved will depend on how a company or project intends to use the component. If, for example, they plan never to move the product to another platform, portability will be irrelevant and should be given a low weight, even zero. Similar considerations can be made for the other factors.

It will also be necessary to adjust the threshold parameter of one or more of the upper limit metrics (type 1 metrics in Figure 42, Section 4.3.6.1). The reason for this is that these metrics are parametrized using the competence limit of the personnel they describe. A quick look through the reusability and quality metrics (Table 7 in Section 4.3.6.3) shows that all the upper limit metrics are concerned with complexity of one kind or another. The threshold that we use will give the metric a value of 0.5, indicating that there is an even chance that the characteristic scored by this metric will cause problems. It is clear that this limit must be personnel-dependent. For example, for a trainee, developing an application with two levels of static nesting may create problems, whereas an experienced software engineer can cope easily with four or five levels of static nesting.

All the suggested metrics, and thus all the criteria and factors, are normalized so that values close to 1.0 indicate a high probability of success, and values close to 0.0 indicate a potential problem in the area described by the metric. This normalization gives two important benefits:

- It is easy to relate to and interpret the scores.

- It is easy to make a simple diagram that sums up the metrics situation for the component.

The presentation of metrics is discussed in the next section.

4.3.8.2 Presenting the results to users

We have chosen to use Kiviat diagrams for presentation of metrics [Verilog90]. This type of diagram represents parameters as vector values plotted on a circle. They provide an easy-to-grasp presentation of assessment results and can be used for factors, criteria and metrics.

The basic diagram is shown below. We have used four factors, denoted by F_1 to F_4, to illustrate the use of the diagram.

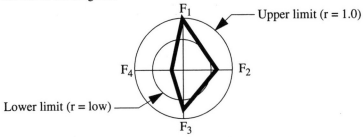

Figure 54 : Example Kiviat diagram

The value denoted "low" is the lowest acceptable score for each characteristic. We see directly that F_4 is much too low in this example, while the other factors are within acceptable limits.

When we combine the Kiviat diagram with the FCM model, it seems natural to use three diagrams with an increasing levels of detail. We decided to use one Kiviat diagram for the factors, one for the criteria and one for the metrics. Examples of all three diagrams are shown in Figures 55-57, taken from the REBOOT toolset.

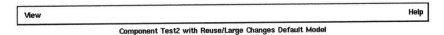

Figure 55 : Kiviat diagram for the Reusability factors

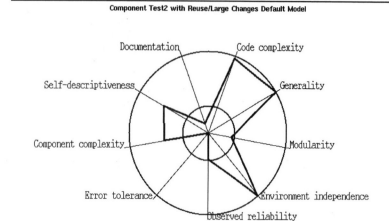

Figure 56 : Kiviat diagram for the Reusability criteria

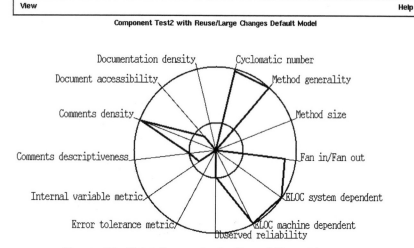

Figure 57 : Kiviat diagram for the Reusability metrics

From Figure 56, for example, it can immediately be seen that the values for *document accessibility* and *internal variable* metrics are below the acceptable limit. Similarly for Figure 57, the values for *method size, error tolerance* and so on are lower than acceptable.

4.3.8.3 Software improvement based on the FCM model

Each metric with a score falling below the acceptable value points to a potential trouble spot in the component. This section describes the recommended action when a metric is below the required level. The approach is based on the FCM model, since the model structure will tell us how to search for opportunities for improvement in the most efficient way.

1. Find the factor in the model with the lowest score.

2. Search through the criteria used to assess this factor. Find the criterion with the lowest score.

3. Search through the metrics used to assess this criterion. Find the metric with the lowest score.

4. If possible, change the component in such a way that the score is increased.

5. Perform a new assessment. If the factor is still below the acceptable value, repeat steps 2 to 5.

The steps are all concerned with different parts of the FCM model. The following diagram shows where each step belongs:

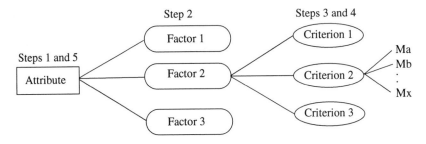

Figure 58 : The relationship between the FCM model and metrics-guided improvement

4.3.8.4 Example of a metrics-guided improvement

In the Kiviat diagrams in the previous section, we see from the factor diagram that the component's *confidence* is much too low. The FCM model tells us that confidence is computed from the criteria *maturity* (observed reliability) and *fault tolerance* (error tolerance). A quick glance at the criteria-level diagram tells us that we should start by improving the component's fault tolerance, as its value is 0.0.

If we turn to the metrics level, we find in the FCM model that fault tolerance has only one metric, computed based on two check-list questions, concerning fault containment and the application of the principle of mutual suspicion for passing parameters. The component can therefore acquire an acceptable assessment by adding fault containment and input and output parameter validation.

In Figure 56 in Section 4.3.8.4, note that even though the *documentation density* metric is also zero, and the documentation criterion has a poor value, the high scores on the other criteria used to assess *understandability*, such as *complexity* and *self-descriptiveness*, are high enough to ensure a sufficient overall score. If this is undesirable, the weights on the criteria documentation density and understandability can be adjusted to lower the overall score.

More testing, to increase *maturity*, or writing more documentation to increase *documentation density*, are logical steps if we want to improve the component's reusability further. The choice between the two approaches is mainly a question of costs and available resources.

4.3.9 *A posteriori* estimates of reusability and quality factors

All factors can be estimated based on observable quantities. To do so, the following data must be available:

* the personnel resources used for integration and acceptance testing

* the number of errors found during integration and acceptance testing

* the number of errors found during integration and acceptance testing that were not adequately handled by the component's internal error control routines, for example exceptions and parameter checks

* the personnel resources used to develop the component

* the size of the component, measured in non-comment lines of source code

* the personnel resources used for maintenance, including error corrections, changes, version updates etc.

* the number of non-comment source code lines developed, changed or removed during the activities measured in maintenance in the previous point

* the personnel resources used for porting the component

* the personnel resources needed to understand the component.

Productivity is computed as follows:

$$Productivity = \frac{\text{Number of non-comment lines of code involved}}{\text{Amount of personnel resources used}}$$

Note that this definition has to be adjusted for reuse as described in Section 4.2.2, when we estimate how much the reused component contributes to the system.

At the present we use the following estimators for the factors:

$$Reliability\,(t)\ =\ e^{-t/maturity}$$

$$Maintainability\ =\ \frac{\text{Maintenance productivity}}{\text{Development productivity}}$$

$$Portability\ =\ 1 - \frac{\text{Cost to port}}{\text{Cost to develop}}$$

$$Flexibility\ =\ \frac{\text{Change productivity}}{\text{Development productivity}}$$

$$Understandability\ =\ 1 - \frac{\text{Cost to understand}}{\text{Cost to develop}}$$

$$Confidence\ =\ Reliability + (1 - Reliability)\,\text{Fault tolerance}$$

Quality estimation for *as is* reuse

Referring to the example in Section , this section shows how *as is* quality is estimated based on field data, an *a posteriori* estimate. Since we also want to use the same example to illustrate model calibration, the two estimates are made to differ markedly.

In the *a priori* estimates we calculated the factor values:

- Reliability = 0.00 for the next 100 hours of operation

- Maintainability = 0.65

With equal weights, this gave us a quality assessment of 0.32, which indicated a low quality component.

After 100 hours of operation, field data is available. One failure was observed, and in the two cases of maintenance, one error correction and one small enhancement, we observed a productivity of fifteen lines of code per person-day, while the development productivity was twenty lines of code per person-day. This information gives us the following *a posteriori* estimates:

- Reliability = 0.34

- Maintainability = 0.75

With the same weights as before, we arrive at a quality estimate of 0.55. This is still low, but considerably better than the *a posteriori* estimate. The calibration activity that results from this discrepancy is discussed in Section 4.3.10.

4.3.10 Calibrating the FCM model

4.3.10.1 The calibration decision

The adaptation and calibration of the product metrics model consists of the following activities:

- Deciding if the factor, criteria and metrics are appropriate for the company.

- Finding the initial values for the model, i.e. the threshold values of metrics and weights for the metrics and criteria. This must be done in all cases before the model is used to assess any software. This activity is described in Section 4.3.10.2.

- Updating the factor values for reused components based on accumulated *a posteriori* data. This activity is discussed in Section 4.3.10.3.

- Updating the model based on consistent or large deviation between the *a priori* and *a posteriori* values. These calibrations are discussed in Section 4.3.10.4.

4.3.10.2 How to set the weights for metrics and criteria

Many methods exist for assigning weights. They range from a solid mathematical basis to a mere formalizing of the assessor's intuition. We use a method balanced between these extremes, *pair-wise comparison*.

This method is simple to use and quite robust. The price we pay for this is that an assessor will not discover any inconsistencies in the pair-wise comparisons. If these inconsistencies are few, however, the method will yield satisfactory results. If we have only two weights, we have to assess these directly through a decision that we consider a to be m times as important as b, and then arrive at the normalized weights from this relation. Thus, we have:

$$m \bullet w_a = w_b \qquad \Rightarrow \qquad \begin{aligned} w_a &= \frac{1}{1+m} \\ w_b &= \frac{m}{1+m} \end{aligned}$$

For a comparison between n criteria ($n > 2$), we start out with an $n*n$ table as shown below. The algorithm is as follows:

1. Compare C<1> to C<2>, C<3> and so on, all the way to C<n>. Each time C<1> is considered to be more important, or is considered to have the greater influence, we

increment the value in the corresponding field in the table. If, for this table, we read ">" as "more important than", the table is completed as shown below.

Table 8 : Pair-wise comparison

Criterion Id (i)	2	3	4	....	....	n	Sum
1: C<1>	1 > i	-	-	-	-	-	S1
2: C<2>	2 > 1	2 > i	-	-	-	-	S2
3: C<3>	3 > 1	3 > 2	3 > i	-	.	-	S3
4: C<4>	4 > 1	4 > 2	4 > 3	.	.	-	....
....	.	.	.	.	.	-	....
....	.	.	.	.	.	.	....
n: C<n>	n > 1	n > 2	n > 3	.	.	n > i	Sn
Sum (S)	n–1	n–2	n–3	....	....	1	n(n–1)/2

2. The weights can now be computed from the following expression:

$$w_i = \frac{Si}{S} \qquad S = \sum Si$$

In some cases, one or more of the sums Si can be equal to zero. To avoid zero weights, these criteria are given the weight of 0.5 and the gross total is adjusted accordingly. The choice of 0.5 is based on the notion of a score that is in between one and zero. It is, however, possible that other choices are as good or better.

It should be remembered that this method was originally intended to compare alternatives, and was not intended for the assessment of individual weights. The results may thus be misleading if it is used in cases with few (less than four or five) alternatives.

4.3.10.3 Calibrating factors and attributes

When we have observed a factor value (*a posteriori*) for a reused component, we need to update the factor and the attributes, reusability and/or quality, that use the factor. There are two important considerations:

1. We must move the factor estimate in the direction of the observed value.

2. We must ensure that we do not overreact so that the estimate oscillates based on the most recent measurement.

We suggest that the non-parametric Bayes estimator is a reasonable way to obtain new factor values. We denote the old factor value by Φ_{old}, the observed factor value by Φ_{obs}

and the new, improved factor value by Φ_{new}. The number of observations that are used to compute Φ_{obs} is denoted by k. The new factor value is then decided from the following formula:

$$\Phi_{new} = \Phi_{old}\frac{u}{u + k} + \Phi_{observed}\frac{k}{u + k}$$

This formula is used repeatedly, so that for the next set of observations, Φ_{new} will take the place of Φ_{old} and u will be replaced by $u + k$.

The choice of u-value is important, especially in the early life of a component. Tentatively, we have decided on $u = 3$. This decision is taken based on the number of observed values needed to make us change our opinion about a factor.

4.3.10.4 Calibration through changes in the model

Constant deviation between the *a priori* and the *a posteriori* values of the factors in a large set of components, or large deviations in some components, can mean that our model is wrong.

The model can be adjusted by changing one or more of the following parameters:

- the factor, criteria and metrics or their composition

- the weights for the factors and criteria

- the threshold values for the metrics or check-lists

- the *a posteriori* definitions

It is difficult to determine the changes appropriate for a given deviation. It is, however, quite simple to test changes and see how they affect the fit between the *a priori* and *a posteriori* values of the components. Note that we should minimize the total sum of deviation over all components. In the following we will only discuss how to change the metrics.

Each metric can be changed in several ways to fit observed data. To simplify this process, we have decided on the following rules (with reference to Figures 42 to 44 in Section 4.3.6.1):

- Type 1 metrics (upper limit metric): Only the 50% threshold is changed. The distance from this threshold to the highest metric value to yield $M = 1$ is not changed.

- Type 2 metrics (optimum value metric): Only the centre value is changed. The distance from the centre value to the 50% limits is not changed.

- Type 3 metric (linear dependency): These metrics are changed by multiplying the metric by a calibration constant.

4.4 Cost estimation

How could you estimate the cost of developing for and with reuse?

4.4.1 Introduction

This section is concerned with two types of cost:

- development *for* reuse: the cost of developing a reusable software component

- development *with* reuse: the cost of developing a system based on one or more reusable components taken from the repository

The rest of this section contains

- an introduction to the COCOMO estimation method

- guidance on how to include extra development costs caused by reusability requirements

- guidance on how to estimate the costs for developing a system when part of the system is realized through reuse

- guidance on how to control the costs during development

4.4.2 Estimating development costs

4.4.2.1 Introduction to the COCOMO method

The COCOMO estimation method for software has a strong commercial basis, and its structure is well suited to our needs. It starts from the assumption that cost is proportional to component size, expressed as the number of lines of code. It is, however, well documented that software development costs can vary quite dramatically, even if the resultant systems are the same size. In the COCOMO model, this variability is attributed to variations in:

- the system's non-functional requirements

- the ability of the people doing the work

- the tools and methods used

In COCOMO, these sources of variation are subdivided into factors called *cost drivers*. These cost drivers allow for a project's deviation from a normal project. For example, a requirement for high reliability is allowed for by using a reliability cost driver greater than one. The COCOMO model thus estimates the cost of building a piece of software from three items of information:

- The size of the system, measured in estimated lines of code (LOC or KLOC)

- The mode of development. The people using the model have to select either *organic*, *semidetached* or *embedded*. For a definition of these terms, see [Boehm81].

- The cost drivers, which describe the project's deviation from a project where all cost drivers are set to a nominal value—the "normal" project. There are fifteen cost drivers, which are multiplied together to give the final cost modifier. We will denote the cost drivers by *f* and an enumeration index *i*. All COCOMO cost drivers are tabulated in Appendix B.

The cost of developing a software component can then be written as:

$$Cost = a \bullet KLOC^b \bullet \prod f_i$$

The two constants *a* and *b* are dependent on the mode of development. [Boehm81] suggests the following values:

- Organic development mode: $a = 3.2$, $b = 1.06$

- Semidetached development mode: $a = 3.0$, $b = 1.12$

- Embedded development mode: $a = 2.8$, $b = 1.20$

Practical experience has shown that the COCOMO model, as all other cost models, must be calibrated to fit any new environment. There are two reasons for this:

- the layout of the code—and thus the information represented on each code line—differs from site to site

- the productivity in a normal project varies from site to site

It is generally agreed that this is best done by modifying the two constants *a* and *b* in the formula above. See for instance [Miyazaki85].

In the rest of this handbook we will for simplicity give the constant *b* a value of 1.0. The use of a linear cost-size relationship makes it easier to discuss relationships between reuse and new development, between reuse and other investments, and so on.

The COCOMO model also has a formula for the estimation of the development time. Once we have found the cost estimate expressed in person-months, the development time in months—T_{dev}—can be estimated as follows:

$$T_{dev} = c \bullet Cost^d$$

As for cost estimation, the two constants used here (*c* and *d*) will depend on the development mode. The values suggested by Boehm are:

- Organic development mode: $c = 2.5$, $d = 0.38$

- Semidetached development mode: $c = 2.5$, $d = 0.35$

- Embedded development mode: $c = 2.5$, $d = 0.32$

The model for development time will need calibration before being used in a particular environment, in the same way as the cost formula.

4.4.2.2 Estimating costs in development for reuse

To estimate the cost of development for reuse by use of the COCOMO model, we map the reusability criteria onto the relevant COCOMO cost drivers. This means that we try to capture and quantify the non-functional requirements that must be met by reusable components in the COCOMO model. The extra functionality we include in the component will automatically be included in the additional lines of code it represents.

If reusability demands high reliability, for example, we include this fact by fixing the reliability cost driver to "high". Some of the extra costs cannot, however, be mapped onto COCOMO cost drivers. These criteria are included as extra code, that is, code that we would not have written if we did not plan to reuse the component.

The criteria in the model for reusable software are converted to costs in one of the following ways:

- *Environment independence*, *maturity*, *modularity* and *simplicity* are converted to cost drivers.

- *Documentation*, *self-descriptiveness* and *fault-tolerance* are converted to extra code; that is, code that would not have been written if the component was not intended for reuse.

- *Consistency*, *testability* and *generality* are ignored in the cost model. The first two criteria are ignored because the extra cost is believed to be small compared to all other costs. *Generality* is ignored because it enters automatically into the cost of writing reusable software as extra lines of code.

Cost drivers for reusability

The following list describes the criteria we converted to cost drivers, and suggested values:

- *Environment independence*
  The cost included here is the extra cost of making a software component environmentally independent from the start. The cost of making an existing component environmentally independent is a different problem. The two cost drivers we considered are the [Herd77] cost drivers f_{10} or f_{12} for scientific software. We selected the cost driver for development on a computer other than the one where the component will be used (f_{12}). We thus use the cost driver value of 1.11 for environment independence.

- *Maturity*
  We have no historical information available when we want to write a new component.

At present, we use the COCOMO reliability cost driver RELY instead. We use a cost driver value of 1.40.

- *Modularity*
  This is the extra cost involved in making a component highly modular, e.g. packaging of functionality in separate functions and blocks of code. This does not affect the amount of code necessary. It does, however, have some impact on the required design effort. In the COCOMO cost model, design represents 18% of the total construction effort. With available experience, we estimate the increase in design effort necessary to be 25%. We thus use a *testability* and *modularity* cost driver value of $1 + 0.18*0.25 = 1.04$.

- *Simplicity*
  We define simplicity as a function of:

  — the number of complex or negative boolean expressions (boolean expressions containing NOT)

  — the number of local and global variables manipulated.

  The complexity and size of the component are also involved. These two factors will not, however, influence the extra cost of writing a reusable component, since they pertain to the problem that the component solves. For the remaining simplicity requirements, we model the extra cost by increasing the effort needed for detailed design. In the COCOMO cost model, detailed design represents 27% of the total production effort. With available experience we estimate the necessary increase in the detailed design effort to be 25%. We thus use a *simplicity* cost driver value of $1 + 0.27 * 0.25 = 1.07$.

Extra code for reusability

The following list describes the criteria we have converted to extra lines of code, and suggested values. To establish a compact notation, we introduced the following acronyms:

- LD_{c_head}: The quantity of comments needed for header and external documentation. We estimate this as $0.15 * SD_{c\_head}$.

- $LC_{failure}$: The amount of extra code needed to achieve error tolerance. We estimate this as $SC_{failure}$ * number of failure conditions.

- LD_{c_comm}: The quantity of in-line comments needed. We estimate this as $0.15* LOC$.

- LC_{p_check}: The amount of extra code needed to control all parameters and external variables to avoid error propagation. We estimate this as SC_{p_check} * (*number of parameters + number of global variables used*).

- LD_{m_head}: The extra quantity of comments needed for a descriptive header for each subroutine or member function in object-oriented design. We estimate this as $SD_{c\text{-}method}$ * 0.15 * *number of member functions*

The values SD_{c_head}, SD_{c_method}, SC_{p_check} and $SC_{failure}$ are of great importance to the cost model. To assign numerical values to these variables, we:

1. Used the general experience currently available at SINTEF and SEMA, to assign starting values to these variables. These values are denoted by the index s for subjective.

2. Collected information from C++ code written in the REBOOT project. These values are denoted by the index e for experience.

3. Made new, improved estimates based on a combination of the collected data and past experience. To combine the data in a statistically sound manner, we will use the approach described in Section 4.3.10.

Our subjective starting values were as follows:

- SD_{c_head} = 40 lines of text

- SD_{c_method} = 5 lines of text

- SC_{p_check} = 5 lines of code

- $SC_{failure}$ = 10 lines of code

All these numbers are averages and so only hold for classes, and not for single member functions. An alternative to using average values could be to use intervals, and give maximum and minimum values for each variable. We do not consider this a useful approach, however.

The following values can be used for the cost of developing reusable software components:

- LD_{c_head} = 6

- LC_{fail} = 10 * *number of controlled failure conditions*

- LD_{c_comm} = 0.15 * LOC

- LC_{p_check} = 5 * (*number of parameters + number of global variables accessed*)

- LD_{method} = 0.75 * *number of member functions*

The total cost of developing reusable components

Our cost model for reusable components can now be written as

$$LOC(\text{As-Is}) = LOC + 6 + 5 \bullet (parameters + globals) + 10 \bullet \text{failure conditions}$$

$$LOC(\text{Small Change}) = LOC(\text{As-Is}) + 0.74 \bullet \text{member functions}$$

$$Factor(mode) = 1.55 \bullet I(mode \in \{As\ Is\}) + 1.81 \bullet I(mode \in \{Small, Large\})$$

$$Cost_{nominal}(mode) = aLOC(mode)^b \bullet Factor(mode)$$

where *mode* refers to the reuse mode, as described in Section 4.3.7.2. To calculate the total cost of building a reusable component, we must include the cost drivers concerning computer attributes (such as turn-around time), personnel attributes (such as analyst capability) and project attributes (such as required development schedule). If we let the relevant cost drivers be denoted by f_i, we have that:

$$\text{Total cost} = Cost_{nominal}(mode)\prod f_i$$

This estimate is only applicable for a company that usually develops components with all cost drivers set to their nominal values. Companies with below-nominal standards will experience higher costs when producing reusable components, while companies with above-nominal standards will experience a lower cost overhead. This can be allowed for in the model by dividing the total cost by the set of cost driver values that the company usually uses for *environment independence*, *maturity* (reliability), *modularity* and *simplicity*. If we denote this set by *Reuse*, the expression for the estimate of the total cost is then modified as follows:

$$\text{Total cost} = Cost_{nominal}(mode)\frac{\prod f_i}{\prod\limits_{j \in Reuse} f_j}$$

We see from this expression that all cost driver-related overheads will vanish if the company already develops highly mature, highly modular, simple and environmentally-independent software.

4.4.2.3 The cost of development with reuse

This section discusses how to estimate the cost of a project in which components are reused in more than one phase of the development life cycle. In Section 4.2.2.1 we described how to measure the benefit of reuse by estimating the size contribution of the reusable component to the system.This discussion was based on the equivalent number of lines of code needed to provided the reused functionality, *EQLOC*. In this section, we discuss how to estimate the actual cost of reusing the component. This estimate is necessary to enable us to decide whether to reuse the component.

We also use the EQLOC method for cost estimation in projects that reuse code. The basic process for this method is as follows:

1. Convert the cost of reusing a software component to a corresponding number of code lines. For example, if the reuse cost is two person-days and our productivity is 20 LOC per person-day, then the *reuse cost equivalent* is 40 lines of code.

2. Add the number of new code lines needed to the reuse cost equivalent, and use this number of code lines in your chosen cost estimation model.

We need a way to convert the number of reused code lines to equivalent code lines. We suggest:

Let S be the set of components in the system. This set is split into two subsets containing new components—S_{new}—, and reused components—S_{reuse}. We need to know the normal distribution of effort on the different phases, denoted by W_{anal}, W_{des}, W_{impl}, and $W_{integrt}$, which sum to 1. This distribution can be company-wide, component type-specific or component-specific.

When we reuse a component, we need to estimate the following:

- the effort to search for and understand any component considered for reuse, converted to the number of lines of code that could have been written with the same effort, LOC_{search}

- the effort to adapt and integrate the component in the remaining life cycle phases, plus any rework of earlier phases caused by the component. This effort depends on how much of the component we adapt.

We assume that the effort is proportional to the component size LOC_j and its complexity $CPLX_j$. The remaining cost drivers are system-dependent. We can now define the factor AAF (*adaptation adjustment factor*) for each component j as:

$$AAF_j = W_{des}Design_j + W_{code}Code_j + W_{integr}Integration_j$$

$Design_j$, $Code_j$ and $Integration_j$ are the portion of design, code and integration work that need to be redone in component j.

The cost of development can be written as:

$$Cost = Cost(search) + \left(\sum_{j \in S_{new}} CPLX_j \, LOC_j^a + \sum_{j \in S_{reuse}} CPLX_j LOC_j^a AFF_j \right) K$$

The project dependent constant K contains all cost drivers except component complexity —CPLX multiplied by the productivity constant.

From the expression above, the equivalent number of code lines can be obtained by dividing the equation above by K. In most cases, the term $Cost(search)/K$ can be ignored and we get:

$$LOC_{equiv}^a = \sum_{j \in S_{new}} CPLX_j \, LOC_j^a + \sum_{j \in S_{reuse}} CPLX_j LOC_j^a AFF_j$$

where LOC_j is the total number of lines of code in the reused component, and the $CPLX_j$ terms are the ordinary COCOMO cost drivers for the reused and original components. Note that we have used different complexity cost drivers for the reused component and the equivalent code. This is appropriate, as the complexity of the reused component can differ from the code we would have written from scratch. Note also that this estimate will change as we discover components for reuse throughout the development of the system.

The development cost for the project, if it had been done from scratch, would have been:

$$Cost = K \sum_{j \in S} CPLX_j \, LOC_j^a$$

We will define productivity as the delivered functionality divided by development cost. If we—as done earlier—use the approximation that functionality is proportional to *LOC*, then we have that:

$$\text{Productivity} \approx \frac{C \cdot LOC}{\text{Cost}}$$

Note that *LOC* here is related to the functionality and is independent of how this functionality is implemented. Thus the productivity increase is given by:

$$\text{Productivity increase} \approx \frac{\displaystyle\sum_{j \in S_{\text{new}}} \text{CPLX}_j \, \text{LOC}_j^a + \sum_{j \in S_{\text{reuse}}} \text{CPLX}_j \, \text{LOC}_j^a}{\displaystyle\sum_{j \in S_{\text{new}}} \text{CPLX}_j \, \text{LOC}_j^a + \sum_{j \in S_{\text{reuse}}} \text{CPLX}_j \, \text{LOC}_j^a \text{AFF}_j}$$

As before we have ignored the search cost term. Since the expression above will just be used to discuss some of the implications of reuse we will simplify it by setting $a = 1$ and assuming constant complexity (CPLX_j) and adjustment (AAF_j). Thus we get:

$$\text{Productivity increase} \approx \frac{LOC_{new} + LOC_R}{LOC_{new} + LOC_{reused}AFF}$$

The number of code lines that we would have written if we had developed the system from scratch. However when reusing a component, we often have to include, understand and maintain code that we did not need. A typical example is code that is intended in order to increase the generality and flexibility of the component. This code, although necessary for the general reuse, is pure overhead for each specific reuser. In order to cater for this, we write:

$$LOC_R = LOC_{reused} - LOC_{roverhead}$$

This gives us:

$$\text{Productivity increase} \approx \frac{LOC_{new} + LOC_{reused} - LOC_{overhead}}{LOC_{new} + AAF \bullet LOC_{reused}}$$

Typically, the conversion factor *AAF* from reused code to equivalent new code will be in the range 0.1 to 0.7. For fixed LOC_{reused} and LOC_{new} values and two different $LOC_{overhead}$ values, we get the following graph:

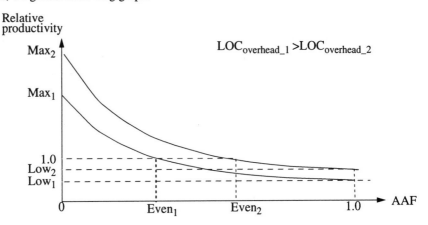

Figure 59 : Relationship between productivity increase and the design adaptation factor

There are three important values to be noted in this figure:

- **Max**: This is the maximum relative productivity that can be achieved for this system with a given amount of reusability, i.e. *AFF* = 0.0.

- **Even**: This is the break-even point for the adaptation factor *AAF*. It defines the reuse overhead that gives the same productivity as development from scratch would have given. Reuse to the right of this value will decrease productivity for the project.

- **Low**: This is the productivity limit achieved when we have to change all the design components included, i.e. *AFF* = 1.0.

These three values can be computed as follows:

$$Productivity_{Max} = 1 + \frac{LOC_{reused} - LOC_{overhead}}{LOC_{new}}$$

$$Productivity_{Low} = 1 - \frac{LOC_{overhead}}{LOC_{new} + LOC_{reused}}$$

$$AAF_{Even} = 1 - \frac{LOC_{overhead}}{LOC_{reused}}$$

When $LOC_{overhead}$ increases, the *AAF* value interval where we get productivity increase greater than one—[0, $1 - LOC_{overhead}/LOC_{reuse}$]—gets smaller and smaller. For large $LOC_{overhead}$ values, a real danger exists that reuse will be counterproductive. To achieve a large productivity increase through reuse, the overhead must be small. This can be realized by making reusable components in such a way that we only need to understand the parts to which we are going to interface.

A simple example is a dictionary handler. We assume that this can be realized through reuse in two ways:

1. We reuse a component called *dictionary handler*. This component takes a name, represented as a string, as input and returns a status value indicating whether the name was entered or whether it was already included in the dictionary. In the latter case, it also returns a pointer to the name.

2. We reuse a set of components. This set includes a hashing algorithm, a component that handles bucket overflow, a search component and so on.

Even though both reuse scenarios give the reuser the same functionality, and the amount of new code needed in the second case is small, more work is required in the second case than the first. This is because, instead of understanding the concept of a dictionary, one must understand all its parts in isolation.

In our opinion, the serious problem of overhead will be greatly reduced when we move from reuse of code to reuse of design components. There are two major reasons for this:

- A design component is on a higher level of abstraction. This makes it much easier to identify the correct reusable component, and so less overhead is introduced

- When making a system or component design, we can be less concerned with details that will only concern the implementation or realization.

4.4.2.4 Reusability and adaptation

This section aims to drive home the fact that reusability is not only a characteristic of the component itself, but is also strongly influenced by:

- the capability of the personnel who do reuse

- how well the component is suited to the specific reuse application

There is a direct relationship between reusability and the adaptation factor (*AAF*). This relationship follows from the following estimator:

$$Reusability = 1 - \frac{Cost_{reuse}}{Cost_{develop}}$$

By inserting the COCOMO estimators for the two costs and denoting the cost drivers for the development and reuse team by (1) and (2) respectively, we get the following relationship:

$$Reusability = 1 - AAF \bullet \frac{LOC_{reused}}{LOC_{reused} - LOC_{overhead}} \bullet \prod \frac{f_i^{(2)}}{f_i^{(1)}}$$

This shows that both the personnel capability level and the amount of extra code, that is, code that is part of the reused component that we do not need, will have a strong influence on the observed reusability. When there is no overhead and both the development and reuse team have the same capabilities, we see that reusability is equal to $(1 - AAF)$. We call this the *nominal reusability*.

The expression above can be further simplified to yield:

$$Reusability = 1 - \frac{AAF}{AAF_{even}} \bullet \prod \frac{f_i^{(1)}}{f_i^{(2)}}$$

If we use the same level of personnel during both development and reuse, the last term will be reduced to one, and reusability can be expressed directly as a function of the adaptation factor.

4.4.2.5 The cost of development for and with reuse – two examples

This section presents examples of how the cost estimation techniques described in the preceding sections can be applied.

Example 1: Development of a component for *as is* or *small change* reuse

We first make a cost estimate for a component that is intended for *as is* and *small change* reuse. From the component's specification, we can extract the following data:

- Raw component size will be 100–200 lines of code. This is our 90% confidence interval, that is, we can be 90% certain that the resultant component will have a size in this range.

- The component will have a total of 10 member functions, with an average number of parameters equal to three.

- We estimate that the number of failure conditions per member functions is four.

- No global parameters will be used.

From these data we find that $LOC(as\ is, small\ change) = 763\text{-}863$. The main reason for the large number of lines of code is the need to control all failure conditions. By reducing the number of possible failure conditions that the component must handle, the cost can be reduced considerably.

The nominal cost interval can now be found as:

$$Cost_{nominal} = [3*0.76*1.81, 3*0.86*1.81], \text{ or } [4.13, 4.67] \text{ person-months}$$

If we assume that all other cost drivers are nominal, this will also be the real cost for the development of the component by the company.

Example 2: Development of a system with *small change* reuse

The next example considers the development of a new system. We plan to implement this system partly through code reuse. The problem is that we do not have a component that exactly fits our needs. We are thus forced to do *small change* reuse. A quick evaluation of the available component tells us that we must rework roughly 10% of the code and 50% of the integration. This gives us $AAF = 0.18$.

The component to be reused has about 2000 lines of code. Of these 2000 lines we need only 1000. In addition we need to understand about 300 lines which handle internal administration. We therefore have $LOC_{reused} = 1300$ and $LOC_{overhead} = 300$. We can now find $AAF_{even} = 1 - 300/1300 = 0.77$. This shows us that this reuse will be profitable.

We estimate that we will need to write about 2000 lines of code from scratch. The complexity for the new code is "low", corresponding to a cost driver of 0.85, while the complexity of the reused code is very high, corresponding to a cost driver of 1.30. This information gives us the following estimates:

$$LOC_{equiv} = 2000*0.85 + 1300*1.30*0.18 = 2004.2$$

If we assume that all other cost drivers have been rated as nominal, we get:

$$Cost = 3*2 = 6 \text{ person-months}$$

If we had written the whole system from scratch, we would have needed $3*(2 + 1) = 9$ person-months. The savings are thus considerable.

4.4.3 Controlling costs during development

Estimating the development cost is only half the job. The other half is to control the development so that we can see how our expenditures and progress develop. This is just as true for development *for* and *with* reuse, as well as for projects that do not use reuse. There are two types of events that need our attention:

1. we discover that we may finish too late

2. we use more of our resources than we had planned to reach the current milestone

The following subsections give short descriptions on how we can detect these two events, and some possible remedies.

4.4.3.1 The milestone chain and produced value

The basis for all project cost control is a good milestone chain. A milestone is defined as an observable and measurable event within a project or activity. The two main considerations to make when setting up such a chain are:

• We need enough milestones to allow us to detect problems early enough to do something about them

• We must avoid setting so many milestones that the overhead in reporting becomes too large

Key project milestones can be annotated with percent of job finished. This can be done both at the activity level and for the entire project. The two figures below show typical examples, the key milestones for a complete product, and the internal milestones for the design documentation:

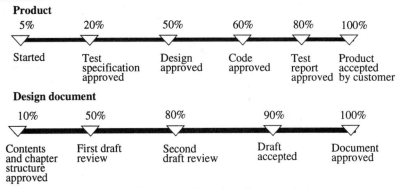

Figure 60 : Two examples of a milestone chain

The percentages show how much of the activity is finished when the milestone has been reached. The produced value is calculated as follows:

Produced value = Percentage value for latest reached milestone* Total activity budget

The milestones with percent-finished indications must always be made at the lowest level of the plan. The key number *produced value* must be calculated at this level and summed to find the produced value for the entire project.

For example, we can use the Design document activity shown above. If we have finished "First draft review" but not "Second draft review" we have reached the 50% milestone. If the total budget for this activity is 200 person-hours, the produced value is 0.50*200 = 100 person-hours worth.

Note that it is not permissible to interpolate between milestones. If we have reached milestone A and expect to reach milestone B in a week, say, we can only report the percent-finished value for milestone A, not something between A and B. If this rule results in too little detail on progress, it indicates that there are too few milestones for the activity.

This method of calculating produced value is error-prone if there are less than, say, ten activities, or if any activity is responsible for more than say 10% of the total produced value of the project.

4.4.3.2 The C/SCSC method for project control

C/SCSC is an acronym for Cost / Schedule Control System Criteria. This method is popular in several branches of industry, both on-shore and off-shore. Its two basic parameters are:

- Deviation from plan = Resources spent – Resource budget

- Deviation in productivity = Resource budget – Produced value

The following diagram shows how this method is used to control a project.

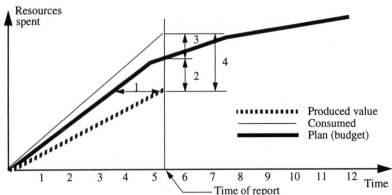

Figure 61 : Example of a C/SCSC diagram

The values needed to get an overview of the project status are marked with 1, 2, 3 and 4 respectively. They should be interpreted as follows:

1. Project time delay. The project needs to be speeded up

2. Productivity deviation. The project's productivity is too low

3. Plan deviation

4. Progress deviation

It is the responsibility of the project manager to decide when the plan or progress deviation is sufficiently large that action is required. Corrective action should consist of the following activities as a minimum:

*   Finding the causes for the observed deviations. Typical causes are bad estimations, unavailability of key personnel, unforeseen technical or managerial problems and so on.

*   Adjusting the activity estimates. This must include both work done till now and the remainder of the project. It is a common observation that if some activities are underestimated, all activities tend to be underestimated.

*   The results of the investigation should be distributed to all personnel responsible for estimation in the company, and be stored for later reference.

4.4.4 When to make a component reusable

When should you decide to invest in development for reuse?

This section examines the decision of making reusable components, compared to other ways to use a company's resources. The problem of resource allocation is treated as an investment problem.

4.4.4.1 The investment problem

The decision to make a software component reusable is a managerial decision. To make an economically sound decision, you need to be able to understand the costs and benefits. You must include the following points in the calculation:

- The extra cost of making a component reusable

- The money saved by each reuse

- The expected number of reuse instances, and how they are spread over the time

- The cost of maintaining the component in the repository

Maintaining the repository includes the following activities:

1. Qualification and insertion of the component.

2. Handling of error reports on reused components.
   Two approaches that can be taken: either we correct the reused component or we make a new, improved version. Both require work.

3. Repository maintenance.
   This includes removing or changing components that are not used, or that receive low reuser satisfaction scores, handling requests for new components and so on.

4. "Back room" activities, for example generalizing or specializing components in the repository.

In addition to the costs associated with these activities, we also have the costs for the resources used by the repository itself, such as extra disk space.

All such costs must be distributed over all reuses of all components. The most reasonable way to do this is to consider the maintenance of the repository as part of the reuse cost. This implies that if the cost of running the repository is M and we expect a total of n reuses per year, each reuse must contribute a sum of M/n. Alternatively, we could grade the amount according to the size of the component reused, and thus measure according to the money saved.

The initial investment, denoted by I in Figure 62, is the cost of making the component reusable. The estimation of I is discussed in Section 4.4.2.

Figure 62 : Investment, adjusted for fixed yearly costs

If we consider the annual costs C to be a lasting commitment, and the rate of interest is r, then the present value of this is $C(1+r)/r$. This amount is a cost which should be subtracted from the annual income.

The savings per reuse is the difference between the development costs for the reused component and the costs incurred if we realize the required functionality through reuse. Let the two costs *cost to reuse component* and *cost to develop component* be denoted by C_{reuse} and C_{dev} respectively. It then follows from our definition of observed reusability that we can write:

$$Reusability \ *C_{dev} \ = \ C_{dev} - C_{reuse}$$

In periods of economic stability, it is customary to assume a fixed rate of interest. The saved cost minus the yearly expenditure divided by the investment, and reduced to its present value is called the *return on investment, ROI*. This is calculated as:

$$ROI \ = \ \frac{C_{dev}}{I} \ * \sum_{i=1}^{m} \frac{Reusability}{(1+r)^{n_i}} - \frac{C}{I} * \frac{1+r}{r}$$

where r is the rate of interest. The condition for profitable investment—in this case profitable reuse—is that $ROI > 1.0$.

Components can conveniently be split into two categories, called *application-dependent* and *application-independent* components. Application-dependent components are those that are specifically linked to a given product line or hardware (for example, an operating system for a specific computer family). Such components will have a life cycle that is dependent on the life cycle of the product. For these components, we must consider where in a product's life cycle we are. Consider the following diagram:

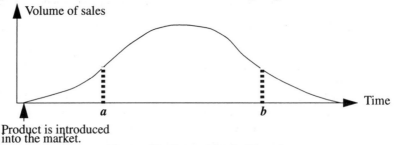

Figure 63 : Product family life cycle

If we enter the market at time *a*, there is a good chance that we will be able to get a fair return on our investments, for example in reusable software components. If, on the other hand, we enter the market at time *b*, developing reusable components will probably not be a wise decision, since the product family will be replaced by a new one in a relatively short time, perhaps rendering our reusable component of no further use.

4.4.4.2 Investment in reuse versus other investments

Before starting to develop reusable components, you should consider alternative ways to invest your resources, such as investing in your company's infrastructure.

Let the symbol LOC_0 stand for the expected total number of lines of code lines written from scratch during a planning period. If we let α be the reuse percentage and $f_i^{(j)}$ denote the COCOMO cost drivers for alternative j, the two cost estimates that we need to compare can be written as follows:

$$Cost_1 = a \bullet LOC_0 \bullet \prod_i f_i^{(1)}$$

$$Cost_2 = a \left((1 - \alpha) LOC_0 + \alpha LOC_0 \bullet AAF \right) \prod_i f_i^{(2)}$$

The first equation represents an alternative in which we invest in improved tools and methods plus education, and the second represents investment in reuse. Obviously it is better to invest in personnel, tools and methods if $Cost_1 < Cost_2$. By manipulating these equations, we get the following condition that expresses when it is *not* profitable to invest in reuse, compared to other improvements:

$$\alpha \le \frac{1 - \prod_i \left(\dfrac{f_i^{(1)}}{f_i^{(2)}} \right)}{1 - AAF}$$

4.4.4.3 Two examples of evaluating investment in reuse

Example 1: Deciding whether to make a subsystem reusable

Our first example is concerned with the decision of whether to make a new subsystem reusable or not. We assume the following situation:

Our current estimate for the component's size is 10 KLOC. It will contain about 100 subroutines. It is our company's policy to minimize the use of global variables, preferably to zero.

The subroutines are split into two groups as follows:

- Group 1: 70 subroutines with an average of three parameters and two failure conditions to be controlled

- Group 2: 30 subroutines with an average of four parameters and five failure conditions to be controlled.

The equivalent number of lines of code is thus given by $LOC_{equiv} = 13230$. The nominal cost of development is Cost = 3*13.23*1.81 = 72 person-months. Without the need for reusability, the cost will be 30 person-months. Since we assume that the same personnel will be used in both cases, personnel cost drivers can be kept out of the estimates.

Our market expectations tell us that we may reuse this subsystem in a new product every second year for the next eight years. The expected reuse cost is 2.5 person-months each time, giving a reusability of 0.97. Our company uses a 10% interest rate for all investment decisions.

The assumptions made above allow us to calculate the return on investment:

$$ROI = \frac{30}{72} \bullet 0.97 \bullet \left(\frac{1}{1.1^2} + \frac{1}{1.1^4} + \frac{1}{1.1^6} + \frac{1}{1.1^8} \right) = 1.02$$

We see that the investment will pay off, but only marginally. To try to increase the profitability of reuse, we can evaluate the effect of putting our best developers on the job of building the reusable subsystem. In this case, we do have to consider the difference in personnel. We have the following estimates:

Initial investment $I = 3*13.23*1.81*0.50 = 36$ person-months. The last term of 0.50 is the effect of using personnel with high capability in analysis and development. The return on investment can now be estimated to be:

$$ROI = \frac{30}{36} \bullet 0.97 \bullet \left(\frac{1}{1.1^2} + \frac{1}{1.1^4} + \frac{1}{1.1^6} + \frac{1}{1.1^8} \right) = 2.04$$

This is obviously a good return. This result is, however, only one of our decision inputs— it must be weighed against the possible extra costs incurred by taking our best personnel away from their current projects.

Example 2:

Our company is planning to move into the engineering software market. Previously, we have only produced small and simple data processing systems. An assessment of our personnel gives them low ratings for all personnel attributes in the COCOMO model.

We expect to produce 1000 KLOC during the next planning period. A brainstorming session with a consultant has convinced us that we—with the planned product line—can introduce reuse in which we will only have to rework 10% of the code and 20% of the integration. This gives an AAF of about 0.1. We also assume that we can obtain a reuse of 30 to 50%.

The alternative to developing for reuse is to send our developers on a series of courses where they will learn the latest methods in systems design and development, and the programming languages C and C++. They expect that the courses will bring the analyst and programmer capability up to "High" and the programming language capability up to "Nominal".

If we ignore the cost of the training courses, our investment decision can be based on the expression deduced in Section 4.4.4.2. We find that:

$$1 - \prod \frac{f_i^{(1)}}{f_i^{(2)}} = 0.5 \qquad 1 - AAF = 0.9$$

We find that the α-limit is 0.55. Since we assume that we can achieve 30 to 50% reuse, it seems that it will be more profitable to invest in personnel training than in reuse. The difference is marginal if the highest estimates turn out to be correct. We can improve on our decision by refining our average reuse percentage estimate.

These two investments can also be combined giving a synergy effect, i.e. both better standard performance and easier to make reusable components.

5 Introducing Reuse

5.1 Introduction

How could you determine and implement a reuse strategy to take advantage of the reuse opportunities in your company?

This chapter describes how to select and introduce appropriate reuse techniques into a company. It is intended to support the introduction of the techniques described in Chapters 1 to 4 (Organizing reuse) and Part B (Practising reuse) of this book.

There are several similar approaches to this problem on which we have drawn, in particular the *Reuse Adoption Guidebook* [RAG92] from the Software Productivity Consortium. Our approach is distinguished by its coupling of the introduction process to the reuse techniques described in Chapters 1 to 4 and Part B.

The aim of introducing reuse into a company is to improve the profitability of the company. It must always be kept in mind that all reuse investments must be at least as profitable as any other investments the company makes.

The chapter is organized as follows:

- Section 5.2 gives an overview of the activities, roles, models and documents involved in the introduction of reuse.

- Section 5.3 discusses in more detail how to determine a company's reuse opportunities, by examining its markets and production methods.

- Section 5.4 provides a method for assessing a company's reuse maturity, that is, the strengths and weaknesses of its reuse introduction and techniques.

- Section 5.5 gives an overview of the legal aspects of software concerned with reuse.

We use the word *company* to denote the organization that intends to introduce reuse, but it could equally be only a part of a company, such as a division or department. This is to avoid the word *organization* which is used elsewhere with other meanings.

5.2 The reuse introduction process

How do you define a process for planning and introducing reuse?

5.2.1 Introduction

This section gives an overview of the factors involved in introducing reuse into a company. In common with any other process, the introduction process consists of four basic elements, described in the following sections:

- Section 5.2.2 describes the activities involved in introducing reuse, with entry and exit criteria for each activity.

- Section 5.2.3 defines the roles involved in each activity, and what they have to do to achieve the goals of the activity.

- Section 5.2.4 describes the models used to analyze the opportunities and the problems of reuse introduction.

- Section 5.2.5 describes the documents where the intermediate and final results of the process are documented, used to communicate both within and without the implementation project.

5.2.2 The activities involved in introducing reuse

What will be the main activities in reuse introduction?

5.2.2.1 An overview of the reuse introduction process

Introducing reuse involves a defined set of activities, those of incorporating or improving the practices of software reuse as a permanent part of a company's culture and way of doing business—a process for institutionalizing reuse. It is a technology transfer process specialized for reuse technology, whose chief targets are software development companies.

As with all other technology transfer processes, it is important to build on, adapt and improve current reuse practices whenever possible. We think of the process as an *implementation* process, even if the company builds on and improves existing reuse practices.

The activities and roles of the process are illustrated below:

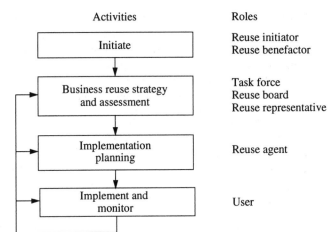

Figure 64 : The reuse adoption process and roles

The rest of this section describes the different activities in more detail. The roles are described in Section 5.2.3.

5.2.2.2 Initiate

The purpose of the *initiate* activity is to get the commitment and resources needed to start the reuse introduction process. We term the person responsible for providing these a *reuse benefactor*. The process starts when a *reuse initiator* identifies long-term reuse potential and the need to improve reuse practices to meet this potential. The reuse initiator can be anyone in the company who motivates the introduction of reuse. The main activity in this phase is to inform management about the potentials of reuse and make them aware of the investment and involvement needed to implement reuse practices. The following activities may form part of the *initiate* activity:

- Executive briefing on reuse, to inform management of the technical and organizational aspects of reuse.

- Identification of how reuse can help achieve the main objectives of the company.

- Preliminary assessment of reuse opportunities in the company. This includes involving middle management in reuse initiation by making them aware of the benefits.

- Collection of previous reuse experience in this or similar companies.

- Identification of other initiatives in the company which can be coupled to the reuse initiative. These can be product, market, process, quality, lead time or productivity improvement initiatives.

The *initiate* activity is completed when the following resources are in place:

- A task force (with money, time and personnel resources) to investigate and define reuse introduction, the next process in the sequence. This can be made up of internal staff or external consultants with reuse experience. The time and personnel outside the task force required to investigate reuse opportunities must also be estimated and allocated. This includes people from all areas of the company—marketing, development, line management, external and internal support, and so on.

- A *reuse board* to monitor the definition of the reuse introduction programme. This board should include those who have allocated resources to the investigation, as well as representatives of areas of the company that will be affected by the reuse initiative. The reuse board should have authority to ensure that the necessary resources from the company are provided to investigate reuse opportunities. The board should meet at least once every two weeks to monitor the reuse task force.

- Management commitment for the investigation. Management (the reuse benefactor) should monitor the investigation through regular progress reports. We also recommend that intermediate results are regularly made available to the entire company through presentations. Managers can show their commitment to reuse by introducing and attending such presentations.

The *initiate* activity could be completed with a "kick-off" meeting where the plan for and personnel working on the next phases are presented. It is important to involve as many as possible of the people who are going to fill reuse roles later on to help spread information about reuse.

5.2.2.3 Business reuse strategy and assessment

The purpose of this activity is to define the company's strategy for reuse, and assess the current state of reuse within the company. To define the best reuse strategy for the company we need to analyze the following:

- The *markets* of the company, to allow us to discover reuse opportunities, such as current or potential customers with similar needs, or customers needing evolving products. This analysis is based on input from a market strategy analysis, ensuring that the company has already identified its preferred markets. If a market analysis is not available, it should be done before the market is analyzed for reuse opportunities. This analysis typically involves the marketing department.

- The *products* of the company, to allow us to discover reuse opportunities within or between product families. This includes both the analysis of existing products for reusable components, as well as analyzing how to restructure the products to achieve more reuse. The structuring of products into subsystems, architectural issues and layering have to be analyzed to get a complete picture of reuse opportunities. The analysis of products includes analyzing the product expertise of the company. We must also take into account possibilities for technology changes that might affect our products. This analysis typically involves product line management.

- The *organization* of the company, to allow us to assess whether it is currently able to take advantage of actual or future reuse opportunities. To do this, it is necessary to look into the roles and interaction of all parts of the company to understand how they can contribute to a reuse strategy. This analysis is typically done in cooperation with the administrative line management.

- The *development processes* and *practices* used in the company, to allow us to understand how they can be adapted or enhanced to incorporate reuse practices. Mature and widespread reuse is greatly facilitated by uniform development processes that incorporate both development *for* and *with* reuse. This analysis is done in cooperation with the process owners and product managers. If the company has a process improvement programme run by a process support group, reuse should be incorporated into it.

We recommend that the analysis is carried out in the form of several 2–4 day workshops in which everyone involved participates. It is best to start with a general workshop where all aspects of reuse are brought up, in which people are allocated to different in-depth workshops. The results of the analysis should be presented to the reuse board regularly. Section 5.3 provides more information on how to analyze the market, product and company. Section 5.4 describes a model to analyze and improve current reuse practices.

The outcome of the analysis should be a reuse vision for the company, together with a set of reuse improvement suggestions coupled to each of the four areas above. These should be presented to the whole company, and personnel should be allowed time to comment before the implementation planning activity is started. The goal of the task force is to develop a set of reuse improvement suggestions—the company can then choose those they believe to be most appropriate. These improvement suggestions can be grouped into short-term and long-term ideas.

The assessment activity is completed when the company has chosen a strategy for the introduction of reuse.

5.2.2.4 Implementation planning

The objective of this activity is to plan the implementation of the chosen reuse strategy. This strategy might incorporate structural changes to the organization of the company, as well as setting up the infrastructure to support the desired reuse goals. Larger structural changes are not discussed here, but might be appropriate in some cases to take advantage of reuse opportunities; different reuse organizations were addressed in Section 1.4.4. The reuse infrastructure includes all five areas covered by Chapters 1 to 4 and Part B of this book, that is, organization, project management, repository management, metrics and development processes (Part B).

The main work in the implementation planning activity is to choose, adapt and plan how to implement the appropriate set of reuse techniques which can best support the chosen reuse strategy. These techniques can be selected from those presented in Chapters 1 to 4 and Part B of this book, as well as other reuse techniques.

This work should be done in close cooperation with those responsible for the areas which are to be adapted to reuse. In this activity the task force therefore changes its role, from analysing current practices and setting reuse goals, to supporting and adapting the practices to achieve the goals.

To facilitate the definition of a complete set of techniques and processes we have introduced a *reuse maturity model*. This defines key areas that should be in place to support reuse. The model can be used to support implementation planning, and to monitor the implementation.

We must also decide how we are going to implement our reuse techniques in the company. Some of the questions which need to be answered are:

- Will we start on a broad basis, or will we experiment with a pilot project?

- How much methodology work are we going to do before we try out reuse on pilot projects?

- How are we going to select, train and support staff for a pilot project?

In this phase it is important to involve people who want to try out the new techniques as reuse agents, and allow them to influence the approach followed.

5.2.2.5 Implement and monitor

Reuse is a broad and elusive goal. It is therefore important to make the goals for each activity, pilot project and reuse agent as concrete as possible. Even though we would ideally like everyone in the company to be involved in all aspects of reuse, it is better for each participant to have a limited focus.

For large companies we recommend that the implementation of reuse is organized around the topics of the chapters of this book:

- Organization

- Project management

- Repository management

- Metrics

- Development for and with reuse (Part B)

The selection of pilot projects to test out reuse techniques is crucial. Here are some guidelines on how to do this:

- Ensure the commitment to, and understanding of, reuse in the pilot project and its management.

- Provide extensive support from reuse agents and experts. This means that the supporters must contribute positively to the goals of the project, not only to reuse.

- Select pilot projects with clear reuse advantages. Analyze the opportunities and risks before committing to a project.

- Understand why the pilot project and their management want to be involved in reuse.

5.2.3 The roles involved in introducing reuse

What roles will be involved in the reuse introduction process?

What are the responsibilities of each role?

Implementing reuse in a company is a complex task, involving many people with different perspectives over a long period. It is therefore important to analyze the different roles in advance, and to motivate the people with their responsibilities in the introduction of reuse. This section discusses the roles listed in Figure 66. Note that transient roles when introducing or improving reuse in a company, for example in the reuse introduction process, are different from permanent roles in the reuse organization responsible for sustaining and supporting working reuse processes (as described in Sections 1.4.5 and 2.3).

Reuse initiator

The reuse initiator is responsible for initiating the introduction process for reuse by researching the reuse potential, and bringing it to the attention of a suitable reuse benefactor.

Reuse benefactor

Reuse benefactors are those who need to give their support to a reuse programme. This involves allocating appropriate resources and encouraging the effort. It is important that benefactors are aware of the complexity and time span of introducing reuse, and that they continuously follow up and reinforce their commitment.

Task force

The role of the task force is to lead the planning and implementation of reuse. The task force should incorporate people who have a thorough understanding of the reuse problem space and solution, and a good knowledge of the organization, processes and products. It can be an advantage to involve external reuse experts as well as internal staff. It is, however, of the utmost importance that internal participants in the task force have good knowledge of the company, and a fair knowledge of reuse.

The task force will change its role as reuse introduction proceeds from assessing the current status and investigating opportunities, via developing reuse improvement suggestions, to supporting the development and implementation of the reuse infrastructure.

This means that it will be in contact with many other parts of the company, and that the composition of the task force may need to change as the work proceeds.

Reuse board

The reuse board exists to supervise and direct the reuse implementation effort. The task force presents alternatives for decisions, gets plans approved, and reports progress to the board regularly. The board directs the implementation effort to keep it in line with the company's overall objectives. The board should consist of representatives from the following groups:

- Strategic product planning and market specialists who know what kind of products and markets will provide the company's business in the future.

- Project leaders who will later lead projects for development *for* and *with* reuse.

- Developers who will do the development *for* and *with* reuse.

- Those responsible for processes and tools that will need to be adapted and enhanced to support reuse.

The reuse board should consist of not more than 4–6 people, and it is important that these people have interest in and some knowledge about the reuse problem space.

Reuse representative

Reuse representatives represent those who are affected by the introduction of reuse, which in most cases will be the entire company. The most prominent groups should be represented in the reuse board, and those groups which are not represented should be identified. Whenever a decision is to be taken which will affect one or more groups these representatives should be consulted. Representatives from all groups should be present at presentations of plans and results.

Reuse agent

The reuse agent is responsible for promoting and improving reuse in his own group or project. Even if reuse is a distributed responsibility for every member of the company, it is important in the beginning to have someone in every group who is able to promote reuse, and can serve as a local reuse "guru". Such people may already exist as an application or component expert in some groups. It is important to have reuse competence represented in all possible groups, from process and tools through product development, test and quality assurance to marketing.

The members of the reuse board and reuse representatives are prime candidates as reuse agents in their own groups, but more agents should be recruited as the reuse implementation effort proceeds. It is also important to have a forum where agents can discuss their experiences and give feedback to the task force.

The reuse agents will have the following responsibilities:

- To apply the reuse processes and tools in their specific environment.

- To increase reuse awareness and build support throughout their group.

- To collect and consolidate data to monitor progress.

- To serve as a reuse expert for their groups.

All these points involve coordination with the task force, who support the reuse agents when necessary, but the aim is to transform the reuse introduction process from a management (provider, task force) to a user (consumer, agent, reuse practitioner) driven process.

The reuse agent is involved in the company's transition from no reuse to mature reuse. This role will be divided into the more permanent roles supporting reuse in the mature reuse organization. These roles are described in Sections 1.4.4, 2.3 and 3.5.

Reuse practitioner

Reuse practitioners are all those who will perform reuse, i.e. the users of the reuse processes. It is important to identify, inform and motivate them as early as possible. If they are involved in the definition of the reuse introduction plan, this will ensure their support in its enactment. All roles in the organization will be involved in reuse, and thus practitioners of the reuse processes. We recommend that you group users into line and product management, project management, repository managers and metrics users (for example quality assurance personnel) and developers to correspond with the topics of Chapters 1 to 4 and Part B of this book.

5.2.4 Reuse introduction models

What models could you use to analyze your company to determine your reuse opportunities?

This section describes models you can use to analyze the introduction of reuse in your company. Three types of models are used in performing reuse implementation process, as shown in Figure 65.

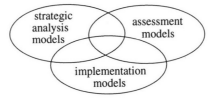

Figure 65 : Basic parts when performing improvement activities

- *Strategic analysis models* are used to analyze the products and markets of the company to find where the company can benefit from reuse. From such models we can derive a set of reuse objectives. These objectives must be in line with the company's overall business objectives. We suppose that the company already has a market strategy which we take as input to the reuse strategy analysis.

- *Assessment models* are used to assess the current reuse status of the company, to determine what must be changed to meet the reuse objectives defined in the reuse strategy. This can involve changes in organization, project management, development processes and product structure.

- *Implementation models* are used to help the company to implement a reuse infrastructure to support its reuse strategy. We use the same model for planning the implementation as for the assessment, the *reuse maturity model*.

The strategy models are discussed in more detail in Section 5.3. Assessment and implementation models are discussed in Section 5.4.

The connection between these models and the activities depicted in Figure 66 can be illustrated as follows:

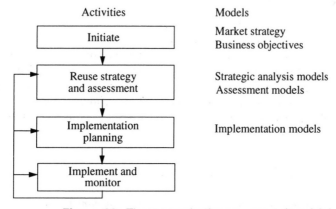

Figure 66 : The reuse adoption process and models

Figure 66 shows in which activity the different models are most heavily used. This does not preclude the models from being used in the other activities—in particular, the assessment model is used during implementation planning.

5.2.5 Documenting reuse introduction

Two kinds of documents are required when implementing a change in a company:

- Documents describing the change, in this case the plan and progress of the reuse implementation process. We call this the *reuse introduction plan*, and describe it in Appendix B. Note that we have chosen to call this document the reuse introduction plan, even if it is used to improve the reuse performance in companies already practising reuse.

- The necessary new and updated process documentation to cover reuse. This can be derived from the material in Chapters 1 to 4 and Part B, and adapted to the needs and existing documentation of your organization.

5.3 Forming a reuse strategy

5.3.1 Introduction

The aim of this section is to provide guidance on how to identify the reuse opportunities of your company, and how to develop a reuse strategy for the company. The main challenge is to identify the business areas and products where the company has the opportunity and motivation to meet its objectives by applying reuse technology. It involves a systematic analysis of reuse opportunities and associated risks involving the products and markets of the company. It is an extension of traditional market analysis, which aims to plan and execute the conception, pricing, promotion, and distribution of products or services. The identification of potential reuse opportunities is strongly correlated with the factors that characterize the company's production.

Before providing the basis for the analysis, we first clarify which objectives can be satisfied by the introduction of reuse. We then examine the different factors characterizing the company's products which must be used as a basis when identifying reuse opportunities and defining a reuse strategy programme. We propose a process for the analysis of the reuse opportunities based on two marketing models in common use, the Porter and General Electric models [Kotler88].

5.3.2 Identifying a company's objectives

Identification your company's objectives clarifies why it wants to introduce reuse. Reuse is not an objective *per se* [RAG92], but a means to achieve general corporate objectives. The reuse strategy must aim to meet these objectives.

Table 9 lists some objectives that can be achieved by reuse. These objectives do not necessarily deal directly with purely economic factors. Initial short-term investments are often more visible than long-term benefits. The more short-term motivations we can find, the better. The reuse implementation strategy at organizational or technical level is strongly dependent on these objectives.

Table 9 : Organizational objectives and possible reuse solutions

Objectives	Reuse contributions
Time to market	Introduction of reuse in customer pre-studies and marketing offers. Speeds up the response to calls for tenders.

Table 9 : Organizational objectives and possible reuse solutions

Objectives	Reuse contributions
More attractive product line	The company's competitiveness can be increased using reuse as an added value to make its product line more attractive to customers.
Quality improvement	A reusable software asset requires a given level of quality, relying on a set of criteria such as understandability, modularity, and so on. By producing and reusing reusable software, the quality of developments will be improved.
Productivity improvement	The company is able to decrease its development costs by reusing existing building blocks, and thus increase its productivity.
Standardization-interoperability	The production of reusable components contributes to the standardization process by becoming *de facto* standards through successive reuse.
Development of evolving products	The development of reusable blocks contributes to improvements in the evolution of the products. It has impact on both corrective maintenance and enhancement of the products.

5.3.3 Analyzing a company's production

A company's production is strongly impacted by the introduction of reuse, since production processes are modified, and the software products produced may have new characteristics. The reuse introduction strategy has to be based on an in-depth analysis of the products, to point out the most potentially successful reuse opportunities. These can then be used as a starting point. The following factors characterize a company's production:

- The type of software products developed by the company.

- The reuse scope available to the company.

- The product level; the level of service offered by the product.

- The product life cycle.

The type of software products

The software company can offer many different products: services, turnkey products, "off the shelf" software, embedded software and so on. The type of product produced or offered influences the type of reusable material available, and the choice of reuse techniques open to the company. In software development, reusable material is mainly software information from the development life cycle, such as specifications, design, code and so on. In activities such as consulting and training, reusable material may be slides, documentation, training courses and so on. The opportunity to capture and reuse procedures, techniques and frameworks should not be missed.

The reuse scope

This characterizes the scope of application domains in which the company is involved (see Figure 8 in Section 1.3.1). We identify three scopes:

- *General* reuse means domain-independent reuse.

- *Domain* reuse means reuse within a specific application domain.

- *Product-line* reuse means reuse within a specific application family.

These terms are defined in detail in Section 1.3. These production factors have to be taken into account in the identification of reuse opportunities, since they determine the target space of future reusers. For example, a general product can be interesting for reuse, in so far as it will serve a greater number of reusers than a domain or application-specific one. But the benefits associated with general components must be also considered together with the level of expertise needed to implement them, and the number that already exist.

The product level

This is the level of service offered by a company. It corresponds to the separation between the product and the user. We distinguish three levels:

- The core product
  The core product is the minimum necessary to answer a specific problem or need. It usually cannot be provided to the user as it stands, but needs higher level "packaging".

- The tangible product
  This corresponds to a layer above the core product. It allows the product to match the specific requirements for platform, user interface and so on.

- The augmented product
  Finally, the value of the product can be augmented by offering additional services such as *installation* and *after-sales services*.

Take the example of database products. The core includes all the software for managing objects. The tangible part includes the presentation layer, for example, such as a graphical user interface for accessing database services. This interface may be able to exist with different user interface standard, such as Motif or OpenLook. The augmented product includes, for example, a query generator tool, or function libraries to build applications on top of a database.

Different products with the same core, that is, answering the same basic need but having different added values, have to be considered together when deciding on a reuse strategy.

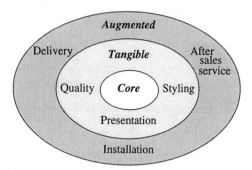

Figure 67 : The three product levels

In the figure, the nearer to the centre the product level, the more independent the product becomes of the customer's specific needs. By arranging its production in such a way, a company can increase its capability to reuse products between different customers.

The product life cycle

A product will at any stage be at some position in its life cycle. A product evolves through different versions, possibly even a complete redevelopment, and maintenance. The future evolution of a product, its frequency of change and so on, have to be taken into account when defining and applying a reuse strategy.

The product life cycle is influenced by factors such as customer demand and technological evolution. Classically, there are four stages in the life of a product: introduction, growth, maturity and decline [Kotler88]. They are shown in Figure 68.

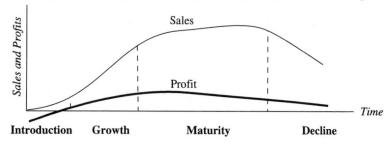

Figure 68 : The product stages

The *introduction* stage corresponds to the period where the product is first brought to the market. The *growth* stage corresponds to market acceptance and substantial profit improvement. The *maturity* stage corresponds to a slowdown in sales growth, because the product has achieved acceptance by most potential buyers. The *decline* stage is when sales show a strong downward trend—the product is obsolete compared with new entrants to the market.

These stages do not include the production phase itself, and concern only the product's life once it has been introduced to the market. When addressing reuse, it is easy to limit our view to the production life cycle of a product rather than its evolution once on the market. This is because we limit the scope of reuse technology to software production. We need instead to consider marketing aspects, by observing the product's behaviour once on the market.

Depending on the point the product has reached in its life cycle, the impact of reuse will be greater or lesser. It is clear that the earlier reuse is introduced in the life cycle, the more impact and return on investment it has.

The study of these production factors throughout the company enables us to differentiate the identified candidate products for pilot reuse applications, using the ratio *effort to be spent* divided by *life of the product*. This study should be coupled with a marketing one; this is described in the following section.

5.3.4 Analyzing a company's market

This section provides guidance on how to identify the best opportunities for a reuse strategy in a company. It does this by describing two market analysis models, the Porter and General Electric models, and showing how they can be applied to the identification of reuse opportunities. The main challenge is to contribute to the overall company's success in those areas where the company wants to lead.

5.3.4.1 Basic concepts

Before presenting the Porter and General Electric models, we need to define some of the basic marketing concepts we use. These definitions are mainly extracted from [Kotler88].

In economics vocabulary, a *market* consists of all the potential customers sharing a particular need, who might be willing and able to engage in exchanges to satisfy that need. The total market of a company usually includes various groupings of its customers. These groups of customers constituting the company's market are called *segments*.

The *market segmentation* is determined by observing variables such as the *consumer characteristics* and *consumer responses*. This market segmentation is important for the definition of the company's strategy, because it gives the company the opportunity to customize its product line for each market segment, and thus to be more competitive.

A *marketing strategy* defines the broad principles by which the company expects to achieve its marketing objectives.

5.3.4.2 The Porter model

Porter provides the following model for studying a company's market, or more especially the different segments of the market. Such a study allows us to identify which market segments are most promising, and thus better suited for investment in reuse. The model considers five elements: *customers, competitors, new entrants, suppliers,* and *substitutes.*

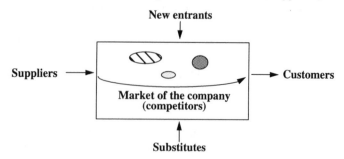

Figure 69 : The Porter diagram

Customers and reuse strategy

Existing customers must be taken into account when defining a company's reuse strategy. By customer, we mean anyone likely to use the products of the company. We can classify customers according to the criteria *origin, diversity* and *influence*:

- *Origin.* We distinguish between *internal* and *external* customers, as they make up two different markets.

  — *External* customers are customers from outside the company, and constitute a competitive market. In such a market, our reuse motivations differ from those for internal customers. It is clear that reuse is a way of gaining an advantage over one's competitors, increasing productivity and quality while decreasing production costs and time-to-market. Competitiveness may also be increased, as prices can often be lowered due to the savings from reuse.

  — *Internal* customers are customers within the company itself. The market is also competitive; the degree of competitiveness between units of the same company depends on managerial policies. Reuse can be a means to make products of better quality. It can also justify the existence of a department or group, when a company has the choice between making components or buying them.

- *Diversity.* The diversity of customers is an important criterion in the choice of a reuse strategy. Faced with a diversity of customers, one of the main problems to be solved when practising reuse concerns its legal aspects. Reuse enforces dependencies between software components and therefore raises potential liability problems between companies. Setting up reuse therefore requires a specific policy on rights and obligations between companies. Legal aspects become more complicated as the number and type of customers increases. Commercial agreements between a customer and the company have to be reviewed if the company wishes to reuse software from one client's application in another client's application. These legal and commercial aspects are considered in Section 5.5.

It is common for some companies to have only one big customer. This makes the related problems easier to tackle. This situation is often found in companies working in very specific domains (e.g. defence or telecommunications) or having clients that are public companies.

- *Influence.* Large customers have a lot of influence. They are able to force prices down, demand more quality or services and trade competitors off against each other. They are sometimes the ones to initiate reuse practice between their sub-contractors (for example the STARS programme from the US Department of Defense [STARS92a,b]).

Competitors and reuse strategy

A market segment is unattractive if it contains numerous, strong, or aggressive competitors. These conditions lead to frequent "price wars", advertising battles and new product introductions. Reuse is a key factor in such market segments, as it gives a company the flexibility to respond to a rapidly changing market.

Suppliers and reuse strategy

Suppliers are usually producers of dedicated packages that solve a specific problem, but need a tailored software layer to build products for end-users. If the distance between the supplier's product and the end-product is not too great, the introduction of reuse into the supplier's company can facilitate the generation of this upper layer, and thus directly affect the customer.

New entrants and reuse strategy

A segment is unattractive if it is likely to attract new competitors who will bring in new capacity and substantial resources, and thus reduce other companies' share of the market.

Substitutes and reuse strategy

A substitute is something that it is possible to sell instead of the product. A segment is unattractive if actual or potential substitutes for the products in the segment exist.

The Porter model allows you to determine the impact of reuse benefits with respect to the organizational objectives and market context of a company. It allows an evaluation of the risks associated with potential customers, and resulting from strategies adopted by competitors.

5.3.4.3 The General Electric model

The General Electric model focuses more specifically on the products of the company and its current position in the market. It uses a graphic template to support a market analysis. The evaluation of a company's production is based on two major dimensions: *market attractiveness* and *competitive position*. To measure these two dimensions, strategic planners need to identify the factors underlying each dimension, and determine how to measure and combine them. The two dimensions have to be customized for each company.

Market attractiveness depends on criteria such as the market's size, annual growth rate, historical profit margins and so on. The competitive position of the company is defined by the company's market share, share growth, product quality and so on. Figure 70 gives a list of possible factors that contribute to these two dimensions.

Market attractiveness	Competitive position
Overall market size Annual market growth rate Historical profit margin Competitive intensity Energy requirements Environmental impact	Market share Share growth Product quality Distribution network Brand reputation Productive capacity Productive efficiency

Figure 70 : Factors for measuring market attractiveness and competitive position

The GE approach consists of locating the different market segments corresponding to the production of the company inside a matrix, and inserting values for each dimension. The resulting matrix is divided into different cells, associated with categories.

Take the example of a software company that produces software engineering products. Each of its market segments is placed within a two-dimensional matrix, which allows us to do a two-way classification.

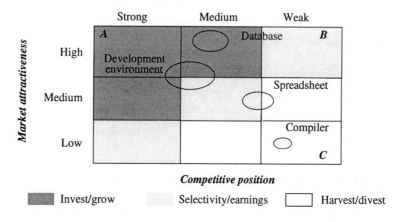

Figure 71 : The General Electric matrix

The resulting matrix is divided into nine cells, which are classified into three areas: A, B and C.

- *Area A.* The three cells at the upper left indicate strong segments, in which the company should invest and grow.

  This area contains markets whose attractiveness is high or medium, and in which the company has a good control of the overall market, or has at least a good competitive position. The company can build long-term strategies for those products in which reuse can be used to advantage. The necessary investment to introduce reuse can then be made with limited risk with respect to the expected lifetime of the product.

  Introducing reuse is a good way to make the company assess its leading position in this market. Reuse is in fact today a technology that begins to report success, in spite of the time needed for it to emerge. Many software product areas have matured and are candidates for benefit from reuse technology, and more and more companies initiate reuse programmes after successes reported by others. If the company wants to keep its leading position in such a market, it should investigate reuse, because its competitors will probably do so as well.

- *Area B.* The diagonal cells stretching from the lower left to the upper right indicate segments that are midway in overall attractiveness. Two types of market form this area:

  — A market that has much interest, but in which the competitive position of the company is not good. The introduction of reuse can be a means to bring the company into a more competitive position for those products whose markets are of interest. Major investments can then be justified (compared to products in area C). The company must first define the objectives it wants to achieve in order to be more competitive. These objectives may be any of those listed in Section 5.3.2. For example, the following all tend to increase a company's competitiveness: ability to respond more rapidly, produce products with better quality, increase production capacity, reduce production costs and thus lowering price.

  — A market that has less interest, but in which the company has good control. As the market is less attractive, the company's profits tend not to be optimized within it. Reuse provides a means for the company to keep its leading position. Reuse can also be used in an interesting way to take advantage of the company's position in this type of market. This consists of analyzing the product involved, finding out what makes the market position of the product strong, and reusing the core part of the product in another product targeted at a new more attractive market. Introducing reuse can therefore be a means to bring added value to new markets.

- *Area C.* The three cells at the lower right indicate segments that are low in overall attractiveness, where the competitive position of the company is not outstanding.

  The company should minimize its investment in these segments unless it decides to change its market segments. As the market is not promising, the introduction of reuse will bring little or no benefit. Reuse practice can be seen as a means to reduce the effort spent on those products that the company cannot delete, for example for contractual reasons. Reuse practice can be limited to the use of techniques or the choice of policies that do not need great effort, and that are efficient in relation to the limited reuse objectives of this case.

5.3.4.4 How to use the models

We suggest using the GE approach as a basis for examining the reuse potential of a company. The resulting matrix shows clearly the most interesting product lines for reuse investment, and for the achievement of the marketing objectives of the company. The results of analyzing the production criteria, and those from applying the Porter model, can then be used to define a reuse strategy for each product line.

5.4 Assessing reuse maturity

How could you determine how well your organization and processes are adapted to reuse?

5.4.1 Introduction

This section describes models you can use to assess the *reuse maturity* of your company in more detail. Reuse maturity is the extent to which a company's reuse practices are defined, managed, measured, controlled and generally effective.

In an organization where reuse is immature, any reuse that does exist is improvised and at a personal level. No processes, methods or tools for the formal support of reuse exist.

In a organization where reuse is mature, it forms an important part of the company's business. Reuse is practised company-wide and on many types of components. Cost-benefit analysis is performed before determining whether a component should be developed for reuse. Roles, processes, methods and tools that support fruitful reuse have been put into operation.

We provide two complementary models for assessing the maturity of reuse within a company:

- Section 5.4.2 describes a reuse maturity assessment model, structured according to Chapters 1 to 4 and Part B of this book, that looks at reuse aspects in detail.

- Section 5.4.3 presents an extension to the Capability Maturity Model (CMM) from the Software Engineering Institute to incorporate reuse practices in the key process areas.

We propose two models because we have found both to be useful. The first is specific for reuse, whereas the other one builds on a general process assessment model.

Several proposed reuse maturity models exist that are similar to our reuse maturity assessment. They all have an assessment of the current level of maturity in common, and provide suggestions for a stepwise improvement. Few of them provide techniques to fill the different levels, however. What distinguishes our approach is that emphasis is put on the stepwise introduction of new methodology and tools.

In addition, you can find some suggested questionnaires to assist you in assessing reuse maturity according to the model described in Section 5.4.2 in Appendix C.

5.4.2 The reuse maturity model

This section describes how the reuse maturity model is structured. The model consists of a set of key reuse areas that capture different aspects of the introduction and improvement of a company's reuse maturity. The key reuse areas correspond to the structure of this book:

- Organization

- Project management

- Repository management

- Metrics

- Development *for* and *with* reuse (Part B)

The key reuse areas are further refined into factors, called *key reuse factors* (KRFs). Each of these factors is modelled according to a maturity scale. This scale describes how a key reuse factor matures, that is, in what sequence the contents of the key reuse factors should ideally be implemented.

5.4.2.1 An overview of the key reuse factors

Table 10 shows the key reuse factors that belong to the different *key reuse areas*. The table contains five columns of KRFs, one for each key reuse area (counting *for* reuse and *with* reuse as one column). The *Reuse Adoption Guidebook* [RAG92] gave valuable input in defining the key reuse factors.

Table 10 : Key reuse factors by key reuse area

Organization	Project management	Repository management	Metrics	Development process	
				for **reuse**	*with* **reuse**
Reuse strategy	External coordination	Component information	Product metrics	Development process integration	
Reuse assessment	Project Planning	Component classification	Process metrics	Type of produced / reused information	
Legal issues	Project tracking	Change management		Analyze variability	Functionality evaluation
Cost and pricing	Staffing	Repository maintenance		Express generality	Reuse cost evaluation
Product line				Costs-benefit analysis	Adaptation/ integration

5.4.2.2 Reuse maturity levels

The *reuse maturity profile* provides a framework for evaluating the current practice of reuse in a company, and its potential. The potential for a company is evaluated for each factor according to a business and marketing study of the company. The way to proceed in analyzing the reuse maturity model is to take each factor in turn, and determine a strategy to reach the potential goal for each factor.

A simple characterization of the reuse factors building on the capability maturity model levels is:

- **Level 1** (chaotic). No planned reuse.

- **Level 2** (repeatable). Reuse is performed on a project-to-project basis, i.e. one project can produce a more general product which can later be reused by other projects, later generations or variants of the initial product. This activity is only performed on a limited project-by-project basis, and there is no overall reuse strategy in the company. Frameworks are a good example of a successful technique at this level.

- **Level 3** (defined). The company has a company-wide reuse strategy, and its processes incorporate reuse. It is possible to reuse components across the company, and the reuse potential of each project is evaluated with respect to the company's long-term reuse strategy. There is a company-wide repository for reusable components.

- **Level 4** (managed). The company's reuse processes and components are quantitatively understood and controlled using detailed measurements.

- **Level 5** (optimized). Continuous reuse improvements occur through quantitative feedback from reuse processes and products, and through testing innovative ideas and techniques.

In the following sections we describe the key reuse factors in each key reuse area, for each level of the maturity model. You should read this material in conjunction with the chapter of the book that describes the relevant topics.

5.4.2.3 Key reuse area 1: Organization

This key reuse area has two parts: the commitment of the company to reuse, and the integration of reuse into the product strategy of the company. The associated key reuse factors are:

- Reuse commitment
  - — Reuse strategy
  - — Reuse assessment
- Product strategy
  - — Legal issues

  — Cost and pricing
  — Product line

Key reuse factor: Reuse strategy

To successfully move a company towards achieving its targeted reuse opportunities, reuse planning is required throughout the company. The following lists the stage of maturity that corresponds to each level in the model:

- **Level 1**: No reuse strategy exists.

- **Level 2**: Reuse strategies are defined, budgeted and executed on a limited scale. Management understands the technical and organizational aspects of reuse.

- **Level 3**: Management develops and implements a long-term strategy for improving the organization's reuse capability, in line with the general improvement programme. The company has organizational structures to support reuse, and is organized to develop *for* and *with* reuse. Reuse is incorporated in standard communication and reporting at all levels. Long-term plans for funding reuse activities exist and are followed up quantitatively.

- **Level 4**: Product-line reuse strategies are developed to benefit from reuse across sets of related products. The reuse strategy is an explicit business and profit factor.

Key reuse factor: Reuse assessment

This key reuse factor defines the extent to which the organization continuously monitors its ability to achieve its reuse goals. The following lists the stage of maturity that corresponds to each level in the model:

- **Level 1**: No planned assessment, and only *ad hoc* firefighting when projects go wrong.

- **Level 2:** The reuse goals and resources of projects are approved by management, and the results are monitored.

- **Level 3**: The organization has a specific group dedicated to the assessment and improvement of the reuse capabilities of the organization.

- **Level 4**: The organization has reuse processes under quantitative control, and can assess any weaknesses in the processes.

- **Level 5:** The organization makes planned improvements of its reuse processes and its organizational structures continuously.

Key reuse factor: Legal issues

It is important for a company to be aware of any relevant legal and contractual constraints and to comply with them. The following lists the stage of maturity that corresponds to each level in the model:

- **Level 1:** There is no awareness of legal or contractual constraints regarding reuse.

- **Level 2:** Legal and contractual constraints on reuse are identified and enforced.

- **Level 3:** Legal and contractual constraints are reduced to increase the potential for reuse.

Key reuse factor: Cost and pricing

The organization must invest in reuse to increase its reuse capability. The investment should be based on a product pricing and funding strategy which supports the reuse strategy of the company. The following lists the stage of maturity that corresponds to each level in the model:

- **Level 1**: If reuse exists, it is not dealt with explicitly when pricing products.

- **Level 2**: Reuse cost-accounting procedures are determined for the development and use of reusable components, i.e. who pays for what and how much? Incentives are established to encourage development *for* and *with* reuse.

- **Level 3**: Product pricing and funding strategies take into account expected costs and anticipated benefits of reuse throughout the product or product line.

Key reuse factor: Product line

The way a company develops its product line has a strong impact on its ability to implement reuse within the product line. Consolidating the product line relies on two sub-factors: the ability of the company to manage its customers' requirements, and its commitment to develop a consistent and adequate product line in the long term. The following lists the stage of maturity that corresponds to each level in the model:

- **Level 1**: The product strategy of the company relies on the vision of individuals.

- **Level 2**: For each product line, all customer requirements are collected, to develop a short-term strategy for product evolution and for integration into the product line.

- **Level 3**: The requirements of customers for a specific product line are anticipated to develop a long-term strategy.

- **Level 4**: An expert (a person or unit) is in charge of the capitalization of the expertise for an application domain and is in charge of developing the product line either for major customers or for a specific marketing area.

5.4.2.4 Key reuse area 2: Project management

This key reuse area determines how well reuse activities are planned and managed at the project level. It also determines how well the organization is able to support the reuse activities of a project.

Key reuse factor: External coordination

Reuse greatly increases dependencies between different projects in the company. The work of the project manager in managing interfaces outside the project becomes a strategic issue. Here are the extra interfaces to be taken into account:

— management of the requirements for the project: liaison is needed not only with the customer, but also with those in charge of defining the product line involved

— coordination with other projects that produce reusable components to be used in this project

— coordination with people that have developed reusable components

— coordination with the repository manager for the acceptance of reusable components developed by the project.

The following lists the stage of maturity that corresponds to each level in the model:

• **Level 1**: No specific interface rules or explicit roles have been defined. The project manager has to handle the work by himself.

• **Level 2:** A member of staff has been appointed to manage software requirements for a specific product line. Management of software requirements for component development is a coordinated activity meeting multiple needs. Project managers negotiate with this member of staff over the requirements.

• **Level 3**: The project manager has specific technical and methodological support from a reuse expert to help cope with reuse aspects. Procedures are set up to allow the project manager to ask for the collaboration of an expert, or with the people that developed the reusable components, to facilitate their reuse.

• **Level 4**: The coordination of all projects working on the same product line is the responsibility of one person, who is in charge of coordinating the projects and managing any potential deadlock between them caused by mutual exchange of components. The project manager therefore has someone to report to, and to complain to if necessary.

Key reuse factor: Project planning

Software project management involves project planning of time, costs and resource estimates, to enable the project to be steered successfully.

Project planning is necessary to manage project's commitments to the customer in terms of resources, constraints and the capabilities of the project. Project planning provides the basis for controlling the software effort and managing the progress of work. The following lists the stage of maturity that corresponds to each level in the model:

• **Level 1**: Project planning does not explicitly take reuse into account.

• **Level 2**: A project management model has been developed to incorporate reuse-specific activities, resources and documentation. The impact of reuse on projects is based on subjective judgement.

- **Level 3**: The project management model is adapted to incorporate reuse activities, resources and documentation. Cost models are developed for reuse-based development.

- **Level 4**: Software project management is a coordinated activity—many projects are coordinated to benefit from the development of reusable components. Cost models are developed to optimize costs between projects.

- **Level 5**: The reuse aspects of the project planning models are continuously improved.

Key reuse factor: Project tracking

This key reuse factor defines to what extent a company has identified reuse activities in its tracking and accounting procedures. Project tracking involves tracking and reviewing project achievements and results against documented estimates, commitments and plans, and adjusting these accordingly. The following lists the stage of maturity that corresponds to each level in the model:

- **Level 1**: No measurement is performed to evaluate reuse-specific activities.

- **Level 2**: *For* and *with* reuse activities are well differentiated from classical development activities. Effort and timing data are collected for further analysis.

- **Level 3**: Procedures for analyzing reuse-specific data collected by project accounting are analyzed on a company-wide basis. The effort of managing and maintaining the repository of reusable components is evaluated and distributed to client projects. Communication overheads due to external coordination between projects are measured. A complete view of the impact of reuse in terms of effort and delays is then possible, allowing reuse processes at the project level to be analyzed and enhanced.

Key reuse factor: Staffing

This key reuse factor deals with the maturity of a company regarding staffing of projects *for* and *with* reuse. Aspects are the reuse roles a project is able to accommodate, and the degree to which the project manager is able to obtain the required competence for the project. For example, 20% of effort should be from people fully capable of developing components for reuse. The following lists the stage of maturity that corresponds to each level in the model:

- **Level 1**: No specific actions are taken to staff the project with reuse competence.

- **Level 2**: The project manager can get people with the required reuse competence for his project.

- **Level 3**: The company allocates people with the required reuse competence to projects based on the available resources and needs of the project.

- **Level 4**: The company allocates people with the required reuse competence to the project taking the long-term development of competence and the product strategy into account.

5.4.2.5 Key reuse area 3: Component classification and the repository

This key reuse area determines how well the company is able to manage the components it produces.

Key reuse factor: Component information

Information stored and extended with the component facilitates its reuse. The following lists the stage of maturity that corresponds to each level in the model:

- **Level 1**: No systematic information exists.

- **Level 2**: Support information exists, such as documentation, component information, administrative information and other related documentation.

- **Level 3**: Reuser experience is included, including who reused it, why, how, and what modifications were required.

- **Level 4:** Process feedback is available because the information saved with reusable components is integrated into the company's organization, process and development methods.

Key reuse factor: Component classification

A classification scheme is necessary to enable effective storage and retrieval of reusable components. The following lists the stage of maturity that corresponds to each level in the model:

- **Level 1**: No support for classification or retrieval is available; storing is not systematic.

- **Level 2**: Storage of components is systematic, but no support for classification and retrieval is provided.

- **Level 3**: Storage of components is systematic, and classification and retrieval are based upon keyword descriptions.

- **Level 4**: Storage of components is systematic, and classification and retrieval are based on a restricted vocabulary with semantic information such as term weights.

- **Level 5**: Feedback from usage of the components is collected and used to refine their classification.

Key reuse factor: Change management

Change management includes the activities performed when components in the repository are updated due to enhancements or bug fixes. The following lists the stage of maturity that corresponds to each level in the model:

- **Level 1**: No specific change management is applied to the components in the repository. Components are copied, adapted and integrated under the control of the project's own configuration management system.

- **Level 2**: The project informs the repository about any adaptations or changes made to reused components.

- **Level 3**: When considered itself reusable, an adapted component is stored and registered as a new version of the component in the repository.

- **Level 4**: The reuse of components is registered, and reusers can elect to be informed about enhancements and changes to the components they have reused.

- **Level 5**: The frequency of change to components is used as an input to repository and component management.

Key reuse factor: Repository maintenance

Repository maintenance is the continuous management of components to ensure that they satisfy the current needs of the company in a cost-effective fashion, and that they are actively used to meet the business objectives of the company. The following lists the stage of maturity that corresponds to each level in the model:

- **Level 1**: No, or *ad hoc* repository management.

- **Level 2**: The repository is continuously maintained, and new components are approved by the repository manager.

- **Level 3**: The repository is regularly inspected to identify obsolete and duplicate components for removal or archiving.

- **Level 4**: Quantitative feedback from the search and reuse of components is actively used to maintain the repository and component classification information.

5.4.2.6 Key reuse area 4: Metrics

This key reuse area quantifies how well the company is able to measure their reuse processes and components. An effective measurement programme is essential to be able to quantify the gains of any new process. This is especially true of reuse, as the merits of development *for* and *with* reuse are very much a cost-benefit question, and without good quantitative data it is difficult to make objective decisions.

Key reuse factor: Product metrics

This key reuse factor defines to what extent a company has applied metrics to evaluate reusable components for quality and reusability. The model refers to the Factor-Criteria-Metrics model described in Chapter 4. This is useful, but it is not essential to use the FCM model if other methods of decomposition exist. The following lists the stage of maturity that corresponds to each level in the model:

- **Level 1:** No measurements are performed to evaluate reusable components. If measurements are performed they are *ad hoc* without clear objectives.

- **Level 2**: Simple subjective judgements are used to rank reusability and quality.

- **Level 3**: A definition of faults exists in the company, and measurements of the number of faults found during acceptance and integration testing are performed based on that definition. The number of faults is used to measure the product's or component's maturity.

- **Level 4**: Consensus about the most relevant criteria regarding quality and reusability exists in the company. Metrics that capture the company's model of the criteria are defined. *A posteriori* factors are defined and measurements are performed according to those definitions.

- **Level 5**: Consensus of the company's model of reusability and quality exists, i.e. the company has decided what factors and criteria they consider important, and the quality and reliability model is defined. Metrics that capture the company's model of factors and criteria for quality and reusability are defined. *A posteriori* factors are defined, and measurements are performed according to those definitions.

- **Level 6**: The company's Factor-Criteria-Metrics model for quality and reusability is continuously improved by calibration procedures.

Key reuse factor: Process metrics

This key reuse factor defines to what extent a company has applied measurements to evaluate their reuse processes. The following lists the stage of maturity that corresponds to each level in the model:

- **Level 1**: No measurements to evaluate and improve the reuse processes are defined. If measurements are performed, they are *ad hoc* without clear objectives.

- **Level 2**: Definitions of lead time and effort for the reuse processes exist and measurements are performed based on these definitions. Bottlenecks are identified, and improvement activities result.

- **Level 3**: A clear definition of faults exists in the company, and measurements of the number of faults found during integration testing, acceptance testing and operation are made. Clear definitions for the types of review remarks are used. Measurements are performed according to these definitions. Error-prone types of reusable components and error-prone reuse activities are identified and improved.

- **Level 4**: The company is able to set up improvement goals and define process measurements that capture the explicit problem areas that are being addressed in the reuse processes.

5.4.2.7 Key reuse area 5: Development process

Key reuse factors for the development process are divided into four different groups:

- **Group 1**: *Development process integration* indicates the integration level of *for* and *with* reuse activities in the development process of the company.

- **Group 2**: *Type of produced and reused information* covers the type of reusable information the company is able to handle in an organized way.

- **Group 3**: *Development for reuse* covers activities specific to development *for* reuse, independent of type of information reused:
  — Analyzing variability
  — Expressing generality
  — Cost-benefit analysis

- **Group 4**: *Development with reuse* covers activities specific to development *with* reuse, independent of type of information reused:
  — Functionality evaluation
  — Reuse cost evaluation
  — Adaptation/Integration

To get a complete picture of a company's reuse maturity for the development process, we must assess maturity of development *for* and *with* reuse for each type of reusable information or component the company wants to handle. Maturity in handling code components can be quite different from that for handling analysis information.

Key reuse factor: Development process integration

This key reuse factor is intended to measure the integration level of the development process *for* and *with* reuse into the development life cycle used by the company. The following lists the stage of maturity that corresponds to each level in the model:

- **Level 1**: Informal reuse.

- **Level 2**: Differentiation of the *for* and *with* reuse activities.

- **Level 3**: Integration of part of the *for* or *with* reuse processes into the development life cycle.

- **Level 4**: Full integration of the *for* and *with* reuse processes into the development life cycle, with explicit links defined between the different *for* and *with* reuse activities.

This factor can be seen as a synthesis of the other factors for development. It can be difficult to give a positive assessment for any of these levels. For example, a company might be on level 4 for code, but on level 1 for requirements, whereas a market analysis might show that it would have been profitable to be the other way around. If this is the case, a more thorough analysis of each phase in the development process is probably needed.

Key reuse factor: Type of produced and reused information

This key reuse factor is common for development *for* and *with* reuse, and concerns the point in the development life cycle at which the company is able to handle reusable components.

The following scale is based on the assumption that the earlier components can be reused in the life cycle, the greater the potential benefits (see Chapter 10). This assumption is based on two facts:

- earlier reuse gives opportunities to reuse larger components, as they can be taken into account in the product design;

- when we reuse a component early, we can reuse documentation produced in later stages of the life cycle as well.

The following lists the stage of maturity that corresponds to each level in the model:

- **Level 1**: Detailed design information including source code with corresponding unit test information is reused. These components can be:
  - components libraries such as libraries of functions associated with a language
  - basic application-domain components

- **Level 2**: Architectural design information is reused. Reusing components in this phase also makes it possible to reuse associated detailed design, implementation, unit and integration tests. These components can be:
  - general components such as user interface subsystems or databases
  - frameworks (application family generic architectures)
  - application domain subsystems

- **Level 3**: Specifications and requirements are reused. Reusing components from this early phase makes it possible to reuse all the later information, and also to negotiate the requirements with the customer.

There is an ambiguity inherent in this key reuse factor, as the scale to evaluate it does not correspond directly to the way we recommend that it is implemented. The first stage is to establish implementation guidelines, because they are the most concrete and the easiest to define. We also recommend, however, that reuse is introduced in earlier phases of the development process like design or analysis, as the pay-off is greater. The important point with this key reuse factor is that reuse capability in later phases must match those in earlier phases, just as an architect must not design a house a builder cannot construct.

We have chosen to divide the type of reusable information by life cycle phases. Some companies might also need to do an analysis by system structure, i.e. system, subsystem, module and class, as they will have different reuse goals and strategies for these different kinds of components. The development of each type of component will affect a different part of the development life cycle, so separate assessments for design of systems, subsystems and classes may be needed, if those are the types of component that concern the company.

In order to get a complete view of the ability of the company to handle the production of reusable components, the following key reuse factors covering development *for* and *with* reuse should be evaluated for each of the development phases of analysis, design, coding and testing:

- Analyzing variability

- Expressing generality

- Cost-benefit analysis

- Functionality evaluation

- Reuse cost evaluation

- Adaptation/Integration

Key reuse factor *for* reuse: Analyze variability

This key reuse factor quantifies the ability of developers to analyze and represent variability in the models used for a development activity. As with the other key factors for development *for* and *with* reuse, these models can be any kind of model used during the development process, i.e. from requirements for the complete system to specifications for a single class. The following lists the stage of maturity that corresponds to each level in the model:

- **Level 1**: No responsibility for variability analysis has been allocated.

- **Level 2**: Projects have allocated responsibility for analyzing and documenting variability, the models are adapted to represent variability, and the goals and effort for the activity are defined and followed up at the project level.

- **Level 3**: The organization has specific support roles for variability analysis, and the goals, efforts and results of variability analysis are monitored at a company level (i.e. on a product strategy basis).

- **Level 4**: The activities and results of variability analysis are measured, and the results are used to estimate future resource requirements.

- **Level 5**: The process and models for variability analysis are continuously improved based on feedback from development projects, and new techniques are systematically tried out and evaluated.

Key reuse factor *for* reuse: Express generality

This key reuse factor quantifies the ability of developers to express generality in the output models for a development activity. As with the other key factors for development *for* and *with* reuse, the output models can be any kind of model used during the development process, i.e. from architectural design for the complete system to implementation of a single class. The following lists the stage of maturity that corresponds to each level in the model:

- **Level 1**: No responsibility for expressing generality has been allocated.

- **Level 2**: Projects have allocated responsibility for expressing and documenting generality, the models are adapted to express generality, and the goals and effort for the activity are defined and monitored at the project level.

- **Level 3**: The organization has specific support roles responsible for expressing generality, and the goals, efforts and results of expressing generality are monitored at a company level (i.e. on a product strategy basis).

- **Level 4**: The activities and results of expressing generality are measured, and the results are used to estimate future resource requirements.

- **Level 5**: The process and models for expressing generality are continuously improved based on feedback from development projects, and new techniques are systematically tried out and evaluated.

Key reuse factor *for* reuse: Cost-benefit analysis

This key reuse factor quantifies the ability of developers to perform a cost-benefit analysis of the alternatives open in development *for* reuse within a development activity. As with the other key factors for development *for* and *with* reuse, the activity could be anything involved in the development process, from architectural design of the complete system to implementation of a single class. The following lists the stage of maturity that corresponds to each level in the model:

- **Level 1**: No responsibility for cost-benefit analysis has been allocated.

- **Level 2:** Projects have allocated responsibility for doing cost-benefit analysis, and the goals and effort of the activity are defined and followed up at the project level.

- **Level 3**: The organization has specific support roles responsible for cost-benefit analysis, the results of which are recorded and used in future analyses, and the goals, efforts and results of expressing generality are followed up at a company level (i.e. on a product strategy basis).

- **Level 4**: The activities and results of cost-benefit analysis are measured, and the results are used to estimate future resources requirements.

- **Level 5**: The processes and models for cost-benefit analysis are continuously improved based on feedback from development projects, and new techniques are systematically tried out and evaluated.

Key reuse factor *with* reuse: Functionality evaluation

This factor measures the capacity of a company to support the understanding and evaluation of the functionality of reusable components. The following lists the stage of maturity that corresponds to each level in the model:

- **Level 1**: No support is given to the user when understanding a component.

- **Level 2:** A set of general guidelines and rules are defined to guide the user in understanding the component.

- **Level 3**: A dedicated organizational structure is defined to support the user in understanding a component. It is possible to access experts in the domain, or to get information from the component builder. Information corresponding to previous reuses has been attached to each component, to enable a reuser to understand the scope of the component.

Key reuse factor *with* reuse: Reuse cost evaluation

This factor measures the ability of a company to estimate the costs necessary to adapt a component. The following lists the stage of maturity that corresponds to each level in the model:

- **Level 1**: No formal support is provided to the developer for estimating the cost of adapting a component.

- **Level 2**: Reusable components are associated with specific information about preliminary experiences of the costs of reusing the component.

- **Level 3**: A collection of previous experiences has been set up, to which the developer can refer to base their estimation. A catalogue of possible adaptations has been defined, with a risk factor associated with each.

- **Level 4**: A generic cost estimation model has been defined to estimate adaptation costs, and validated through preliminary experiences.

Key reuse factor *with* reuse: Adaptation/Integration

This factor measures the experience and ability of a company in adapting and integrating reusable components when developing applications. The following lists the stage of maturity that corresponds to each level in the model:

- **Level 1**: The adaptation and integration activity is done in an informal way.

- **Level 2**: Specific techniques and guidelines are used for adapting and integrating components. Traceability facilities are available to help the user to propagate adaptations from the high-level phases to the code and test activities associated with the component.

- **Level 3**: The development environment integrates automatic generation tools that are able to support adaptation.

5.4.2.8 Other reuse factors ("non-key")

The identification of a set of key reuse factors has been the subject of a lot of discussion within the REBOOT project. We have attempted to choose a set of orthogonal factors which completely measure the reuse maturity of a company. The following is a list of candidate factors which we decided not to include, but that might be useful for some companies. The list includes the reasons we used for not identifying each factor as key.

- Training. This is implicit in all key reuse factors.

- Subcontract management. This has little explicit influence on reuse, and is partly incorporated in legal and contractual issues. However, as it is a key process area it is also incorporated in the reuse extension of the Capability Maturity Model described in Section 5.4.3.

- Software quality assurance. This has little explicit influence on reuse. However, as it is a key process area it is also incorporated in the reuse extension of the Capability Maturity Model.

- Tool support. This is implicit in all key reuse factors.

- Component quality. This is covered by *development for reuse* and *metrics*.

- Component integrability. This is covered by *development for reuse* and *metrics*.

- Component awareness and accessibility. This is covered by *component classification*.

- Component reusability. This is covered by *development for reuse* and *metrics*.

- Component value determination. This is covered by *cost-benefit analysis* in development *for* and *with* reuse.

- Component evaluation/verification. This is covered by *development for and with reuse*.

- Needs identification. This is included in *analyze variability* in development *for* reuse.

- Continuous process improvement. This is covered by *process assessment*.

- Product standardization. This is covered by *development for reuse* and *product line*.

5.4.3 Reuse extensions to the Capability Maturity Model

How could you integrate reuse with a capability maturity model?

This section provides a reuse extension to the Capability Maturity Model (CMM) developed by the Software Engineering Institute [Paulk91]. The arguments for making a reuse extension to the CMM are:

- Planned reuse is very dependent on process maturity.

- The CMM provides a well understood, comprehensive and accepted framework which is easy to extend.

The rest of this section is structured as follows.

- Section 5.4.3.1 to Section 5.4.3.3 give a short overview of the CMM.

- Section 5.4.3.4 provides an overview of the additions we made to incorporate reuse into the model.

- Section 5.4.3.5 to Section 5.4.3.8 detail the additions for each maturity level of the CMM.

Section 5.4.3.1 to Section 5.4.3.4 can help you decide whether you should base your reuse introduction on the CMM. Section 5.4.3.5 to Section 5.4.3.8 are intended to be read together with the original CMM model.

5.4.3.1 An overview of the Capability Maturity Model

A five-level maturity model

The CMM is a framework characterizing the elements of an effective software development process. The CMM describes an evolutionary improvement path from an *ad hoc*, chaotic process to a mature, disciplined process.

In an immature organization, software processes are generally improvised by practitioners and their management during the course of a project. Even when a software process has been specified, it may not be rigorously followed or enforced. The immature organization is reactionary and managers are usually focused on solving immediate crises. Schedules and budgets are routinely exceeded because they are not based on realistic estimates.

A mature software organization possesses a company-wide ability for managing software development and maintenance processes. The processes mandated are consistent with the way the work actually gets done. These defined processes are updated when necessary, and improvements are developed through controlled pilot tests and/or cost-benefit analyses. Roles and responsibilities within the defined process are clear throughout the project and across the organization.

The amount of planned reuse that can be achieved increases with the maturity level, because the company is better able to institutionalize reuse practices.

The structure of the Capability Maturity Model

The CMM defines five maturity levels, as shown in Figure 72. Each maturity level is a well-defined plateau on the path towards becoming a mature software organization. Together they define an ordinal scale for measuring the maturity of a company's software process and for evaluating its software capability.

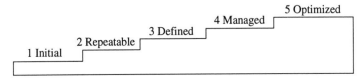

Figure 72 : The five levels of the Capability Maturity Model

Each maturity level is characterized by a set of *key process areas*. Each key process area is described by goals and five common features. These are:

- *Commitment to perform*. This describes the actions the organization must take to ensure that the process is established and will endure.

- *Ability to perform*. This describes the preconditions that must exist in the project or organization to implement the software process competently.

- *Activities performed*. This describes the roles and procedures necessary to implement a key process area.

- *Measurements and analysis*. This describes the need to measure the process and analyze the measurements.

- *Verifying implementation*. This describes the steps needed to ensure that the activities are performed in compliance with the process that has been established.

Each common feature consists of several key practices. To attain the goals of a key process area the key practices of all common features must be present.

The key practices also tell you what to focus on when trying to make your organization more mature. If the organization is immature (at Level 1) the improvement activities should be focused on fulfilling the key process areas at Level 2 before focusing on the key process areas at Level 3, and so on.

5.4.3.2 The key process areas

This section briefly describes the five levels of the Capability Maturity Model and the corresponding key process areas on each level.

Level 1: Initial

The software process is *ad hoc* (and occasionally even chaotic). Few processes are defined, and success depends on individual effort.

Level 2: Repeatable

The process capability of companies at this level can be summarized as *stable* for planning and tracking the software project, because a disciplined management process provides a project environment for repeating earlier successes.

The key process areas are:

- *Requirements management.* Both technical and non-technical customer requirements must be established and maintained. Changes to requirements must be dealt with.

- *Software project planning.* A plan that describes the estimates and the commitments for the work to be done is defined and issued, making it possible to manage the progress of the work.

- *Software project tracking and oversight.* Software accomplishments and results must be tracked and reviewed against commitments, estimates and plans, and must be adjusted according to the actual values. (Note that 'oversight' in the CMM model refers to supervision.)

- *Software subcontract management.* Subcontractors must be selected, commitments must be established, work must be established and the subcontractor's performance and results must be tracked and reviewed.

- *Software quality control.* Software products and activities are reviewed and audited to ensure their compliance with applicable processes, standards and procedures.

- *Software configuration management.* Baseline items are selected and monitored within projects. Changes to them are controlled.

Level 3: Defined

The software process for both management and engineering activities is documented, standardized, and integrated into a company-wide software process. All projects use a documented and approved version of the company's process for developing and maintaining software.

The key process areas are:

- *Organizational process focus.* The company must develop and maintain its standard software processes.

- *Organization process definition.* A project must define the processes it intends to employ and the measurements that will be performed.

- *Training programme.* The staff (including managerial staff) must be trained in a way that ensures their ability to perform their work appropriately.

- *Integrated software management.* Project activities are managed according to a defined procedure, and with the help of historical data.

- *Software product engineering.* Software product engineering involves building and maintain the software system using appropriate state-of-the-art tools and methods.

- *Intergroup coordination.* A disciplined interaction and coordination of project groups is performed to address system-level issues and activities.

- *Peer reviews.* A methodical examination of all work is performed following defined procedures.

Level 4: Managed

Both the software process and products are quantitatively understood and controlled using detailed measurements. The key process areas are:

- *Quality assurance.* Measurable goals for product quality and process quality are established, and corrective actions are taken during the projects to ensure customer satisfaction.

- *Process measurement and analysis.* Measurements are carried out on the company's processes. The measurements are analyzed and adjustments are made to the processes to stabilize their performance.

Level 5: Optimizing

Continuous process improvement is enabled by quantitative feedback from the process and through testing innovative ideas and technologies. The key process areas are:

- *Process change management.* Process improvement goals are defined and improvements are systematically identified, evaluated and implemented.

- *Technological innovation.* New technologies are identified, selected and evaluated, and appropriate technologies are incorporated in the company.

- *Defect prevention.* The introduction of types of defects that have appeared in earlier systems is prevented in future projects.

Note that a company should focus on management processes before focusing upon engineering processes—Level 2 focus upon the management process and Level 3 on both management and engineering processes. It may seem easier to define and implement an engineering process than a management process, but without management discipline, the engineering process is in danger of being sacrificed to scheduling and cost pressures.

5.4.3.3 Management understanding and commitment

Achieving a higher level of process maturity in a company is incremental and requires a long-term commitment to continuous process improvement. It is necessary to define an evolutionary path that increases the company's software process maturity in a stepwise manner.

Continuous process improvement is based on many small evolutionary steps rather than revolutionary innovations. The Capability Maturity Model provides a framework for organizing these evolutionary steps into the five maturity levels that lay successive foundations for continuous process improvement. Senior management is often impatient for results, and occasionally attempts to reach Level 5 without progressing through Levels 2, 3 and 4. This is counter-productive, as each level forms a necessary foundation from which to construct the next.

5.4.3.4 The reuse Capability Maturity Model

The reuse extensions to the Capability Maturity Model are structured as additions to the key process areas of the CMM for each level. The specific additions to each key process area are as described in Section 5.4.3.1:

- Goals

- Commitment to perform

- Ability to perform

- Activities performed

- Measurement and analysis

- Verifying implementation

Since this section is intended to be read in connection with the original CMM model [Paulk91], we have sometimes simplified the key practices, for example by dropping phrases like "according to a documented procedure". This should be implicit. The numbers in parentheses refer to the relevant areas of the original CMM model.

5.4.3.5 Capability Maturity Model level 2: Repeatable

At Level 2 the company is performing reuse on a project by project basis. Reuse goals are incorporated into the goals of the project, approved by management, and followed up by the project manager.

There is no formal coordination between projects, and the company has not (yet) institutionalized a complete reuse programme.

Most companies entering a reuse programme will be on Level 2 as they try out pilot reuse projects. The key reuse process areas at this level are:

- Requirements management

- Project planning

- Project tracking and oversight

- Subcontract management

- Software quality control

- Software configuration management

There are no additional reuse-specific key process areas at this level.

Requirements management

The purpose of reuse requirements management is to provide mechanisms to record and handle requirements from different current and future customers (development *for* reuse), and negotiate current requirements with customers based on the possibility of reusing components (development *with* reuse).

- Goals

  — Requirements are classified according to customers, and a cost-benefit analysis for each customer and requirement is performed to determine which requirements to incorporate (new).

- Commitment to perform

  — A written company policy for managing requirements includes specification on how to manage requirements from several current and future customers, and to negotiate requirements with customers based on the possibility of reusing components (1).

- Ability to perform

  — The responsibility for analyzing requirements of current and future customers is established (1).

  — The allocated requirements include reuse requirements (2, 3 and 4).

- Activities performed

  — The market potential (probability and profit) of each current and future customer is evaluated (new).

  — Reuse requirements are classified and reviewed for singularities, conflicts and benefits (1).

- Measurement and analysis

  — Measurements of the status of requirements are kept per customer (development *for* reuse) or per reused component (development *with* reuse).

- Verifying implementation

  — The activities for managing the reuse requirements, i.e. different customers and potential reusable components, are reviewed with the project manager (2).

Project planning

The purpose of reuse project planning is to determine the reuse goals of the project and to incorporate reuse activities into the project plan. This includes activities to develop both *for* and *with* reuse.

- Goals

  — Reuse is taken into account when estimating and planning the project (1-3).

- Commitment to perform

  — A written company policy for planning a software project specifies that the reuse goals of the project are included in the project plan, and reviewed and approved by affected groups and senior management (2).

- Ability to perform

  — The statement of work for the project includes reuse goals (1).

- Activities performed

  — The selected software life cycle incorporates reuse activities (5).

  — Reuse goals are incorporated into the project's software development plan according to a documented procedure (6).

  — Reuse goals are documented in the project plan (7).

  — Estimates for software size, cost and effort, critical computer resources and schedules take reuse into account, according to a documented procedure (9-12).

  — The risks associated with reuse are identified, assessed and documented (13).

  — Plans for the project's reuse support are prepared (14).

- Measurement and analysis, Verifying implementation

  — No additions.

Project tracking and oversight

The purpose of reuse project tracking and oversight is to provide adequate visibility into the reuse activities and their results, so that management can take effective action when reuse performance deviates from the reuse goals.

- Goals

  — Actual reuse results are tracked against goals and plans (1).

  — Changes to reuse goals and commitments are agreed by those affected (3).

- Commitment to perform

— The policy for managing a reuse project specifies how the project manager is kept informed about the reuse status and issues requiring agreement on changes to reuse goals and plans (2).

- Ability to perform

  — Project managers explicitly assign responsibility for reuse activities (2).
  — Software mangers are trained in managing the reuse aspects of a project (4).
  — First-line software managers receive orientation about reuse goals and progress of projects (5).

- Activities performed

  — The reuse goals and activities in project plans are updated to reflect accomplishments (1).
  — External reuse commitments are reviewed with senior management according to a documented procedure (3).
  — Approved changes in reuse goals are communicated to the project members (4).
  — The size of the reused components (both those developed for reuse and those reused) is measured (5). The size measured for reused components includes both the actual size of the reused component, and a size estimate of a component with the same functionality developed from scratch. In development *for* reuse we estimate the size of a component developed without reuse requirements in addition to the size of the reusable component.
  — The effort, cost, schedule and technical progress of the reuse activities are tracked (6 and 8-9).
  — The risks associated with reuse are tracked (10).
  — Reuse measurements (size and effort) and re-planning data are recorded (11).
  — Periodic internal and formal reviews include reuse activities and progress (12-13).

- Measurement and analysis, Verifying implementation

  — No additions.

Subcontract management

The purpose of reuse subcontract management is to incorporate reuse goals into the selection of subcontractors, and to incorporate reuse into the establishment and tracking of commitments.

- Goals

  — The reuse goals are incorporated in the selection of the subcontractor (new).

- Commitment to perform

  — The policy for managing a software subcontract specifies handling of reuse (1).

- Ability to perform

  — Those involved in establishing and managing the subcontract are trained to take reuse into account (2).

  — The specification of the technical aspects of the subcontract includes reuse goals (3).

- Activities performed

  — The procedure for defining and planning subcontract work incorporate reuse goals, e.g. specific components to be reused, or specific components to be developed for reuse are explicitly specified (1).

  — The evaluation criteria for selecting a subcontractor includes reuse ability (2).

  — The contractual agreement includes reuse commitments (3).

  — Reuse is incorporated in the subcontractor's development plan (4).

  — Reuse goals are tracked, changes resolved, reviewed, tested and evaluated together with the rest of the subcontractor's commitments (5-13).

- Measurement and analysis, Verifying implementation

  — No additions.

Software quality assurance

The purpose of reuse software quality assurance is to provide management with appropriate visibility of the reuse processes used and the reusable components built. Software quality assurance is particularly important for reusable components, as they will be reused in other products. Low quality will therefore have consequences outside the current product.

- Goals

  — Reuse is explicitly incorporated in the software quality assurance plans and activities (new).

- Commitment to perform

  — The policy for software quality assurance specifies the responsibilities for quality of reusable components (1).

- Ability to perform

  — Members of the software quality assurance group are trained to understand the reuse processes and products (3).

- Activities performed

  — The quality assurance plan specifies how the reuse goals will be assured (1).

  — The quality assurance group reviews reuse activities to verify compliance (4).

  — The quality assurance group audits designated reusable software work products to verify compliance (5).

- Measurement and analysis, Verifying implementation

  — No additions.

Software configuration management

The purpose of reuse software configuration management is to establish and maintain the integrity of the reusable and reused software components. This includes keeping reuse of both existing and new components under configuration management.

- Goals

  — Reused software components are identified, controlled and available (2).

  — New reusable software components and changes to reused software components are controlled (3).

- Commitment to perform

  — A written company policy for implementing software configuration management specifies how to handle reuse of components within and between projects (1).

- Ability to perform

  — A board having authority for approving and managing the reusable components exists (1).

  — Adequate resources are provided for managing the reusable components (3).

  — Members of the software engineering group are trained in the objectives, procedures and methods for searching, using and maintaining the reusable components (4 and 5).

- Activities performed

  — The software configuration management plan covers activities to manage reuse of components and new reusable components (2).

  — The repository configuration management system supports the use of items from other libraries (3).

  — Reusable components under development are identified (4).

  — Change requests to reusable components are tracked, controlled and propagated according to a documented procedure (5 and 6).

  — Reusable components are created, their status recorded, reported and audited according to documented procedures (7-10).

- Measurement and analysis, Verifying implementation

  — No additions.

5.4.3.6 Capability Maturity Model level 3: Defined

At Level 3 reuse is carried out on a company-wide basis. Project reuse goals are derived from the company's long-term reuse goals, incorporated into the goals of the project, and followed up by strategic product coordinators. There is a formal coordination between projects, and the company has institutionalized a complete reuse programme.

There are two additional reuse-specific key process areas at this level, *product reuse coordination* and *reuse repository management*. The complete list of key reuse process areas is:

- Product reuse coordination (new)

- Reuse repository management (new)

- Organization process focus

- Organization process definition

- Training programme

- Integrated software management

- Software product engineering

- Intergroup coordination

- Peer review

Product reuse coordination

The purpose of product reuse coordination is to establish the long-term reuse goals of the company and to coordinate the company's development processes to achieve these goals.

- Goals

  — The reuse goals of the company are established (1).

  — The reuse goals of each project are derived from the reuse goals of the company (2).

- Commitment to perform

  — The company follows a written policy for establishing company and project reuse goals.

- Ability to perform

  — Adequate resources and funding are provided for product reuse coordination.

  — The individuals responsible for product reuse coordination receive the required training.

  — The other software groups receive periodic orientation about the goals, plans and activities of product reuse coordination.

- Activities performed

  — The company's reuse goals are established, the results assessed and goals revised according to a documented procedure.

  — Each project's reuse goals are established from the company's overall goals according to a documented procedure.

  — The project's reuse plans, activities and results are periodically reviewed by the product reuse coordinators according to a documented procedure.

  — The project's reuse achievements are evaluated according to a documented procedure.

- Measurement and analysis

  — Measurements are made and used to determine the effectiveness of product reuse coordination.

- Verifying implementation

  — The activities for product reuse coordination are reviewed with senior management on a periodic basis.

  — The software quality assurance group reviews and/or audits the activities and work products for product reuse coordination and reports the results.

Reuse repository management

The purpose of reuse repository management is to establish and maintain a company-wide repository of reusable components and experience.

- Goals

  — The company's reuse repository is established (1).

- Commitment to perform

  — The company follows a written policy for using the reuse repository.

- Ability to perform

  — Adequate resources and funding are provided for reuse repository management.

  — The individuals responsible for reuse repository management receive the required training.

  — Other software groups receive periodic orientation about the goals, plans, activities and services provided by the repository management.

- Activities performed

  — The company's reuse repository is established and periodically revised according to a documented procedure. The type of reuse repository is derived from the reuse goals of the company. The procedure typically specifies:

- Which components the repository will contain.
- How they are classified.
- How they are maintained.
- How projects can use the repository.
- How the repository is maintained.

— The activities of reuse repository management are planned and documented.

— Each project uses the reuse repository according to a documented procedure. The procedure specifies:
    - How to search for components.
    - How to insert components, and what information they must contain.
    - Quality criteria for components.
    - Who will provide help and assistance with the use of the repository.

— The effort needed to perform reuse activities when inserting and retrieving components from the repository is recorded according to a documented procedure.

— Feedback on the repository in general and the individual components in particular is collected according to a documented procedure.

- Measurement and analysis

    — Measurements are made and used to determine the effectiveness of reuse repository management.

- Verifying implementation

    — The activities for reuse repository management are reviewed with senior management on a regular basis.

    — The software quality assurance group reviews and/or audits the activities and work products for reuse repository management and reports the results.

Organization process focus

The purpose of organization process focus is to develop and maintain an understanding of the organization's reuse processes, and coordinate the activity of specifying and improving these processes.

- Goals

    — Reuse process activities are coordinated throughout the company (1).

    — The strengths and weaknesses of the reuse processes used are identified relative to a reuse process standard (2).

    — Organization-level reuse process development and improvement activities are planned (3).

- Commitment to perform

    — The policy for coordinating software processes explicitly addresses the reuse processes (1).

- Ability to perform

    — The training of the group responsible includes reuse technology (3).

    — The orientation of the company's software process activities for other groups includes reuse process aspects (4).

- Activities performed

    — The assessments performed explicitly address reuse processes (1).

    — The plan for software process activities explicitly incorporates reuse according to the reuse goals of the company (2).

    — The activities of the company and projects for developing and improving their reuse processes are coordinated at company level (3).

    — The use of the reuse process database is coordinated on the company level (4). (The reuse process database is where the company stores historical information about the running of reuse processes.)

    — New reuse technology in limited use is monitored and transferred to other parts of the company when appropriate (5).

    — Training in reuse processes is coordinated throughout the company (6).

    — Affected groups are informed about the reuse process activities (7).

- Measurement and analysis, Verifying implementation

    — No additions.

Organization process definition

The purpose of organization process definition is to develop and maintain a usable set of reuse process components that improve reuse performance.

- Goals

    — The standard software process for the company incorporates reuse activities (1).

    — Reuse information from the use of this process is explicitly specified (2).

- Commitment to perform

    — The company's software process components include reuse processes (1).

- Ability to perform

    — Those performing these activities receive adequate training in reuse technology (2).

- Activities performed

    — The procedure for developing and maintaining the software processes explicitly treats reuse processes, and specifies that they should satisfy the company's reuse goals (1).

— Reuse processes are documented (2).

— The influence of reuse on the approved standard life cycles is documented and maintained (3).

— Guidelines for tailoring standard reuse processes are developed and maintained (4).

— The company's software process database incorporates reuse process data (5).

— The library of process-related documentation includes reuse plans and experiences (6).

- Measurement and analysis, Verifying implementation

— No additions.

Training programme

The purpose of the reuse training programme is to develop the reuse skills and knowledge of the individuals so they can perform their roles effectively and efficiently.

- Goals

— The reuse training activities are planned (1).

— Reuse training, both organizational and technical, is provided (2).

— Individuals in the company received the necessary reuse training (3).

- Commitment to perform

— The training policy explicitly specifies the reuse training needed (1).

- Ability to perform

— Members of the training group have the necessary skills and knowledge in reuse (3).

- Activities performed

— Projects' training plans explicitly cover reuse training (1).

— The company's training plan covers reuse training (3).

- Measurement and analysis, Verifying implementation

— No additions.

Integrated software management

The purpose of integrated reuse software management is to integrate the reuse software engineering and management activities into a coherent, defined software process based on the company's standard processes.

- Goals

— The project's reuse processes are based on the company's standard reuse processes and integrated with the project's software processes (1).

— Reuse activities are planned and managed according to the project's software processes (2).

- Commitment to perform

    — The policy for planning and managing the project specifies that each project documents, performs and records its reuse processes (1).

- Ability to perform

    — The individuals responsible for developing the project's software processes receive suitable training in how to tailor and manage the reuse processes (2-3).

- Activities performed

    — The project's reuse processes are developed by tailoring the company's standard reuse processes according to a documented procedure (1).

    — The procedure for revising the software processes explicitly includes how to treat the reuse processes (2).

    — Reuse activities are developed and revised following a documented procedure (3).

    — Reuse activities are managed in accordance with the project's defined software process (4).

    — The company's reuse process database is used for planning and estimating reuse activities (5).

    — The size, effort, critical computer resources and risks connected with reuse activities and reusable components are estimated, managed and recorded according to a documented procedure (6, 7, 8, 10).

    — The influence of reuse on the critical paths and schedule of the project are managed according to the documented procedure (9).

    — The project reviews explicitly include review of the reuse goals and performance (11).

- Measurement and analysis, Verifying implementation

    — No additions.

Software product engineering

The purpose of reuse software product engineering is to incorporate reuse practices (development *for* and *with* reuse) into software engineering activities.

- Goals

    — Reuse is defined and integrated into all software engineering activities (1).

- Commitment to perform

    — No additions.

- Ability to perform

  — Skilled individuals and tools are available to perform reuse activities (1).

  — Members of the software engineering technical staff receive suitable training in reuse technology (2). Examples of such training include the principles of:
  - Analyzing, representing and reusing variability in requirements.
  - Representing and adapting generality in the design, code, test and documentation.

  — Members of the software engineering technical staff receive orientation in related reuse technology (3).

  — Project managers and all software managers receive orientation in reuse aspects of the software project (4).

- Activities performed

  — Appropriate reuse methods and tools are integrated into the development process (1).

  — The selected process for requirements analysis supports and incorporates analysis of variability in requirements, and reuse of existing requirements (2).

  — Variability in the requirements is incorporated as generality in the design. Reusable components are searched for, evaluated, adapted and integrated according to the project's defined process (3).

  — The generality in the design is represented in the code and documentation. Reused components are integrated according to the software process (4).

  — Testing of reusable components is defined in the process (5).

  — Integration, system and acceptance testing of systems containing reusable components are defined in the process (6 and 7).

  — The documentation needed to support reusable components is defined in the process (8).

  — Data on defects are collected for each reusable component (9).

  — Consistency is maintained across software work products for reusable components (10).

- Measurement and analysis

  — Measurements are made to determine the reusability of reusable components (1).

  — Measurements are made and used to determine the status of reuse activities and reusable components (2).

- Verifying implementation

  — No additions.

Intergroup coordination

The purpose of reuse intergroup coordination is to establish a means for the software engineering group to participate with other engineering groups (inside and outside the project) so that the project is better able to discover and take advantage of reuse opportunities.

- Goals

  — The reuse potential and reuse goals of the project are agreed between all affected groups (1).
  — Intergroup issues concerning reuse goals and opportunities are identified, tracked and resolved (3).

- Commitment to perform

  — The policy for interdisciplinary engineering teams specifies how to handle reuse issues (1).

- Ability to perform

  — No additions.

- Activities performed

  — Development *for* and *with* reuse is taken into account when establishing system requirements (1).
  — Reuse activities and issues are monitored and coordinated by representatives of the project's software engineering group working with other engineering groups (2).
  — A documented plan is used to communicate intergroup reuse commitments, and to coordinate and track the work performed (3).
  — Critical dependencies involving reuse are identified, negotiated and tracked according to a documented procedure (4).
  — Reusable components produced are reviewed by representatives of the receiving group to ensure that the components meet their needs (5).
  — Representatives of the project engineering groups conduct periodic reuse reviews and interchange of information (7).

- Measurement and analysis, Verifying implementation

  — No additions.

Peer review

The purpose of reuse peer reviews is to assure the reusability of the components early and efficiently. Reuse peer reviews involve a methodical examination of reusable components to assure that they satisfy the requirements for a reusable component.

The reusability of a component is assessed when the component is produced (development *for* reuse) and when it is reused (development *with* reuse). When developing *for* reuse the main concern is to ensure that the component has the potential for reuse in the future, for example adequate generality, quality etc. When developing *with* reuse, the focus is to ensure that it is appropriate to reuse the component in the current context.

- Goals

  — The reusability of components is assured (new).

- Commitment to perform

  — The company policy for peer review specifies that peer reviews are used to assure the reusability of the components (1).

- Ability to perform

  — Reviewers receive required training in how to assure the reusability of a component (3).

- Activities performed

  — The documented procedure to perform reviews incorporates information on how to assure the reusability of the component, such as check-lists (2).

- Measurement and analysis, Verifying implementation

  — No additions.

5.4.3.7 Capability Maturity Model level 4: Measured

At Level 4 the company has quantitative control over its reuse activities. The project and company have quantitative reuse goals which are monitored. The key reuse process areas at this level are:

- Quantitative process management

- Software quality management

- Software reusability management (new)

Quantitative process management

The purpose of quantitative reuse process management is to quantitatively control the performance of the reuse process. For this key process area we mainly need to include the reuse processes in quantitative control procedures, and to establish resources, procedures and competence to do so.

- Goals

  — The reuse performance of the software process is controlled quantitatively (2).

- The reuse capability of the company's standard software process is known in quantitative terms (3).

- Commitment to perform

  - The policies for measuring, quantitatively controlling and analyzing the performance of the process specify how to measure and control reuse activities (1 and 2).

- Ability to perform

  - A group exists for coordinating the quantitative reuse process management activities (1).

- Activities performed

  - The project's plan for quantitative reuse process management is developed according to a documented procedure (1).
  - The strategy for reuse data collection and quantitative analysis are determined based on the project's defined reuse processes (3).

- Measurement and analysis, Verifying implementation

  - No additions.

Software quality management

The purpose of reuse software quality management is to develop a quantitative understanding of the quality of the company's reusable components and achieve specific quality goals. These goals are established at the company level and are achieved through the reuse projects.

- Goals

  - The quality management activities of the company are planned (1).
  - Measurable company goals for the quality of reusable components are defined, and these goals are used to establish the quality goals of the projects (2).
  - Actual progress towards the goals is quantified and managed at the level of both individual projects and the entire company (3).

- Commitment to perform

  - The company and each project follow written policies for managing reuse software quality (1).

- Ability to perform

  - A group exists for managing the quality of reusable components.

- Activities performed

— The quality plan for the company's reusable components is developed and maintained according to a documented procedure (new).

— The project's software quality plan supports the quality plan for the company's reusable components (1).

- Measurement and analysis, Verifying implementation

— No additions.

Software reusability management (new)

The purpose of software reusability management is to develop a quantitative understanding of the effectiveness of the company's reusable software components, and to achieve specific reuse goals.

- Goals

— Software reusability management activities are planned (1).

— Measurable company goals for reuse are defined, and these goals are used to establish the reuse goals of the projects (2).

— Actual progress towards the goals is quantified and managed at the level of both individual projects and the entire company (3).

- Commitment to perform

— The company follows a written policy for establishing measurable company and project reuse goals.

- Ability to perform

— Adequate resources and funding are provided for software reusability management.

— The individuals responsible for software reusability management receive suitable training.

— Other software groups receive periodic orientation about the goals, plans, measurements and activities of the software reusability management.

- Activities performed

— The company's quantitative reuse goals are established, measures taken, results assessed and goals revised according to a documented procedure.

— Each projects' quantitative reuse goals are established from the company's overall goals according to a documented procedure.

— Projects' reuse plans, activities, measures and results are periodically reviewed by the software reusability management according to a documented procedure.

— Project's quantitative reuse achievements are evaluated according to a documented procedure.

     — Quantitative data (effort used, effort saved, errors) from reuse processes are collected on a component basis and used to establish whether individual components and the total repository satisfy the reuse goals.

- Measurement and analysis

     — Measurements are made and used to determine the effectiveness of software reusability management.

- Verifying implementation

     — The activities for software reusability management are reviewed with senior management on a periodic basis.

     — The software quality assurance group reviews and/or audits the activities and work products for software reusability management and reports the results.

5.4.3.8 Capability Maturity Model level 5: Optimized

At the optimized level the company focuses continuously on reuse improvement. The company has the means to identify weaknesses and improve the reuse processes proactively, to achieve its reuse goals. Data on the effectiveness of reuse processes are used to perform cost-benefit analyses of new reuse technologies.

    Teams at this level analyze their reuse performance to determine causes for their failures and successes, and lessons learned are systematically disseminated throughout the company. There are three key process areas at this level:

- Defect prevention

- Technology change management

- Process change management

Defect prevention

The purpose of reuse defect (failure) prevention is to systematically identify weaknesses in the reuse processes or components, and to seek their cause so that they can be prevented from recurring.

- Goals

     — Reuse defect prevention activities are planned (1).

     — Common causes of reuse failures are sought out and identified (2).

     — Common causes of reuse failures are prioritized and systematically eliminated (3).

- Commitment to perform

     — The company and projects follow written policies for reuse failure prevention activities (1 and 2).

- Ability to perform

  — Organization-level and project-level teams exist to coordinate reuse failure prevention activities (1 and 2).

- Activities performed

  — The project develops and maintains a plan for reuse failure prevention activities (1).

  — At the beginning of any reuse activity, the team meets to prepare for the activity and the related reuse failure prevention activity (2).

  — The causal analysis meeting is performed after each reuse activity to evaluate the reuse process and the reusable components. In particular failures to reuse a component or to develop a component for reuse are analyzed (3).

  — Reuse failure prevention teams meet on a periodic basis to review and coordinate the output of the causal analysis meetings (4).

  — Reuse failure prevention data are documented and tracked between the coordinating teams (5).

- Measurement and analysis, Verifying implementation

  — No additions.

Technology change management

The purpose of reuse technology change management is to identify new reuse technologies and track them in the company in an orderly manner.

- Goals

  — Incorporation of reuse technology changes is planned (1).

  — New reuse technologies are evaluated to determine their effect on quality and productivity (2).

  — Appropriate new reuse technologies are transferred into normal practice throughout the company (3).

- Commitment to perform, Ability to perform, Activities performed, Measurement and analysis, Verifying implementation

  — No additions.

Process change management

The purpose of reuse process change management is to continually improve the reuse processes used in the company with the intention of improving software quality, increasing productivity, and decreasing lead time.

- Goals

  — Continuous reuse process improvement is planned (1).

— Participation in the company's reuse process improvement activities is company-wide (2).

— The company's standard reuse processes are improved continuously (3).

• Commitment to perform, Ability to perform, Activities performed, Measurement and analysis, Verifying implementation

— No additions.

5.5 Legal aspects of software

How can you protect your legal interests when you buy and sell reusable software?

5.5.1 Introduction

This section describes the current situation concerning legal aspects for software, including reusable software components.

Software legislation does not consist of a unique set of dedicated laws, but is an adaptation from different old, well-established fields of law. An example of this is copyright law. The legal mechanisms for protecting software include trade secrets, copyright and patent laws; the next section gives an overview of these.

An excellent and very understandable introduction to the legal aspects of software can be found in [Remer82]. This book contains detailed descriptions of various kinds of contracts (non-disclosure agreements, licence agreements between developer and vendor, warranty disclaimers and so on). Even though the book is written from an American point of view and necessarily contains specialities which are not valid world-wide, it describes the concepts well. It contains a number of sample contracts with a very detailed explanation of each of the important clauses, and provides alternatives which may also be used. Examples of licence agreements in German and in English can also be found in [Pagenberg89].

Licence agreements set up by different computer program vendors provide another important source of information. Some of them have licence agreements that vary from country to country. We also found some examples of licences and copyrights for public domain and free software.

5.5.2 Trade secrets, copyright and patents

Trade secrets, copyright and patents are all legal concepts that apply to different aspects of software. This section provides a brief explanation.

5.5.2.1 Trade secrets – protection of "know-how"

What you can protect as a trade secret

Software may include "know-how" that can be protected as trade secret. Know-how can be defined as a body of information, that is secret, substantial and identified in any appropriate form (EEC Regulation No. 556/89 of 30 November 1988). An example is proprietary information that leads to a commercial advantage.

Obtaining protection and duration of protection

As long as know-how is secret (that is, not publicly visible), it is protected. You must therefore limit the number of people who gain access to the know-how. If you want to transfer your software to others you must oblige them to keep the know-how secret by signing a non-disclosure agreement before delivery. Failure to do this can compromise the legal status of your software to contain know-how, and therefore your protection. It can also of course result in your customers failing to keep the know-how secret.

Violation of a non-disclosure agreement

When a party to the agreement fails to keep the know-how confidential, he violates the agreement and the other party may have a right to claim damages from him. Once the confidentiality of the know-how has been violated, you cannot prevent others from using it unless it is protected by a patent.

5.5.2.2 Copyright protection

The EU has adopted a directive on the legal protection of computer programs [Council directive]. The member states of the EU were required to bring into force provisions in their national law to comply with the Directive by 1 January 1993. This section therefore discusses copyright protection as defined by the directive.

What you can protect by copyright

A copyright protects works of literature, art and science (technical works belong to this category). Software (computer programs and the design material) are defined in legal terms as literary works. Protection is applied to the expression of the software, but not to ideas and principles underlying it. However, you can patent an idea; see Section 5.5.2.3. Software is only protected if it is original in the sense that it is the author's own intellectual creation. Most computer programs fulfil this criteria.

Obtaining protection and the duration of protection

Copyright protection begins with the creation of an original program and ends 70 years after the death of the last surviving author. The duration of protection can be shorter under national law, but it must be at least 50 years. When the software is an anonymous work the duration of protection is calculated starting from the day the software was made available to the public.

No further conditions such as registration or copyright notices must be fulfilled for the protection to start. It is, however, sensible to place a copyright notice on a program to show that the program is protected and you will enforce your rights. This notice should have a form like this:

> © Copyright SoftComp, 1994
> All rights reserved

Whenever somebody runs the program or lists its source the copyright notice should be displayed to denote that the software is not in the public domain. Instead of © you can also use (C), but it is obligatory to put ©, (C) or Copyright.

Besides displaying the copyright notice when the program starts, and in the source code, you should also mark any distribution media such as tape streamers, floppy disks and so on with the copyright notice. The year should be that in which the program was published. After the year you should write either the name of the programmer or the name of the company as appropriate.

The rights of a copyright holder

The owner of the copyright has the right to:

- reproduce the software

- alter the software

- distribute the software

and can exclude anyone else from doing any of the above.

A lawful buyer of the software is allowed to make a back-up copy and can observe, study or test the functioning of the program, providing that he does so by using the program in a way that he is entitled to do. He can also reproduce and translate a program to obtain information necessary to achieve the interoperability or compatibility of an independently created program, when the information necessary to achieve interoperability has not previously been made readily available.

5.5.2.3 Patent protection

Most European countries are members of the European Patent Convention. This convention is used to discuss patent protection. Other countries have similar bodies, such as the American Patent and Trademark Office [PTO].

What you can protect by patent

Patents are granted for technical inventions that are new and involve an inventive step. The invention can be:

- a product (hardware)

- a process or method which describes how a product (such as a computer) works; an algorithm is such a process

- a process to produce a product.

Patents will not be granted for:

- a mathematical method

- a scheme, rule or method for performing mental acts, playing games or doing business

- a computer program

to the extent that the invention relates to these subject matters. For example a mathematical method which is a step in a process among other technical steps will not hinder the granting of a patent. The distinction between patentable or not-patentable methods is difficult and can only be determined with legal advice.

Obtaining a patent

To obtain a patent you have to make a patent application for your invention and file it at a patent office, for example at the European Patent Office in Munich. The application should contain:

- a request for the grant of a patent

- a description of the invention, which discloses the invention in a form that would enable it to be carried out by a person skilled in the art

- one or more claims which define for what protection is sought

- drawings referred to in the description or the claims.

The patent office will examine the application to determine whether the invention described is new and involves an inventive step. If the examination is successful a patent will be granted and protection starts. Patent protection ends 20 years at the latest after the date of filing.

The rights of a patent holder

The patent holder has the right to prevent the use of the patent by all third parties not having his consent.

He can prevent anyone else making a patented product, advertising it, putting it on the market or using it. He can prohibit anyone from using or offering a patented process. If the patent is infringed he can sue the infringer. He also can settle the case by making a licence contract and obtaining a licence fee. The patent holder is free to choose which approach he pursues.

5.5.2.4 Conclusions

In most cases the situation is clear:

* Computer programs acquire a copyright by virtue of their creation.

* A patent can only be obtained under particular circumstances.

For more information about legal protection of computer programs, see the European Council directive issued on 14 May 1991, published in the Official Journal of the European Communities on 17 May 1991 [Council directive]. In addition, the importance of good legal advice in this area cannot be underestimated.

5.5.3 Establishing contracts to protect your software

A good collection of non-disclosure and licence agreements can be found in [Remer82], and [Pagenberg89]. The samples provided there form a solid base for establishing one's own contracts for most purposes. Be careful about using samples as they stand; you need the help of a lawyer to adapt them for your special circumstances. For example, the country or countries in which you plan to market your product or services play an important role.

5.5.3.1 Non-disclosure agreements

A non-disclosure agreement is a very good means for securing your important trade secrets. Besides stating that you are serious about taking care of them, it will tell those that sign to do so as well by binding them from disclosing the secret. By signing, the signatory becomes legally liable for any harm caused by disclosure.

Non-disclosure agreements should be used for anyone outside the company who will have access to your trade secrets. Examples are potential customers or licensees, potential investors, external evaluators, or bankers. Non-disclosure agreements are also often used for employees as well as for contractors hired for a specific fixed-term job.

When establishing a contract between a company and employees or contractors, a non-disclosure agreement should be included that covers all trade secrets. These should be as concrete as possible. Besides technological issues such as programs, non-technical trade secrets such as customer lists should be included. The duration of such agreements should be indefinite, to protect you after employees or contractors have left. It is also recommended to set up specific non-disclosure agreements for important projects. They can be made much more specific than the more general ones that form part of a contract of employment. Non-disclosure clauses often form part of licence agreements.

5.5.3.2 Licence agreements between developers and vendors or customers

A licence agreement is the most important type of contract between developers and vendors or customers. This kind of contract merits a closer look if both the development and marketing of software is to be successful. Software requires a considerable effort to take it from the original idea to a program that can be sold.

The licence agreement is also known under the synonyms of *licence contract*, *royalty contract*, or *royalty agreement*. The licence agreement describes the relationship between the developer and the vendor or customer in detail, as well as the program which is the subject matter of this contract. An exact description of the deliverables must be provided together with the terms for payment to the developer. Other important topics include restrictions of the licence such as geographical, market scope, or computer type, delivery schedules, program maintenance terms, modification, training, warranties, copyright, indemnification, contract termination, and arbitration.

5.5.4 The legal impact of software reuse

Studying different fields of law from the perspective of software reuse does not show that a dramatically different approach is required in reuse than for software in general. All the legal protection means mentioned so far such as copyright and patent hold true for reuse.

There is one specific difference in that with reuse, software with different legal categories may reside in the same repository. These categories may be summarized as follows:

- strategic knowledge confined to an organization

- non-strategic knowledge which has commercial value

- non-strategic knowledge which does not

The type of product tends to be different between reusable components and classical software products. The former deals largely with specification, design and source code, whereas the latter is concerned more with binary code and user documentation.

The strength of protection you have to set up depends on the form in which you intend to distribute your software—as compiled executables or libraries, or as source code. If you distribute in the form of compiled code, the licence contract for a vendor as well as for an end-user need be no different from those set up for commercially available software products. The case is slightly different if you plan to publish the source code of your program. Since the user has free access to use and change the source, a more rigid approach must be established to protect your trade secret.

The recommendation in this case is to include a rigorous non-disclosure agreement in the licence for the end-user. This can prevent the end-user from giving your program source code to third parties. Contracts with vendors do not seem to be a problem here, as they need not differ from existing contracts that include source code. The use of the program in compiled form as part of a development should (as always) include the copyright notice of your program.

The scenario described above is the normal one. The program is used as is, no changes or additions are made. But what happens if the customer starts adapting the program source code to fit his needs? You do not want the adapted source to be distributed freely or as part of a product in source code form by the end-user. The best practice again is to establish a rigorous agreement that binds the end-user not to give away your source code.

One question arises from the above: will reusable components other than standard components like data structures, database, or user interface libraries be sold as products? We feel that domain-specific components will be the trade secret of a company wanting to protect their business. Giving away such components would limit their market, and create great potential for competitors in a market segment important to the company.

5.5.5 Summary

We have looked at legal aspects of software relevant to non-reusable software as well as to reusable software. We have found no particular cases for reusable software that do not already occur. Copyrights, trademarks, patent law, non-disclosure agreements and licence agreements hold in the same manner for reusable software.

This section can help you to determine what protection is appropriate for your software, as well as helping you to obtain information on contracts with vendors and customers. Nevertheless, it is highly advisable to consult a lawyer if you want to apply for a patent or to set up a licence agreement.

Part B
Practising Reuse

6 Development *for* and *with* Reuse

6.1 Introduction to Part B

Development *for* and *with* reuse is the core of reuse. Development *for* reuse is concerned with the development of reusable components while development *with* reuse is concerned with the development of systems with reuse of components.

It is predicted that development of software based on reusable components will take over from development from scratch. Software development will evolve from the composition of simple code statements to the synthesis of large components from smaller ones. Terms like "mega-programming" are used, especially within the STARS programme [STARS92], to distinguish this form of component engineering from ordinary programming.

These predictions (or hopes) depend on a clear understanding of:

- what it takes for a component to be reusable and how we can create such components

- how we reuse it

- how we can manage components and find the correct one from many

These questions are summarized within the STARS conceptual framework for reuse processes (Figure 73) used within the STARS project for studying reuse.

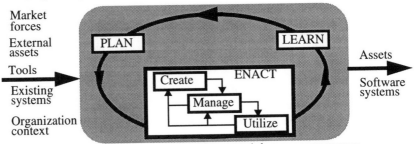

Figure 73 : STARS conceptual framework for reuse processes

The ENACT part of this conceptual framework is related to the twin life cycle model, which distinguishes between development *for* (*create* in Figure 73) and development *with* (*utilize* in Figure 73).

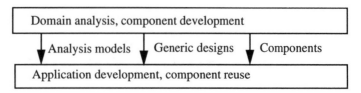

Figure 74 : The twin life cycle

Figure 74 illustrates the twin life cycle model by showing the connection between development *for* and *with* reuse. In this part of the book we discuss:

1. general guidelines on how to adapt development methods to reuse

2. specific guidelines on how to adapt object-oriented development methods to reuse

3. an adaptation of selected development methods to development *for* and *with* reuse

4. examples of reuse-adapted development methods in applications

5. a re-engineering method for reuse.

The main objective of the development *for* reuse process is to develop or re-engineer reusable components. Different organizations use different models and notations for requirement and implementation models, and these may not support reuse. It may not be feasible to introduce completely new models and notations, but rather to extend and broaden the use of the existing ones. Although we strongly advocate object-oriented development methods, we also provide support to other paradigms.

We have grouped all aspects of development *for* and *with* reuse together in a separate part of the handbook, as they are mutually dependent. For example, the development *with* reuse process often places requirements on components developed *for* reuse. The remainder of Part B of the handbook is organized as follows:

*   Chapter 7 provides a set of reuse support guidelines that are independent of the development paradigm. It also provides guidelines on how to adapt an existing development process to reuse.

*   Chapter 8 presents the various types of object-oriented components, object-oriented techniques, and the object-oriented life cycle model used by both development *for* reuse and development *with* reuse methodologies.

*   Chapter 9 describes a methodology for developing reusable object-oriented components. This methodology focuses on the development of object-oriented components, but we also take into account that most of today's software is not written using this methodology.

- Chapter 10 explains how to reuse object-oriented components in the different development phases—how to find, evaluate, adapt and integrate existing components in a new system.

- Chapter 11 presents a re-engineering method. This method describes how to transform non-object-oriented code to object-oriented code.

- Chapter 12 presents an example of the adaptation of the Cleanroom development process [Mills87] to incorporate reuse and object-oriented development. The purpose of this example is to show how a non-object-oriented development process can be adapted to reuse.

7 Generic Reuse Development Processes

7.1 Introduction

In this chapter we discuss development *for* and *with* reuse at an abstract level, independent of any specific development process or system structure. We try to answer the following questions:

- What is a reusable component?

- What constitutes reusability?

- How do we represent reusability?

- How do we develop *for* reuse?

- How do we document a reusable component?

- How do we test a reusable component?

- How do we develop *with* reuse?

- How do we incorporate reuse in a development process?

We attempt to provide answers to these questions that are independent of the software development paradigm, and irrespective of whether we are considering reuse "in the large" or "in the small". However, the answers do need to be adapted to the specific development process and component types of each company and project.

The information we provide in the following sections has been developed from our experience in the REBOOT project, specifically in introducing reuse in different development processes for our customers.

7.2 What is a reusable component?

7.2.1 A morphology of software development

To describe what a reusable component is, we subdivide software development as a three-dimensional activity using the following categories:

- The *structural* dimension represents the system breakdown into subsystems, modules and classes. We define these artifacts as components. The two classical reasons for such a decomposition are:

  — it breaks the problem into smaller, more manageable pieces
  — it enables parallel work

  The standard procedure when decomposing a system is to do as much analysis as is necessary for the decomposition, define the interfaces between the subcomponents, then specify each subcomponent as the combination of the relevant interfaces and the relevant part of the analysis model.

- The *abstraction* dimension represents the refinement of the system from requirements, through analysis and design (intermediate models) to implementation (solution model). The main reason for representing the system by different models is to bridge the conceptual gap between the customer's requirements and the executable system.

- The *layering* dimension represents different "abstract machines", platforms, or interfaces which come between the end-user and the hardware. These layers are used to ease the construction of applications and make them more portable. There is a structural and abstraction dimension within each layer. Each layer or platform consists of both an interface which gives access to the resources and a library which facilitates the use of the layer. For example, in the Unix operating system, the interface is represented by system calls, whereas everything else is the library.

  This model is illustrated in Figure 75.
  As we can see from the figure, the abstraction dimension recurs at each structural level, where the design on one structural level (e.g. subsystem) becomes the requirements for the next lower level (module). This means that each component type has some information relating to specification, analysis, design, implementation and test.
  Even if it is not shown in the figure, the structural and abstraction dimensions are repeated within each layer. An example system with three layers is an end-user application building on a fourth-generation language building on an operating system.
  We may also introduce (or take into account) specific requirements in a given layer or structural level, such as distribution, error tolerance, implementation platform and so on. The number of layers, levels of decomposition and abstraction models used will be dependent on the application domain and the size of the application.

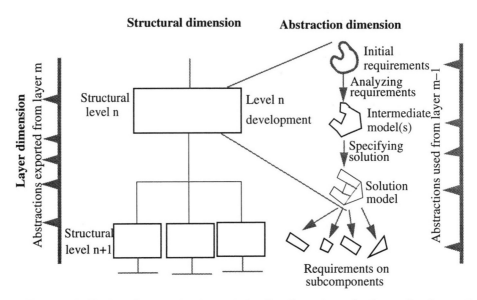

Figure 75 : The layering, structural and abstraction dimensions of software development

7.2.2 Definition of a reusable component

Given this characterization of software development, we can now define what we mean by a reusable component:

> *A reusable component is any component that is specifically developed to be used, and is actually used, in more than one context.*

A reusable component can thus be on any level in the structural dimension, from a single class to the entire system. A component can also come from any layer of the system. For example, abstract data types will be used in all layers. Each reusable component will also have its own abstraction dimension, from its own requirements to the requirements on its subcomponents, from which the specification of the subcomponents can be derived.

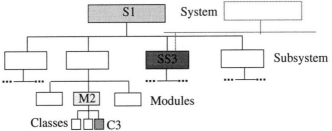

Figure 76 : A system structure with several reusable components

The development and reuse of components is illustrated in figure 76. Here we have shaded the components which are developed for reuse (S1, SS3, M2 and C3). We have also shown that SS3 is reused in another system, illustrated by dotted lines in the figure—thus the dotted system incorporates SS3 from S1. We see here that development *for* and *with* reuse penetrates the entire system structure, and we can reuse components at any level.

Even if we discuss components as software modules, directly "pluggable" into a target system, a reusable component may in fact consist of other types of information. Some examples are:

- Source code components which are intended for reuse *as is*.

- Abstract components which are intended for reuse by specialization. In this section we are mainly concerned with this type of component.

- Guidelines and standards for components. These include everything from simple guidelines to a complete process for constructing components in a given domain.

These examples of reusable components can be thought of as templates which are used to construct actual components faster and better than starting from scratch. Every reusable component can therefore be characterized by:

- the set of actual components they will be used to produce

- the effort needed to produce the actual component from the reusable component.

This discussion indicates that the reusability of a component is not a binary property, but that each component has a *degree* of reusability. Note that as we reuse and specialize the abstract components, we produce a set of less abstract components (instantiations) which can also be reused.

Based on this understanding of what a reusable component is we can define development *for* and *with* reuse as:

- Development *for* reuse is the planned activity of constructing a component for reuse in contexts other than the one for which it was initially intended.

- Development *with* reuse is the search for, evaluation, adaptation and integration of existing components in a new context.

In some cases, development *for* reuse is also called *domain engineering* whereas development *with* reuse is called *application engineering* [SPC92].

This discussion has been focused on component-based reuse. A layer, such as an operating system or fourth-generation language, can be considered as a large component on which the systems on the next layer are based. The decisions to develop such a layer is in principle the same as when we decide to develop a smaller component for reuse:

- How much it costs to develop

- How much we save each time we reuse it

- How many times it will be reused

In the following sections we focus mainly on reuse in the structural dimension. This is because the reuse aspects of developing a layer or a smaller component are principally the same. The following connections between reuse in the structural and layer dimensions exist:

- Development for reuse on a structural level extends the functionality of the layer below. If this functionality becomes stable and is generally useful it can be migrated down to the subsequent version of the layer below. For example, reuse between applications can lead to extensions of a fourth-generation language.

- Development for reuse in a lower layer of the system level provides more general interfaces, thus serving more applications in the layer above.

A layered architecture usually reflects a mature understanding of the domain, and reuse in the structural dimension evolves naturally into reuse in the layered dimension. That is, class and module reuse evolve into the lower layer whereas system and subsystem reuse evolve into the next layer. Thus when we talk about *level* we mean structural level.

Even if we can reuse at any level, the potential for profit increases with the size of the reused components. The risk of attempting to develop or reuse a large and unknown component must not be underestimated, however. It is also important to search for reusable components early in the abstraction process. This is because the probability of being able to reuse a component decreases drastically with the number of design decisions taken.

7.3 What constitutes reusability?

What distinguishes a reusable component from a non-reusable one? A reusable component is developed in one context and is intended to be reused in other contexts. To be able to reuse a component, it must fulfil a reuser's need for a specific functionality. The clue is to foresee this need, and define a component so that as many reusers as possible can profit from using it, thus:

Reusability is useful generality

Even if non-functional criteria like confidence and understandability are of major importance when it comes to reuse, it cannot be overlooked that the first and most important criterion for reuse is functionality. If a component does not solve our problem, we do not need it.

As different reusers usually have different requirements for the same component, it is not profitable to construct one "concrete" component for each reuser. It is better to construct general components that can be specialized, parametrized or configured by different reusers. This means that we need components that are as general as possible. We must, however, also consider the cost of understanding, adapting and integrating a general component, as well as any performance penalties. These factors indicate that we must carefully weigh the amount of generality we build into a component. The conflict is illustrated in the following simplified figure:

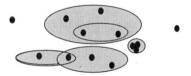

Figure 77 : General components and specific requirements

Here different reusers' specific requirements are illustrated with black points, the distance between the points represents the difference in requirements, and the reusable components are shaded ellipses, the larger ellipses representing more general components. The cost of evaluating, understanding and adapting a reusable component can be thought of as proportional to the cost of contracting one of the ellipses to the size of a specific point. We must therefore balance generality with the cost of adaptation. The only way to get this balance right is by making a thorough analysis of the current and potential requirements. A similar process is described as *instance-space analysis* in [Barnes91].

Reusability has a scale—there are degrees of reusability. This is illustrated with the size of the shaded ellipses in Figure 77, and by the degree of shading of components in Figure 76. We have to make a conscious decision about how reusable a component will be. This decision should be explicitly based on expected needs, their probability and benefits, and not based on habit or what is easiest to do.

The word *useful* in our definition of reusability is important, as it conveys the message that even the most general component is not reusable if no one needs its functionality. We must therefore ensure that we invest in the components with the largest market potential, i.e. a large enough number of potential reusers.

We defined development for reuse as the planned activity of constructing a component for reuse in contexts other than that for which it was initially intended. Development for reuse therefore extends and generalizes the requirements of the component for the current user, so that requirements for future reusers are captured, and the component can be reused.

When we develop for reuse, the main aim is to identify potential reusers with similar requirements, and analyze the variations between their requirements. Development for reuse is all about identifying and analyzing these needs, anticipating similar needs, and designing a general solution which can be economically adapted to satisfy as many requirements as possible [Barnes91]. Any additional reuse requirements must be as well specified and testable as ordinary requirements from the original customer [NATO-STD].

Requirements for a reusable component can be represented by a specialization hierarchy, in which we allocate common requirements as high in the hierarchy as possible. Different specializations represent functionality which differ for different users or contexts. A simple example from the world of transportation is used below to illustrate the concept:

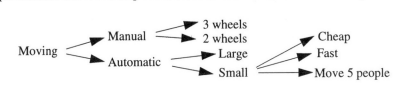

Figure 78 : A requirement specialization hierarchy

Note that some of the concepts are more like design decisions than functional requirements (e.g. two or three wheels, instead of "stability"), but this is normal in any kind of requirements specification. It is not always obvious which requirements are contradictory, as this often depends on the design.

Analyzing requirements from potential customers leads to a better understanding of the original customer's requirements. This might well lead to early discovery of hidden or undiscovered requirements from the original customer, which would otherwise lead to expensive rework if discovered later in the development process.

7.4 How can you represent reusability?

When we decide which requirements it is economical to include in a reusable component, we must decide how best to represent the reusability or generality.

This is a design activity in which we must take into account what is technically a good solution, and whether potential reusers will be able to understand and adapt the component easily. This is related to the work we do in the abstraction process for each level of the system. In this dimension we have the necessary design freedom to make a design tailored for reusability.

In analyzing several reusable components, we have found that it is possible to identify several general techniques which may be applied independently of component size (the structural dimension) and the development process step (the abstraction dimension). We decided to focus on the following five techniques. Although we do not claim them to be complete or orthogonal, we have found them to be very useful in practice:

* *Widening*. This means identifying a set of requirements that are not contradictory, then making a general component that satisfies all of them. In the transportation example in Figure 78, this could be *Fast* and *Move 5 people*, which would be satisfied by a SAAB 9000. The advantage with this approach is that the component can be reused *as is*. The disadvantage can be the cost of the component, with respect to:

    — initial development, i.e. it is expensive to develop all the functionality at once, and the component may become unnecessarily complex

    — being obliged to understand irrelevant functionalities when reusing the component

— resource consumption, e.g. space and efficiency

- *Narrowing.* Here we identify functionality common to several customers which can be represented by an abstract component. We can choose to place an abstract component at any level in the requirements hierarchy. Consider the following abstraction hierarchy:

Figure 79 : An abstraction hierarchy

When we want to make a new vehicle, such as a monocycle or a convertible, we will specialize *Bike* or *Car* respectively, rather than implementing it from scratch. The principle of reuse by inheritance is well known within object-oriented development, where it is most commonly applied to classes. There is no reason why it should not be applicable to larger components such as modules, subsystems or entire systems.

- *Isolation.* Different requirements can be isolated to a small part of the system, and the rest of the system constructed relatively independently of whatever specialization is chosen. In the transportation example shown in Figure 78, we might isolate the *Cheap* and *Fast* requirements in the engine, and construct the rest of the car to the same specification.

A special case of isolation is *parametrization*, where we recognize that some requirements can be expressed by parameters. In the transportation example, we can imagine the number of wheels or the size to be such parameters. Other examples are *indirection* and *abstract interfaces*, that is, using pointers to objects where we only specify the required interface, and leave the rest of the object unspecified. Layered architectures are a special case, where we isolate variable parts in different layers. Isolation is a much-used technique in making components independent from the underlying system, for example the operating system, hardware or database server.

- *Configurability.* Configurability means that we make a set of smaller components, that can be configured or composed in different ways to satisfy different requirements. For the car we could imagine, for example, a modular middle part to the chassis to enable us to built different sizes of car (one or two middle modules respectively) and an engine with a variable number of cylinders. This is an even more viable approach for optional requirements.

Configurability exists on a scale ranging from a strict framework, where we can only compose the system according to given rules (see [MacApp89] and [Campell92]), to a general-purpose library that allows us to build systems from very general "bricks". This can be compared to the popular Lego toys, which provide everything from general-purpose kits to very specialized ones. Interesting work is going on to try and categorize object-oriented design patterns that can be reused [Gamma93]. These are the kinds of structures that can be used to achieve configurability.

- *Generators*. Different requirements can be satisfied by making a "new" application-domain-specific language with which one can describe an application. Executable code can then be automatically generated from the application description. This approach requires a mature knowledge of the application domain and a considerable investment. In our example an application generator would be like a car plant where the customer could specify the car on the drawing board, and pick it up at the end of the assembly line. Application generator reuse corresponds to reuse in the *layering* dimension.

  Even with application generators we can use component-based reuse, because the programs for the application generator can be reused. By doing this we move the reuse problem one layer up.

These techniques are not orthogonal, as the examples show—we can use more than one technique to represent the same generality. Which technique we use is a design decision. It is important, however, that designers are aware of these techniques, because they tend to appear in different guises, and a decision to use any of them will affect a component considerably.

For example, object-oriented framework technology is based mainly on a combination of the *configurability* and *narrowing* techniques, resulting in a set of abstract classes with predefined communication mechanisms. The Synthesis approach to development for reuse [SPC92] focuses on *parametrization*, here called *decision models*. These models are used both to analyze the variability in the requirements and to represent the generality in the design. Configuration management systems also represent variability by version selectors that can be categorized as a special case of parametrization.

A similar characterization is made in [Barnes91] where two strategies are identified:

- adaptive reuse corresponding to *isolation*

- compositional reuse corresponding to *configurability*

Barnes also argues that parametrization and generators are two sides of the same coin, and that there is a connection between parametrization or isolation and narrowing, if we consider functions as parameters. That is, an object-oriented virtual function may be considered as a special case of a function parameter.

Design for reuse is an iterative process, in which one compares different design alternatives with the requirements, as are all design activities. The freedom to choose which reuse requirements are to be incorporated, and how to represent them, increases the need to iterate and evaluate different alternatives.

When we have decided how to represent the generality, we must decide *when* the reused component will be coupled with the system being developed. Although this concerns development *with* reuse, this decision must be taken during development *for* reuse. There are three possibilities here, corresponding to different stages in the development life cycle: development-time coupling, build-time couple and run-time coupling.

- *Development-time coupling*. This means incorporating the component in our new system in the form of its source code. Development time reuse can be reuse *as is* or reuse with modifications, in which we adapt the component during development.

Development time reuse is possible in all phases of the abstraction process—analysis, design, code and test. Changes to the code or specification of the component fall into this category.

- *Build time-coupling*. Here the reusable component is part of the build specification, and the build tool fetches the component automatically each time the system is built. Build time reuse is reuse *as is*—the component is never changed. Any variability is managed by narrowing, configuring or parametrization, using techniques such as inheritance, pre-processors, configuration management systems and libraries. This form of reuse is similar to the use of an interface from the layer below.

- *Run-time coupling*. Here we can change the component as the system is running, in the same way that we can change a car from a person carrier to a cargo carrier by folding down the rear seat. Run-time coupling is quite common in telecommunication and other real-time systems where it is very expensive or unacceptable to stop and restart a system. Dynamic link libraries are a special case of this technique.

The two dimensions of *how* to represent generality (widening, narrowing, isolation, configurability or using generators) and *when* to represent generality (development, build and run time coupling) can be combined quite freely. Different combinations are sometimes used within the same reusable component for different requirements, giving considerable design freedom.

7.5 How do you develop *for* reuse?

How should you develop reusable components? We have argued that development *for* reuse is independent of both component size (the structural dimension) and life cycle phase (the abstraction dimension). We have also found that a component can have different degrees of generality. This means that we can try to identify the steps in a general development process for reuse independently of:

- where the component is in the system structure, for example an entire system or a single class

- what kind of development model we use to represent the requirements and solution

We list below the steps we have found necessary to follow in development for reuse. The resources we put into each of these steps depends on the size of the component:

1. Capture the initial requirements, collecting the set of requirements to make an initial solution.

2. Define an initial solution or identify previous solutions to the same set of requirements. It is best to keep the solution in a form that customers can understand and validate. In the case of re-engineering, the result of this step should be the identification of previous solutions. A cost estimation for developing the actual solution should be made or

updated at this time.

3. Identify possible generalizations. This is the inventive step in which we try to see the generality in our requirements and our solution, based on both the requirements and the initial solution. At this step the component's reuse potential should be discussed with the product management and the plan for following steps should be refined.

4. Identify potential reusers and collect their requirements. Potential reusers are important to ensure that the generality we include in our component is really justified.

5. Estimate the cost and benefit of added functionality. For each added requirement we must estimate:

   — the benefit for reusers who will use it

   — the extra cost (e.g. time to understand, remove) for reusers who do not need it

   Each potential reuser should also estimate the effort needed to develop the functionality he needs from scratch, and the probability that he will reuse the component.

6. Analyze the added requirements with respect to invariants and variation. This is the step that involves making a requirements hierarchy such as that illustrated in Figure 78. The hierarchy usually impacts the initial solution, and we should therefore be prepared to modify it if necessary.

7. Propose a generalized solution with specializations and cost estimates. Here we reconcile the different requirements into one solution by applying techniques to represent generality from the appropriate models.

8. Present the solution to reusers and reuse experts for validation and approval. Each reuser must ensure that the solution covers his requirements. He should also refine the estimate of how much it will cost him to reuse the component. The reuse expert's role is to ensure that the solution is satisfactory, to check that the proposed specializations are appropriate.

   Based on this input, we can decide if we will develop the component for reuse. All the estimates made during the analysis of requirements and solutions should be saved to enable comparison with actual data (see Chapter 4). Note that this step is taken before we start the bulk of the development effort.

9. Develop and document the solution. This is the final step where we implement the component or system. If we are developing a high-level component (Figure 76) we may repeat this process for reusable subcomponents. We discuss the documentation needed separately in Section 7.7.

These steps are generic and can be applied at any stage in the development process and system structure. They do not necessarily form a strict sequence: we may iterate over steps 4 to 8 several times.

We frequently observe that this more elaborate analysis process can be profitable even if we choose not to develop the component for reuse. For example the search for a more general solution and the study of other potential reusers can uncover hidden requirements from the original customer, lead to a more complete and adequate solution, and avoid costly changes later in the development or maintenance phase when problems arise due to missing functionality.

7.6 How do you develop *with* reuse?

We can identify some generic activities in development *with* reuse just as in development *for* reuse, regardless of component, model or type of artifact reused. These are listed below:

1. Identify the components needed to build the application and which could be reused, derived or adapted from existing reusable components[1].

2. Formalize the requirements for these components in terms of search conditions, and search for candidate components. The search for components can start as soon as we have some idea of the needed functionality. Early retrieved components can serve as a basis for refining the requirements.

3. Evaluate the retrieved candidates. During the analysis phase it may be possible to negotiate requirements with the customer—if the customer can save 90% of the cost by sacrificing 10% of the functionality, he should at least be aware of the option. It might also be that the retrieved components provide some functionality which the customer might want in addition to the functionality he has specified.

4. Choose the best candidate and investigate the chosen component thoroughly. Detailed understanding may lead you to reject the chosen component and consider another candidate.

5. Adapt the component if necessary, and integrate it (possibly with adaptation) into the application.

Steps 2, 3 and 4 may need to be iterated until we find a suitable component. For subcomponents, these activities can be run in parallel with the search and adaptation of the component. For example, we may know that we need a graphical library, and start searching for it immediately.

Even though we talk about a customer and an application as if they were the end customer and the entire application, these steps are equally applicable at any level of the system structure. The customer for lower-level components will be the designer at the level above the component.

Even if we decide not to reuse any component after evaluating several potential candidates, we probably gain from the experience by discovering hidden customer requirements and using retrieved components as prototypes. Chapter 4 discusses a proposal

---

1. These components can be of several types: 1) Specific components which can be reused as is, 2) General components which must be specialized or 3) Libraries or other configurable components.
Note that in some cases (e.g. in a mature domain), guidelines, standards and application generators may be of benefit, but here we mainly deal with components which will compose the application.

to quantify this effect and how to estimate the benefits of reuse concerning productivity, quality and lead time.

To evaluate the reusable components and the search mechanism, the search condition and the retrieved and evaluated components should be recorded together with the reuse decisions and effort used to search, evaluate and understand the components. This subject is dealt with in more detail in Chapter 3.

We have treated development *for* and *with* reuse separately. This does not mean that we cannot interleave these processes—the opposite is usually true in a mature reuse process. We therefore regularly reuse components at a lower level while developing for reuse at a higher level, and we often isolate subcomponents for potential reuse while reusing a component.

7.7 How do you document a reusable component?

Documentation is the glue between the producer and the consumer of the reusable component. It is an important means for the producer to communicate the purpose of the component to the consumer. Documentation must be tailored to the process of development with reuse.

In system development we can distinguish between different forms of documentation:

- Engineering documentation (such as project plans, test plans, and so on). This is documentation produced during all development stages from analysis to test. This documentation is usually not part of the product documentation.

- Product documentation. This is documentation accompanying the product that contains information for those who will use the product after its release, such as users, system administrators, sales staff, and installers.

- Maintenance documentation which contains information (such as requirements and design specifications) for those who will maintain or evolve the product.

To enable reuse, some of the maintenance documentation needs to be converted to product documentation. Engineering documentation should also be made accessible so that later projects can learn from the experiences of those who built the product. When we introduce reuse the distinction between these three forms of documentation decreases.

From an analysis of the different steps of development with reuse described in the previous section, we can understand the need for specific reuse documentation better:

1. For *searching*. The reuse repository must be organized so that a suitable set of candidate components can be retrieved. As the reuser is likely to be searching for components early in the development process, his understanding of the requirements may not be so clear. The repository should compensate for this by providing possibilities for finding related components. Automatic retrieval systems such as those described in [Prieto-Díaz87], [Karlsson92] and [Sindre92b] are constructed for this purpose. Chapter 3

describes the classification approach recommended by the REBOOT project in more detail.

2. For *evaluation*. When a set of candidate components is retrieved we need to evaluate them to select one that we will try to reuse. For this purpose we need evaluation information. This should consist of one or two pages that describe the component and give an overview of its functionality.

3. For *investigation*. When we select a component we intend to reuse, we need to understand how to use it. This is like a user reference manual for the component, which can helpfully incorporate examples of use.

4. For *adaptation*. Many components developed for reuse are intended to be adapted before they are reused. The different approaches for representing this adaptable generality were described in Section 7.4, and should be reflected in the documentation:

— *Widening* does not constitute any problems in documentation.

— *Narrowing* relies on object-oriented concepts like inheritance and dynamic binding. We need to document the functionality of the abstract component, and then describe how it is supposed to be specialized.

— *Isolation* requires a combination of *as is* documentation and specific documentation for what needs to be provided.

— *Configurability* requires that we document the key mechanisms used to configure the components, that is, how the components are intended to be connected and communicate with each other, and which components can be connected together.

Documentation for planned adaptations is the most important for reuse at this stage. A component can also be modified more radically than the planned adaptations, if they prove insufficient for a reuser's needs. In such a case, an entire set of maintenance documentation is required to support this activity.

5. For *integration*. Here we need to incorporate the documentation of the reused component into our existing system. The reused component is going to be part of a system, and needs to be documented as such. When we develop the component for reuse by adaptation there are two alternatives for the product documentation:

— Prepare the documentation for incorporation in the system documentation. This means that the total life cycle documentation from analysis to test should be prepared for this adaptation, so that the component can be incorporated into the new application in the same way as a component developed from scratch. This is the traditional way to document maintenance and enhancement of existing systems.

— Prepare the documentation so that only the adaptations are documented. This means that we can reuse the general documentation *as is*, and add our adaptations as separate documentation.

The strategies to use will be determined by the type and scope of the reusable component. A component to be reused once with minor adaptations in a similar application will be reused more readily if the documentation of the adaptations is incorporated. Documenting just the adaptations is more suitable for a generally reusable component. The special object-oriented mechanisms of frameworks and inheritance fall naturally into the latter case.

It is also important to include any relevant negative information with the component, i.e. what lies outside the intended scope of the component. This information is acquired from the steps in points 5 and 8 of the development for reuse process described in Section 7.5.

7.8 How do you test a reusable component?

Testing a reusable component has to be performed by both the producer and the reuser of the component. The producer must check that the component is as adaptable as intended, and test the correctness of the component's general functionality. The reuser has to test the adapted and integrated component. The effort needed to reuse the component will be reduced if good test documentation is provided with the component.

For reuse *as is* the testing provided by the producer can be quite comprehensive. The component should be provided with a large set of test cases. Guidelines for integration tests should also be provided. The reuser should assure himself that this set adequately covers his use of the component, and optionally make and test additional cases.

For reuse with adaptations the problem of providing test support for the reuser is more difficult. Ideally we should prepare tests for the adaptations as we do for the component itself, as described in Section 7.4. Some ideas on how to prepare tests for different techniques are:

- *Widening*. Tests can be prepared as for a component reused *as is*.

- *Narrowing*. Tests can be prepared by allocating the general test cases to general components. How to provide abstract test cases which can be specialized together with the component should also be investigated.

- *Isolation* is similar to narrowing, where just the test cases for the adaptations are isolated.

- *Configurability* represents a challenge when it comes to testing, because it is difficult to deduce suitable system tests from test cases for individual components. The best solution is to provide guidelines and standards for testing the system that contains the component. These guidelines should include testing of any communication mechanisms the component provides.

7.9 How can you incorporate reuse in a development process?

An existing development process can be adapted to development *for* and *with* reuse by applying the general definitions presented in the previous sections. A development process can be characterized by the following facets:

- The models used to analyze the problem and express the solution.

- The various processes performed when working with the models.

- The documents or components where information about the models is stored.

- The roles involved in the processes, in particular those of the customers and the developers.

This section analyzes how to adapt each of these facets to incorporate reuse. It is a prelude to the following chapters of the handbook, which provide more detail and guidelines for using specific techniques in development *for* and *with* reuse.

The first question to be answered is "which type of component is going to be the most profitable for your company?". Having decided which component types should be made reusable, we focus on the reusers of these components. Their characteristics will decide the next two facets—which models and activities we should use to enable them to reuse the components. It is also possible to analyze this question from the viewpoint of development technology, by starting with the models and activities where we see the greatest opportunities for improving reuse capabilities.

Components

There may be opportunities for reusable components anywhere in the system structure, for example in the system, subsystems, modules and classes. For any particular development we have to analyze what system structure is used. Based on the system structure we can identify component types. In addition we need to ensure that the information provided with the components is appropriate for reuse:

- Do we have an appropriate abstraction dimension for each component, that is, do we have all the information we need from the requirements, the design and the coding for the component?

- Are the reusable component types properly isolated—do they have a well-defined interface to the rest of the system?

We must also evaluate whether the component types we currently use are appropriate for the kind of reuse we want to achieve.

Reusers

Types of reusers have to be identified at each level in the system structure. We have to identify potential reusers, and what kind of components they may be interested in. For these component types we have to identify the capabilities of the reusers who are going to adapt and integrate the components in new applications required. For example, will they be able to specialize a complex abstract class, or adapt the component to their development context successfully? The answers to such questions will guide the type of reusable component produced, and its associated documentation. They are important to allow us to produce reusable components that are suitable. If the reusers have little development experience, this fact should be taken into account.

Models

There are generally three different types of models used in development processes:

- *Requirements models* are used to capture and understand the customer's requirements, i.e. the problem domain. There can be several different models, each covering separate aspects or views of the system. Some examples are:
  - functional models covering what the system should do
  - non-functional models such as distribution models describing how the system is to be distributed, performance models, reliability models, and so on
  - sales models covering requirements for how the system is presented to the sales organization
  - maintenance models covering requirements for how the system is to be maintained

  These models must be enhanced to represent the variability in requirements, as described in Section 7.3.

- *Intermediate models* are used to transform the requirements models into something nearer the implementation model. An intermediate model is either a pure transformation of one model, or the merging of two or more models into one. Examples are a hierarchical decomposition with specifications of the subsystems, a transformation to a more efficient representation, and the distribution of the functionality in the functional model over the distribution model. These models should be enhanced to incorporate the different ways of representing variability, as described in Section 7.4.

- *Implementation models* are the final result of the system development. They usually consist of source code organized in some system structure with build information for deriving the executable code. In this model all the requirements expressed in the requirements models must be represented. Apart from functional requirements, the software must be distributable according to the distribution requirements, the sales organization must be able to present the different functionality, both core and optional, and the maintainers must be able to easily update and enhance the system.

The choice of models must be in accordance with the results of the analysis of component types, customers and reusers, and not just depend on the process model.

Activities

When we have identified the reusable components, who the reusers are, and how generality will be represented in our models, it is time to adapt the development process to take development *for* and *with* reuse into account. We then have to identify where in the process model the general activities outlined in Section 7.5 and Section 7.6 should be inserted to achieve development both *for* and *with* reuse.

7.10 Conclusion

In Chapter 7 we have proposed answers to some fundamental questions about software reuse. These answers result from work done within the REBOOT project, where we have been working with these questions while adapting different processes to development both *for* and *with* reuse. We have applied these principles by adapting several processes, including the Cleanroom development process [Mills87], an object-oriented development process, and a proprietary development process for telecommunication systems. This is described in detail in Chapter 12.

The important lesson we have learned is that development for reuse is complex. If making a good design is difficult, then making a good reusable design is even harder, and any amount of process description cannot substitute for the skill, imagination and experience of a good designer. A process can only support the creative work, and ensure that things are done and recorded properly.

8 Object-oriented Components, Techniques and Life Cycles

8.1 Introduction

The reuse approach relies on the concept of reusable software components produced and stored in a common repository. This section describes the different types of components involved, and presents specific reuse techniques. It describes an object-oriented life cycle model that can be used as a basis for defining the life cycles of development *for* and *with* reuse.

8.2 Types of object-oriented component

There are two main types of object-oriented components: *solution-based* inheritance hierarchies and *domain-based* frameworks.

A solution-based inheritance hierarchy is application domain independent and consists of a number of classes associated by inheritance. The abstract classes exist at the top of the inheritance hierarchy and the *leaves* are the concrete classes.

An *abstract class* is a class designed to be used as a template for specifying subclasses rather than objects. It has no instances and is only partially defined: it lacks implementations for some of its operations, though it may implement them as undefined operations. The subclasses, which have instances (concrete classes), must implement these undefined operations to complete the implementation.

Although there are several solution-based inheritance hierarchies available (see Figure 80), it is not an easy task to choose a class library for an organization. The choice partly depends on the compromises that the class library developers have made to satisfy a wide range of demands. The same drawbacks also hold for object-oriented frameworks.

However, most frameworks are developed in-house and for specific domains, therefore it is easier to give priority to different aspects. The most severe problem today seems to be that many solution-based inheritance hierarchies are not efficient enough to be used because they have too many internal dependencies, and the readability of the library is poor.

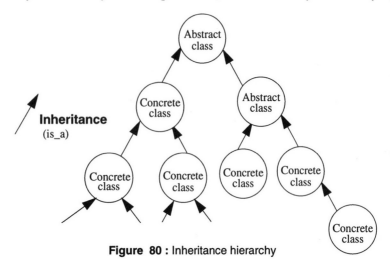

Figure 80 : Inheritance hierarchy

However, efficient class libraries are available. A common denominator among these seems to be that their classes are arranged in a "forest" structure. This means that there are several solution-based inheritance hierarchies in the class library. Some classes from different hierarchies may form aggregates, but they still do not capture the behaviour or functionality of an application in the same way as framework components.

An object-oriented framework (see Figure 81) is a type of class library with tightly coupled classes where the classes cannot be extracted from their context, and the whole framework must be reused as a component—although it can have optional parts that can be stripped out if necessary. *Messages* are extensively used in a framework, so the classes are not just associated by inheritance (using one or more inheritance hierarchies).

A framework describes how to implement all or part of an application in a particular problem domain. It is a general architecture for the domain and its classes describe the objects in the domain and how they interact. An *instantiation* of a framework is an ensemble of objects that work together closely to solve a particular problem. A framework should hide the parts of the design that are common to all instances, and make explicit the pieces that need to be customized.

The distinguishing feature of an object-oriented framework is that the flow of control between the framework and the application is bi-directional. A conventional base system is used by an application by issuing calls to library routines. Through the use of dynamic binding, the object-oriented framework can make calls back to the application. The framework may therefore include general functionality where only the details have to be specified by the application. In powerful frameworks, calls from the framework to the application are more common than in the other direction, something which has caused object-oriented frameworks to become known as "upside-down libraries"

Reusing a framework typically comprises two activities:

1. Defining the new classes needed

2. Configuring a set of objects

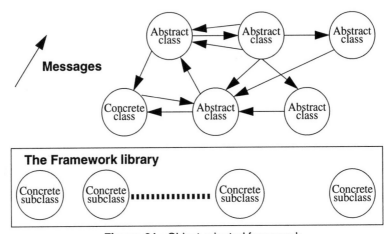

Figure 81 : Object-oriented framework

A mature framework will have a large library of concrete subclasses—the framework library. These classes can be specific to one or more applications. Frameworks by themselves are, however, seldom ideal and most applications must define new classes as well.

Some well-known frameworks are:

- The first implemented framework, the Model-View-Controller (MVC) [Krasner88]. MVC is a user interface framework written in Smalltalk. The terminology of frameworks and the underlying ideas were developed at Xerox PARC by the Smalltalk group.

- Choices [Campbell87]. This is an operating system framework written in C++.

- The user interface framework MacApp [Wilson90] for the Apple Macintosh. Using the MacApp user interface framework relieves the developer of much of the work of constructing the user interface for an application, and forces it to follow the Macintosh user interface style guide.

8.3 Object-oriented techniques and reuse

Traditional class-based object-oriented programming languages offer a given number of mechanisms that allow the user to develop reusable components. They may be differentiated by their usefulness as a support for specialization and generalization techniques. This section presents the fundamentals of object-oriented development with a focus on specialization and generalization for reuse. Chapter 10 covers some of these techniques in more detail.

8.3.1 Specialization

The inheritance mechanism supported by the object-oriented paradigm provides a powerful means to redefine the functions of a component when specializing for adaptation.

Inheritance mechanism

The inheritance relationship (as shown in Figure 82) is a structuring mechanism specific to object-oriented languages. It means that a new class is developed by stating how it differs from already existing class(es), and the new class inherits all properties—attributes and member functions—provided by its existing classes. A big advantage is that the existing class can be reused over and over again.

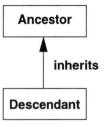

Figure 82 : Inheritance

The usual way to use inheritance is to define classes providing general services such as list manipulation, drawing objects, window display and so on, and to create more specific classes inheriting from these, or to enrich the base class with extra features.

A set of components can therefore be represented as a set of hierarchy trees, or *directed acyclic graphs* with multiple inheritance. When inheritance is properly used, classes in graphs are organized according to their degree of generality, with the most general classes at the top of the graph and specific classes at the bottom of the graph. Chapter 10 provides guidelines on how to do this. This kind of relationship is useful, as it enables developers to see how components are derived from each other. It is important to use inheritance to create new classes, as it allows a user to gain a better understanding of a class just by looking at the inheritance graph.

8.3.2 Generality

A component should be as general as possible to allow it to be reused over and over again. A general component can be more easily adapted to specific contexts. Generalization makes the components applicable to a wider range of applications, but it can require that they be factorized to separate independent design aspects. The following subsections describe how generalization can be supported by various features of object-oriented development, some pitfalls, and how avoid them.

Dynamic binding

This mechanism is used in object-oriented technology. Inheritance allows a reuser to redefine member functions of a component. Support for generalization makes it possible to create superclasses for already existing classes, enabling the creation of classes that describe commonalities among existing ones. The superclass comprises all the common properties of a set of classes, such as common member functions.

Of course many properties are not common, otherwise inheritance would not be necessary. For example, it is essential to be able to redefine member functions of a derived function, and to be able to invoke the correct redefined member function for an object if only its base type is known.

In C++, the mechanism for this is to address an object through a pointer, which provides a reference to the object. The pointer is declared to be of type *pointer (reference) to base class* and the relevant base class member function is declared as *virtual*. A C++ reference manual such as [Stroustrup90] can provide a more complete explanation. A virtual member function indicates that if the member function is called for an instance of a derived class that is only known as being an instance of the base class, the member function of the derived class is called. If the member function is not redefined in the derived class, the member function of the base class is called.

In the case of a call to a member function through a pointer to an instance, the underlying mechanism (*late binding*) generates a small execution overhead. Most of the time this is negligible in comparison to the power that the virtual member function mechanism provides.

Each virtual member function declared in a base class should also be defined with a default body. This ensures that the derived class does not necessarily have to redefine the member function if the default member function satisfies its needs. The base class member function can also be defined as abstract *(pure virtual* in C++*)* if it must be redefined by the derived class—this occurs if no default body can be specified.

Extra parameters and constants

Each constant (numeric or string) in the body of a member function is by nature an implementation constraint for the component. Such a constraint can be relaxed by allowing the reuser of a class to modify the value of the constant easily. This is possible by passing the value for the constant as a parameter to the member function, or by defining the value as a constant, if possible at the component level. A default value can be given to a constant passed as a parameter.

Even if constants are still embedded in a class, they must be able to be easily located and modified. However, all constants in the code might not need to be replaced by parameters or by constants at the component level. Only constants whose values might need to change should be treated like this. For example, constants in formulas cannot always be changed as the formula might produce invalid results.

Parametrized programming

Parametrized programming is a powerful technique for the reliable reuse of software. In this technique, modules are parametrized over very general interfaces that describe the properties of an environment that are required for the module to work correctly. Parametrized programming increases reusability, but moves reusable components away from their end-users (a specific "deparametrization" layer must be provided with each reuse).

The basic idea of parametrized programming is to maximize program reuse by storing programs in an as general form as possible. It is then possible to construct a new program module from an old one by just instantiating one or more parameters. The process of parametrization turns a procedural interface into a functional interface. The higher a function is located in a call hierarchy the more parameters it accesses. The main function of a program will have parameters for all global data of the entire program. Parametrization therefore violates all the principles of data abstraction. Hidden design decisions are made visible throughout the direct and indirect accessing functions.

8.3.3 Using both generalization and specialization

To determine superclasses, common properties of object classes have to be detected, combined and moved to a superclass. If we are comparing two classes that only share one property, the superclass would only have that property. For example, a class *animal* with four legs and a class *chair* with four legs share the property of having four legs, and so a superclass derived from that property would seem to be a class comprising all things that have four legs. This is obviously not right—the superclass should not be so general that it becomes meaningless.

Suppose that we look at an object class *car* and an object class *van*, then we could define a superclass *automobile with four wheels*. Comparing a car with two mirrors and a van with two mirrors should result in a class of four-wheeled automobiles and not in a class of automobiles with two mirrors.

This example demonstrates that if we try to construct superclasses out of their subclasses, we have to consider carefully which classes to compare. The number of classes to be compared, and possibly a predefined number of classes that should share some members to build a superclass, will influence the appearance of the superclass.

The generalization and specialization mechanisms allow the user to adapt a component after the high-level phases of software development, at least as low as the general design phase. This phase provides a first set of high-level classes, making it possible to carry out a first set of adaptations to the class hierarchy.

8.3.4 Other mechanisms in object-oriented programming

Extension

Extension can be viewed from two different aspects. The first is inheritance structure, in which new classes can be created and inherit the features of the abstract class. The second is that new instances of a class can be created that can be used to communicate with other objects in the system. This can be done easily, since other objects will not be affected by the new object. This makes it easier for the reuser to adapt and extend a component.

Association

The *association* relationship is present if a member function uses another class and has neither an aggregation nor a generalization/specialization relationship. An association can be viewed as a client-server relationship.

Aggregation

Aggregation is a strong form of association in which an aggregate object is "made of" components. Components are "part of" the aggregate. The aggregate is semantically an extended object that is treated as a unit in many operations, although physically it is made of several lesser objects [Rumbaugh91].

Polymorphism

Polymorphism means that an object which sends some stimuli does not have to know the receiving object's class. In other words, the caller provides only a request for a certain event, while the object that receives the call knows how to perform the event.

Abstraction

Abstraction means that aspects that are important for some purpose are isolated, and aspects that are currently unimportant are suppressed. By using abstraction, the freedom to make decisions is retained for as long as possible. For example, in system development the focus is on what an object *is* and *does*, while the implementation decisions are handled later in the development [Rumbaugh91].

Encapsulation

Encapsulation consists of separating the external aspects of an object that are accessible to other objects from the internal implementation details of the object, which are hidden from other objects. This ensures that only methods on the class should access its implementation [Rumbaugh91].

8.4 The object-oriented life cycle

8.4.1 Introduction

When describing an object-oriented life cycle that includes reuse, it is more profitable to adapt an existing software development life cycle (see Figure 83) to the development of reusable components and to their exploitation, rather than develop one from scratch. The generic and classical object-oriented life cycle we start from is derived from existing object-oriented methods including that of Booch [Booch91], the Shlaer and Mellor object-oriented method [Shlaer88] and the *Object-oriented modelling and design* method by J. Rumbaugh [Rumbaugh91].

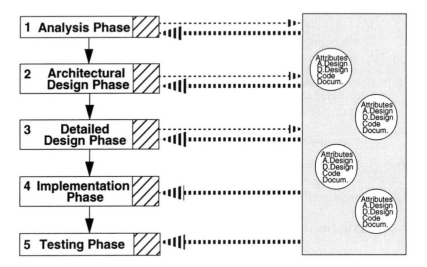

Figure 83 : The development life cycle

8.4.2 The analysis phase

The analysis phase is the starting point for classical software development. The main goal of the analysis phase is to define the requirements from the point of view of the subsequent clients or users. The requirements analysis is concerned with the performance, quality, and behaviour of the software to be developed, and also with the environment into which the system has to be embedded.

In the analysis phase a formal model is developed from the client's requirements. The closer this model is to reality, the easier it is to trace the real-world structures in the software and to integrate changes and extensions in a natural way. The result of the analysis is a description of the system that is abstracted as far as possible from the environment in which the system will be implemented.

The analysis activities should produce both *data* and *dynamic* models of the requirements. In the data models, the system and its environment are organized around objects. The resulting models describe the objects of the system, their attributes, and the relationships between the objects. The dynamic models describe the interaction between objects and the time-dependent behaviour of the objects and the system.

The analysis process can be described as shown in Figure 84.

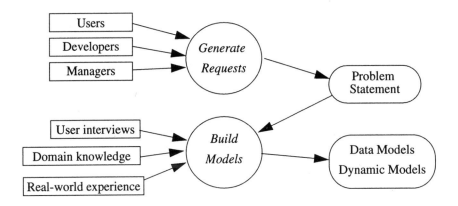

Figure 84 : Overview of the analysis process

The data modelling step

The first problem in data modelling is to identify the concepts and map them to objects. This can only be done from practice and experience. Various object-oriented analysis (OOA) methods exist and offer guidelines to help identify the different elements of the system. That proposed by Shlaer and Mellor suggests focusing on the question "What are the objects in the problem?" and observing the following aspects:

— Physical entities: these are the manipulated objects of the system

— Roles: these represent all roles played by people or organizations

The dynamic modelling step

Dynamic modelling is a description of aspects of a system concerned with control, including time, sequences of operations, and interactions of objects. Aspects to consider are:

• *Incidents*. Incident objects are used to represent an occurrence or event; something which happens at a specific time.

- *Interactions.* Interaction objects generally have a transaction or contract quality, and relate to two or more objects in the model.

The dynamic modelling step can be formalized by using different templates:

- The *state diagram* describes the behaviour of a single class of objects, but can also be used to model the behaviour of a system and subsystem. It represents a succession of *states* connected with *events*. An event is something that happens at a point in time and that triggers switching from one state to another.

- Another type of diagram describing the dynamic behaviour of the system is the *message diagram*. It represents the exchange of messages between different objects.

Use cases

Another OOA method is that proposed by Jacobson [Jacobson 92]. He starts by focusing on *use cases* (similar to the dynamic modelling). When a user uses the system, he performs a sequence of transactions in a dialogue with the system. This sequence is a use case. Jacobson differentiates between what exists outside the system (actors) and what should be performed by the system (use cases). When the systems behaviour has to be changed, the appropriate actor and use case is remodelled. After finding all the use cases, the focus is shifted to finding the objects needed.

By using this approach, the objects that are really needed are found, instead of finding all possible objects (both necessary and unnecessary ones).

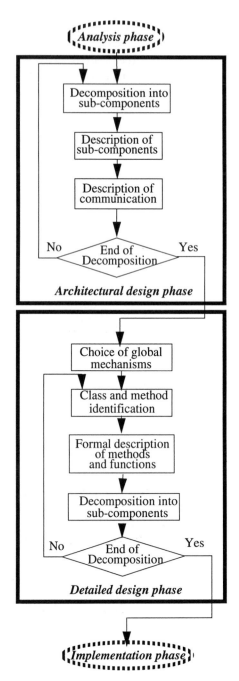

Figure 85 : The stages in object-oriented analysis and design

8.4.3 Object-oriented design

This section describes a model of an object-oriented design process, that will be used as a basis for describing the integration of reuse activities. During the design, decisions are made about how the problem will be solved. This is done at a high level and at increasingly detailed levels. The design process is divided into two phases:

— the *architectural design* phase
— the *detailed design* phase

These are illustrated in Figure 85.

During the architectural design phase, a high-level description of the application is made based on the application specifications. The application is split into sub-components with a description of the communication between them. During the detailed design phase, these components are mapped onto classes, and then fully defined during the implementation phase.

The architectural design phase

In the architectural design phase, application specifications are translated into high-level components and the communication between them is defined. It is in this phase that the overall structure and style of the application is decided upon.

The first step in the architectural design is to divide the system into subsystems. An application is often divided according to its data and functionality. This decomposition provides subsystems, and each subsystem encompasses aspects of the system that share some common property—similar functionality, the same physical location, or execution on the same kind of hardware. Since the specification of the application is not necessarily object-oriented, we are not always able to map its results directly onto the design (the process of identifying objects). The following three steps are applied to each identified component (object or subsystem) that is considered complex enough to warrant it, the first component being the application itself. The steps of architectural design are:

* *Decomposition into sub-components.* In this step, the component is decomposed into smaller sub-components. Either a sub-component is identified as an object, or it is considered as a subsystem, where parts of the component can be identified as corresponding to a functionality or a set of functionalities that the component must provide.

* *Description of sub-components.* In this step, each sub-component (object or functional sub-component) identified is described.

* *Description of communication.* In this step, communication between all sub-components is specified. A message expresses a directed interaction between two components.

The decomposition process ends when the designer has identified all the objects that describe the system without considering target language features.

The detailed design phase

In the detailed design phase, all components which have been identified during the architectural phase are formally described and refined if necessary. This phase includes the following four steps:

- *Choice of global mechanisms.* Since the detailed design of several subsystems can be done simultaneously by several teams, all common choices must be made at the beginning of the detailed design phase. The most common example of a global mechanism to be determined at this stage is to decide how to handle *collections* of components, since the concept of collection of components does not directly belong to the programming language. For object-oriented languages, implementing such a collection as a specific class is one option, for example the classes *Bag, Stack* ... in the National Institute of Health Class Library. *Genericity* can also help to define such collections. Any other classes implementing global mechanisms must be identified, such as mechanisms to store meta-information about classes, mechanisms for persistency, for memory management and so on.

- *Class and inheritance identification.* Similarities between the objects from architectural design are studied, such as similar concepts and similar services provided. This must be done so that similar objects can be defined as instances of the same class. During this step, all classes of the application as well as the inheritance relationships among them are described. Each class is formally described by means of attributes, methods and so on.

- *Formal description of methods and functions.* Here, all functions of a subsystem and all methods of objects are formally described by specifying their interface using the target programming language syntax. Their dynamic semantics, such as pre/post conditions, class invariants and concurrency properties, and body are also described.

- *Further decomposition into sub-components.* Some components need to be further decomposed, and this leads to the identification of sub-objects. This step is similar to the architectural design phase, since objects are first identified and then their interaction is described.

The transition from architectural design to detailed design

The boundary between architectural design and detailed design phases is not straightforward. Only general rules can be given for evaluating when the architectural design phase can be considered as finished and when the detailed design phase shall begin, as shown in Figure 85.

All concepts used by the end-user to describe the application must have been identified during the architectural design phase. New components identified during the detailed design phase are only for implementation purposes.

The general design phase is done by one team having an overall view of the application, whereas the detailed design phase may be done by several teams working in parallel on different high-level components. The description of each component must therefore be sufficient to allow it to be designed without the knowledge of the other components' descriptions apart from their interfaces.

8.4.4 Implementation phase

The implementation phase follows the detailed design phase, when all components (in this case classes with their attributes and methods) have been identified and described using the target programming language. During this phase, the programmer or programming team has to map all components onto the target programming language.

The input to the implementation phase is a detailed description of the component classes, interfaces and external definitions specified within the formalism of the target programming language. The output of the implementation phase is a set of implemented components ready to be tested.

There is no strict boundary between the detailed design, implementation and testing phases since inconsistencies discovered during the implementation phase require a return to the detailed design phase. On the other hand, components are often tested during the implementation phase rather than just at the end.

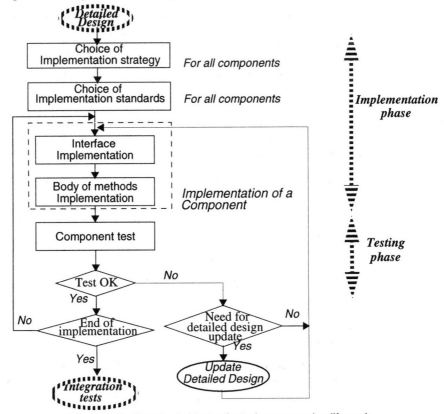

Figure 86 : Standard object-oriented programming life cycle

A general way of implementing an object-oriented application composed of a set of classes is graphically described in Figure 86. The testing phase appears on the figure to show the possible loops with the implementation phase.

The implementation phase is composed of the following steps:

- Choice of an implementation strategy

- Choice of implementation standards

- Implementation of components

The corresponding activities are discussed in detail below. Most of these activities are not specific to object-oriented programming, and are present in older standard programming approaches. However, we shall point out the specific features relating to C++ in these activities.

8.4.4.1 Choice of implementation strategy

The first programming activity step is the choice of an implementation strategy for sequencing the implementation of the components of the application. An application implemented using an object-oriented methodology is composed of many objects (instances of classes) working together at run-time. These objects are related in two ways:

- *run-time* dependencies (*use* relations, like operation calls or attribute use)

- *structural* dependencies (such as *subclassing* relations)

Both kinds of relations may influence the implementation sequence of the object classes composing the application. There are two major problems to cope with when implementing components in a random way:

- a component can only be fully tested when all components it calls or uses are fully implemented;

- there can be no high-level simulation of the application before all components are developed.

Two types of objects have to be implemented:

- basic *low-level objects* (like lists, stacks, dates…) which are used by many other objects and are quite independent

- complex *high-level objects* which use other objects to "sub-contract" part of the services they provide

The user can choose between a *bottom-up* or *top-down* implementation strategy. The first approach consists of implementing the basic components first and the second approach consists of implementing high-level components first.

- Bottom-up approach

  The *bottom-up* approach consists of developing low-level objects first. Low-level objects are often the most independent ones. Examples of such objects are Date, Time, List, String or components specific to an application domain, such as Complex and Matrix for mathematical applications. This approach favours *unit testing*, since the components are almost autonomous. It also favours the development of components shared among several programming teams working in parallel.

- Top-down approach

  The *top-down* approach consists of developing the high-level objects first. The high-level objects implement the main functionalities of the application, and usually sub-contract work to lower-level objects. This approach favours *prototyping* since the main functionalities of the application can be called at the beginning. However, high-level components depend on others that are implemented later and therefore they cannot be tested before lower-level components are tested. It is necessary to simulate calls to methods not yet implemented, or to implement a skeleton of the required components without the body of their methods. In this way, high-level components can be compiled and executed even if the objects they depend on are not yet implemented.

- Hybrid approach

  Both approaches present their advantages and disadvantages. The two approaches are independent: the application can be prototyped (a top-down development method), while low-level objects are being implemented or reused from a repository (simultaneous bottom-up development). They can therefore be combined to define a *hybrid approach* that provides greater freedom to plan and schedule the work.

8.4.4.2 Choice of implementation standards

During this step, all considerations common to the components are decided. This includes the following activities:

- Definition of coding standards

  Standard conventions for the target language must be defined or reused from an earlier project. These conventions include the definition of the structure of files, naming conventions and rules for use of language mechanisms such as references, in-line functions and so on.

- Debug and test policy

  Although not directly belonging to the programming activity but rather to the testing activity, the debug and test policy must be defined before the implementation of components starts. The debug and test policy defines the required coverage level for tests and how debug information will be included in components.

8.4.4.3 Implementation of components

In a programming language such as C++, the implementation of a component includes the following steps:

- Definition of the interface of a component

  The external interface of the component (i.e. its public methods and attributes) that was defined during the detailed design phase is completed to include the internal definition of the component (i.e. its protected and private attributes and methods).

- Implementation of methods

  The implementation of the methods of a component is done in an incremental way:

  — *skeleton implementation*: the method skeleton is first realized as an empty body with a correct return type.

  — *simulation implementation*: the body of the member function is implemented by simulating what the member function must really do. This simulated behaviour can be as close to the desired behaviour as is practical.

  — *full implementation*: the final phase is to implement the entire behaviour of the member function fulfilling all standards previously established.

These steps are normally followed by unit testing of the component in the test phase.

8.4.5 Testing phase

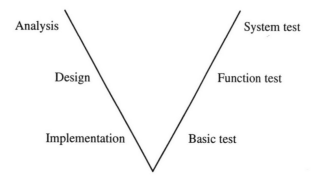

Figure 87 : V life cycle

In the classical V life cycle (see Figure 87), the testing activity recovers each phase of the development life cycle. Thus, the information developed during analysis and design phases is verified in the corresponding system and functional testing phases. It should be easier to handle and associate test information with a component in a reuse-based approach, as comprehensive documentation should have already been produced in the definition of the reusable component.

9 Object-oriented Development for Reuse

What is the best method of developing for reuse? Chapter 7 gave a general overview of the development for reuse process. This chapter proposes a method that addresses the development of *domain-based frameworks*, as this is the most complex object-oriented component. The method is general enough to make it suitable for the development of other object-oriented components.

The first section describes a development for reuse process (see Figure 88). The following sections present development guidelines for the analysis, architectural and detailed design, implementation and test phases.

The chapter presents a set of guidelines appropriate for development for reuse. The guidelines provided are divided in three categories for each phase. The first category addresses system development in general, the second category addresses object-oriented system development, and the third category is specific to development for reuse. The notation used in the chapter is taken from [Rumbaugh91].

Some parts of this chapter are not specific to object-oriented development methods, and most guidelines also apply to non-object-oriented development. The proposed method is not related to any specific object-oriented method.

9.1 The development for reuse process

9.1.1 Introduction

Development for reuse implies the analysis and formalization of domains that lack theoretical foundation, for example the domain of compiler design. The group dynamic technique we present in the next section is appropriate for such domains. The following sections discuss the other aspects of the development for reuse process:

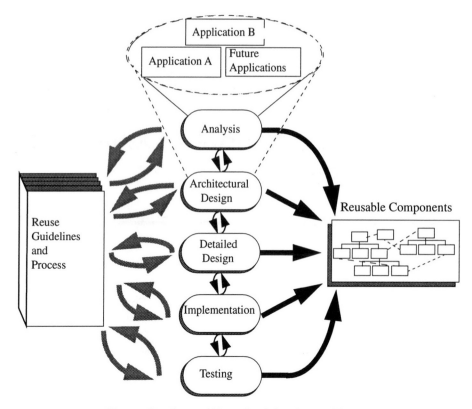

Figure 88 : General life cycle of development for reuse

- iterations between analysis and component development
- life cycle aspects
- development activities:
    — Defining the domain
    — Collecting applications in the domain
    — Analyzing sample applications and developing models and components
    — Preparing reuse support
- solution-based components
- adaptations of the object-oriented life cycle
- the maintenance process

9.1.2 The group dynamic technique

Interviews in isolation with a single domain expert are a slow and tedious method of analyzing or modelling a domain, and the result is only one person's view of the problem. What is really needed is a common view of the domain, or several common views where each view focuses on a certain aspect. Interviews are often sequential, and although they can be conducted in parallel, a lot of time will be consumed in the synthesis of model from the different experts. Collected facts may be contradicted or no longer valid at the end of a prolonged interview process. It is also time consuming to resolve incompatible views. The problem is highlighted in a development process for reuse, where people with different backgrounds will participate.

One solution to this problem is to let several people work together. The Swedish Institute of System Development, SISU, has developed a modelling process called group dynamic modelling [Willars91]. In this process, the model is developed jointly by all the people who would otherwise have been interviewed in one or more individual sessions (see Figure 89). The same approach is used in the technique known as *joint application design* (JAD) [Wood89]. It allows the model to be completed in a much shorter time, and any inconsistencies due to differences of opinion can be dealt with immediately.

One factor that makes this technique successful is that the base of participants is sufficiently broad to cover all the important aspects of the domain—managers, users, or people representing different products can all be involved at the same time. It is important to ensure that everyone present is actively participating and contributing. Notations used should therefore be very simple, or adapted to the modelling group. No observers should be present.

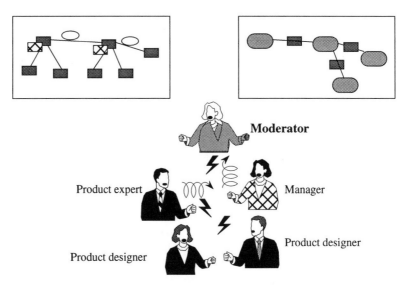

Figure 89 : A group dynamic modelling session

Allowing a group of people to work together on a single graphical model can be achieved by drawing the model on large plastic sheets, typically one sub-model on each sheet. To allow easy editing and rearrangement, the nodes of the model can be put on paper slips that are stuck to the plastic sheets. Arrows are drawn directly on the plastic sheet with a regular white-board pen. The size of the sheet makes the models more visible to all involved. It also stimulates creativity by requiring people to move around and actually pick up, touch and move elements of the model. Experience has shown that physical activity is so important that nobody should be allowed to sit during the creative parts of a session. Involving multiple senses in the creative process is achieved by using consistent colouring of the paper slips: one colour for concepts, one colour for properties and so on. This makes even complex models quite easy to read for experts and novices alike.

By far the most critical factor for successful modelling is the knowledge, experience and personality of the *moderator*. The moderator must maintain the rhythm of the session, by alternating between creative periods in smaller groups and analytic periods where the whole group listen to and discuss each other's results. The moderator must also be able to resolve quickly mistakes that beginners often make. A typical mistake is to confuse the name of a concept with what it denotes, which may lead to meaningless discussions about the proper name for the concept. Alternatively it may be that one name has been used for two distinct concepts, which sometimes can be resolved by a specialization/generalization manoeuvre.

The models used in SISU's method are usually used in business modelling, but are general enough to be used in the modelling of most problems. However, the models and notations used should not be regarded as fixed, but can be adapted to each organization and the phenomena to be modelled. When targeting reusable components, a conceptual model including inheritance should be used for analysis purposes, and class and object diagrams (at least) should be used for design purposes.

9.1.3 Iterations between analysis and development

Development for reuse does not imply a number of activities to be done in sequence, but rather interleaving activities that are iterated. This is particularly true when developing reusable domain-specific components.

The external view (requirements specification) and the internal view (re-engineering) of different applications are analyzed at several stages in the development process. The analysis effort is driven partly by new models, so the development activity starts from the beginning of the process. The development activities iterate between analysis models, designs and implementations. Reuse guidelines and success criteria enforce modifications of current versions of the components, which later affect the analysis of other applications.

It is an open question when the outside view, the inside view, or a specific level of detail of an application should be analyzed. However, it should be feasible to start the analysis and development process with the outside and inside views of two applications and a set of future requirements. This should be done without going into details except for the main function of the application, which should be dealt with in detail. In this way, the chosen models as well as the process itself can be assessed very early, and it will be possible to answer such questions as:

- Do the models describe the reuse aspects of the development adequately?

- Is the process cost-effective?

This approach also provides an early framework for all views of the domain, and the most important parts (the main function of the family of products) will be stable first.

9.1.4 Life cycle aspects of development for reuse

Development for reuse is not an activity that is part of the classical development life cycle. Even if analysis, design, implementation and testing are activities in the development of most pieces of reusable software, development for reuse should go on in parallel with the software life cycles of a company's products. Development for reuse interacts with all projects. This interaction results in development of new reusable components, modified components, and so on, as shown in Figure 90.

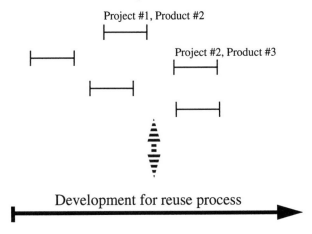

Figure 90 : Development for reuse process

9.1.5 Domain analysis in development for reuse

Domain analysis is the identification of classes and objects that are common to all applications within a given domain, or to related parts of the same application. In [Berard93], a set of activities for domain analysis is presented; these are also discussed in Chapter 8. We used this set of activities as a basis for extension to include development for reuse. The resulting development process for object-oriented domain-specific reusable components comprises the following activities:

- Defining the domain

- Collecting applications in the domain

- Analyzing the applications in the domain and developing models and components

- Preparing reuse support

These activities are not intended to occur in a strict sequence, but rather iteratively. The sections that follow describe the activities in more detail.

Defining the domain

The objective is to define the domain as narrowly as possible, but still keep relations to adjacent domains visible. Domain-specific components should be kept separate from product-specific components and general-purpose components.

The domain models may include textual, graphical and executable models. These models should explain and describe the domain and the relations between different components. The main models should be organized around objects. The domain models do not have to include all types of components, but should focus on domain entities and key domain artifacts. However, all types of components to be used in the domain must be identified and characterized. Taxonomies, quality and reusability requirements, should also be decided on.

Collecting applications in the domain

Reusable information can be found in old products. Specifications, analysis, designs, code, test cases and so on of old and often non-object-oriented software provide potentially reusable components, albeit with the effort of re-engineering. This re-engineering may include removal of domain-specific dependencies from general-purpose components, and product-specific dependencies from domain-specific components. These activities must be cost-effective. The developers must assess whether it is worthwhile to analyze the applications. Poorly documented, unstructured and uncoordinated applications are not likely to produce many reusable components. Very old applications might not be representative of current or future practices.

Future applications in the domain must also be investigated. New requirements might yield new domain abstractions and identify needs for new solution-based components.

Analyzing sample applications and developing models and components

During scanning and documentation of old products or off-the-shelf software, different models of the domain as well as reusable components are developed. Analysis models may serve as domain models as well as reusable components, as illustrated in Figure 91.

Analysis of user requirements yields a set of models that capture different views of a system, the environment of the system and the requirements that the system must fulfil. Some organizations use only informal textual descriptions, but reuse aspects can still be taken into account. For object-oriented software development, which uses classes as the

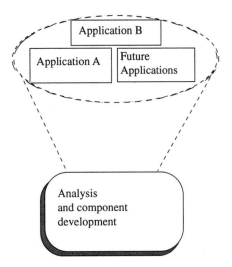

Figure 91 : Collecting applications

primary building blocks, a crucial part of the model should describe the concepts people use within the domain. The conceptual model should include inheritance, to allow commonalities in the concepts and static structures of the applications to be captured.

Process models and functional models can capture dynamic views, representing the behaviour or the functionality of a system. These models often allow decomposition of the specification into several levels of detail. Commonalities in the behaviour or functionality of the products can then be captured at the higher levels in these models. Also informal textual specifications can be adapted to facilitate reuse. Different requirements and descriptions can be separated into different views and different levels of abstraction.

Models used to support reuse and the increasing number of applications, future as well as existing, drive the process of development for reuse. In this process, the people involved must identify common requirements, domain abstractions, behaviours, and so on. The resulting models must clearly separate the invariant parts—the parts likely to remain unchanged between reuse instances. We call this a *variability analysis*.

The analysis models are the main input to the design and implementation process for reuse. Genericity and high-level abstractions, captured in the analysis models, must be retained in the design and implementation. If the first phase focuses on real-world objects and relationships, this second phase should focus on the software inventions or components used in existing products.

The models used in existing object-oriented design methods, such as class hierarchies and object models, are necessary but should be improved in development for reuse. For example, in an object-oriented framework much behaviour is captured in abstract classes and their interaction. The models used in the method should be extended to capture such relations as well.

Extended design models should be used when analyzing the design and implementation of existing applications. The development process is driven by these models, the increasing number of applications and level of detail, in the same way as the analysis process. The following activities take place in the development for reuse, as a minimum:

- identification of candidate reusable components

- identification of variations, specializations, generalizations, configurable parts, etc. of the component

- re-engineering to increase the reusability of the components using development guidelines

- documentation and re-engineering the component to fit in the extended design models

Preparing reuse support

The reuser must have some guidance concerning reuse of the components. These guidelines should help to decide when to reuse a component and when not to. They could also state a specific order of activities to be carried out when a component is reused. Especially complex components such as object-oriented frameworks should be accompanied by such a description. A "reusers' manual" is useful, and should describe how to adapt and configure the component or components to different requirements.

The development process should also include some acceptance criteria reflecting a reuser's point of view. The following is a check-list that covers some typical acceptance criteria:

- All "expected" application analysis models should be extracted or developed with reuse of the generic models.

- All "expected" application designs and implementations should be efficiently extracted or developed with reuse of the generic specification and design.

- Invariant parts should be separated from variant parts in the analysis documents.

- Invariant parts should be separated from the variant parts in the designs and implementations.

"Expected" analysis models include existing as well as predicted variations of the applications in the domain. Only samples can be checked, but these criteria are still valuable. They also drive the development process.

9.1.6 Solution-based components in development for reuse

Applications in very different domains often share a set of similar software artifacts. These artifacts, or *solution-based components*, are independent of the actual domain and useful as building blocks for different implementation purposes. Some examples are container classes, classes for concurrency management, and so on.

The development process for solution-based components differs from the development process for domain-specific components in the following ways:

- Less effort is spent defining functional requirements compared to non-functional requirements.

- Most solution-based components are well known and do not require extensive models.

- Applications from a wide range of domains should be collected.

- The applications should be used to identify the needs and requirements for components rather than identifying new ones. However, some components will be found in the applications, e.g. components interfacing hardware and system software, and so on.

- Variability analysis does not really concern a component's functionality, rather non-functional requirements such as time and space.

Different domains may put different requirements on these common components. Examples of such requirements are:

- The components should be efficient, not only at run time, but also at compile and link time. Also the binary size is important.

- The components should be portable.

- The components should have consistent and complete interfaces.

- The components should have simple interfaces.

9.1.7 Adaptations of the object-oriented life cycle for reuse

An ordinary object-oriented life cycle (see Chapter 8) should form the basis for development for reuse. The following activities must be taken into account.

- Include variability analysis in the general analysis phase within the object-oriented life cycle. Model a wide variety of applications, not just one.

- Focus on objects in the general analysis and design phase from the start. This may inhibit early division into parallel work, but it will increase reusability in the long tun.

- Keep domain-specific, product-specific and general purpose parts separate as far as possible.

Both analysis and design should include models that support reuse. The design phase should be given more consideration than in ordinary development; for example, design prototyping should be included. Methodology support from a reuse expert may also be necessary in the design phase. Reuse guidelines should be added to each development phase. These guidelines are used to increase the reusability of the components. The reusability should be checked in reviews of each phase.

9.1.8 Maintenance in development for reuse

Reusers should give feedback on components, log component extraction and make requests for components that are missing, as this gives valuable information to the component developers and maintainers. Quality problems must be identified and dealt with both when developing new components and when maintaining existing components. Each reuser should be notified when a component is modified, and especially if faults have been corrected and new versions issued.

Modifications of a component's interface, semantics or re-organization of the components can be difficult to manage in ordinary projects. For example, a new version of a library is released, and maintenance of the old version ceases. A development project using the old version then faces the risk of finding faults in it during testing and of being forced to maintain it themselves. In a situation where all development is done in-house, this scenario can be avoided, but this implies a lot of work if the components are not stable.

Since some changes to the reusable components are so inconvenient to manage, they must be avoided as far as possible, preferably by ensuring high quality components with a high reusability. A common problem in object-oriented development is building a small general-purpose library and then using inheritance for code sharing when extending the library. Under these circumstances, it is very hard to understand how and why components are related, and it becomes very difficult to make modifications.

Recording a reuse history is important, to enable modifications or validation of quality models and reusability models, as well as for validation of development guidelines. It might be tempting to start modifying the old components, but as said before, this should be avoided as far as possible.

9.2 Analysis in development for reuse

9.2.1 Introduction

Developing reusable software for a particular domain requires a thorough domain analysis. The analysis should collect knowledge from different sources and produce a consistent and sufficiently complete model of the domain. Focus should be upon modelling the domain, not just an application within the domain.

9.2.2 Generalities of analysis

Traditionally, the only inputs to the analysis phase are requirement specifications for specific applications, either formalized or unformalized. With such specific input it is hard to produce a general enough basis for the subsequent design work. However, use of group dynamic techniques can dramatically improve the analysis outcome—these were described in Section 9.1.2.

The analysis phase should always be iterated, using the output as input for a second, third, fourth etc., analysis. This facilitates understanding of the domain, which is essential when producing reusable software. Examination of existing applications and standards within the problem domain provides a large part of the necessary input.

The output of the analysis phase can also be improved by reviewing the conceptual model. Experience has shown this to be a very good technique, as faults are detected and corrected, and not propagated to subsequent development phases. Results from the reviews can then be used as additional input in subsequent analysis iterations.

Analysis is not a mechanical process. It has no formal methodology, and requires human communication to clarify ambiguities and misconceptions. Some models describe a problem better than others, and different models satisfy the needs differently in different projects. Possible results from the analysis phase are:

- A conceptual model. This is the single most important model and should capture the key abstractions. Figure 92 shows part of a conceptual model from the Fire Alarm example described in Appendix A:

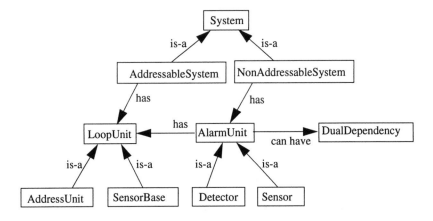

Figure 92 : Part of a conceptual model

- A preliminary design model. This is a refinement of the analysis models.

- A detailed requirements specification. This is based on the preliminary requirements and results from modelling sessions.

- A flow/concurrence model. Data flows between classes should be described in this model. Figure 93 shows the information flow for the Dual Dependency unit in the Fire Alarm example.

- A limitations/performance model. Performance requirements placed on the component should be described in this model.

- A goal model. No special notation is needed in this model—keep it simple.

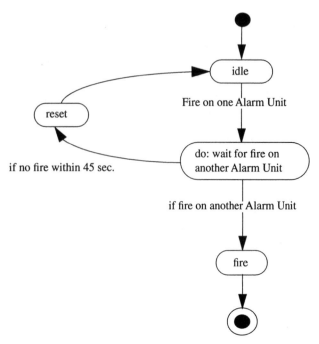

Figure 93 : State diagram for a Dual Dependency unit

- Other models. If the notation used does not describe the essentials in a satisfactory way, additional models may be used.

9.2.3 Steps and actions in analysis

Analysis is a seamless development process, iterative rather than sequential. There are a number of steps to follow:

1. Analyze the initial requirement specification received from the customer (if any). Read the specifications received from the customer to get an overview of what is to be done. Figure 94 shows an example.

2. Conduct a Group Dynamic Modelling session, see Section 9.1.2. Use an experienced moderator and make sure the group consists of differently skilled people. Possible outputs from this session are any of the models previously mentioned.

3. Write a detailed requirements specification. Extend the initial requirements using the results from step 2 if necessary.

4. Formalize and document the models from step 2. Use a notation that describes the essentials of the component in a satisfactory fashion. Documentation of the models is vital for the reuser.

Basic requirements

All fire alarm systems, existing as well as forthcoming, must be developed from a single base system. Our lead time and cost for maintenance must be decreased by more than 50%. The ultimate goal is to have zero defect software. In case of fire the fire brigade must be called within 1 second. The requirements must also be met using as little RAM memory as possible.

System 1 requirements

The system shall comply with the European fire alarm standard EN 54. It shall contain 1 fire brigade panel (FBP) but be expandible to 10 FBP's. Each central unit (CU) shall be able to handle 1000 sensors, detectors etc. Alarms shall be distributed to and presented on all central units. One of the CU's is the main unit. The others are slave units. In case of communication failure one of the slaves must automatically become the main unit. All faults must be detected and presented on diodes on all FBP's and on control panels (CP's). The system shall contain an external alarm transmitter. This device could have a service called alarm annunciation. When the alarm annunciation service is activated personnel are given 45 seconds to acknowledge the alarm and another 5 minutes to investigate the alarm. The fire brigade will not be notified within this time.

Figure 94 : Requirements specification from the Fire Alarm example

5. Exploit and refine the analysis models into preliminary design models. Translate and refine the analysis models using a suitable notation, preferably one that the developers are used to.

An analysis model will probably be incorrect after one iteration of steps 1 through 5. If a defect is found in one step, go back to the previous step or steps and correct it. This iteration is shown by the shadowed arrows in Figure 95.

9.2.4 General guidelines for the analysis phase

These guidelines are intended for use when performing analysis for reuse. Most of the guidelines are applicable in all object-oriented software development processes. All guidelines are important to reuse even if many of the guidelines are not reuse-specific.

Guideline 1 : Gather information from as many different sources as possible

A system based on the view of one person is not likely to fulfil the actual requirements, current or future. In order to obtain a stable component, the developers should gather information from as many different sources as possible. These sources could be the customer, external domain experts, other project members and so on.

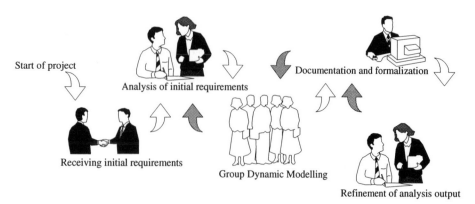

Start of project

Analysis of initial requirements

Documentation and formalization

Receiving initial requirements

Group Dynamic Modelling

Refinement of analysis output

Figure 95 : The analysis process

Reuse aspects

It is more likely that all requirements can be found and dealt with if several sources of information are used. This is a basic step in producing a component that is based on proper reusable abstractions.

Guideline 2 :   Capture all requirements as parts of the analysis models

The goal of the project is the fulfilment of functional and non-functional requirements, as well as visible and invisible requirements. Visible and functional requirements are usually found in requirement specifications and in group dynamic modelling sessions. Invisible requirements, which are often non-functional, might be harder to find.

In the goal model, which is a high level overview of requirements, all goals and their relationships should be clearly visible. This model should help to identify invisible requirements.

Reuse aspects

The complete understanding of requirements is essential in all software development projects. When developing for reuse, it is even more important to capture invisible and non-functional requirements, since these are often aimed at improving reusability of the component. It might sometimes be hard to express these requirements in words, hence the invisibility. Models describing the requirements facilitate understanding.

Guideline 3 :   Use a notation that is easy to understand

To minimize development time, errors due to misunderstandings must be eliminated. Use a notation that leaves no room for misunderstandings. One example could be different colours in the conceptual model to express concepts, relationships and characteristics.

Reuse aspects

In order to facilitate reuse of the component in the future, it is essential that the models are easy to comprehend for the reuser. When the component is used or altered, it is mainly the analysis models that are used to determine how to subclass or change the architecture.

Guideline 4 :   Present the models in a clearly visible way to all project members

This can be done by putting all models produced in the analysis phase on large plastic sheets on the wall. If group dynamic modelling has been used, this will already have been done.

Reuse aspects

It is vital to the project that all project members are motivated and feel that they are part of the project. Making it easy for project members to discuss and refer to the models, by presenting the models clearly, promotes quality and reusability of the component.

Guideline 5 :   Refine and formalize the analysis models

Use a notation that emphasizes what is important in the component, for example use a notation with clear flow models for action-driven components. Refine the conceptual model with respect to redundant classes, look for higher abstractions and so on.

Reuse aspects

Higher abstraction levels are likely to be found during refinement. The component is validated from a set of models—perhaps several conceptual models can be used as a basis for validation. This ensures that the best possible solution is used.

Guideline 6 :   Conduct a formal review of the outputs from the analysis phase

Errors discovered and corrected by project members in an early phase dramatically minimize development time.

Reuse aspects

A thorough examination of the analysis output may result in new, previously undiscovered requirements that have to be dealt with to obtain a fully reusable component. A review of the abstraction level might result in new, even higher abstractions, thus improving reusability.

9.2.5 Object-oriented guidelines for the analysis phase

Guideline 7 :   Use inheritance to express specialization on types

Using inheritance structures is an important reuse-promoting technique that supports extension and refinement. It can be directly applied to the conceptual model, promoting abstractions. Figure 96 shows an example of inheritance in the Fire Alarm example (see Appendix A).

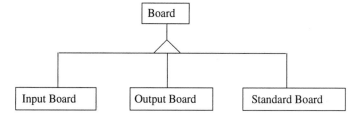

Figure 96 : Generalization/Specialization

Reuse aspects

Inheritance structures identified in early phases are likely to be problem-domain specific, contrary to solution-specific structures that are likely to be identified in later stages, and are thus likely to remain unchanged.

9.2.6 Reuse-specific guidelines for the analysis phase

Guideline 8 :   Analyze existing applications within the domain and identify commonalities

This guideline is especially applicable if the developers have little or no knowledge about the problem domain. Different solutions exist because different applications have been developed. Consult the customer and/or external experts to find the proper abstractions, and then put them in a general model.

A major problem concerning this guideline is the availability of applications. It may be that the developers have no access to the information needed to analyze the applications. However, this guideline should be applied if possible.

Reuse aspects

Proper abstractions are found more easily if existing applications are examined. Abstractions that are common in several applications may remain stable in the future. Existing applications can be used to model scenarios of events that can be used in a later stage to test the reusability of the component.

Guideline 9 :   Generalize in such a way that future alterations of the component are supported, i.e. introduce high level abstractions

The requirements placed on the component will probably not be stable. Requirements may change even shortly after the completion of the component, or while it is still being developed. High level abstractions give the component the desired extensibility.

Reuse aspects

Abstractions at a high level facilitate alterations of the component without having to restructure the architecture, merely by creating subclasses from it.

Guideline 10 :   Pinpoint variants among existing and future systems within the domain

Reuse aspects

Use of inheritance to point out differences between systems will force the analysis participants to focus on finding established, stable abstractions that will remain unchanged over a long period. The abstractions are also likely to remain stable when new systems are developed.

9.3 Architectural design for reuse

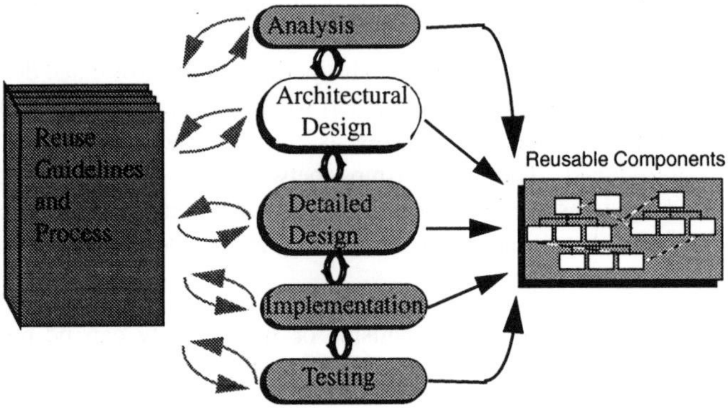

Figure 97 : The architectural design phase of the development for reuse life cycle

9.3.1 Introduction

In this section, architectural design for reuse is described by means of a set of development guidelines. The guidelines are applicable for object-oriented development; any ordinary object-oriented methodology or notation can be used when developing components. The guidelines presented positively affect both reusability and quality when combined with the development methods used in an ordinary system development project.

9.3.2 Generalities of architectural design

The architectural design focuses on system decomposition into subsystems. A subsystem groups several objects or classes, and may also include other subsystems. Subsystems may be used in both analysis and design/implementation. Object-oriented architectural design also comprises identification of classes and their main responsibilities and interactions.

One problem in the design phase is a rapid increase in complexity, due to an increasing number of classes, methods, attributes and so on. Subsystems are introduced to manage the system more abstractly. Through subsystem decomposition, a hierarchical structuring of the system is accomplished, with the system itself at the highest level. In this way, the complexity can be decreased, allowing the whole design of a large system to be grasped on a high level of abstraction.

Strong functional cohesion is an important property of a good subsystem. Here, *function* is an external description of the subsystem. It describes what the subsystem does, but not *how* it does it. A subsystem with strong functional cohesion is a subsystem that performs one function or provides one well-bounded behaviour [Booch91]. This function must be anticipated at a higher level of detail. The subsystem may be described as a set of more detailed functions, but these functions can only be described as one function at a higher level. A subsystem in an object-oriented design may be described in the same way as composed of a set of objects (and subsystems) with different responsibilities [Wirfs90], that is, knowledge to maintain and actions that can be performed. These objects collaborate to fulfil a greater responsibility or function.

The object is the primary abstraction in object-oriented development, and it is important to focus on objects from the start when structuring a system and its requirements. As many domain objects and classes as possible should be identified before subsystems are introduced. The relationships between the objects should also be identified before subsystems are introduced. A quick functional decomposition into subsystems at several levels allows early division of work among development teams. However, this approach has several drawbacks:

- similar classes, mechanisms or functionality can be built into different subsystems developed by different people, resulting in redundancy and unnecessary work

- strong coupling between subsystems, because it is hard to foresee all the interaction between subsystems at this stage

Even if we advocate a focus on objects and classes, it is not feasible for large systems to produce a detailed specification of all classes and objects before subsystems are introduced. Private responsibilities and method signatures, as a minimum, should not be dealt with before subsystems are introduced. In larger projects, a high-level decomposition may be necessary earlier. For instance, it may be feasible to define a subsystem at each logical node in a distributed environment. Existing products which may form part of the system may also encourage an early high level decomposition.

In [Jacobson 92], a set of criteria for selecting subsystems is presented:

- When a system is to undergo a minor change, this change should concern no more than one subsystem at the lowest level. This means that the criterion for subdividing the subsystem is predicting what the system changes will look like, and then making the division on the basis of this assumption. A subsystem should therefore preferably be coupled to only one user category, since changes are usually caused by a user category.

- Each subsystem should have high cohesion.

- The subsystems should have weak coupling—there should be a very limited communication between subsystems.

- Try to encapsulate optional behaviour or functionality into subsystems. A subsystem can be a compulsory unit, but it can also be an optional unit. Optional subsystems are not only those that are optional in a specific delivery or in a specific system or product. Anything that *could be* optional should be taken into consideration.

The criteria above are important for reuse. High cohesion and low coupling are properties which are desirable in any system. Optional subsystems are very important for reuse within a family of products. Possible combinations of optional functionality or behaviour should be supported by the reusable components associated with the family of products. The first step should therefore include identifying and subdividing optional functionality.

The different members of a family of products may address slightly different requirements. The differences that can be predicted should be supported by associated reusable components. Some requirements cannot be foreseen; this will cause changes in the reusable components or in the specific software for a product, or in both. Even if the precise changes cannot be predicted, it may be feasible to predict which objects or classes will be affected by a change. These objects and classes should be grouped together to minimize the effect of the new requirements.

In application projects we have observed that it is almost impossible to reuse a module or subsystem *as is* from old products in a family of products, because commonalities and specifics are mixed. Because of this, we always need to modify all modules or subsystems above the class level. If we think it is important to reuse products *as is* as much as possible, the products must have been divided into invariant levels instead. Of course, we must also develop for reuse. A prerequisite for reuse *as is* and any other successful reuse of complete modules is how well we separate independent aspects in the implementations. The extent to which we need to modify our reused modules depends on this separation. Such analysis should therefore be part of a development for reuse process.

Subsystems can be used as a tool for enhancement of an object-oriented design. We identify subsystems to simplify the patterns of collaboration among objects. Without such simplification, communication paths could flow from nearly any class to any other [Wirfs90]. The guidelines presented later in this section will explain how this simplification can be made.

9.3.3 Steps and actions in architectural design

This section presents some activities that should be common to architectural design in most object-oriented methods. These activities are based on the design method presented in [Wirfs90]:

1. Identify the objects/classes required to model the system. A lot of guidelines exist for identification of objects and classes, such as "Look for noun phrases in the requirements specification". Many objects may already have been identified in the analysis phase.

2. Assign system responsibilities to specific objects. This implies determination of the operations each object/class is responsible for performing, and what knowledge it should contain (see Figure 98). A common guideline here is "Look for verbs in the requirements specification". Another approach is to perform walk-throughs or scenarios of the system. These *use cases* [Jacobson92] start with some stimuli and should use as many system capabilities as possible. The places where something must occur as a result of input to the system should be recorded and the necessary actions should be identified. Note that private responsibilities should be deferred and no precise method signature should be used. The relationships between classes should also be examined. Identify generalization/specialization relationships ("Is-a" or "Is-kind-of") and move common responsibilities to the identified superclasses (see Figure 99). Differentiate between responsibilities requiring different implementation for each subclass and common implementations. Identify aggregates or containment

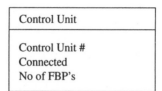

Figure 98 : Knowledge of the object and class

relationships ("Is-part-of" or "Has-a"). Figure 100 shows an example from the Fire Alarm system described in Appendix A. Some classes may contain other classes and have some responsibility for them.

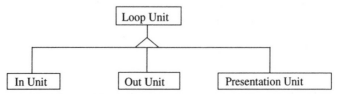

Figure 99 : Generalization and specialization

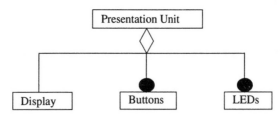

Figure 100 : Aggregation

3. Analyze how the objects work together. Look at each class and for each of its responsibilities decide if the class is capable of fulfilling the responsibility itself. If not, determine which other classes it can collaborate with. An object collaborates with another if, to fulfil a responsibility, it needs to send the other object any message. Use cases are also valuable in this activity.

4. Refine the inheritance hierarchies and collaborations. Look for objects and classes that share certain responsibilities. Determine if it is feasible to factor out these shared sets of responsibilities into superclasses. Distinguish between abstract and concrete classes. Abstract classes exist to factor out behaviour that is common to more than one class, and to put it in one place for a number of subclasses to make use of. Designs for a family of products will reveal more generalization and specialization relationships compared with a design for one system. In this stage it is also helpful to search for mechanisms common to different inheritance hierarchies that can be used for flexible communication between objects, such as an *event handler* class: see the fire alarm system in Appendix A.

Before subsystems are introduced in an object-oriented development we assume that at least activity 1, 2 and 3 have taken place, but subsystems may also be introduced after activity 4.

When a draft design consisting of objects and classes is ready, subsystems should be introduced. The paths along which information flows should be recorded as well as the frequency of communication. Classes which collaborate with everybody or nobody should be dealt with. Optional subsystems should be identified first. Classes that are likely to be changed at the same time are also candidates for subsystems. Look for strongly coupled classes. The coupling between two classes is a measure of how much they depend upon each other. A strong connection can be both a large number of different messages or one frequently used collaboration. All such groups of classes are potential subsystems. Additional requirements should also be fulfilled, for example the classes should work together to implement one unit of functionality or role, and the classes should form a meaningful abstraction. The coupling to other classes and subsystems should also be low.

The identified subsystems stress where the coupling should be low. It may be necessary to revise the first design to maximize information hiding and low coupling. The classes in each subsystem should collaborate with as few classes and subsystems as possible outside the subsystem. In addition, as few classes as possible in a subsystem should collaborate with classes and subsystems outside their subsystem. These basic rules apply at any level of the system organization. These guidelines imply that a class in a subsystem is less likely to be affected by changes to other parts of the system. This is also true for the subsystem itself.

It may be hard to decide to which subsystem a class belongs. One guideline [Wirfs90] is that a class is part of a subsystem only if it exists solely to fulfil the goals of that subsystem. For example, a subsystem for printing may consist of a *Server* class and a class hierarchy for different types of printers. The *Server* class may be implemented by using a class *Queue* for queuing purposes. The *Queue* class should, however, not be part of the subsystem, because instances of this class are, or could be, used by a wide range of classes outside the printing subsystem.

This method of decomposing a system into subsystems differs very much from ordinary decomposition, since it advocates a bottom-up rather than a top-down approach. In some cases, we may be forced to do top-down decomposition, but then we will be faced with a much larger uncertainty about the final modularity of the system. Even if the pace of a development project can be greater (due to parallel working) when early top-down subsystem decomposition is used, the modularity and the reusability of the system will be lower. We therefore recommend a bottom-up approach for the introduction of subsystems in a project developing for reuse. Since the architectural design has a large impact on reusability, it may also be valuable to try out different designs (design prototyping) and compare their reusability. Some design activities and results may be shared among the designs, such as the identification of objects.

Subsystems should be viewed as a component type. Other object-oriented reusable component types are concrete and abstract classes, class libraries and object-oriented frameworks. Subsystems extend the module concept. They should be viewed as an information hiding mechanism by treating them as an integral whole, or "black box". Just as classes can be general or abstract, we should allow a subsystem to be viewed as general.

In this way, we can use subsystems to describe object-oriented frameworks, for example, which are intended to capture the invariant parts of a design for a family of products.

9.3.4 General guidelines for the architectural design phase

The following guidelines are extracted from [Wirfs90] and [Jacobson92].

Guideline 11 :   Make optional parts of the system as subsystems

A subsystem can be a mandatory system unit, but it can also be an optional unit. Anything that *could be* optional should be considered for building as a subsystem.

Reuse aspects

Optional subsystems are very important to reuse within a family of products. Possible combinations of optional functionality or behaviour should be supported by reusable components associated with the family of products, because different combinations are likely to appear in requirements for new products.

Guideline 12 :   Distribute system intelligence evenly

A responsibility should be assigned to the class to which it logically belongs. However, in some cases, it may not be clear to which class the responsibility does belong. The developer should then establish a principle to determine how to distribute the responsibility, and follow that principle in the remainder of the design.

Reuse aspects

A very "intelligent" object knows and manages a lot of information, can do a lot of things and affect many other objects. Such a class or subsystem will be hard to subclass or adapt. Distributing the intelligence among a variety of objects allows each object to know about relatively fewer things. Such objects will be easier to modify. The only advantage of the procedural approach is that it may be easier to see and understand the control and information flow.

9.3.5 Object-oriented guidelines for the architectural design phase

Guideline 13 :   Make subsystems of strongly coupled classes that implement one unit of functionality

Making a subsystem of strongly coupled classes which implement one unit of functionality is a good way of managing the design at an abstract level.

Reuse aspects

Classes in the subsystem are likely to be affected at the same time and by the same change in requirements, and are suitable for reuse as a unit.

Guideline 14 :   Factor common responsibilities as high as possible in the inheritance hierarchy

If a set of classes all support a common responsibility, they should inherit that responsibility from a common superclass. Create a common superclass if it does not already exist and if a good abstraction can be found.

Reuse aspects

This guideline helps in finding the most suitable abstraction—no inadequate responsibilities are inherited, a few must be added and redefined. This means that more behaviour can be reused.

Guideline 15 : State responsibilities as generally as possible

Try to find a common way of expressing similar responsibilities. This may help in finding new abstract classes.

Reuse aspects

This guideline helps in finding the most suitable abstraction for reuse by inheritance.

Guideline 16 : Minimize the number of collaborations a class has with other classes or subsystems

Classes should collaborate with as few other classes and subsystems as possible. Fewer collaborations means that the class is less likely to be affected by changes to other parts of the system. One way to accomplish this is to centralize the communications flowing into a subsystem. You can create a new class or subsystem to be the principal communications intermediary, or you can use an existing one for the role.

Reuse aspects

This guideline implies that a class is less likely to be affected by changes to other parts of the system.

Guideline 17 : Minimize the number of subsystems

By properly encapsulating classes and subsystems within a subsystem, it becomes easier to manage complexity and adapt to change. A well-designed subsystem has a few classes or other subsystems that directly support its responsibilities, and a larger number of collaborations between internal classes and subsystems.

Reuse aspects

This guideline implies that only minor changes of the subsystem may be necessary when other parts in the system are changed, because only a few parts (classes, subsystems) are dependent on parts outside the subsystem.

Guideline 18 : Make subsystems out of classes which are likely to be affected by the same minor change in requirements

The members of a family of products address slightly different requirements. The differences that can be predicted should be supported by associated reusable components. Some requirements cannot be foreseen, causing changes in the reusable components or in the specific software for a product, or maybe in both. Even if the precise changes cannot be predicted, it may be feasible to predict which objects or classes will be affected by the same change.

Reuse aspects

Such objects or classes should be grouped together to minimize the effect of the new requirements.

9.3.6 Reuse-specific guidelines for the architectural design phase

Guideline 19 :   Create as many abstract classes as possible

See whether the classes might encapsulate behaviour that could be reused by existing and future subclasses. Look for common attributes and duplicated responsibilities. Look for further useful abstractions. If you don't have, or cannot foresee, at least two subclasses of a candidate abstract class, reject it.

Reuse aspects

This guideline helps in finding the most suitable abstraction—no inadequate responsibilities are inherited, a few must be added and redefined. Defining as many abstract classes as possible means you have factored out as much common behaviour as you could possibly foresee [Wirfs90].

Guideline 20 :   Introduce subsystems late in the architectural design phase

A quick functional decomposition in subsystems in several levels allows early division of work among development teams, but it has several drawbacks for reuse.

Reuse aspects

A more detailed class and object design allows a better division into subsystems. Subsystems could also be introduced for streamlining the communication between objects in the design. A very low coupling can be achieved in this way.

9.4 Detailed design for reuse

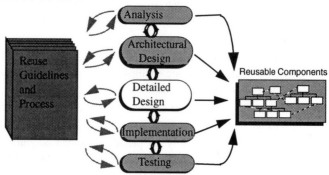

Figure 101 : The detailed design phase of the development for reuse life cycle

9.4.1 Introduction

In the detailed design phase, the class and its methods are constructed and defined. The guidelines presented in this section describe how to perform detailed design to make the components as reusable as possible. It is very important to consider reuse aspects when constructing classes and methods, since they are the interface to the component for the reuser.

9.4.2 Generalities of detailed design

Each of the following guidelines covers a specific aspect of the detailed design phase, but some common points can be identified:

- There are several advantages to introducing inheritance: the components will be smaller, easier to understand and to modify, and thus to reuse. Advocating that inheritance must be exploited more does not necessarily mean that a designer should develop a class hierarchy any further. In some cases a new inheritance hierarchy should be developed, and instances from the different class hierarchies can then work in collaboration.

- The protocol is the interface to the classes, the methods of the class that are public. By using a standard protocol, objects achieve a similar interface, i.e. the same method names.

- Polymorphism (described in Section 9.5.2) reduces the number of different interfaces that have to be taken into account. Standard protocols are not just important with respect to polymorphism, they also help when interconnecting objects, and can serve as a basis for a shared vocabulary among programmers.

- Large classes should be avoided. In some cases a large class models an abstraction that could be split into a number of new abstractions. In other cases, a large class should be transformed to a small inheritance hierarchy.

9.4.3 Object-oriented guidelines for the detailed design phase

Guideline 21 :   If general properties of some classes can be identified and viewed as making up a generalization or abstraction of the classes, create a superclass for this generalization, gathering the identified general properties using inheritance

This is a "bottom-up" guideline, used when generalizations are found during the construction of classes. However, the division into generalizations and abstractions of the structure is preferably performed in earlier development phases when the structure of the component is being developed.

Reuse aspects

By capturing commonalities in higher abstractions such as superclasses, subclasses can focus on differences. The reuser can then find the most suitable abstraction from which to inherit. If commonalities are not captured in higher abstractions, the reuser is forced to make large modifications and/or extensive redefinitions.

Guideline 22 :   Use multiple inheritance rarely

Multiple inheritance may cause difficulties when reusing the component. Most object-oriented languages have problems when managing multiple inheritance, especially if the inheritance structure is ambiguous. Referring to Figure 102, the problem then is that class D will inherit the methods from A twice, once from B and once from C. A solution to this problem is to make D abstract and overload the multiple methods from B and C. In the overloaded methods you should specify if you want to use the method from B or C.

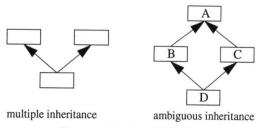

multiple inheritance   ambiguous inheritance

Figure 102 : Multiple inheritance

Multiple inheritance is not common in the real world and it is important to focus on modelling the real world. It makes little conceptual sense to imply that an object is an instance of more than one thing at the same time. If multiple inheritance is necessary, at least try to avoid ambiguous inheritance.

Reuse aspects

Inheritance structures will be simpler if multiple inheritance is avoided.

Guideline 23 :   If an operation X of a class is implemented by performing a similar operation on another class, then that operation should also be named X (recursion introduction)

Recursion introduction is important with respect to standard protocols, which in turn allow polymorphism to be used more extensively. For example, if a method *Draw* of class *Picture* is implemented by calling a similar method for classes of type *Shape*, the similar method for *Shape* should also be called *Draw*.

Reuse aspects

The reuser will only have to manage a limited set of method names and protocols, and can focus on functionality and/or performance aspects of similar components instead. It should also be easier to interconnect objects.

Guideline 24 :   One task – one method. Each method should perform only one task to keep it simple. For example, decompose a method called *put_and_print* into two methods, *put* and *print*

Reuse aspects

The protocol of the class will be easier to understand and thus to reuse.

Guideline 25 :   Subclasses should be specializations

Use of inheritance just to achieve code sharing should be avoided. Subclasses must be true specializations of the superclass. Misuse of inheritance will make maintenance more difficult and inhibit reuse.

Reuse aspects

The standard use of inheritance is to implement specialization relationships. In order to not confuse the reuser, other usages of inheritance should be avoided. When developing with reuse, code sharing is of more interest, but it should not be implemented by inheritance.

Guideline 26 :   The top of a class hierarchy should be abstract

The abstract class at the top of an inheritance hierarchy enforces the standard protocol and prepares for polymorphism. Only the leaves of a class hierarchy should be concrete.

Reuse aspects

It is often better to inherit from an abstract class than from a concrete class. A concrete class must provide a definition for its data representation, and some subclasses are likely to need different representations. Since an abstract class does not have to provide a data representation, future subclasses can use any representation without fear of conflicting with the one they inherited. Also, in a concrete superclass it is easy to make over-restrictive assumptions about specializations. If you find you need to instantiate a superclass, it probably indicates a fault in your design.

Guideline 27 :   Keep a small total protocol for a class

The total protocol for a class consists of all methods defined in the class and all methods inherited from its superclasses that are not redefined or overloaded. Classes should represent abstractions. If many different methods (say 25 or more, including the inherited methods) are available for the lowest class in the hierarchy, then it must represent a complicated abstraction. It is likely that such a class, and the other classes in the hierarchy, are not well defined and probably consist of several different abstractions. This hierarchy may be a candidate for several smaller and less complex class hierarchies instead.

Reuse aspects

It is hard to reuse large classes. It is easier to understand and modify or subclass a few smaller classes from different inheritance hierarchies instead.

Guideline 28 :   Keep classes small—avoid introducing too many methods

When a lot of new, rather than inherited, methods are introduced in a class within a class hierarchy, it is probable that the class can be divided into one superclass and one subclass, and that suitable abstractions can be found. It should be possible to find at least one more subclass if the division is to be maintained.

Reuse aspects

It is harder to reuse from a large class than from a small inheritance hierarchy where common behaviour is extracted to superclasses. The reuser can find the most suitable abstraction from which to reuse, requiring very few redefinitions and no unnecessary methods, by subclassing.

9.4.4 Reuse-specific guidelines for the detailed design phase

Guideline 29 :   Use abstract classes as far as possible in inheritance hierarchies

An abstract class is designed to be reused and acts like a template for concrete classes. It enforces the use of standard protocols and highlights the generalities in a class hierarchy. One way to increase reusability further is to use abstract classes on several levels of the inheritance hierarchies.

Reuse aspects

It is often better to inherit from an abstract class than from a concrete class. A concrete class must provide a definition for its data representation, and some subclasses are likely to need different representations. Since an abstract class does not have to provide a data representation, future subclasses can use any representation without fear of conflicting with the one they inherited. In a concrete superclass it is easy to make too restrictive assumptions about specializations.

Guideline 30 :   Class hierarchies should be fairly deep and narrow

Experience from systems developed today shows that class hierarchies are often too shallow and too wide. If there are more than ten subclasses directly below one superclass, it is recommended to look for a new abstraction level.

The disadvantage of having too deep a hierarchy is the difficulty of comprehending its behaviour, since the methods are spread in the hierarchy. When making a class hierarchy, the focus must be on modelling the real world and mapping the class hierarchy to normal abstractions. Each new abstraction level should add at least one new behaviour.

One way of starting the transformation of a shallow class hierarchy is to look for subclasses that implement the same method and then try to migrate the method to a new common superclass.

Reuse aspects

By capturing commonalities in higher abstractions (superclasses), subclasses can focus on differences. The reuser can find the most suitable abstraction, requiring very few redefinitions and no unnecessary methods, by subclassing.

Guideline 31 :   Factor implementation differences into new abstractions

Not all problems are solved by extending the inheritance hierarchy. Some implementation differences are better treated by introducing a new class hierarchy, from which instances act as components or parts in instances from the first class hierarchy.

Templates may also be used for this purpose. This is not described further as it is not supported in all object-oriented programming languages.

Reuse aspects

Too deep and large an inheritance hierarchy can be hard to understand. One way of avoiding this is to try to identify new abstractions that are parts of the abstraction in the hierarchy. It will be easier for the reuser to find and adapt a few small abstractions to use when configuring the large abstraction than to try to comprehend and adapt one large abstraction.

Guideline 32 :   Favour uniformity over specificity in naming conventions

For example, in the Eiffel libraries, all names on operations in the data structure library have been standardized. The basic operation for inserting an item is called *put* for all structures, instead of *push* of stacks, *enter* in arrays, *add* in queues and *insert* in hash tables.

Reuse aspects

The reuser will only have to manage a limited set of method names and protocols, and can focus on functionality and/or performance aspects of similar components instead. It should also be easier to connect objects.

Guideline 33 :   Keep method signatures consistent

Methods that have similar functions should have the same names, the same type and the same return value type.

Reuse aspects

This guideline support standard protocols and polymorphism.

9.5 Implementation for reuse

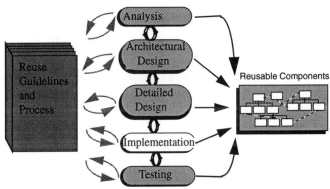

Figure 103 : The implementation phase of the development for reuse life cycle

9.5.1 Introduction

It is important to implement and use the structure of a component correctly. Relationships between classes are set up at the design stage, but they must be properly implemented. This section presents a set of guidelines for programming for reuse in C++. The guidelines for implementing reusable components take some advantage of C++-specific implementation techniques, but some of them are also applicable to all programming languages. Some guidelines are general object-oriented programming guidelines, others have a specific focus on reuse.

Some basic implementation techniques are presented first, followed by a set of examples focusing on reuse. These examples are then used in the programming guidelines.

9.5.2 Generalities of implementation for reuse

The relationships between classes identified in the design should be preserved or transformed in a standardized manner in an implementation for reuse.

Generalization/Specialization

In object-oriented programming languages, we represent the *is-a* relationship by inheritance. In C++ the generalization/specialization relationship, such as "a rectangle *is-a* shape", is implemented by public inheritance.

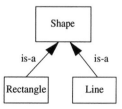

Figure 104 : Generalization/specialization relationship

Example 1

```
class Shape {....};
class Rectangle:public Shape {...};
class Line:public Shape{...};
```

Aggregation

The aggregation relationship expresses the containment "object A has an object B", or "object A consists of object B and...". For example, a line is part of a rectangle, or a rectangle has four lines. In C++ the aggregation relationship is implemented by declaring the related objects as private or protected attributes.

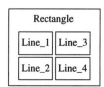

Figure 105 : Aggregation relationship

Example 2

```
class Rectangle:public Shape {
private:
   Line Line_1, Line_2, Line_3, Line_4;
};
```

Associations

The association relationship is present if a member function uses another class and it is neither an aggregation nor a generalization/specialization relationship, that is, the class does not contain the other class but it uses it for some other purpose. An association can be viewed as a client-server relationship. This relationship is called *knows* or *uses-a*.

In C++ the association relationship is implemented by taking a reference, or a pointer to an instance of another class, as a parameter.

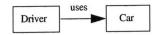

Figure 106 : Association relationship

Example 3

```
class Driver:public Person {
public:
    void Accelerate(Car &The_Car) {...};
};
```

There can be cases when a class relationship cannot be categorized into any of the three above. One such example is similar classes, such as sets and lists. Such an *is-like-a* relationship may be implemented in C++ by declaring one class as a private or protected attribute of the other. In this case, the *is-like-a* relationship is implemented as an aggregation, since the *is-a* relationship is not applicable here.

Figure 107 : Is-like-a relationship

Example 4

```
class List{
public:
    void Insert(void* Element);
};
class Set {
public:
    int Count(); // New method
    void Insert(void* Element)
    { the_List.Insert(void *Element);}
private:
    List the_List;
};
```

Polymorphism

Polymorphism means that an object which sends stimuli, such as a call to a method in another class in C++, does not have to know the receiving object's class. In other words, the caller provides only a request for a certain event—only the object that receives the call knows how to perform the event. Dynamic binding, which is often confused with polymorphism, means that the stimuli from the caller are not bound to a certain method in the called object's class until the call is executed, that is, the corresponding method is resolved at run-time.

In C++, polymorphism means that a method's signature may be the same for a number of different classes, while each class contains different implementations for the method. These different classes must belong to the same inheritance structure. You can prepare for dynamic binding by declaring methods as virtual in the base classes, while their implementation is declared in the subclasses. This postpones the need for specification until execution time. As a result the specific class type is not known until execution time when using dynamic binding.

For example, the class *Shape* has a method *Draw*, which may differ for different types of shapes. The class *Picture* contains a number of shapes. When the *Draw* method is performed on an object of class *Picture*, each of its shape objects should be drawn. The shapes may be *circles*, *lines*, and *rectangles*. Depending on the class of the *Shape* object, the corresponding implementation of the *Draw* method is executed.

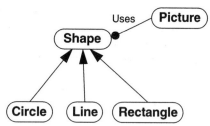

Figure 108 : Class structure

Example 5 An implementation with polymorphism:

```
class Shape {
public:
   virtual void Draw()=0;
   // Must be implemented in the subclasses
};

class Circle: public Shape {
public:
   void Draw() {// Draw a circle}
};
```

```
class Line: public Shape {
public:
   void Draw() {// Draw a line}
};

class Rectangle: public Shape {
public:
   void Draw() {// Draw a rectangle}
};

class Picture {
public:
   void Draw();
private:
   ListOfShapes theShapesOnTheScreen;
};

void Picture::Draw() {
   Shape *aShape;
   while (!theShapesOnTheScreen.IsEmpty()) {
       aShape=theShapesOnTheScreen.Next();
       aShape->Draw();
     // With polymorphism the
   } // object knows its specific implementation
}     // of the method
```

Abstract classes

An abstract class is a partially defined class. It lacks implementations for some of its operations, though it may implement other operations in terms of the undefined operations. An abstract class cannot be instantiated to an object. It is used as a template for subclasses and describes a small-scale design.

The opposite to abstract classes are concrete classes. These can be instantiated. To use an abstract class it must be subclassed to a concrete class. The concrete subclass must implement these undefined operations to complete the implementation.

A class cannot be declared as abstract in C++, but by declaring the constructor as protected and by having at least one pure virtual method, the class cannot be instantiated.

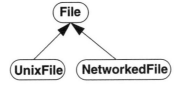

Figure 109 : Inheritance example

Example 6

```
class File {// Abstract class
protected:
   File() {
   // Protected constructor. Inhibits from being
   // instantiated.
public:
   virtual void Read(...) = 0;
   // Abstract method and pure virtual.
   // Inhibits from being instantiated and
   // enforces this method to be implemented
   // in the subclasses.
   virtual void Write(...) = 0;
   // Abstract method and pure virtual
   virtual int Size() = 0;
   // Abstract method and pure virtual

   void SetDate(...);
   // Implemented and should not be overloaded

   virtual void Copy(File* aFile);
   // Implemented and may be overloaded

   void File::copy(File* aFile) {
   char buffer[BlockSize];
   for (int i=0; i <= this->Size(); i++ {
      this->Read(buffer);
      // Uses the abstract methods read and write
      aFile->Write(buffer);
      // without dealing with how the
      // abstract methods are implemented
   }
}

class UnixFile : public File { // Concrete subclass
public:
   void Read(..);
   // Implementation of reading a buffer from a Unix file
   // This method must be implemented in the concrete class

   void Write(...); // Implementation of write in Unix

   void Size(); // Implementation of the size of a Unix file
}
```

```
  :
  :

main() {
   File my1File;
   // Compilation error! You cannot instantiate objects of an
   // abstract class

   File *my2File;// It is OK with pointers to abstract classes

   my2File = new UnixFile;// OK! UnixFile is concrete
   my2File = new File; // Compilation error! Abstract class.
}
```

In Example 6, class *File* is an abstract class that provides a specification of all subclasses, such as their *Read* and *Write* operations. The method *SetDate* is a fully implemented method. Notice that the *Copy* method will use the *Read* and *Write* methods defined in the subclasses.

9.5.3 Programming examples

In this section different key mechanisms of object-oriented development are described in the form of C++ examples. These examples used to illustrate the programming guidelines.

Encapsulation

Instead of making a component that consists of function calls, try to encapsulate the methods into an object-oriented interface with common parameters declared as private attributes. *Class* is the smallest possible reusable component in object-oriented development.

Example 7 A bad non object-oriented component with functions for handling files:

```
void ReusedFileWrite
   (const FileP& F,const FileType aType, char ch) {...}

charReusedFileRead
   (const FileP& F, const FileType aType) {...}

void ReusedFileCopy
(      const FileP& FromFile,
       const FileP& ToFile, const FileType aType) {...}
```

Example 8 A good object-oriented component with a class and its methods in an object-oriented design:

```
class File {
public:
   File(const FileP& theFile, const FileType aType) :
```

```
        myFile(theFile),myType(aType) {};

    void Write(const char theChar);
    char Read();

    void Copy(const FileP& toFile);
    File& operator=(const File& ToFile);
    // Copy by assignment,
    // e.g. file F2 is copied to F1 (F1=F2)

private:
    FileP& myFile;
    FileType myType;
};
```

Visibility of members

In the C++ programming language, a definition of the visibility of members is essential. Members are declared as either public, private or protected:

- A *public* member can be called by any function or method.

- A *private* member can be called only by methods of the class or by *friends* of the class.

- A *protected* member can be called by methods of the class and its derived classes, or by *friends* to the class.

The notion of protected members can be used to prepare a class for reuse. Class members that are related only to the specific class's implementation must not be exported. They can be declared as private or protected.

Implicitly-generated member functions

The following member functions are automatically generated by the compiler and should, to avoid ambiguity, be explicitly written by the programmer:

- The default constructor (X::X())

- The copy constructor (X::X(const X&))

- The assignment operator (X& operator= (const X&))

- The destructor (X::~X())

It is possible to inhibit a class from being instantiated by making the constructor protected, or even private. Making the copy constructor and assignment private or protected inhibits copying of one object to another. In the case of protected, it is possible to call the method from derived classes.

Using const

A good general guideline is to use const whenever possible. It allows you to specify a semantic constraint, the compiler will enforce that constraint, and the reuser will also know that the component has this constraint.

Const can be used to tell the compiler and the reuser that certain parameters are not modified when the method is executed. This is implemented by declaring a parameter, or a pointer to a parameter, as const. It is then impossible to change its value in the implementation of the method. This is valuable information that gives a reuser control over parameters sent to methods.

Example 9

```
class Thing {
void SetA(char newCh); // newCh can be modified

void SetB(const char newVal);// newVal cannot be modified

void SetC(char *newStr);
   // The pointer can be modified
   // The data can be modified

void SetD(const char *newStr);
   // The pointer can be modified.
   // The data cannot be modified

void SetE(char * const newStr);
   // The pointer cannot be modified.
   // The data can be modified

void SetF(const char * const newStr);
   // The pointer cannot be modified.
   // The data cannot be modified
}
```

Const can also be used to tell the compiler and the reuser that a method does not change any attribute in the object. This is also very important information for a reuser, since it states that a method can be called without the risk of changing the object's state, that is, the method has no side-effects on the state of the object. All *Get* methods should therefore always be declared as const.

Example 10

```
class Thing {
public:
   void Set(float val);
   //This method can change the state of the class

   void Get() const;
   // This method does not change the state of the class
```

```
  void DoSomething() const;
  // Does not change the state of the class

  void DoSomethingElse();
  // May change the state of the class
}
```

When creating a const object, calls to methods not declared as const will result in compiler warnings.

Example 11 Class Thing declared as in Example 10:

```
const Thing aThing(someInitAttributes); // Const object.
  :

Result = aThing.Get();
// Ok! Get is a method declared as const

aThing().DoSomething();// Ok!

aThing.Set(8);
  // Error! Can't set/modify attributes on a constant object

aThing.DoSomethingElse();
  // Error! This call will change the state
  // of the object. Impossible for a constant
  // object.
```

Virtual methods

Class inheritance gives a programmer the power to organize code in new ways, enabling support of software reuse. Code common to several classes can be collected in a base class, and derived classes can augment the behaviour of the base class to define more refined and specialized operations. Common data and member methods are collected in the base class. A variable declared as a base class pointer can be used to address an object or any of its derived classes, and can invoke any of the common base class member functions of the object. Each object is treated in terms of its general type, the base class of the hierarchy.

Example 12

```
class Shape {
   //class Shape is an abstract base class
public:
   virtual void Draw() = 0;
   virtual void Move() = 0;
   // other common methods
};
```

```
class Line:public Shape {
public:
   void Draw() {...}
   void Move() {...}
       // Any class that shall be able to
       // instantiate objects has to have an
       // implemented (or derived implemented)
       // version of each virtual function
...};
......
Shape* aShapepointer;
aShapepointer = new Line;
aShapepointer->Move();
....
```

If we consider the code for redrawing shapes:

Example 13

```
class ShapeContainer {
private:
   Shape *contents[maxNoOf];
public:
   void Redisplay() const;
};
void ShapeContainer::Redisplay() const {
   for (int i=0; i<maxNoOf; i++)
      if (contents[i])
         contents[i]->Draw();
         // calls the right method Draw for
         // something known as a Shape
};
```

If the application is extended, for example by adding new types of shapes, this code does not have to be modified.

It is also possible to define a default body for a virtual method if the method is called for an object that is just an instance of the class, that is, not of one of its subclasses. For example, a class *Polygon* can define a method for determining the surface of the polygon using a complex algorithm. If a class *Square* is created as a subclass of *Polygon*, the method for determining the surface can be redefined since the algorithm is then obvious.

It is often best to define a method as virtual. If a better implementation of a method is found after the class has been produced, a class can be derived from it properly. The cost of using virtual methods in an application is low. Virtual methods should not be avoided for the sake of execution time efficiency. When the late binding mechanism is used effectively (calling a virtual method) only one additional pointer reference is needed compared to a classical method. Avoiding use of late binding results in more lines of code, making the class less extensible and less reusable.

Focus on relationships rather than internal representation

It is important to focus on relationships rather than on internal representations. Recall Example1: a *Triangle* consists of three *Lines*. In this case we might incorrectly conclude that *Triangle* should be a specialization of *Line* (Examples 14 and 15).

Example 14 (bad)

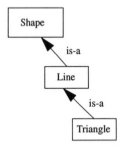

Figure 110 : A bad *is-a* relationship

```
class Shape {....};
class Line:public Shape {...};
class Triangle:public Line {...};
```

Example 15 (a better solution)

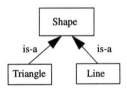

Figure 111 : *Is-a* relationship

```
class Shape {....};
class Line:public Shape {...};
class Triangle:public Shape {...};
```

Please note that there is also an *aggregate* relationship between *Triangle* and *Line* (that is, Triangle *has* three Lines).

Inheritance and accessing via base class pointers

When using inheritance, it is possible to add new member functions in derived classes, but the functions cannot be accessed in terms of their base class interface. This is a quite restrictive model of inheritance and leaves no room for run-time dispatching of new methods, the way in which derived methods are most powerfully used. If the programmer has to deal explicitly with every class in an inheritance hierarchy, the inheritance feature offers no abstraction power. Programmers would have to explicitly convert the base class pointer to the correct derived type. To do this, he would of course have to know the type.

In Example 16 explicit downcasting is used for executing the correct method, in Example 17 an explicit check on the object type is performed and in Example 18 access via a base class pointer is used.

Example 16 In this example, explicit downcasting is used to find the correct method to execute. This causes undesirable dependencies to the subclasses of the base class (bad).

```
class Shape {
public:
   virtual void Draw() = 0;
   // This implies all Shapes can be drawn, but
   // does not describe how,i.e. pure virtual.
};

class Line:public Shape {
public:
   void Draw() const {...};// OK Draw is virtual
   void Move() {...};
   // not good, Move ought to be virtual in
   // base class Shape. All shapes can be moved
};

class Circle:public Shape {
public:
   void Draw() const {....}
};
......
Shape* aShapepointer;
aShapepointer = new Line;( (Line*) aShapepointer )->Move();
   // explicit downcasting
   // conversion is necessary
....
```

Example 17 In this example, an explicit check on the object type is performed before deciding how to execute the corresponding method. This creates dependencies and problems when new types of *Figures* (new subclasses of *Figure*) are defined (bad).

```
enum ShapeType { Line = 1, Circle = 2,....}

class Shape {
public:
   virtual void Draw() = 0;
   virtual void Move() {...}
private:
   ShapeType This_Shape_Type;
      // public! and
      // initialized through constructor
};
```

```
class Line:public Shape {
public:
   void Draw() {...}
   void Move() {...}
};
class Circle:public Shape {
public:
   void Draw() {....}
   void Move() {...}
   void Fill() {...}
      // cannot be in base class Shape
      // only closed Shapes can be filled
};
......
Shape* aShapepointer;
aShapepointer = new Circle;
if ( aShapePointer->This_Shape_Type == Circle )
   aShapepointer->Fill();
   // okay!?- but the check on object type will give
   // dependencies and problems when adding new types of
   // figures. Not good C++ style
....
```

Example 18 In this example, access via a base class pointer is used. An empty method is defined in the base class for all methods implemented in the subclasses. All *Figures* can potentially be filled, but nothing happens if the object is not a *ClosedShape*.

```
class Shape {
public:
   virtual void Fill() {};
      // Empty method. Do nothing if not implemented in subclasses
   virtual void Draw() = 0;
};

class ClosedShape : public Shape {
public:
   virtual void Fill() = 0;
      // Pure virtual method. Must be implemented in the subclasses

class Line:public Shape {...};
class Circle:public ClosedShape {....};
......
Shape* aShapepointer;
aShapepointer = new Circle;
aShapepointer->Fill();
   // 'Fill' without thinking about the specific object type.
   // If it is not a ClosedShape, it will do nothing.
```

The solution proposed in example 18 is not feasible for all types of problems. The implementation must map onto the real world, that is, it may be correct to ask a *Line* to fill itself (that is, *Figure* has a virtual method *Fill*) but it is not correct to ask a *Car* to *Dive* just because both *Cars* and *Submarines* are a means of transport (that is, the base class *MeansOfTransport* has a virtual class *Dive*).

Inheritance with cancellation

Inheritance with cancellation allows you to cancel base class properties in a derived class. It is possible to simulate this in C++ by using private inheritance. Inheritance by cancellation should normally be avoided, as it increases complexity in the inheritance structure. In any case it is likely that it is really another type of relationship (*has-a* or *is-like-a*) that has been wrongly implemented with inheritance (*is-a*).

In Example 19, the class *Set* is inherited from *List* but with cancellation, that is, not all public members are inherited from the superclass, only *Count* and *Insert*. In Example 20, however, the *List* is modelled more reasonably as an aggregate in *Set*.

Example 19 (bad)

```
class List{
public:
   void*  Head();
   void*  Tail();
   int    Count();
   void   Insert(void*);
};
class Set:private List{
public:
   List::Count; // Make the Count method visible
   void   Insert(void* Element) { } // A new Insert method
};
```

Example 20 More appropriate according to object-oriented development concepts:

```
class List{
public:
   void*  Head();
   void*  Tail();
   int    Count();
   void   Insert(void*);
};
class Set{
public:
   Count() {return myList.Count();} // Make the Count method visible
   voidInsert(void* Element) { } // A new Insert method
private:
   List myList;
};
```

9.5.4 Object-oriented guidelines for the implementation phase

Guideline 34 :   Do not use multiple inheritance just to minimize code

Multiple inheritance will complicate the inheritance structure, which is especially true for ambiguous inheritance structures (which should in any case be avoided).

Reuse aspects

The structure will confuse the reuser, and ambiguous inheritance may be introduced when classes in the component are inherited. Multiple inheritance decreases simplicity, which among other things affects maintainability.

Guideline 35 :   All methods intended to be overloaded or redefined in subclasses must be declared as virtual

When defining the methods of a class, the methods intended to be subclassed should be defined as virtual. See also Examples 12 and 13.

Reuse aspects

Defining methods as virtual tells a reuser which methods are intended to be redefined. If a non-virtual method is redefined, the reuser must be more careful, since he will be reusing the class differently from how the developer of the component intended. Unfortunately there is no mechanism in C++ to make it difficult or impossible to overload a method.

Guideline 36 :   Do not cast down the inheritance hierarchy unnecessarily

Casting down in an inheritance structure is performed by explicitly calling a method lower in a class hierarchy. This creates dependencies in the hierarchy beyond the inheritance structure. The objects should identify themselves by using polymorphism. See Examples 16, 17 and 18.

Reuse aspects

Extensive administration of object types inhibits reuse. If a component uses a number of base class pointers and uses downcasting, then the reuser must continue to use downcasting if new subclasses are used in the component.

Guideline 37 :   Try to avoid inheritance with cancellation

Inheritance with cancellation is the situation in which there are restrictions to inheritance made by the subclass, that is, the subclass decides which methods to inherit. Cancellation contradicts the specialization relationships in an inheritance structure. Instead of using inheritance with cancellation, re-examine your inheritance structure. See Examples 19 and 20.

Reuse aspects

There will be an unclear interface for the subclass in an inheritance structure with cancellation. This interface is harder to understand for a reuser than a client-server relationship (*has-a* or *is-like-a*). When developing with reuse, inheritance with cancellation might be used, but we generally recommend a client-server relationship instead.

Guideline 38 :   Do not use private inheritance

Private inheritance in C++ is not an object-oriented concept and it is not used in any object-oriented design methodology.

Reuse aspects

Private inheritance may confuse the reuser, since it is difficult to examine what is inherited and therefore what is reused.

Guideline 39 :   Keep classes small—avoid large total protocols

Classes should represent abstractions. If a class has a lot of methods it may represent a complicated abstraction. It is likely that such a class is not well defined and probably consists of several different abstractions. Every class with more than about 25 methods, including inherited methods, should be inspected for potential modification.

Reuse aspects

It is hard to reuse a large class. It is easier to understand, modify or define subclasses from a few smaller classes in different inheritance hierarchies instead.

Guideline 40 :   Keep classes small—avoid the introduction of too many methods

When a lot of new (not inherited) methods are introduced into a class in a class hierarchy, it is probable that this class can be divided into a superclass and a subclass, and that suitable abstractions can be found. If there are, say, ten or more methods, it may be possible to find at least one more subclass.

Reuse aspects

It is harder to reuse from a large class than from a small inheritance hierarchy where common behaviour is extracted to superclasses. The reuser can find the most suitable abstraction to reuse by subclassing. This has the additional advantage of requiring very few redefinitions and no unnecessary methods.

Guideline 41 :   Keep the number of method arguments small

The number of arguments may be reduced by breaking the method into several smaller ones, or by creating a new class that represents a group of messages. Every method with more than three arguments (except constructors) should be inspected for potential modification.

Reuse aspects

Methods with many (say more than five) arguments are hard to read and therefore hard to reuse. It is less likely that standard protocols can be found when the number of arguments is large.

Guideline 42 :   Keep methods small

Every method with more than twenty lines of code should be inspected for potential modification.

Reuse aspects

It is easier to reuse by subclassing if the superclasses have small methods, since the behaviour can be changed by redefining a few small methods instead of a few large ones. The smaller methods are easier to understand and modify. It is also easier to identify common behaviour when the methods are small. This common behaviour may be migrated to an abstract superclass which can then probably be reused *as is*.

Guideline 43 :   Declare member methods `const` when possible

By declaring a member method as `const`, it is impossible to change its attributes in the implementation of the class; that is, member methods declared as `const` do not change the state of a class. It is only possible to call methods declared as `const` on a `const` object. See Examples 10 and 11.

Reuse aspects

Declaring member methods as `const` shows a reuser the methods that do not change any attributes in the object. There is therefore no risk of changing the state of an object by calling these methods. Unfortunately, there is no mechanism in C++ to express an intention to change the state of an object. This guideline forces reusers to use the methods as the developer intended, for example in redefinitions. Misuse is therefore prevented.

Guideline 44 :   Declare parameters `const` when possible

By declaring a parameter or a pointer to a parameter as `const`, it is impossible to change its value in the implementation of the method. See Example 9.

Reuse aspects

Declaring parameters as `const` clearly shows a reuser that the parameters, or pointers to parameters, are not changed in the implementation of the method. There is therefore no risk in passing a parameter that it is not intended to change to such a method. Misuse is therefore prevented.

Guideline 45 :   Always make destructors virtual in the base classes

This will stress correct deallocation of memory in an inheritance hierarchy. If a base class pointer is used to point to a class hierarchy in the component, and an object from the hierarchy is deleted, the destructor of the most derived class is called first. It will then continue to call destructors all the way up the hierarchy. If the destructors are not virtual, only the destructor for the declared object is called.

Reuse aspects

If a component is reused by subclassing any class in the component, and base class pointers are used, there may be memory allocation problems when an object is deleted. If the destructors are declared virtual in the base classes, the amount of work for the reuser will be decreased when using subclassing.

Guideline 46 :   Eliminate `switch` statements on object types

Use polymorphism instead of explicitly checking the object type. Object types can be simulated in C++. In Example 18, `enum` variables are used to identify object types. See Examples 16, 17 and 18.

Reuse aspects

When checking object types, unnecessary dependencies on other object types are created. When a new object type is needed whilst reusing the component, it has to be modified by inserting another check, for example. By using polymorphism instead, the component will be more adaptable.

Guideline 47 :   Specify attributes as private

This hides data representation and keeps the interface stable even if the type of the attribute is changed.

Reuse aspects

The reuser should not have to worry about the implementation, if possible. The interface for the reuser is the public and protected methods. The developer has the responsibility of making a suitable interface for the reuser. By using this interface, the component is reused correctly, and misuse is prevented.

Guideline 48 :   Use protected methods instead of protected attributes in the base class, for interfacing the subclasses

By using methods for the interface, the internal data representation can be modified without changing anything in the subclasses.

Reuse aspects

If a component can be reused using inheritance of any of its classes, the developer can control how it is reused by giving the reuser a well-defined interface, that is, public and protected methods.

If the component is exchanged for a new version with another data representation, the interface for the reuser is the same. This makes exchanging an old version with a new one easy.

Guideline 49 :   Avoid using *friends* if possible

The *friend* concept violates encapsulation and makes reuse more difficult. It is better to make some member functions *friends* than to make a whole class a *friend*.

Reuse aspects

The *friend* relation introduces relations in a component that are difficult to follow and handle by the reuser.

Guideline 50 :   Avoid implicit `inline`, that is, implementation and code in header files

The implicit `inline` violates encapsulation and shows the implementation to the reuser. Use explicit `inline` instead.

Example 21 Implicit inline (bad):

```
class Currency {
public:
    float GetSwedish() const {return(myDollars * 8.52);} // Bad
```

Example 22 Explicit inline:

```
// File: file.h (header file)
class Currency {
public:
    float GetSwedish() const;
}
// File: file.cc (source file)
:
inline float Currency::GetSwedish{return(myDollars*8.52);}
```

Reuse aspects

When the data representation is changed in a component, the interface seen by the reuser, as contained in the header file, should not need to be changed—the reuser should not have to concern himself about the implementation.

9.5.5 Reuse-specific guidelines for the implementation phase

Guideline 51 :   Inhibit classes intended to be abstract from being instantiated

Make the *virtual* methods pure virtual and specify the constructor as *protected*. See Example 6.

Reuse aspects

Making methods that should not be instantiated virtual forces a reuser to subclass the abstract class before using it, and forces subclasses to contain a homogeneous protocol. This guideline prevents misuse, as it forces the reuser to investigate which methods he can redefine.

Guideline 52 :   Implement implicitly generated class methods: *constructor, destructor, copy constructor* and *assignment*

To keep the control and to avoid unexpected behaviour when an object is created, copied and destroyed, prohibit the compiler from implementing implicitly-generated methods by implementing them yourself. This is especially important for classes with dynamically allocated memory and classes that have *uses-a* relations with other classes.

Reuse aspects

This will show the reuser how to use the class and how to implement these methods if the classes in the component are inherited. Misuse will be prevented.

Guideline 53 :   When copying or assignment makes no sense, hide the copy constructor and the assignment operator in the private part of the class specification

Reuse aspects

This will inhibit the reuser from performing unintentional operations with the component, preventing misuse.

9.6 Verification, test and certification

9.6.1 Introduction

This section discusses the certification of reusable components, the methodological aspects of performing test activities when developing *for* reuse and how the result of these activities can be reused when developing *with* reuse.

Testing is concerned with:

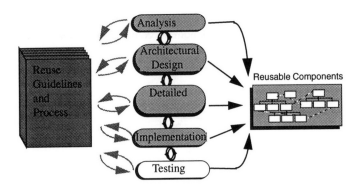

Figure 112 : The testing phase of the development for reuse life cycle

1. Reducing the number of faults.

2. Enuring that a component meets its requirements.

There are two approaches to this: proving the correctness of the reusable component, or performing testing. The first approach is briefly described in Section 9.6.2. Testing of components developed using object-oriented methods is covered in Section 9.6.3.

9.6.2 Proving correctness

One means of removing faults from code is by performing proofs of correctness. This involves mathematically verifying the code, and thereby proving that it is correct. This idea is attractive, mainly for software where the number of possible behaviours is large and they are not easy to test. The drawback is that such techniques require a large amount of work, as it is almost like rewriting the code. It is difficult therefore for large software components, especially where the interfaces with other components are complex.

If a component is proved correct, it has an infinite reliability if the proof has been correctly performed. This means that if a component is developed for reuse and proved correct, it will be failure-free as long as it is used in accordance with the specified interface.

Development for reuse

When developing for reuse, there are three aspects that help decide whether a proof of correctness should be performed:

1. The size of the component.

2. The number of times a component will be reused.

3. The importance of the reliability of a component.

The choice of whether to use a mathematical proof is based on a combination of all these factors. If the component is going to be reused with modification, the correctness proof must also reflect this. The component and the proof of correctness must be strongly linked to make it easier to reuse both the component and the proof. It is important that modifying the proof is as well documented as modifying the component.

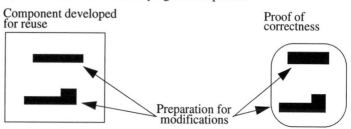

Figure 113 : Preparation for modifications both in the component and in the proof of correctness

When developing for reuse there are a number of different ways to represent generality. For a definition of these methods, see Section 7.4.

- *Widening*. This approach means that all requirements are covered, from both the current customer and any anticipated customers. In this case the proof of correctness should cover the anticipated modifications. It will not therefore be necessary to re-perform the proof of correctness when developing with reuse. It is important nevertheless to both document and store the proof of correctness, since it is possible that the component will be reused with modifications.

- *Narrowing*. If this approach is used it is possible to perform a separate proof of correctness for the higher level of abstraction. The specific functionality then has to be proved after it has been developed. It is important that the proof is performed separately for the general level of abstraction, so that the adaptations are easier to change when the component is reused.

- *Isolation*. This approach is like narrowing, but instead of isolating specific functionality to a lower abstraction level, it is isolated in a specific part of the component. For this approach it is important that the proofs for the invariant parts are performed separately.

- *Configurability*. When this approach is used it is possible to perform proofs of correctness of each of the components that will be combined to provide the specific functionality.

- *Generators*. It may be difficult to perform proofs of correctness for generators, as it is difficult to cover all the possible combinations that a generator can produce.

Guideline 54 : If a component is small and will be reused many times, or if it is vital that it is totally reliable, it is better to perform a proof of correctness than to use conventional testing

Development with reuse

If the component is likely to be modified when it is reused the proof of correctness must also be modified and re-performed. For minor modifications it is, however, possible that parts of the initial proof can be reused. It is also possible to prepare the proof to make it easy to modify in line with the modifications to the component. The initial proof of correctness can therefore be used as a support in proving the correctness of modifications.

9.6.3 Object-oriented testing in development *for* and *with* reuse

Testing software that has been developed using object-oriented techniques does not differ much from ordinary software testing. The purpose in both cases is to:

- verify the realization of the system

- verify that the system is correctly designed in accordance with the requirements

- remove faults from the code

The next section describes a general model for testing that is used when discussing development *for* and *with* reuse. This model then forms the basis for a discussion of testing strategies. We look at different types of test used for object-oriented testing. Finally we examine how testing should be performed in development *for* and *with* reuse.

Test model

The test model to be used in development *for* and *with* reuse is a description of the interface that a component "sees". This model is made up of two types of descriptions:

- Test cases

- Test beds

The test cases describes a sequence of stimuli given to the system. The test cases also

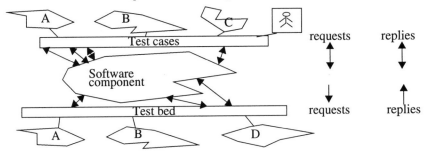

Figure 114 : The test interface to a component

contain the expected responses from the component when a specific stimulus is applied. This means that the test cases describe part of the component's environment that requests something from the component, such as sending a stimulus to it, or responds to requests from the component based on earlier stimuli. This interface could be with other components or users. The *test bed* is the part of the component's environment that it uses to receive the information necessary to perform the requested actions.

All the test cases and test beds that are used should be directly coupled to the component under test. The idea is then to couple test cases and test bed descriptions to the specific component, components or users that will communicate with the component under test. This makes it easier to integrate components. When components are integrated, it is possible to identify parts of earlier test cases and test beds belonging to the original components that still constitute the interface to the new component. The final result is that the only test cases that remain are the ones describing the external use of the system. The remaining test bed then describes external sources that the system uses to fulfil its task.

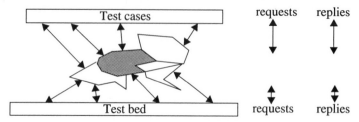

Figure 115 : The total interface to a number of integrated components

In some cases it is useful if the test cases and test beds are coupled to the specific requirements they are testing. This makes it easier to sort out test cases associated with requirements that do not need to be tested if only parts of the component's functionality are reused. It would be easier, if widening is used for example, to test only the relevant functionality of the component. It is also important to record which test cases have been executed to ensure full test coverage.

It is possible that a component contains functionality that should be separately tested. This is the case when a component contains specializations describing its behaviour in a specific application, for example. This can occur when generality is represented by narrowing or isolation. It is important that the test bed allows for parts of the component that might be replaced when the component is reused. It will then be possible to test the general parts of the component. Test cases must also test the functionality of both the general and specific parts of the component. This makes it possible to use the test cases when testing the general functionality of the component through basing the responses on the behaviour of the test bed—see Figure 116. It is still necessary to keep the original test bed and test cases that are not modified by the functionality represented by the internal test bed.

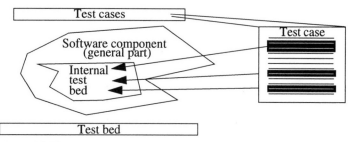

Figure 116 : Additional test bed and adapted test case for testing general functionality

When specific parts of the component have been implemented, the test cases and the parts of the component corresponding to the functionality of the specific parts of the test case have to be modified. It might also be necessary to create new test cases to cover the functionality of the entire component. This is shown in Figure 117.

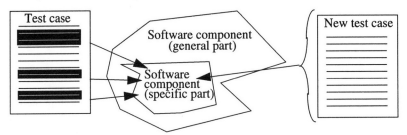

Figure 117 : Adapted test cases when testing the entire component

When narrowing is used it might be helpful to use multiple test beds. This means that a separate test bed is created for each specialization of the component. Each test bed then represents a specific specialization of the general component. It will then be possible to test the general functionality of the component in several steps dependent on the generality required.

Guideline 55 :   Couple specific test cases and test beds to the component they are intended for

Guideline 56 :   Couple specific test cases and test beds to the component, components or users they are intended to represent

Guideline 57 :   Couple specific test cases and test beds, or parts of them, to the parts of the component that represent specific functionality

Guideline 58 :   Record the test beds used and for a component

Object-oriented testing

Traditional testing includes the following types of testing:

- Unit tests

- Integration tests

- System tests

These test types relate to the system structure as shown in Figure 118.

Unit testing

Traditionally testing begins at a low level with unit testing. Unit testing means testing a single software unit. An object-oriented system consists of a number of objects which communicate with each other. These objects contain both data and behaviour that make them "larger" units than in traditional system development. There are two different methods for carrying out unit testing:

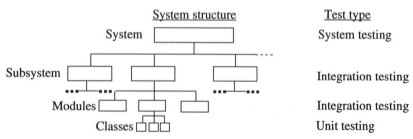

Figure 118 : Test types in relation to the system structure

- Structural testing (*white-box* testing). This means testing with a knowledge of the internal structure of the unit. Different criteria exist for deciding how structural testing should be performed, such as code coverage or branch coverage.

- Specification testing (*black-box* testing). This testing strategy means testing based only on the implementation specification of the unit. In this type of testing no knowledge of the internal structure of the implementation is needed.

Integration testing

The purpose of integration testing is to verify that different units developed and tested separately are working together properly. Integration testing in an object-oriented development process is performed at an earlier stage, since communication is of major importance for system development. Integration testing is therefore easier when object-oriented techniques are used.

System testing

The purpose of system testing is to compare the system to its original objectives. It is important to note that system tests are not limited to systems, and can be applied to any product that has stated objectives. The main reason for system tests is that they provide the first possibility of actually testing initial requirements. Unit testing and integration testing are all aimed at verifying derived requirements. System testing is of course not possible if the project has not produced a set of measurable objectives for its product.

Testing in development *for* reuse

All of the above test types may be needed when developing *for* reuse. When testing, it is important to note the aims of the testing in terms of reusable components. Possible reuse aims are listed below:

- Unit testing

    — Aimed at testing a reusable component. Needed when the reusable component is a unit.

    — Aimed at testing part of a reusable component. Needed when the reusable component is made up of a number of units of which the unit to be tested is just one.

- Integration testing

  — Aimed at testing a reusable component. Needed when the integrated software units or modules form a reusable component.

  — Aimed at testing part of a reusable component. Needed when the integrated software units or modules form part of a reusable component.

  — Aimed at testing integrated reusable components. Needed when one, some or all of the integrated software units or modules are reusable components.

- System testing

  — Aimed at testing a reusable component. Needed when an entire system forms the reusable component.

  — Aimed at testing integrated reusable components. Needed when one, some or all of the integrated subsystems are reusable components.

Generally this will lead to three different cases:

1. Testing a number of software entities from which one, some or all are reusable or reused components. The test cases and test bed from the reusable component(s) can be reused when the internal communication modules in the integrated software have been removed.

2. Testing a reusable component. In this case testing should be performed in accordance with the way in which the generality is represented in the component. This is further described below.

3. Testing of an entity that will form part of a reusable component. It is necessary to prepare the testing of the reusable component. This means that for each software entity that has to be tested, test cases and test beds should be created as described in the test model. It is then easier to derive test cases and test beds for the reusable component.

Any combination of these cases is possible. When testing a reusable component it is important to consider its generality. The various ways to represent generality were described in Section 7.4. All these influence testing when developing a reusable component, as follows:

- *Widening*. Using widening means including all the requirements for a component in one solution. In this case is important to only test objectives that have been based on the original requirements. Based on the test model presented earlier, it is only necessary to perform test cases that are coupled to the requirements for the specific use of the component. It is also important to record which parts of the test cases and test beds were used when testing the component.

- *Narrowing*. Using narrowing means creating an abstract component in which all the common functionality is gathered. Here it is necessary to represent the different levels of specialization by actual test beds. It is also important that the specializations are coupled to parts of the test cases. Through this it is possible to test general functionality separately from testing the entire component.

- *Isolation.* Isolation means that the various requirements are isolated to a small part of the system. In this case it is necessary to identify in the test cases which parts belong to general functionality and which parts belong to specific functionality. Test beds are then created that represent the specific functionality to make it possible to test the general functionality.

- *Configurability.* Configurability means the possibility of connecting smaller components to form a system that fulfils the customer's requirements. The components must have a well-specified interface to make it possible to configure the system. In this case it is necessary to test each of the components only once, and then test the entire system. This is possible because of the well-specified interface and the static behaviour of each of the components. It is also relatively easy to derive test cases and test beds for the entire system based on the test cases and test beds of the single components. Note though that the system's configuration may be dynamic—each separate configuration may require a separate set of tests.

- *Generators.* Generators are like new languages, and the range of possible applications is very large. This has to be taken into account when a generator is used. Guidelines for testing applications should be provided with the generator but they can never be more than guidelines because of the large range of applications possible.

Testing in development *with* reuse

When testing during development *with* reuse, it is important to distinguish between the different ways that generality is represented.

- *Widening.* If widening has been used, it is important to examine which of the requirements have been covered by earlier tests. It is then possible to only perform tests of the additional requirements.

- *Narrowing.* When narrowing is used it is important to start testing from the correct specialization level of the component, that is, the level where modifications have been introduced. The old test cases can be used if the parts covering the specialized functionality are exchanged to represent the new functionality.

- *Isolation.* If isolation has been used it is necessary to update the test cases to exchange the parts corresponding to the specific functionality. This means that testing can be performed based on test cases derived from the original reusable component.

- *Configurability.* Here it is only necessary to check whether a specific configuration has been used before. If so, it might not be necessary to test at all. If not, it is relatively easy to derive test cases based on those for each of the components in the system.

- *Generators.* Applications developed with a generator have to be tested according to the guidelines provided with the generator.

10 Development with Reuse

10.1 Introduction

This chapter describes our approach to development *with* reuse, the methodological aspects of the development of applications using existing reusable components. It presents a set of guidelines for each of the phases of a project developing with reuse.

We need to adapt an existing software development life cycle to a development using existing components. Starting from a classical object-oriented life cycle model for software development, we point out the specific steps that could be devoted to reuse, and the necessary changes to integrate reuse with the step.

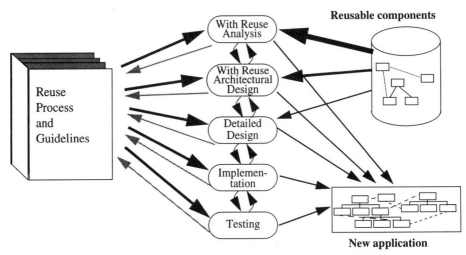

Figure 119 : General life cycle for development with reuse

The first section presents a set of aspects concerning *with* reuse development. We then describe the specific *with* reuse activities. Having presented a common reuse process for each development phase, we address the phases used in classical life cycles, basing our study on the OMT methodology described in Chapter 8:

- *with* reuse analysis

- *with* reuse architectural design

- detailed design

- implementation

- testing

The last part of the chapter focuses on the impact of reuse on non-classical but currently used life cycles: rapid prototyping and the spiral life cycle.

10.2 Specific aspects of *with* reuse development

This section presents the assumptions we make when approaching development *with* reuse.

Implement reuse as soon as possible in the development life cycle

In order to be effective, reuse of software components has to be integrated into the overall development process, and should include method and tool support for reuse. You should investigate reuse of existing components from the first phases of development. It is possible to identify potential reusable components in each phase, such as analysis, as well as in the design and implementation phases. The impact of reuse on the overall application will vary with the phase of development. The V-development life cycle illustrated in the figure below shows the potential impact of reuse for the different phases of the life cycle.

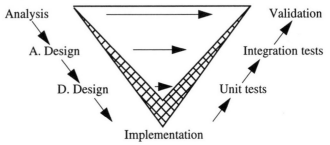

Figure 120 : V life cycle model

The earlier reusable components can be used in the life cycle, the more impact it will have on the remaining phases. Reusing architectural components has a large impact on the overall application and is highly profitable. Reusing high-level components leads to the reuse of all associated information, such as source code and test information. Reusing low-level components, such as general data structures, is also profitable, contributing mainly to the quality of the applications.

Domain analysis

Domain analysis is an activity specific to development *for* reuse, and is detailed in Chapter 9. It aims to provide a minimum set of information to support the creation of reusable components and their reuse in future applications. It consists of identifying, collecting, organizing and representing the relevant information of the domain by studying:

- existing systems and their development histories

- knowledge captured from domain experts

- underlying theories

- the anticipation of customers' requirements

- emerging technologies within the domain.

Domain analysis results have their main impact on the analysis and architectural design phases. The results are close to those of a classical analysis activity, and usually include different models of the domain (object, functional and dynamic), generic software architectures for the most relevant applications in the domain, a taxonomy, a classification of components in the domain, and a set of generic requirements for each system in the domain.

Standardization

A major problem with reusability arises from the incompatibility of interacting components. Industrial standards, suitably adapted for reuse, help to obviate this problem. Standards address not only application domains, but techniques as well. Some well-known standards are:

- POSIX communications and operating systems

- CCITT telecommunications

- ISO 9126 qualification of components

- ISO 9001 process quality assessment

Many development techniques have submitted to standardization, and should now take the practice of reuse into account.

Depending on the level of standardization of a domain, procedures for reusing components may vary. If the domain is already standardized, the application architecture and the main components for building domain applications should already be well defined. You can build an application using standard structures and components, mapping your needs to them. This can also lead to adaptation of the application's *requirements*, rather than to the adaptation of components. This is unusual in classical software development, and can offer a new way of working.

10.3 *With* reuse-specific activities

When developing *with* reuse, you should integrate several specific reuse activities into the classical software development life cycle. Activities such as the retrieval, evaluation and adaptation of pre-existing components are new and essential for the successful reuse of components. The process of reusing existing components is the same in all development phases, and includes the reuse-specific activities shown in Figure 121.

If you have already identified a component during a previous phase, some of these activities may be skipped, such as *searching* and *selection*. *Identification of components requirements* then consists of transferring the part of the component relevant to the current phase.

Identification of components requirements

Searching

Understanding

Investigating possible adaptations

Selection

Adaptation - Integration

Reporting

Figure 121 : Reuse-specific activities

The sections that follow describe these activities, and highlight those specific to development *with* reuse by placing them in italics. More detailed information is provided in the sections describing the impact of reuse on each development phase.

10.3.1 Identifying requirements for reusable components

This consists of understanding the application and determining the software components needed to implement the solution. Identifying potential reusable components occurs at each level of the development life cycle, for example in the analysis as well as the design or testing phases.

When the domain is already standardized, or when a domain analysis is available, main components are probably already identified. In that case you can probably identify a major proportion of the components immediately. For example, standard subsystems may be defined. The most relevant data from domain analysis for use in identifying subsystems are:

— the **object model** and domain taxonomy in each phase of the life cycle

— the **list of requirements** in the analysis phase

— the **architecture** in the design phase

Guideline 59 :   Use different abstraction levels for the requirements depending on the phase of the development. The earlier in the development life cycle, the more general must be the requirements

Formulating requirements is a primary step in identifying potential reusable components. In many cases, opportunities for reusing components fail just because the requirements do not map onto existing components. As different people have different ways of handling the same problem, it is difficult (but crucial) to understand how a proposed component fits a particular requirement.

- To enable high-level components to be found for reuse in the analysis phase, requirements must be as general as possible. If you focus on specific requirements, you reduce your chances of finding candidate components.

- It is easier to identify low-level components such as lists or other data structures from very specific requirements. This is particularly the case for components to be incorporated during the detailed design or implementation phases. Such low-level components are characterized by having only a few simple links to their external environment.

10.3.2 Searching for reusable components

Searching consists of retrieving a set of components that fit the identified requirements. The resulting set of components must be large enough to allow you to evaluate several alternative solutions to your problem and select the best. To support the selection of components for reuse, search and retrieval mechanisms should not be too selective, and should provide:

- An inventory of existing components, including references to ancillary information attached to the components.

- A repository of components that gather and store all available reusable information.

- Facilities to consult either the inventory or repository of components, including browsers, hypertext and classification.

- Retrieval tools based on keywords, classification or indexing mechanisms which are able to retrieve a set of components from sophisticated queries. Such tools should preferably include relaxation mechanisms to enlarge the search scope of queries.

If these features are available in a repository, they help to ensure that the set of retrieved components is as close as possible to your requirements. The resulting set of components may include standard components corresponding to the application domain or application family in which you are interested.

Guideline 60 :   Enlarge the scope of the search as widely as possible within the company, and do not ignore external sources of reusable components

When searching for components, people too often restrict their search to the local environment, instead of widening the searching scope to other company departments and to external suppliers.

- The success of a search for components depends mainly on their accessibility. It requires efficient communication and inventory procedures. This is particularly important when components are not stored in a common repository.

- The external market for software components is currently limited to general purpose components, or general components belonging to a number of specific domains such as user interfaces and operating systems.

Guideline 61 :   Use the *taxonomy* put forward by the company

The search-term space used by the searching tools must fit the taxonomy defined for each application domain of the company. This taxonomy results from analyzing the domain, and promotes the use of a common vocabulary for the domain.

10.3.3 Understanding retrieved components

Understanding existing software is one of the main limitations to the reuse of existing components. The cost of understanding existing software at all levels, not only at the implementation level, is usually seriously underestimated. This cost has been estimated for maintenance at 40 to 70 percent of the total. This figure may reasonably be assimilated into the required effort of understanding a component when reusing it. Two aspects have to be considered when understanding a component:

- The *functional* aspect corresponds to understanding the functionality offered by the component. You should start by considering the component as a black box and focusing on its interface, and examine the internal implementation if you need further details.

- The *non-functional* aspects include qualitative ones such as the efficiency, portability, understandability and reliability, together with other aspects such as platform characteristics, structure and interrelationships between various entities within the component.

Guideline 62 :   Use the appropriate view of a component to understand it

The understanding process varies greatly between different individuals. Many research programmes have studied the problem of understanding software for reuse. The main finding is that a combination of different views is a very powerful method to enhance software understandability.

Such multiple views are provided by several development methodologies and supported by tools facilities. For instance, OMT proposes three models for modelling a problem: an object model, a dynamic model, and a functional model. As the best way to address a problem depends strongly on the developer's own culture, we recommend you begin with the view with which the developer is most familiar, either the static, dynamic or process view of the problem.

Guideline 63 :   Use domain analysis results, if available, to understand the characteristics of the component

Domain analysis results are a good support for understanding the purpose of available components and the context of their use in the application domain. They mainly impact the high-level phases of the development.

- The *classification* of the component provides a broad view of its functional and non-functional characteristics. For example, the classification scheme in the REBOOT environment gives information based on the following facets: *abstraction, operations, operates-on* and *dependencies.* These are described in Section 3.4.

- The *generic requirements* provide information on the context of use of a component, that is, the functional and non-functional constraints on the component within the application domain.

- The *object model* describes the structure of the component and its relationships with other components.

- The *functional model* provides information on the behaviour of the component.

- The *dynamic model* gives information on the control and sequencing aspects associated with the use of the component.

- The *architecture* describes the place of the component in the system decomposition.

Guideline 64 :   Consult experienced people

Three sorts of people can help you understand a component: the domain expert, the developers of the component, and previous reusers. However, some or all of these people may not be available. Efficient communication procedures ease such a consulting process.

Guideline 65 :   Carry out a complete study of a high-level component so that you fully understand it and can make an appropriate selection if time allows

A high-level component describes the architectural design of a system or subsystem. It is a composite element that contains atomic and other composite components. High-level components may gather all the information on the rationales used during the development of an application. Understanding them is a costly activity and often involves exploring lower-level parts of the component such as the code. For example, the possibilities of adaptation of a framework are very limited, considering its behaviour and inherent mechanisms. The selection of frameworks such as the user-interface frameworks InterViews or ET++ determines the whole behaviour of the resultant system. Such a choice cannot be undertaken without a preliminary and accurate study of the framework, including its architecture, inherent mechanisms and behaviour. You may even have to explore the code to understand the framework thoroughly.

10.3.4 Investigating adaptations

Once you have acquired a good understanding of the retrieved components, you need to investigate the adaptations needed to make them fit your requirements (or vice-versa). You should start by evaluating the distance between the component you need and those you have retrieved, and how much it will cost to adapt them.

It may turn out that there is a great difference between the environment in which the component is to be reused and the one for which it was developed. The effort to adapt the reused component has to be evaluated carefully to enable you to judge whether less effort is needed to develop a new component. In a few domains, such as mathematical and statistical applications, reuse can often be achieved without adaptation. In most cases, however, software components cannot be carried from one application to another without changes. Adaptation involves removing the inappropriate parts and replacing them; this may in turn affect other parts of the component, provoking additional adaptations.

The boundary between investigating adaptations and pure adaptation activity is shady. The result of your investigation may vary from a coarse estimate based on the cost models proposed in Section 4.4, to a very detailed one that includes a detailed description of the adaptations required, taking into account its technical aspects. Depending on the context, you may already have done some of the adaptation work during the investigation phase.

Guideline 66 :   Study the technical solutions for implementing adaptations based on your chosen mode of reuse

We distinguish between several modes of reuse: *black box*, *grey box* and *white box* reuse, which reflect the way in which adaptations are applied to a reused component.

As is   **--> Black box** Encapsulation, inheritance
Few changes   **--> Grey box** Inheritance, in-line adaptation
Major changes   **--> White box** Program changes

Figure 122 : Reuse modes and adaptation of components

- *Black box* reuse consists of reusing a component *as is*, that is, without considering its contents. The component itself is not modified. The adaptation consists of customizing the component to fulfil the application needs. Encapsulation and inheritance are two techniques you can use to customize a component without modifying its content. Encapsulation allows you to define a new layer on which build new functionality. Inheritance is specific to object-oriented development. It is described in more detail in Section 8.3.

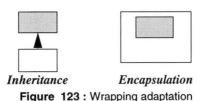

Inheritance   *Encapsulation*
Figure 123 : Wrapping adaptation

- *Grey box* reuse consists of reusing a component by applying *few* changes to the component to customize it, that is, in-line adaptation. Such adaptations can include renaming variables, changing method calls, and changing an implementation part. You can use inheritance to modify the component definition or behaviour by overloading.

- *White box* reuse consists of reusing a component by applying *major* changes to customize it. The component can be changed quite drastically in its structure and behaviour.

Guideline 67 : Determine the appropriate level of investigation of components depending on the component type and the types of requirements to be fulfilled

Investigating adaptations provides you with the necessary information to enable you to select the appropriate alternatives between several components. This can be very costly, depending on the level of detail used to evaluate the adaptation costs. As you may need to repeat such investigations on several components, you should be aware of the associated costs. The level of information necessary to select a component is very different depending on the type of the components and of the type of requirement involved.

Guideline 68 : Evaluate the distance between candidate components and the requirements

You can think of the distance between the retrieved components and the requirements as having a functional and non-functional aspect. The functional distance corresponds to the distance between required functionalities and those that the component provides. The non-functional distance includes qualitative properties such as the portability, efficiency, understandability and reliability characteristics of the component, and also the platform considerations.

Formal specifications for the functional aspects can help you judge such distances. Evaluating non-functional aspects relies on the use of quality or reusability models based on metrics, as described in Section 4.3.

Consider the three following adaptations when reusing a component, if X is the required component and Y the retrieved one:

1. Y -> X

2. X -> Y

3. X <-> Y

- In approach (1), you modify the existing component to fit your requirements.

- In approach (2), you modify your requirements to fit the existing component. Doing this obviously impacts people working on previous phases, and impacts the customer during the analysis phase. In large applications, it is usual for different teams to be assigned to each development phase. The relationships between the different teams can be illustrated with a customer-provider relationship as shown in figure 124.

- Adapting requirements requires that you notify and negotiate with the teams involved in the previous phase. You need to iterate this negotiation until your proposed requirements

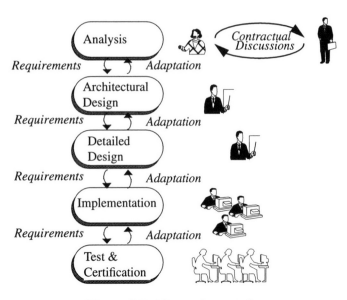

Figure 124 : The requirements flow

modification has no further impact. At the highest level of requirements, those for the entire system, it is the customer that is involved.

- In approach (3), there is a modification of both the initial requirements, and of the existing components. As for approach (2), this requires you to negotiate any modification of requirements with the appropriate people.

Guideline 69 :   When using evaluation models based on metrics, consider the different evaluation levels of *metrics, criteria, factors*

You can carry out a quantitative evaluation on metrics, criteria and factor levels of detail, such as those defined in the *Factor-Criteria-Metrics* product models described in Chapter 4. Each level corresponds to a different view of the non-functional requirements that impact different development phases:

- *Factors* are used in the analysis phase to fit to customer requirements.

- *Criteria* are used in the design phase.

- *Metrics* are used in the implementation and documentation phases.

Guideline 70 :   Do not forget to study the adaptations you need to integrate the component into the application development

This aspect is often forgotten and sometimes discovered too late in the development process. You often meet three types of problem when integrating an existing component into a new development:

- Integration of a complete reusable component for more limited needs

  A classical situation is to reuse a complete component, but only use one or two of the services it provides. This can occur for example when using a complete library in which only some components are needed. It mainly concerns the implementation phase, where the code of a complete component can be voluminous and not needed in its entirety. The problem of reusing only parts of a component is an implementation problem and is not addressed by object-oriented concepts. It is sometimes supported by compilers or other programming language mechanisms. For example, the C++ mechanism *genericity* offers this kind of support. When you instantiate a generic class for a specific type, the compiler only generates the associated code for that specific type.

- Redundance in functionality

  This happens when integrating different components that provide the same functionality in an application.

- Conflicts (object names, communications, and so on)

  Object name conflicts occur when separately developed software components use the same identifier for different objects. For example, if two libraries that provide a class with the same name are linked, a link error occurs for the multiple definition. In this case, one of the class identifiers has to be renamed. It is better to modify your own code rather than the library source code—in most cases you do not have the choice, because you do not have the library source. This kind of conflict causes problems in the low-level phases of development, but should be considered in the design phase.

10.3.5 Selecting a component for reuse

Selecting a component consists of choosing a solution from those possible using the candidate components. This can depend on any of the following factors:

- economic factors

- quality and delay factors

- the constraints of the application domain and the development environment

- future reuse objectives

- legal aspects

- your company's reuse policy

If several solutions all meet the customer's requirements, cost arguments become dominant. A customer may also be willing to relax some requirements out of economic motivations if this does not conflict with the constraints of the application domain.

In some cases, there is too little information to be able to select one component from the retrieved set of components. You may then decide to select a subset of the proposed components, and delay your final choice to a later phase. For example, you may decide that you need a *list* as an implementation mechanism, select two or three list mechanisms that seem appropriate in the design phase, and make the final choice during the implementation phase.

Guideline 71 :   When selecting components, you should choose standardized ones in the absence of any other criteria

10.3.6 Adaptation and integration of reusable components

This consists of implementing your selected adaptations, and integrating the component into your application. Once you have adapted the component, it is possible that it constitutes a new potentially reusable component.

Guideline 72 :   Use a project-wide or module-wide prefix for each outstanding global name

Longer prefixes reduce the likelihood of clashes with other prefixes. New or adapted *String* classes should be called something like *My<Project>String*, where *<Project>* is the project-specific part of the name.

Guideline 73 :   Define a standard communication protocol

When integrating adapted components into the application, you should consider the communication aspects. If the communication protocol is not fixed for the application under development, you are strongly advised to use the same one as that used in existing reusable components to avoid possible conflicts.

Guideline 74 :   When making adaptations of a component in a given phase, do not forget to carry this information forward to the following phases

For high-level components containing information about each phase of the life cycle, the adaptation process is as follows:

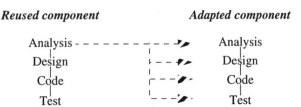

Figure 125 : Adaptation process model

10.3.7 Reporting on the reuse of a component

This activity differs from the previous ones because it is included in the *with* reuse development process, without being specific to the reuse activity itself. Its existence is justified because of its value in contributing to the further reuse of the component—it is a part of what we previously referred to as *information support*. You should make a report when you have reused, or tried to reuse, a component. This increases the reusability of the component because your experience of reusing the component is stored together with its documentation. Information of particular interest includes:

- a description of the reuse environment

- any problems you experienced in reusing the component, especially in understanding, integrating and adapting it

- what it cost you

All this information should be stored with the reusable component, so that other people who want to reuse the component can benefit from it. For example, the REBOOT toolset offers a reporting function. This consists of a set of questions to be answered by the reuser that deal with testing, effort saved or spent on adaptation, error tracking, critical points and modifications. The answers are then stored as part of the reusable component, allowing others to consult them in context. The reuse report can also contain recalculated quality attributes for the component.

10.4 Common reuse process

The introduction of reuse into a classical life cycle development phase has two different impacts. The first is the introduction of the activities specific to reuse, as described above. The second is a highlighting of the steps in the conventional life cycle that benefit from reuse; this is usually the first step within each development phase that determines the strategy to be applied in a phase.

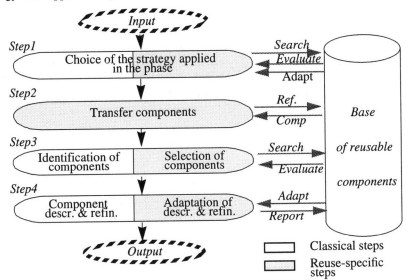

Figure 126 : *With* reuse common process for each phase

The resulting process is illustrated in Figure 126, and includes the following steps:

- Step 1: Determining the strategy for the phase

This step should be integrated into the beginning of each phase. It consists of selecting and adapting the strategy for the development of the phase. For example in the implementation phase, the choice of a development strategy may be bottom-up, top-down or mixed. The bottom-up strategy consists of implementing the basic components first, while the top-down approach (used for prototyping) consists of implementing high-level components first. The choice of development strategy should make use of reuse reports for previous experiences with similar systems.

- Step 2: Transferring components

This specific reuse activity should be integrated as the second step of each classical development phase. For example, the transfer activity in the design phase deals with the integration of the design part of the components found during the analysis phase. Depending on the nature of these components, the requirements and the type of analysis method used, integration can directly determine almost all the structure of the system.

- Step 3: Selecting components

This reuse step should be handled in parallel with the classical steps that correspond to the identification of components within each phase. It includes all the reuse activities from the identification of the requirements for the component to the selection of the component. It concerns high-level and low-level components, such as subsystems in the architectural design phase, and implementation mechanisms during the implementation phase.

- Step 4: Adapting and integrating components

In parallel with the classical steps dealing with the refinement and description of components already identified, this activity is performed as soon as one reusable component has been selected for integration. If no adaptation is needed for a reusable component, it can be extracted *as is*.

10.5 The phases of development with reuse

10.5.1 The analysis phase

Generalities

The analysis phase includes activities from *requirements capture* to *modelling the application world*. Analysis consists of capturing the customer's requirements to provide a contractual agreement and a basis for the design and implementation phases. Analysis also has to provide a precise, concise, understandable, and correct model of the application and

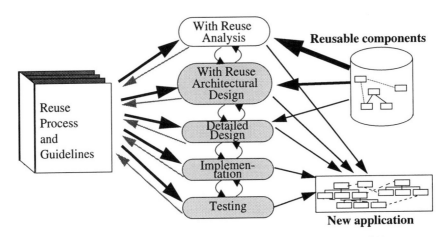

Figure 127 : The analysis phase of the life cycle for development with reuse

its functional aspects. Following the OMT development methodology, it provides the *object*, *dynamic* and *functional* models.

Introducing reuse at this stage has a major impact on the overall application development. Practising reuse consists of synthesizing a solution to a problem based on pre-defined solutions to sub-problems. The analysis phase describes the solution; you can immediately follow it by considering reuse possibilities. Using and modifying previous analysis results increases the benefits later in the development life cycle. These components also often have design and implementation parts that you can reuse with modification.

With reuse-specific activities in the analysis phase

This section describes how you can reuse requirements when you analyze the requirements for a new system, the impact of reuse on the acquisition of domain knowledge, and on the static, dynamic and functional analysis of the system.

- **Reusing requirements**

  Requirements expressed by a customer not only concern functional aspects of the software, but also describe non-functional aspects such as performance budgets that constrain execution time, size, and any environmental constraints within which the software must operate, such as interfaces, modularity, documentation, packaging and so on. The requirements influence the selection of components for all phases of the life cycle development, as shown in Figure 128.

Figure 128 : Development decisions categories

You can associate components that correspond to higher-level phases with different designs or implementations, depending on the requirements for the components, as illustrated in Figure 129. You can classify such requirements according to the phase of the project that they impact.

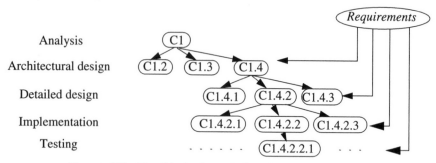

Figure 129 : Possible implementations for one component

This classification maps the decisions made at different phases of the development life cycle. Reuse of existing requirements statements can have a number of advantages, including:

— Providing consistency among related systems

— Establishing *de facto* standards

— Increasing reliability due to use of proven implementations

— Reducing overall risk

- **Reuse impact on the acquisition of domain knowledge**
  In reuse, you can formalize the knowledge acquisition to be performed during the analysis phase in two steps. The primary action to be undertaken is the *identification of the domain* or application family in which you are interested. This starts with checking the customer's problem against the base of reusable components to see whether any of the referenced domains match the domain of the problem. The second action is the *search for domain knowledge*. It is essential for a developer inexperienced in the domain, and relies on extracting all the domain knowledge from the repository of reusable components as a basis for acquiring further knowledge about the domain. Domain knowledge in the repository can be used to give an analyst an introduction to previous analysis in this problem domain, and thus give him a starting point for his analysis of the customer's specific problem. It may also be used as a basis for developing the customer's requirements, by providing a developer with the means to formulate new questions to the customer (see Guideline 77). The main benefit of using an information repository in this phase is that domain knowledge may be easily transferred to the analyst if stored with a component. As domain knowledge is the basis for all analysis, the benefits can be substantial.

- **Reuse impact on the object, dynamic and functional modelling of the system**
  Identifying analysis components can be difficult, as components may be somewhat fuzzy

at that stage. This makes automatic *searching* more difficult. Even though reuse in the analysis phase is desirable, it should not be applied if the problems overshadow the benefits. The identification problem is also due to the heterogeneous information that is manipulated during this first phase of analysis. The components found may be part of any domain, not just the target domain of the application under development. This makes it possible to reuse across application domain boundaries, desirable in large companies working in several domains.

Specific reuse guidelines

Guideline 75 :   Identify reuse opportunities during the specification phase, and identify specific reuse requirements that support them [NATO91a,b]

The system requirements establish the structure in which reuse of components is possible. Requirements influence the choice of reused components for all phases of the development life cycle. You could associate components that correspond to the higher level phase with different designs or implementations, depending on the requirements of the components, as illustrated in Figure 129.

Guideline 76 :   Do not over-specify requirements [NATO91a,b]

The presence of implementation details in the requirements for a new application can prevent you from reusing available components. The best opportunities for reuse arise when the system specification describes only necessary functionality and performance, and allows a system designer to select operational specifics. This gives you the freedom to identify reusable components that can help provide the required capability.

Guideline 77 :   Use the domain analysis to determine and validate new application requirements

Domain analysis results, and especially the domain scope definition, should be used by the requirements analyst to determine if a new application required by the customer is within the domain for which a set of products is already available. If the application is within the domain, the analyst can use generic requirements to negotiate the capabilities of the application with the customers.

Domain analysis identifies and makes explicit the knowledge about a class of problems and supports the description and appropriate solution to these problems. The output of domain analysis consists of:

- a context analysis that defines the domain which is modelled

- the domain modelling itself, to provide a static description of domain concepts

- an architectural model, that establishes the structure of software in the domain.

It therefore constitutes a base for knowledge acquisition.

If an object model is available such as that defined in the OMT methodology, or an entity-relationship model, it can be used by the requirements analyst to acquire knowledge about the domain entities and their relationships.

Guideline 78 :   Use the products from domain analysis to understand the context in which the application takes place, and its dynamics

Since domain analysis models are obtained by observing different applications in the same domain, it provides a good means to understand how the domain works. Models such as the OMT ones provide good support in this respect.

Guideline 79 :   Use available documentation as much as possible when learning about a reuse repository

During the analysis phase the way to tackle a library of components and to *understand* it, is to first examine any documentation available that describes the characteristics and behaviour of the library.

10.5.2 The architectural design phase: system design

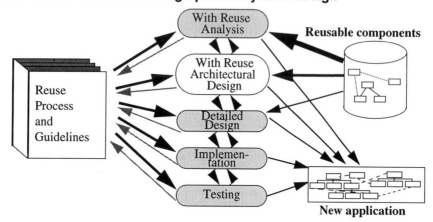

Figure 130 : The architectural design phase of the life cycle for development with reuse

Generalities

Architectural design consists of defining a high-level strategy for solving the problem and for building a solution. It corresponds to the OMT system design phase described in Chapter 8. Considering the "state-of-the-art" in reuse, the most important benefits we can currently expect correspond to the introduction of reuse within this phase. Reuse in the design phase is different from reuse in analysis, even in object-oriented development where the borderline between analysis and design is less clear.

Reusing design components is essential to achieving code reuse, and is valuable even if the corresponding code is not reused. The design process differs depending on the scale of the components to be reused. You can reuse small-scale components directly as individual classes or objects.

With reuse-specific activities in the architectural design phase

The major problem inherent in the architectural design of applications from existing reusable components lies in:

- the difficulty of building up a knowledge of predefined solutions

- applying that knowledge to structuring the application problem in term of sub-problems for which solutions already exist.

This is really the problem of knowing about what components already exist and *identifying* suitable candidates. Using a standard architecture facilitates this task. When a standard architecture is available, the problem is then to introduce within that architecture the specific needs of the new application, that is, its *adaptation* to the new application. One way to do this is to use frameworks.

Using frameworks

A framework describes how to implement the whole or part of an application in a particular problem domain (see Section 8.2). It is a general architecture for the domain and its classes describe the objects in the domain and how they interact. The following figure shows an example of a framework in the fire alarm application described in Appendix A.

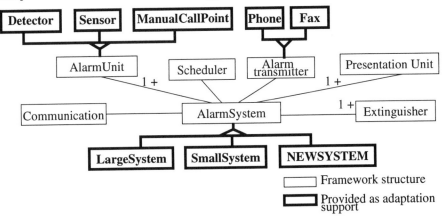

Figure 131 : OMT object model of the fire alarm framework with adaptations

There are two types of objects in a framework:

- the objects that are the basic blocks of the framework

- the objects provided to anticipate future adaptations; these are usually created using inheritance

The previous figure shows an example. The "Alarm Transmitter" has been refined into two different specific devices (phone and fax) for transmitting the alarm, ready to be used for the new developed application.

Reuse impact on the object, dynamic and functional modelling of the system

The *evaluation* of a framework's structure and behaviour within the architectural design phase requires investigating the detailed design and implementation parts of the framework. A study of the most significant branches of the framework is generally sufficient for a complete *understanding* of its specific behaviour. You have to take such new transitions between the different phases of the classical development life cycle into account when introducing reuse into a project.

Specific reuse guidelines for using frameworks

Guideline 80 :   Select well-documented frameworks

High-level components should be well documented, easily understandable and illustrated by examples of use.

Reuse aspects

When reusing high-level components such as frameworks, developers have made the observation that evaluating such high-level components has to be done mainly by reading the documentation. An important criterion for the evaluation of high-level components is the existence of accompanying examples of use. Developers evaluate the generic architecture framework by reading the documentation, examining the code and doing tests with given examples.

Guideline 81 :   Consider detailed design for framework evaluation

When evaluating a framework, the developer should carry out the detailed design of the main mechanisms provided by the framework to understand its behaviour.

Reuse aspects

The evaluation of a framework is difficult because its architecture is generally complex. Since this type of component will become the main part of the system, we suggested that developers do some detailed design work to study the behaviour of the component. When they have enough knowledge about how the component interacts with other subsystems, the remainder of the adaptation can be left to the detailed design phase.

Guideline 82 :   Preserve the strategy implemented in the framework when adapting it

Use specific object-oriented mechanisms like encapsulation or inheritance to make the architectural adaptations to a framework, so that you remain consistent with the initial architecture of the framework.

Reuse aspects

Reuse of high-level components, such as frameworks, has shown that most of the implementation strategy is determined by the generic architecture of the component. Future adaptations should therefore fit the main strategy implemented in the framework. Framework components are not adapted like general components. Adapting such a component is like implementing a whole system or subsystem. You adapt them by designing and implementing subclasses and subsystems, and you should leave this until later in the detailed design and implementation phases.

Guideline 83 :   Keep the life cycle sequencing for framework adaptation

Apart from the necessary evaluation of the framework, postpone the identification of classes to the detailed design phase.

Reuse aspects

Reusing a framework defines the set of objects and classes already determined by the framework structure. Adapting classes that have already been identified can lead you to define new classes or objects directly rather than postponing the task. Even if this approach seems attractive at first, it is not recommended because the resulting set of classes may be too rigid for the architectural design phase.

Guideline 84 :   Use inheritance to customize reused frameworks

You can customize frameworks for a specific application using *refinement adaptation*. This involves leaving the structure of the framework unchanged but adapting the individual classes in the framework. The best way of doing this is to use inheritance.

10.5.3 The detailed design phase: object design

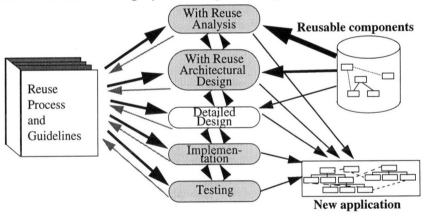

Figure 132 : The detailed design phase of the life cycle for development with reuse

Generalities

In the detailed design phase, all classes and associations are fully defined. Object-oriented design is an iterative process. When one level of abstraction is complete, the developer brings the design down to a finer level of detail. It corresponds to the OMT object design phase.

With reuse-specific activities in the detailed design phase

The selection activity described in Section 10.3 impacts two major steps of the detailed design process:

- It gives valuable inputs to the classical object-oriented detailed design step that deals with the *choice of global mechanisms* (see Section 8.4.3). Basic features such as error-trapping or persistence have to be selected at least at the beginning of the detailed design phase. Standard mechanisms can be reused at that stage.

- The selection activity supports the developer in *mapping objects into classes, objects and templates* by searching and evaluating existing components in the repository. It provides references to predefined classes that correspond to already complete abstractions.

The *adaptation* activity concerns the class and template descriptions of reused components. Adaptation is performed using parametrization or specialization techniques.

Integrating the component can bring a new problem, depending on the formalization used in the design phase. When a component fits the development method (object-oriented component with object-oriented development, or structured development), integration is simplified. When the component does not fit the development method, integration is more difficult. Two suggested integration approaches are:

- When the reused component from a structured development is used in an object-oriented one, one way to facilitate its integration is to encapsulate it within an abstract data type with visible interfaces.

- To integrate an object-oriented component into a structured environment, include the object wherever it is used.

10.5.4 The implementation phase

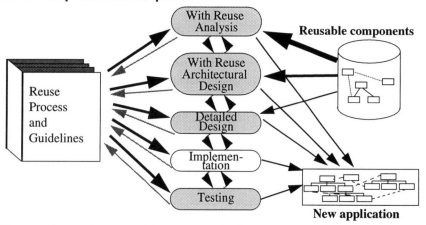

Figure 133 : The implementation phase of the life cycle for development with reuse

Generalities

The transition from the detailed design phase to the implementation phase is quite straightforward—components and their interface must be implemented. Reuse activities within the implementation phase appear in two different ways:

- Informally, by reusing implementation standards like documents retrieved from a previous development.

- Formally, by reusing code from existing components identified in the design phase. The corresponding code can be reused *as is*, or adapted to the requirements of the application.

With reuse-specific activities in the implementation phase

The main reuse activities within the implementation phase consist of understanding and adapting the component's code, and then integrating it in the overall development.

Understanding the code can be achieved in previous analysis and design phases, as a means of understanding the component, described in Section 10.3.3. It is often an expensive activity, often due to lack of appropriate documentation. Any *adaptations to the code* should be documented to describe the adaptations made.

A classical situation when *integrating* a component is to use only one or two services provided by it. This can occur for example when using a complete library in which only some components are needed. It mainly concerns the implementation phase, where the code of a complete component can be voluminous and not needed in its entirety. The problem of reusing only parts of a component is an implementation problem and is not addressed by object-oriented concepts. It is sometimes supported by compilers or other programming language mechanisms. For example, the C++ mechanism *genericity* offers this kind of support. When you instantiate a generic class for a specific type, the compiler only generates the associated code for that specific type.

Specific reuse guidelines

Guideline 85 : Using browsers during the implementation phase is very useful in understanding components

Guideline 86 : Establish implementation standards that facilitate the ease and safety of code reuse

Implementation standards should include the following points:

- Choose naming conventions to avoid name conflicts, and also to increase the understandability of the component.

- Standardize basic mechanisms, such as exceptions, help procedures and so on.

- Avoid global data items.

Guideline 87 : Control and document each modification performed on the component

This contributes to the documentation of the reusable component and so enhances its future reusability, and supports version control.

Guideline 88 : Rename programming entities when necessary

C++ distinguishes the following programming entities: *classes, member functions, attributes* and *types*. There may be several reasons to rename them, due to name conflicts.

Apply the following implementation guidelines to avoid global names, and thus conflicts:

- Use member functions instead of global *friend* functions and non-member functions.

- Use static member data instead of global non-member data.

- Use a project-wide or module-wide name for each remaining global. Longer prefixes reduce the likelihood of clashes with other prefixes.

You may also need to rename a C++ entity when reusing it simply to respect such project-wide naming conventions. In each situation, you must keep the naming coherence when modifying an identifier, that is, each reference to the entity involved has to be updated. In all cases it is preferable to modify your own code rather than library source code to resolve the conflict.

Guideline 89 :   Keep the naming coherence

When you modify an identifier, you have to update every reference to it. The following references are possible in C++:

- *Class*. Creation of objects of this class. Declaration of the class in modules where it will be used

- Function call

- *Member function*

- *Attributes*. Access to the attribute

- *Types*. Creation of an object of this type

The problem of global declaration does not exist for member functions and attributes, because they are implicitly or explicitly qualified by the class name. In this case, a name conflict can only occur when two classes are merged. You should limit the use of functions. It is preferable to link them to a class by declaring them within a class.

Guideline 90 :   Keep coherence when manipulating programming entities

This applies to both the moving and the deletion operations.

Moving operation

The moving operation needs strong control of the coherence of the produced code. The object has a given scope depending on where it has been defined. Moving it has consequences for references to it.

When an entity is moved, you must exercise strong control on the new visibility of moved objects. Suppose in Figure 134 that you want to reuse the class *Town*, but define the class *Street* at a global level. In this kind of movement, the new access to attribute and member functions is the same. The code to be modified concerns only the declaration and access to objects of class *Street*.

Consider that you want to reuse two classes from different sources, for example the classes *Glider* and *Airplane* in Figure 135. You therefore decide to create a more generic class and to introduce an inheritance relation. With this kind of movement, you have to check the following points:

- Private members that are moved into the newly inherited class must be declared as *protected*, to be accessible by the objects of the inheriting classes.

```
Class Town {
      class Street {
      string Name;
      private string Type;
      private string Location;
      void Print();
      string GetStreetType(string);
      string GetStreetLocation(string);
      }
      Street * ListStreet;
      Street * GetStreetType(String);
      string GetStreetLocation(String);
}
```

Figure 134 : Example: Street and Town classes

```
Class Glider {                                 Class Airplane{
      private string registration;                   private string registration;
      private int TimeOfFly;                         private int TimeOfFly;
      private string make;                           private string make;
      boolean                                        boolean
         AuthorizedToFly(string);                       AuthorizedToFly(string);

      string GetRegistration();                      string GetRegistration();
....                                                 . . . .
      boolean AuthorizedAcrobatics;                  date LastEngineControl;
      string HookType;}                              string EnginePower;}

   Class Flying {

         protected string registration
         protected int TimeOfFly;
         protected string make;
         virtual string GetRegistration();
         .......
         virtual boolean
            AuthorizedToFly(string);}

Class Glider: public Flying {              Class Airplane : public Flying {
      boolean                                    date LastEngineControl;
         AuthorizedAcrobatics;                   string EnginePower;}
      string HookType;}
```

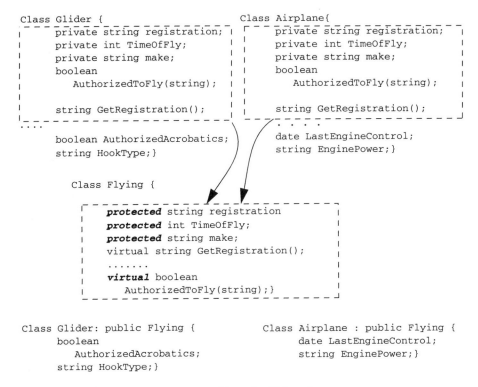

Figure 135 : Example: Flying classes

- Each member function allowed to read or modify private members must be moved into the generic class and declared as *virtual*.
- Other common member functions should be declared as *virtual* in the newly created class.

Deleting operation

- Before deleting an entity, first verify that it is not used elsewhere.

- Before deleting a type, first verify that no object is declared or otherwise used (*casting*, sizeof and so on) with this type.

- Before deleting a class, first verify that it is not inherited by another class, and that no object of this class is created or otherwise used.

- Before deleting a function, first verify that it is not called anywhere.

10.5.5 The testing phase

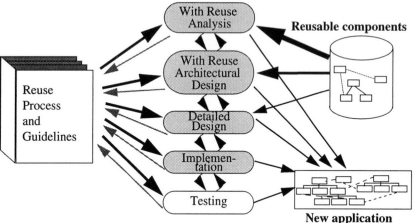

Figure 136 : The testing phase of the life cycle for development with reuse

Generalities

Testing is usually decomposed into four steps:

- Choosing a strategy
  This consists of finding a test strategy that will be applied during the whole testing phase. It includes points such as the rate of success for the tests, the test coverage used to determine when the system is considered to be fully tested, and the development order for testing (high-level components and then low-level components, or vice versa).

- Developing test suites
  This consists of developing testing scenarios and allocating material such as:

  — software required to simulate a testing scenario

  — specific software for supporting testing, such as a test coverage tool

  — the human resources required to complete the testing

- Executing test suites on the system
  The order of execution of tests is defined as part of the test strategy. The running of each test suite must be independent of any other suite.

- Reporting the results of tests

  In this step, the results of executed tests are recorded. Test failure may require a return to one of the previous development phases. A result is not valid if it does not fulfil the conditions given in the test strategy. All results must be recorded.

With reuse-specific activities in the testing phase

One of the main interests of the testing phase is the ability to reuse test components (test cases, test data, environments and so on) from the repository. You should consider test information as self-contained components within the repository; this will help their general reuse. Test information has to be packaged with additional information (such as the components to which the tests have been applied, modifications, statistics and so on), so that it can be reused efficiently.

Reuse impacts the choice of testing strategy insofar as global testing strategies, such as *statistical usage* testing, can be reused between applications that have a similar execution context.

The next step consists of adapting test scenarios and needed material to test components of the system. At the moment little information exists on planned reuse during the test phase of an object-oriented system, as our experience of introducing reuse in testing is limited. However, the reuse of global testing strategies between similar applications appears to offer a promising approach.

10.6 The impact of reuse on development life cycles

The reuse of high-level components poses a number of questions about the best way to integrate reusable components into each phase of the development life cycle.

A major difficulty is the fact that you have to reconsider a reusable component at each phase of the life cycle, and reactivate a part of the reuse process to reuse the component within each phase. This chapter describes a scenario to illustrate this difficulty, and proposes several strategies for reusing a component. It ends by describing some commonly used development life cycles and their suitability for the integration of reuse.

10.6.1 Reusing a component in different phases of a development

This section describes an example that illustrates the difficulties you might encounter when reusing a component throughout the development life cycle. The scenario illustrated in Figure 137 describes the reuse activities required in each phase of the development life cycle for a component.

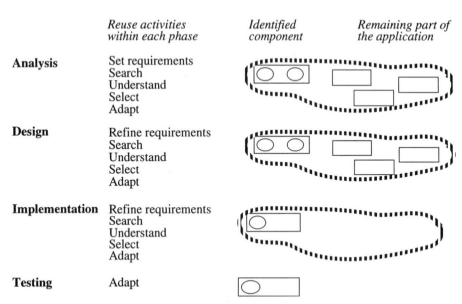

	Reuse activities within each phase	Identified component	Remaining part of the application

Analysis   Set requirements
             Search
             Understand
             Select
             Adapt

Design   Refine requirements
             Search
             Understand
             Select
             Adapt

Implementation Refine requirements
             Search
             Understand
             Select
             Adapt

Testing   Adapt

Figure 137 : Example: Reuse of one component all over the development life cycle

- Analysis phase
  Suppose you identified the need for a component when performing the analysis. You would then carry out the *set requirements, search* and *understand* activities at the analysis level, selecting a set of components that fit the requirements. However, as the requirements at that stage are imprecise, you postpone a final selection to a subsequent phase.

- Design phase
  During the design phase, you must remember that a set of components has already been retrieved to fulfil the requirements of the analysis phase. You need to reconsider the set of candidates found in the analysis phase in the light of the new requirements of the design phase. You carry out the *Set Requirements, Search* and *Understand* activities again to refine the set of candidate components for these new requirements. You may find again that the requirements at the design phase are too high-level for the type of components to be selected, and again postpone your final selection.

- Implementation phase
  The requirements are now well defined at the code level, and you reconsider the first three activities (*Set Requirements, Search* and *Understand*). You make your final selection of component and adapt its code. You then update the design and specification parts of the components to match.

- Testing phase
  You take all the adaptations made to components in the coding phase into account in the testing phase, adapting the test suites to the modifications of the external view of each component (such as its interface).

Many similar scenarios can be envisaged, highlighting the fact that several specific reuse activities have to be re-executed several times during the reuse process. The most common is the adaptation of one component in all subsequent phases when the component has been selected very early in the development process. The following section describes different strategies you can apply to reusing a component in the development process.

10.6.2 Strategies for reusing a component

There are several ways to reuse a component.

- You can choose to reuse the component in a discontinuous way in each development phase, focusing on the part of the component associated with the current phase, and reporting the adaptations for later phases. For example, you could reuse and adapt the analysis, architectural and detailed designs within the appropriate phases of the development, rather than carrying this out separately as a single activity for each component. This has the advantage that the component is treated in a consistent context of the application in the current phase. The drawback is that some of the understanding activity must be repeated to trace the adaptations previously made.

- When selecting a component, you can choose to adapt all its associated parts at once. This optimizes the understanding process by performing all the adaptations required by the following phases in a single step. The drawback is that it could be difficult to perform and validate the adaptation before the remainder of the application is implemented.

- You could employ a mix of these two approaches, depending on the type of component and stability of the requirements on it.

The choice of strategy relies on the following criteria:

- Reuse process mapping
  Reuse activities have to be divided amongst the different phases depending on the availability of requirements for the relevant selection of a component, and the necessary adaptations of the components. For example, a component identified during the design phase has to be integrated or adapted into the design, and its associated implementation part has to be integrated or adapted in the coding phase. Some reuse-specific activities require a significant effort in understanding and adaptation. Understanding a component is a prerequisite to its adaptation. It is a challenge to distribute the reuse tasks so that you benefit from previous work and a well-defined context.

- Reuse efficiency
  It may be more efficient to reuse and adapt the design of a subsystem, and re-implement it entirely, than to reuse some of the implementation parts of a component.

- Distribution of work
  The problems mentioned above are worse when different people work on the different phases of the life cycle. In a sequential life cycle, how can we avoid redundant work between the analyst, the designer and the programmer dealing with the same reusable

component? Each of them has to thoroughly understand the component to properly integrate it into the phase on which he is working. How can we highlight the adaptations made in the high-level phases so that we propagate them to the following phases? This question is even more acute when the analyst, designer and programmer roles are completely differentiated.

- Scheduling and time interval
  You have to take these two factors into account when reusing a component between phases of a project. For example, when understanding and adapting a component, even if these are performed by the same person, the knowledge acquired about a component rapidly fades in the interval between two adaptations of the same component.

The following section examines the appropriateness of sequential and iterative development life cycles based on the considerations presented in this section.

10.6.3 Different life cycle types for the reuse of components

This section describes two of the most common iterative development life cycles, *prototyping* and *spiral*, and compares their adequacy to a sequential approach.

Prototyping life cycle

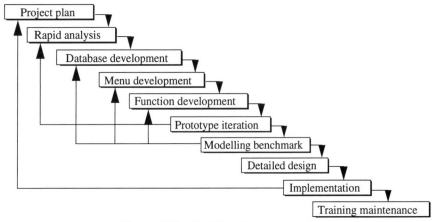

Figure 138 : Rapid prototyping model

The objective of prototyping is to bridge the gap between the systems designer and the customer by providing a demonstration of the application to the customer rapidly.

There are two main motivations for using this approach. The first is to identify the user's requirements. The resulting prototype is used as a contractual support for the system specifications. The second reason is to test the feasibility of the system if the domain of the application is poorly understood.

Spiral life cycle model

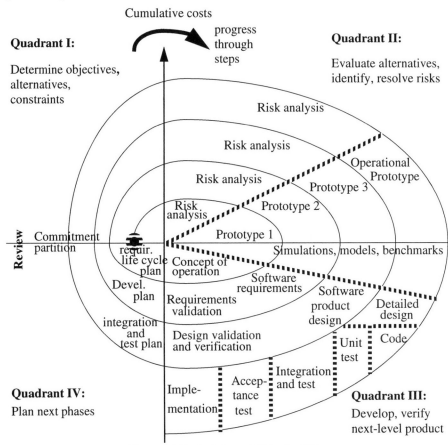

Figure 139 : Spiral model [Boehm88]

The spiral model [Boehm88] corresponds to a *risk-driven* approach—a development method designed to minimize development risks—that provides a user with the means to test different options and requirements for the system at an early stage. It is based on a cyclical approach. Each cycle of the spiral contains the following steps, as illustrated in Figure 139:

• Identification of the targets of the product, the implementation alternatives for this part of the product and the constraints that influence the application of the alternatives.

• Evaluation of the alternatives and identification of the associated risks.

• Development of a more detailed product with minimal effort.

• Product review and schedule for the following cycle (if any).

Comparison of the life cycle models

What are the advantages and drawbacks of the use of these life cycles for the reuse of existing components, compared with a sequential approach? The advantages and disadvantages of each approach are discussed below.

The conventional sequential development life cycle model

One of the main reasons for using a conventional development life cycle is that basically it describes the correct and necessary activities of a software development process in the right order. The results of each phase are validated, enhancing the quality of the produced components. The Waterfall model implies that the entire software product is determined by the end of the analysis and design phases. Such an approach requires a very precise knowledge of the system at the analysis phase, and makes no provision for changes while the project is in progress. A drawback is that the early specification of product requirements can result in a mismatch between the user's requirements and the created system.

However, there are several difficulties for reuse inherent in software life cycle models such as the Waterfall model proposed by [Boehm88]:

• System development and the development of individual components are performed only with regard to the product in progress. The result of a strict use of a conventional life cycle model is software that is extremely difficult to modify and extend. The monolithic structure of the developed system and the specialization of its individual components tend to prevent efficient reuse.

• In the Waterfall model, difficulties are not raised by the activities performed in the individual phases, but rather by the sequence and strict separation of the phases, the interactions between the phases, and the requirements and composition of the intermediate products between each phase. Each phase is self-contained with respect to the preceding and succeeding ones, resulting in a lack of planning for the inclusion of later modifications. As the separate phases are self-contained and the intermediate products are frozen, the end-product is realized completely isolated from any changes in the environment, and no allowance is made for changing user requirements. This is an important limitation for reuse of pre-existing components, as the reuse of components often requires the ability to change the requirements for the component.

Use of rapid prototyping and spiral life cycle models

A major advantage of iterative life cycle models such as rapid prototyping and spiral models is the incremental creation of the software that results. The whole iteration can be executed for every component of the whole project. Several spiral runs can take place simultaneously. Changes in the requirements that result in changes to the components or the reuse of existing components can be reacted to appropriately. This is because such models are suitable for the whole project as well as for the development of individual components. For example, the integration of modifications and new requirements only recognized in the development phase can influence the development of other components in other spiral runs. These models present the flexibility required for reusing a component as discussed in Section 10.6.2.

You can consider the repository of reusable components as a basis for rapid prototyping when using this type of model. The evaluation of the resulting prototype will give new input to the analysis. In this way the analyst is able to speed up the iteration life cycle of the project.

The use of the spiral model provides a means to test the development options for an application in a limited context with controlled risks. It can focus attention on options involving the reuse of existing software at an early stage, favouring the reuse of existing components.

The spiral model includes validation steps that you can use to measure the quality of the performed software and to evaluate the options for each significant step of the development. Such a process favours the evaluation of *with* reuse activities and the rationales for reusing components.

10.7 Conclusion

We have demonstrated in this chapter that the activities specific to development *with* reuse are compatible with classical object-oriented development. Their integration into the object-oriented development life cycle is easy, and provides significant support to the developer. The process of development *with* reuse must be an integrated part of the overall development life cycle, so that developers are aware of the steps where they can incorporate reuse, and are stimulated to do so.

11 Re-engineering for Reuse

11.1 Introduction

Re-engineering software for reuse in another context provides the chance to keep the knowledge embodied in the software available for future systems, and to save a considerable amount of work.

Re-engineering for reuse describes a further possibility for the development for reuse. It focuses on the problem of re-engineering an existing system in such a way that parts of the system become reusable, as reusable components, in other systems or other contexts.

Object-orientation and object-oriented programming are regarded as some of the most promising approaches for mastering the challenges of software development in the future. The great advantages of object-orientation are the ease of maintenance, and the high degree of reusability of object-oriented programs, or parts of programs such as object classes.

Unfortunately, most of today's software is not written in this way, so the maintainers of these systems cannot benefit from the advantages provided by object-oriented methods and tools. There is, however, a strong demand to migrate existing systems in a way that allows newly developed tools and techniques to become applicable.

Besides building reusable objects from scratch, existing systems offer a broad range of potentially reusable components even though they were not implemented in an object-oriented way. The methodology for re-engineering for reuse addresses the problem of retrieving reusable components from non-object-oriented software. The method presented here is also applicable to object-oriented programs.

This chapter presents:

- The objectives of re-engineering for reuse

- When to apply re-engineering for reuse

- The difference between re-engineering for reuse and re-engineering

- The necessity of a defined re-engineering for reuse method

- The scale of extractable reusable components

- The kinds of components that can be extracted with re-engineering for reuse

- The foundations of re-engineering for reuse methods

- How to apply re-engineering for reuse

11.1.1 The goals of re-engineering for reuse

What should be your objectives in re-engineering for reuse?

When should you apply it?

Our re-engineering method does not tackle the problem "How can we transform non-object-oriented code into code written in an object-oriented language?". A transformation like this would depend on the particular object-oriented programming language. Within the work described here, we concentrate on the development of a method for retrieving objects regardless of the programming language actually used. This means that we base our method on as few language-dependent features as possible. However, the result of the method is a set of reusable objects written in a non-object-oriented language, consisting of a set of functions and data structures for a problem domain.

Transformation of the retrieved objects into an object-oriented language can be carried out afterwards and should be supportable by automatic tools like program translators. This is not considered in the scope of this discussion, however.

Our method for retrieving reusable objects from non-object-oriented code has three main objectives:

- It tries to develop a way of retrieving reusable objects that is less costly than rewriting the code, enabling you to detect code that is worth reusing. The method presented here aims at a reuse of both design information and parts of the code. This requires an inspection of the source code that goes far beyond pure design recovery. We do not claim that the reuse of source code is the only thing worth considering, but we have concentrated on it because it seemed the most fruitful approach.

- The application of our method provides a methodological background for supplying the reuse repository with really reusable objects. Thus it is an important means to get reuse started.

- From a user's point of view, these techniques will help you migrate smoothly from non-object-oriented software to object-oriented software. It supports you in understanding existing software systems and reducing your maintenance effort.

It is not our intention to re-engineer a complete system using this method; only parts of it are extracted and re-engineered in a way that enables them to be treated as reusable components. The problem of re-engineering a reusable component to adapt it to the needs of a special application is not part of the method described here.

11.1.2 An overview of this chapter

This chapter describes a method for retrieving reusable objects in existing applications, and its application is described. The description of the method is purely methodological in that activities are described that are carried out during the different steps of the method. This is not a description of how to use a specific set of tools. To some extent the method is applicable without tool support, but its efficiency is limited in such a case.

We start with some reasoning about the need and usage of a re-engineering method. After this, we present our key ideas about how such a method could work, and discuss some basic techniques that might be useful.

The next section then presents our method for retrieving reusable objects with the help of three scenarios to demonstrate how it could work. Differences and commonalities with other approaches are discussed and, finally, we show how the REBOOT toolset can be used to support this method. The development of this method has strongly influenced the development of the re-engineering services of the REBOOT toolset. These services provide the best support to the user available at this time.

11.2 Some reasoning about re-engineering for reuse

11.2.1 The need for re-engineering for reuse

Why might it be necessary to have a defined re-engineering for reuse method?

The retrieval of reusable objects from non-object-oriented code is still largely an unsolved problem, regardless of its importance and the potential benefits. There are several reasons why it is useful and profitable to develop a method for retrieving reusable objects:

- Objects extracted from existing systems can be expected to have a certain degree of reliability because of its use, allowing errors to be detected.

- Many methodologies and environments concentrate on the development of new systems, and their support ends after the first release of the software. It is a well-known fact that software systems may deteriorate during their lifetime due to changes and quick bug corrections that do not conform with the initial intentions. A methodology is needed that supports the user and tells him how to handle existing systems. This is necessary for non-object-oriented as well as object-oriented systems. Even if the components of the system were designed for reuse but not stored in a base of reusable components, there is a danger that these components will have deteriorated too, and the same work is needed to retrieve them.

- Objects retrieved from existing systems represent knowledge about the domain of the application they have been extracted from. This knowledge and the experience associated with it are not in a form suitable for reuse, and it may be very hard to retrieve them in any other way.

11.2.2 Re-engineering for reuse versus re-engineering

Is there a difference between re-engineering for reuse and re-engineering?

There is a basic difference between re-engineering for reuse and re-engineering an entire system:

- *Re-engineering* tries to recover or reverse-engineer the design of a system, and to change the system afterwards to make it more flexible, maintainable, understandable and so on. It aims at the system as a whole.

- *Re-engineering for reuse* goes for the pieces. It tries to split a system into building blocks. Some of these might be reusable, others are discarded.

Re-engineering for reuse tries to find reusable parts which may be taken as black boxes, with a clearly definable behaviour and defined interfaces. The internal realization should not be of interest to the reuser and should not depend on nor affect other parts of the system. Re-engineering for reuse concentrates on finding and extracting those reusable parts out of existing software. Parts which are not considered for reuse are ignored. The original system remains unchanged; the reusable parts are extracted, modified and used outside the system.

The decision whether to re-engineer a system or just to use it as a resource for components for re-engineering depends on many factors:

- Is the system still in use? If not, you can only use it to extract reusable parts.

- What can you gain by re-engineering the system? Longer life-span? Better portability? Better extensibility?

- Are major changes in the requirements and hardware or software environments expected?

- Is it possible to share the costs for re-engineering with future reusers of parts of the system?

- Is it possible to share maintenance costs with reusers?

You need a thorough analysis of costs and benefits to decide which approach to take. In the following sections, we focus on re-engineering for reuse. The methods presented there are also valid and applicable for re-engineering.

11.2.3 The applicability of re-engineering for reuse

The method described here focuses on the extraction of reusable pieces of source code. Just as in development for reuse, where the use of a component was planned at development time, re-engineering for reuse plans and enables the reuse of components that already exist. It requires an investment at development time to enable future reuse.

Source code is not the only thing you can reuse—design and architectural concepts are reusable as well. If you attempt to reuse source code that is extracted from its original context, you also have to recover its design and understand it. Even if you do not succeed in reusing the code, nothing prevents you from reusing intermediate results such as design concepts or other knowledge that was gained during the re-engineering activities.

Contrary to other methods that aim only at the reuse of concepts and designs, the method proposed here is based on a deep and profound knowledge of the concrete realization of the system from which components are extracted. This makes it also suitable for use during the development of complex systems, to help developers master the complexity, to keep an overview over the system, and to avoid getting lost in details of implementation.

11.2.4 The scale of reusable objects

What scale of components can be extracted by re-engineering for reuse?

The size of components extracted by re-engineering for reuse has a strong impact on their reusability. It is not only reusability that counts here, but the reuse benefit of such a component. Reusability and reuse benefits do not follow the same conditions. Very small components such as functions have a very high reusability, but the benefit achieved when reusing such components is not very high. Very large and complex components may seldom be reused, but the benefit of doing so is very high because of the complex functionality which is recoverable.

We therefore aim at medium-scale objects. For small objects, the benefit we would obtain would not be worth the effort of retrieving them—a new implementation would be easier and cheaper. For very large components the problem of finding and extracting them from existing systems is not so great because they might be complete subsystems, or may have already been designed for reuse. Design with reuse, enabling further use of such large components, is the harder problem in this case. Medium-scale components that we want to extract should consist of several hundred lines of code and have a clearly describable purpose and functionality. In terms of object orientation, these components can be considered as objects in the domain of the application from which we are trying to extract them. In that sense, domain analysis provides a very important aid for re-engineering for reuse, by assisting you in getting the knowledge you need about the system containing the components.

If you look at the components that have been extracted for reuse in one domain and are reused in another domain, you will find that their size and granularity are not only determined by the structure of the original system. The similarity of the two domains is another important factor. The more similar the two domains are, the more likely it is that they may contain the same objects which may be found and reused. If the domains are not similar at all, they will probably share only small objects of general use. If the domains are similar, the common objects may be rather big and complex as they may be key abstractions which are common to both domains.

11.2.5 Candidate components for re-engineering for reuse

What kind of components can be extracted by re-engineering for reuse?

Some types of components are more likely to be reusable than others. Selecting the right components in a recovered design helps limit and focus the work required:

- You can expect designs and structures in which the principle of distinction between *policy* and *implementation* is realized to contain reusable components. Implementation components should realize context-independent services, whereas policy components provide higher-level functionality realized by combining the services of the implementation components. Policy components cannot be reused easily as they usually differ from application to application. If the principle of distinction between policy and implementation is not realized, the chances of finding something that may be reused become smaller. Sometimes, especially in recovered designs, it is difficult to see whether this principle has been followed or not, and you can only find out by inspecting the code.

- If you can find a clear abstraction for an element of the design easily, this indicates a conceptual entity. This does not necessarily mean that conceptual entities have been realized as entities in the source code. The opposite holds: if it is not possible to find a proper abstraction for an entity that you consider to reuse, this implies that it is probably not reusable.

Here are a number of examples of the kinds of components that can be reused and what cannot:

Reusable components

- Communication facilities and Inter-Process-Communication-components, providing the communication between arbitrary components that follow a fixed protocol.

- Components that represent devices like disk drives, I/O-devices, mice, joysticks and so on.

- Foundation classes that realize some basic functionality that may be applied in many cases.

- Components that realize substantial parts or abstractions of the application domain.

Non-reusable components

- "Glue" components, mediators between components and adaptation components

- "Wrapper" components that are used to encapsulate other components. These should be rewritten as they are not general enough in most cases. This applies only for the wrapper component itself, and not for the component that is wrapped.

- Policy components. Basic operations realized by implementation components may be applied in many different places but their combinations, realized by policy components, will probably differ in different applications.

11.2.6 When to apply re-engineering for reuse?

The most important applications of re-engineering for reuse are:

- browsing through an existing system looking for parts that might be reusable

- searching for the parts of something that is known to be in the system.

These two possibilities are used later on to explain our method and its usage. These are not the only ways that this method could be applied. However, just to apply the method for the sake of finding reusable components may be very expensive in some cases, and more costly than rewriting the components from scratch.

You can also use the method proposed below as an aid to understanding existing systems. You can use it completely or partially whenever you need a profound understanding of a system and its interrelationships.

11.2.7 Is extracting components from existing systems worth the effort?

You can use the re-engineering method described in this chapter to extract components from structured systems and incorporate them into object-oriented systems. You can therefore use the method to convert parts of systems in such a way that they may become a part of an object-oriented development. Converting a system or parts of it in this way offers many advantages such as improved maintainability. You have to look carefully to see if such a conversion is really worth the effort. The following points are relevant:

- If fundamental structures in a program are missing, conversion makes little sense and rewriting is cheaper.

- If the system depends on non-object-oriented tools like toolboxes that must be linked into the code, the system cannot be made totally object-oriented.

- If the system takes full advantage of system-level resources such as interrupts, system calls, and so on the code will be hard to transform into true object-oriented code.

- The higher the coupling between application components—modules, procedures, or whatever—the harder it will be to transform it to an object-oriented design.

These points apply regardless of what method you use for retrieving objects in non-object-oriented code or for converting whole systems. You can find more information about these aspects in [Duntemann90]. We believe that conversion has more advantages than disadvantages, however.

To reduce the risk of working on a system that is not worth the effort because it does not contain parts that might be reused, REBOOT's method incorporates support for the early phases. It takes the above points into account, and applies metrics that help you decide whether your program is a good candidate for reusable objects or not.

11.3 The methodology for re-engineering for reuse

What are the foundations of a method for re-engineering for reuse?

What steps and activities are required for re-engineering for reuse?

11.3.1 The idea

Our basic idea for finding reusable components in existing code is to start from the source code of the system and try to find parts or groups with a strong inner coupling. We can then take these groups as candidates for reusable components and evaluate them later.

To put this idea of finding reusable objects into practice, we have to look for techniques that might be useful. Besides methods for converting programs to object-orientation, there are other techniques like *grouping* or *classification* that might help us to achieve our goal. Reorganizing or regrouping of functions and data is a far from new idea. Even if the goals of these techniques were different in the past, we can profit from work that has been done in those areas and extract important hints for our re-engineering method.

11.3.2 Parametrization

Parametrization is a frequently recommended method for increasing the reusability of a program or a function. It replaces access to global variables by newly-generated parameters of the accessing function. This helps to make a function more transparent, and it becomes easier to see its type and dependencies. It is much easier to provide a variable accessed as a parameter than to ensure there are global variables of exactly the name and type required when trying to reuse a parametrized function. Dependencies through parameters are easier to control (even though they still exist). You can find examples showing how parametrization works and how you can use it to find objects in [Garnett90].

Parametrization turns any procedural interface into a functional interface in which all the accessed data are provided as parameters. This creates functions with huge lists of parameters. The higher a function is located in a call hierarchy, the more parameters it accesses. The function *main* will have parameters for all the global data of the entire program. In programming languages that do not support data abstraction, parametrization is a commonly-used technique to realize abstract data types as global data together with a set of access functions. Access to the global data is only done via these access functions, and knowledge about the existence and the concrete realization of the data items is not needed in the rest of the program. With parametrization, this information is spread throughout the program, and knowledge about the existence of the abstract data types involved is lost. In that sense parametrization violates data abstraction. Hidden design decisions are made visible throughout the direct and indirect accessing functions. Even if this is only an intermediate result, it may cause problems in some cases, and there is certainly a loss of information.

11.3.3 Grouping

Finding components or functions that belong together and grouping them is (apart from human intuition) the most important technique to help find strongly connected components. Grouping can be carried out after parametrization using common parameters to detect groups, or it can be based on the access of individual data items, functions and so on. We think that grouping based on the access of individual software features is better suited for retrieving reusable objects than grouping on the basis of common types.

Grouping by software features

Information-sharing heuristics can be based on the non-local names that procedures use. More formally, a non-local name is any name whose scope includes two or more procedure bodies. We always assign a unique identifier to each of these names, to distinguish multiple declarations in different scopes. Every non-local name is a potential feature name. Every non-local name appearing in the body of a procedure is a feature of that procedure.

Sometimes two or more procedures are placed together in the same module because they are called from the same procedures. For example, whenever procedure A calls procedure B, not only does A receive the feature "calls B", but B receives the feature "called-by-A".

Similarity between two objects is a function of common and distinctive features, and that similarity increases monotonically with a growing common feature set, and decreases monotonically with a growing distinctive feature set.

The *similarity number* measures the properties of the similarity of two objects and assigns weights to the individual features. The significance of a feature is estimated by its Shannon information content:

Weight(f) = $-$log(Probability(f))

where the probability of f is the number of all procedures that have feature f. This gives rarely-used identifiers higher weights than frequently-used identifiers, in keeping with the idea that rare names are more likely to be hidden in modules than frequently-used ones.

Finding objects by grouping

Grouping bases its calculations on the access or use of individual features. These features of a function might be calls of functions, being called by functions, access of global data, use of macros and constants, and use of data-types. We need a *similarity measure* to group the most similar functions or procedures together. We group functions around the data they share to achieve this. Every feature has a certain significance that indicates how much it contributes to the context, meaning or property of the function. This helps to group functions around those data items that are most important to them. We do not need a classification scheme, facet or template to determine which objects belong together. Grouping can handle any program without modifications, and form groups of functions that share common features.

You can find an example of how this kind of grouping can be supported by tools in a tool called Arch[1]. Arch is a graphical and textual "structure chart editor" for maintaining large software systems. It extracts cross-reference data from the code itself and, using the current subsystem tree as a guide, creates several kinds of graphical and textual views of the cross-reference data, at varying levels of detail. Arch provides a clustering algorithm that groups related procedures into modules. In order to improve the quality of existing modules, Arch provides a "critic", which identifies individual procedures that apparently violate good information-hiding principles.

The importance of data

You can find some hints on how to use data items to restructure a software system in [Zimmer90]. This approach is based on the idea of finding state invariants and linking data items by "data cobwebs". The concept of a data cobweb does not describe all the kinds of complexity within a program. It is meant to describe only complexity that arises because of interrelationships between data items within a program. A program with N data items has $N(N-1)/2$ potential data connections, because there are this many possible pairings of data items. Modularity can reduce this number in two ways: it can make some potential data cobwebs impossible, and it can create contexts in which potential data cobwebs need not be considered.

Where we want to find objects in a given system, the relationships between data items give us a strong indication of which ones belong together. Vice-versa, the most important criterion when grouping data items into a module or whatever is that the module should have a coherent purpose.

The user's skills and knowledge

We have discussed a number of techniques that may support you in your task of finding objects in non-object-oriented code, or converting the whole program to object-orientation. It is our belief that these tasks have to be interactive, and that the user plays the most important role. Even though there are reports of tools that claim fully automatic behaviour, we are doubtful about the value and quality of the created objects. The understanding of meaning, purpose, and functionality of a reusable object is the key to the reuse of this object. This understanding, however, cannot be created automatically—it has to be interactive and tools can only give support. An example showing how further information that is found in documentation and other sources can be used is found in [Brown92].

We have respected the importance of the user when developing our re-engineering method, and consequently it is highly interactive.

---

1. Arch has been developed at Siemens Corporate Research, Princeton, NJ and is described in more detail in [Schwanke89] and [Schwanke90].

11.4 Retrieving objects in non-object-oriented code

This section describes and defines our method for retrieving objects in non-object-oriented code in detail. It explains it in three steps, with the help of three scenarios to demonstrate how the method works and how you can apply it:

- The first scenario describes the situation when you are browsing through a software system and looking for potentially reusable components without concrete knowledge of the system or its components, and without a concrete idea what you are looking for. In fact, this is the most difficult situation that could appear and also the most unlikely. We use this scenario purely to describe the applied techniques and to point out the important aspects. It discusses how different architectural styles may influence this method.

- The second scenario takes the opposite situation into account. You know about the existence of a component that you want to reuse in the investigated system, and you try to find this component with all its parts. This situation is much more likely to appear and we use it to demonstrate how the method might be applied.

- In the third scenario we look at real life and show how re-engineering for reuse is incorporated into a software development process.

It is possible to think of a number of further situations in which this method could be used and of further ways to incorporate it into different processes. You should be able to decide how to apply the method in those cases from the scenarios below.

11.4.1 Browse and harvest

To browse through a software system and see what might be reusable without an idea of what you are looking for is a bottom-up way of working. It might be argued that it is not very realistic for a considerable amount of work to be undertaken on an uncertain chance of finding something that might be reused later on. It will not occur often—it is more likely that after a first browsing step you have an idea of what you might reuse, and you can then switch your strategy to search for these things.

The most difficult way of working is to browse through the software and try to find something without having any idea what you are searching for. We start the explanation of our method with this scenario in mind.

Figure 140 gives a rough overview how this method works. The individual steps are explained below.

Step 1: Analyze software and create cross-reference information

In order to give our investigations a solid base we need reliable information about the software under investigation. We do not rely on documentation or specification, but analyze the code and extract cross-references. Unfortunately, cross-references produced on demand by some compilers are not sufficient for this purpose. You also have to consider

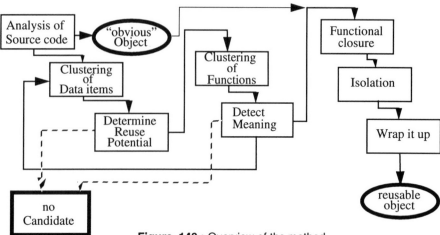

Figure 140 : Overview of the method

redirections and accesses via pointers, which raises the need for control- and data-flow analysis. In this step you must transform the software into a representation that contains all the information that can be obtained directly from the source code, enabling the calculation of control- and data-flow dependencies. Control- and data-flow analyses are needed to detect dependencies not visible in "normal" cross-reference information. Examples are:

• calls of functions via pointers to functions

• other redirections that represent a control-flow dependency

• the flow of data that relates variables that seem to be unrelated by "normal" cross-references

The completeness and correctness of this calculated information is crucial to the success of the whole method. All assumptions and calculations that are carried out later depend on it.

Documentation, however, can be of great help in understanding the system. We treat documentation as background information with a value that has to be approved. There are good chances of detecting possible objects in the documentation, so it might provide several hints.

Step 2: Find objects that are obvious

These are objects known from documentation or other reasons. If you were very lucky in browsing through the cross-references created in the first step, you might guess some objects. In many cases these objects will realize objects of the real world of the application. An additional analysis of the domain of the investigated program will help your understanding and is strongly recommended at this point.

For obvious objects, you can switch to the process of finding objects that you know, described later. When you have finished extracting these objects, you have to take them out of your cross-reference information that you use to find further objects, and follow the next steps.

Step 3: Find closely related data items

The use of *cluster* techniques based on a similarity measurement, or the conceptual distance between objects, seems to be the most appropriate technique for finding objects. We make use of the concept that objects contain private data shared by the members of the object and hidden from the outside world. In this step we try to find data items that belong conceptually together and could be taken as the private data of the object you want. To achieve this, we first apply cluster strategies to data items. These strategies are based on the conceptual distance between data items which can be calculated in various ways. Data items are related to each other by data flow. Thus data flow relations should be the base for the analysis of closely related data items. The use of data items in functions (i.e. cross-reference information) is another source of information that may indicate closely related data items. This is because the use of data items in a function represents a design decision. The purpose of a function establishes a certain context in which a data item appears.

In the following we explain the clustering of data items in more detail. We base our calculations on cross-reference information. You could also base it on the number of control-flow branches between the items, combined with the length of these branches. We are still experimenting with which calculation or which combination of calculations is best suited here.

There is a further good reason for using cross-reference information. The premise for objects is encapsulated data, that is, the information-hiding principle. What does a group of related data and functions following the information-hiding principle look like? The functions accessing the data items of the group should have a coherent purpose and so should not access other data items. Functions that serve a different purpose and use other data should not access the data items of the group. This can be expressed by cross-references rather than by data flow. If data flow references result in a group of data items and the group (together with its accessing function) violates the information-hiding principle, it cannot be easily turned into an object.

The relation between two data items V_1 and V_2 can be weighted by

- CommFunc (V_1, V_2) is number of functions that use both V_1 and V_2;

- SharedTypes (V_1, V_2) is number of types that V_1 and V_2 share in their declaration;

- SameMod (V_1, V_2) is 1 if V_1 and V_2 are declared within the same module, 0 else;

- Rel (V_1, V_2) := CommFunc (V_1, V_2) + C_1 × SharedTypes (V_1, V_2) + C_2 × SameMod (V_1, V_2);

This equation also takes into account that two variables may share the same types in their definition, and that they may be declared in the same module or apart from each other. This information may also help you to define that they "belong together". This relation can be represented in a graph with a node for each data item. The edges are undirected and weighted by Rel(V_1, V_2). The problem of finding closely related data items now

corresponds to the task of dividing the data item graph into subgraphs (clusters) with the
following features:

- There are many connecting edges within the cluster. Data items are used together in the
  same functions.

- The edges within the cluster have high weight values. Data items are used by some
  functions.

- There are few connections from nodes within the cluster to nodes outside. Only few, if
  any, data items are used together in the same function with data items outside the cluster.

- These connections have lower weight values. Only a few functions use data items within
  and outside the cluster.

Figure 141 describes the steps of a simple algorithm that might be used for that purpose.

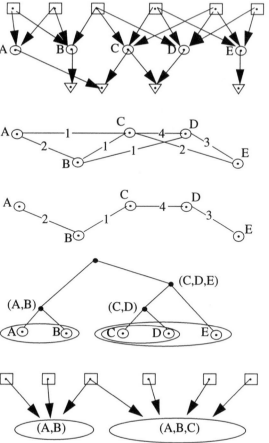

The graph shows access of data
items in functions and use of types
for data item definition.

⊡ Function
⊙ Data item
▽ Type

1) Weighted graph for data items.
The edge weights correspond to
the number of common functions
and types for two data items each.

2) Minimal coherent graph for data
items. Only edges with maximum
weight remain.

3) Cluster tree. The nodes
represent data item subgraphs that
are created by cutting edges with
minimal weight in the minimal
graph.

Graph showing access of functions
to data item clusters.

Figure 141 : An example for the clustering of data items

This cluster algorithm severs weak connections in the data item graph and in this way divides the graph into subgraphs. You use it as follows:

1. Construct the data item graph. Nodes correspond to data items V_i. Edges are weighted with the value of $Rel(V_1, V_2)$.

2. Construct a minimal graph such that the graph is coherent, and for each node only the edges with highest weight values are present. Removing any edge of the minimal graph will result in a non-coherent graph.

3. Remove the edge with the lowest weight value from the minimal graph. By definition the graph will be separated into subgraphs. Iterate this step. The subgraphs will themselves be divided. For each step the nodes of a subgraph represent a cluster, resulting in a hierarchical structure, a cluster tree.

A good design following the information-hiding principle should result in a balanced cluster tree. A bad design does not yield a partition, but a degenerated tree with a single main path. This is a very valuable input for the next step, the definition of the reuse potential of a given piece of software.

This way of handling data offers the advantage that it keeps data items together that belong together, and thus avoids producing a large number of small and meaningless "objects". Later we apply cluster techniques again to group the functions around the clusters of data items we retrieved in this step.

Step 4: Determine the reuse potential of the analyzed program

If you want to reuse parts of existing programs and to turn them into objects without a complete reimplementation, the source program must be of a certain quality. A program with a design that violates the data-hiding principle, without a reasonable internal structure, cannot contain candidates for reusable objects. This does not mean that the whole program must be well structured. You might detect a reusable object within a program that has a very poor internal structure, but for that reusable part of the program some assumptions about "structuredness" will hold.

The evaluation of analysis results for properties like structuredness, or data abstraction of the whole program or parts of the program, is what we call *determining the reuse potential*.

The results of cluster algorithms applied to the initial cross-reference information, and some metrics on these clusters, are a very reliable indicator of the quality of the investigated program in the sense of being suited for retrieving reusable objects. These results were obtained in the previous step when you tried to find closely related data items. What you have to do in this step now is to evaluate the results of Step 3 and decide whether or not your program is a reasonable candidate for retrieving reusable objects.

A program that contains parts that might be reused will contain hints about their existence that will show up in the clustering of data items. The cluster-algorithms return a cluster tree in which the closest related items are grouped together and the closest related of these groups are grouped in subtrees, and so on. Well-structured programs lead to cluster trees with numerous groups at the leaf level of the tree and a fairly well balanced tree. In a program with accesses to global data all over the program, on the other hand, such independent groups of data items are missing. The cluster tree obtained is unbalanced. There are only few clusters at the leaf level of the tree and single data items are added to these groups in higher levels of the cluster tree. In an extreme case, the cluster tree consists of one branch containing almost all data items and a few single data items in the other branch(es).

Depending on the appearance of the tree, you can judge whether your program is a suitable candidate for browsing and harvesting reusable components.

Step 5: Cluster functions around the clusters of data items

Having decided that your program is worth the effort for retrieving reusable objects, you now have to try to apply cluster algorithms to the functions of the program. You should try to assign the functions to those clusters of data items to which they have the strongest relationship, or alternatively to that cluster of data items that is most important to the function. The clustering of functions is based on the accesses to individual features as described before.

This clustering of functions around clusters of data is easy as long as a function accesses only data items of one cluster. As soon as more clusters are involved, you have to decide which cluster is the appropriate one. You can do this by calculating the similarity of functions, and assigning the function to the cluster that already contains the functions that are most similar to the one you are trying to assign. You can find more details on how to do this in [Schwanke89] and [Schwanke90]. Another possibility is to define a metric for the inner coupling of a cluster, and to assign the function to that cluster that increases its inner coupling when the function is added. Such a metric could be realized by using the similarity of functions as described above, or in other ways. A very simple way would be to define the inner coupling by the ratio of access inside the cluster to the access outside the cluster.

All this reasoning does not take the importance of a function to a cluster into account. This importance is very hard to measure with a tool. Therefore, you should have the ability to mark a function as being important to a cluster by assigning a weight to it.

Step 6: Take the clusters as objects and try to identify their purpose and properties

At this point human interaction and understanding is required. You need easy access to the corresponding parts of the source code and the related documentation to ease the task.

Trying to determine the purpose of an object might lead to the insight that further data items have to be added to an existing cluster. In this case you have to go back to Step 3 in the method and iterate until the retrieved clusters have reached a size and quality such that you can identify their purpose or reject them as candidates for reusable objects. You can omit Step 4 from the iteration.

Step 7: Try to get a functional closure

So far, you have reached the point of having found object(s), identifying their meaning and purpose, and acquiring an idea of their functionalities. To achieve a functional closure you have to add those functions to the object that contribute to its overall functionality (imagine the object offers some kind of simple functionality such as type-conversion). These are probably functions that do not access the data structures of the retrieved object.

A possible path to follow at this point is to start from the meaning of the object and to list all functionality needed for that purpose. Detailed cross-checking between the parts that are available and those that are needed will lead to further functions that have to be retrieved.

Step 8: Isolation

At this step you can attempt to isolate the object from its environment. This consists of replacing accesses to the object's internal data items and providing access routines. You also have to eliminate accesses to data structures outside the object by the object's methods, or if this is not possible, use parametrization. If neither method is feasible because the functionality of the object depends on a specific structure or data item outside the object, you should discard the object. If the object depends on functionality in the rest of the code it is possible that you can also turn the external functionality into an object, and that the two objects together can then form a reusable component. You should check this.

Step 9: Wrap it up

If necessary, establish an object-oriented wrapper around the retrieved object to ease its possible further use within an object-oriented environment. Such a wrapper provides an object-oriented interface to the old systems, but still maintains the code in its original language. You can find more information on how to do this in [Dietrich89]. You should customize the format and shape of the wrapper according to the requirements and conventions used for the repository of reusable objects where you will store the object.

Wrappers are not very well suited for reuse, because in most cases they are not general enough to meet the requirements of all potential reusers. For that reason, treat this step with caution. There are two possible ways round this problem:

- If it is likely that the re-engineered component has to be adapted before it is applied in the new application, delay the creation of the wrapper until the adaptation activity.

- If the re-engineered component is a solution-based component applicable to a number of possible applications, you should devote sufficient effort to the development of a wrapper to make it as general as possible.

The impact of architectures

The architecture of a software system, or its architectural style, has a strong impact on the method of retrieving reusable objects from it. To be successfully applicable to building a software system with a certain architectural style, our re-engineering method has to take the style into account. Depending on the architectural style used by the system under investigation for component extraction, you may need to perform certain additional actions to enable the successful application of the method.

The crucial point here is that there are no commonly agreed architectural styles on which we can base our method. There are some widely known and accepted principles that we will use for future work, but for which we are unable to tackle all possibilities. This section contains some examples to show how the method of finding reusable components described above can be applied in accordance with the architecture of a given system.

Data used by a program are often located in a database or a special layer that controls all data. In this case, all accesses to the data are realized by an access function to the database or the data layer. This seems to destroy our ideas of clustering related data items, because we cannot "see" the data access any more. Fortunately, this is not the case. Even if data are held in a database, you can still determine which function accesses which data item. You have to use the parameters of the accessing functions used to determine the data item to do this. The only difference from the method we described above is that you have to use clusters of access functions with special values for their parameters. This requires a data-flow analysis to detect it. However, complicated address arithmetic may spoil your efforts in certain cases so that it becomes impossible for you to determine which data item is accessed by static analyses.

You can handle abstract data types in a similar way. In many cases, however, it will be sufficient to use type-based cluster-techniques that do not require further analyses.

There are two possible procedures to follow when trying to extract reusable components, especially for layered architectures:

- Disregard the layers and group functions, access-functions and data items without taking the layer into account.

- Respect the layers and try to find reusable parts within one layer.

The second approach will in the long run lead to large-scale reuse of layers or parts of layers. To enable it, standardization efforts for layers and their interfaces are needed. Standardization is one of the most urgent questions when talking about reuse, not only in connection with layered architectures.

User requirements, run-time constraints, environmental conditions, or other reasons may sometimes lead to decisions about the architecture of the system. Knowledge of the actual architecture and the reasoning behind it is an essential aid to the task of retrieving reusable objects from an existing system. The architecture of the system strongly influences the way you have to look at the system, and the way you work when you want to extract components.

We showed above how our proposed re-engineering method could be modified to become applicable to a specific architecture. A lot more work is required in this area to enlarge the number of architectural styles that have been explained. Object-oriented architectural principles and basic mechanisms have especially to be covered in this area. Another very important aspect of this area is the question of reusability across architectural styles, and the adaptation needed to enable the transition from one style to the other.

The latest research trends in object technology are moving towards sets of collaborating objects or *object patterns* [Buschman93]. Patterns form an entity of event and space in which the event happens. Patterns are characterized by:

- the problem: the kind of functionality and the non-functional properties achieved by the pattern

- the context: when to use the pattern

- the description: the structure that solves the problem and its dynamic behaviour

- the name: expresses the intent of the pattern.

You can think of patterns as abstract high-level building blocks for a software architecture. Every design pattern has an infinite number of realizations, but the structure and behaviour described by the pattern are often applicable without change. Some examples of such patterns are "envelope-letter", "collection-iterator", or "model-view-controller". A lot of research is going on in the area of design patterns, and catalogues of patterns are being built up. This might be a step towards further standardization of software architectures. As the use of patterns begins to evolve during the design phase, there is a chance that design patterns may also be useful for re-engineering. Patterns might be applied during re-engineering in two possible ways:

- to detect sets of collaborating objects rather than isolated objects

- to learn more about patterns and their application by collecting their realizations in real systems.

You could apply patterns for re-engineering purposes. For example, if during re-engineering you detected an object that might be part of the realization of a design pattern, you could use the object as a starting point to find other objects participating in the pattern. To have a real chance to find these objects, you must use the description of both the static and the dynamic behaviour of the pattern to find the objects and to determine whether the pattern was really applied. The dynamic behaviour of patterns is described by sequences of messages passed between the objects that participate in the pattern. This type of analysis puts even stronger requirements on the analysis of the system you are investigating to properly reconstruct the system's behaviour. If you achieve this, there is still a further problem to solve. Patterns may be used in a combined way, which makes it even harder to identify them in existing systems.

There is a long way to go until re-engineering for reuse can effectively support the finding of realized design patterns in existing systems. In spite of this fact, design patterns seem to be becoming important for software architectures, and if re-engineering techniques and tools become mature enough to retrieve them, we will have made a big step forward.

11.4.2 Searching for known parts

The wish to retrieve reusable components from existing software systems appears very often when you know that such components exist in the investigated system. To be more precise, you know that a certain functionality is realized in the system and you want to extract a component that realizes it. Unfortunately, in many cases the required functionality is not realized in one component that you can extract and reuse *as is*. In some cases functions contributing to the required functionality might be scattered all over the program.

The difficulty is now to identify all the pieces in the program that realize the required functionality. This leads us to a further method of retrieving reusable objects. The most difficult task when browsing and harvesting components, to determine the meaning of a group of functions and data items, has disappeared in this situation. You also do not have to take the entire system into account, but can concentrate on a part of it.

In the following we show how you can use this method to solve the problem described above.

Step 1: Analyze software and create cross-reference information

The starting point for your work is again the cross-reference information of the investigated program.

Step 2: Browse and search for names

The next step is now to browse through this information and search for function names that give a hint that they might be used to realize the functionality you are looking for. You can use normal search functions to support this task.

You must inspect the source code of the retrieved candidates either to strengthen your suspicion that a function is part of the component you are searching for, or to reject the function as a candidate. At this point you depend very much on in-line comments in the code, and hopefully the use of meaningful names. You need a strong coupling between the cross-reference information used for browsing and guessing candidates, and the corresponding source code, to avoid tedious searching in source files.

Step 3: Detect key data items and create clusters of data items

You use the retrieved functions as one or more starting points for the following steps depending on whether they are connected or not. *Connected* means that control-flow or data-flow connections between the functions exist, that is, the functions call each other or they share data in a direct or indirect way.

Starting from these functions or groups of functions, take the data items accessed by the functions as starting points for clustering data items. The crucial thing at this point is that you have to capture the key data items in this step to obtain results that are useful. This is not trivial, especially if these data items are hidden, protected in abstract data types, or hidden in any other way. Refer back to the section on the impact of architectures for further strategies to use in this case.

Step 4: Cluster functions around the clusters of data items

After you have created groups of data items, you have to group functions around these data clusters. You could repeat this step several times, using different criteria to decide which functions to add to the cluster, if the results are not satisfying. You could use criteria that incorporate functions into the cluster that access the data items directly or via a certain number of indirections. Access to data items cannot, however, be your only criteria, because functions that are used by other functions already in the cluster may also be needed even if they do not access common data. Another technique you could use here would be to calculate the transitive closure with various levels of indirections.

Step 5: Evaluate the retrieved "object"

The next and very important step is to evaluate the retrieved cluster of data items and functions. There are a number of questions that you need to answer.

If you started with more than one starting point for clustering data and functions, the most interesting thing is to see whether or not these different points have been joined together in one cluster. If not, it means that you have retrieved totally independent clusters, and there are doubts whether this result can be correct. Different reasons for this kind of result are possible.

The first possibility is that you made an error when selecting your initial functions. This means that you must withdraw the corresponding cluster. Another possibility could be that your initial functions have led to several independent clusters that deal with similar things. An example of this might be if you were searching for a component that prepares output for a graphics display. In the actual system you may have selected two functions, one belonging to the component you want, and the other to a component independent of the first that prepares output for a backup medium. In a few cases, redundancy in the system, which can be for various reasons, could have led to independent clusters.

It might also be that the overall functionality you want is realized by independent parts of the system. In this case you need more than one retrieved cluster to build up the required component.

After this step is finished and you have removed all obsolete or wrong clusters, you need to check whether all the functionality you require is provided by the cluster. If any functionality is missing, you need to start a new iteration to search for the missing functionality.

Step 6: Try to get a functional closure

You have to achieve a functional closure when further functions have to be added to the cluster to realize its entire functionality. Further on, you need to check the cluster to see whether it contains parts that do not contribute to the functionality you want, and that can be removed from the cluster.

Step 7: Isolation

Finally, you have to isolate the parts of the cluster and extract them from the system, and determine the interfaces you need.

Step 8: Wrap it up

If necessary, establish an object-oriented wrapper around the retrieved object.

11.4.3 Integrating re-engineering for reuse into software development

Re-engineering for reuse is not completely isolated from other activities in the software development process—it is strongly coupled and is interleaved with other activities.

The method for re-engineering for reuse we have described so far delivers components that may be reused *as is* or *with changes*. The retrieved components fulfil a number of requirements for reusable components such as high internal cohesion and low coupling to other parts, due to the techniques used to extract them. The degree to which generality and application independence were taken into account is determined by the original development, and not by the re-engineering for reuse process. You may need to make further adaptations to the components, depending on how well the retrieved component fits the requirements for its new application. These adaptations are the same as for other reusable components, and therefore we include the adaptation activity into the development with reuse process, and exclude it from re-engineering for reuse.

In most cases re-engineering for reuse will probably be driven by a concrete need, such as establishing reuse for the first time. This is the case especially when you search for something in an existing system. You search for it because you already have an idea how you could reuse it, and because you have a concrete need. This concrete need, your planned reuse of the component, brings in the aspect of *variability*, which was probably not taken into account when the system was originally developed. The re-engineering method described previously does not take variability into account. You have to combine a domain analysis with re-engineering to bring the aspect of variability into re-engineering for reuse, by driving the re-engineering process with a concrete need for generality.

Taking a detailed look at a software development process that comprises re-engineering for reuse, you start off with a given problem to solve. Analyzing as many applications as possible in the same problem domain leads you to an understanding of the domain, and to the discovery of common and distinctive (invariant and variant) parts of applications in the domain. With this knowledge you may, according to your specific needs, start to design your application, design a framework for a class of applications in that domain, and build up a model of the entire domain.

Common parts that you discovered during the analysis tend to be key abstractions of the investigated domain. These parts are good candidates to re-engineer for reuse, or if this is not possible, to develop for reuse. They can become parts of the framework, if it is your goal to develop a framework and if the corresponding part of the domain is covered in that framework.

It should be clear which parts you need to re-engineer, which to develop for reuse and which to develop without reuse (because they are specific to the application) when you do the first design of your new application. You can now be clear what you need to search for and re-engineer, and why. The components you find might not fit all your new requirements, of course, but this can happen just as easily with components which were retrieved from a repository too. They still have to be adapted.

This example may demonstrate how development *for* and *with* reuse, domain analysis and re-engineering for reuse are interwoven. In real life they do not appear in isolation, but are strongly coupled. As indicated in the picture above, the development process that incorporates re-engineering for reuse is still a development *with* reuse process, because we

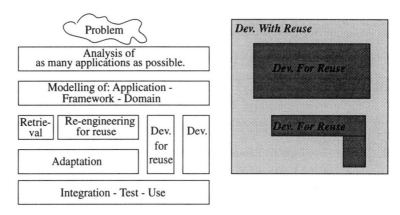

Figure 142 : Re-engineering in a "normal" development

intend to reuse knowledge and artifacts developed previously. Domain analysis and domain modelling comprise analysis for reuse, and re-engineering for reuse is a part of development *for* reuse. This development for reuse runs in the context of a development *with* reuse process.

For some activities it might be difficult to decide to which kind of development they belong, but this is unimportant. The essential thing is that the nesting of the different types of development processes sets up the environments, scopes and conditions for the inner processes which simplifies their execution.

This is certainly the case for re-engineering. It becomes much easier to evaluate candidate components, to check whether they fit the needs of the new application, and discard them if they do not. This way of working in a given context introduces a number of intermediate checks and points at which candidate components can be eliminated that make re-engineering for reuse faster and easier to do. That does not necessarily make the re-engineering more productive, of course. If the components in an application were realized in a way that prevents them from being reusable, the best that a re-engineering method can do is to show as early as possible that the components are not reusable.

11.4.4 Re-engineering for reuse in the fire alarm domain—a brief discussion

The fire alarm framework used as a common example throughout this book provides the possibility of demonstrating how re-engineering for reuse may be applied in practice. The system itself is described in Appendix A. For the development of a fire alarm framework, there are no old fire alarm frameworks that could be partially re-engineered, but there are a number of old fire alarm systems. These systems have to be investigated thoroughly and understood to give us a sufficiently broad base for the development of a framework. The fire alarm systems investigated provide a rich field of reusable components that could be harvested. A lot of the objects in the framework represent real objects in the fire alarm domain that appear in most of the fire alarm systems. These objects are very good candidates to search for and to re-engineer for reuse. Examples of these kinds of objects are devices such as detectors, sensors or displays.

To find and to re-engineer such objects, we have to apply a strategy as described in Section 11.4.2. It is very likely that a narrow interface to these objects exists and that they may be isolated without too much effort. If this is not the case, an abstraction of the device does not exist in the software under investigation, which will become obvious very soon during the analyses. This will mean that the original designer did not use the abstraction of a device such as a sensor in his model of the system, and we therefore cannot find and re-engineer it.

The profound knowledge of the domain necessary for the development of a framework enables you to judge the quality and adequacy of a retrieved component, not only from the implementation point of view but also from the point of representing a valid and good abstraction of reality.

11.5 Measuring your success

The simplest measurement of success in re-engineering for reuse is to count the reuses of your re-engineered components. You should try to determine what the reuse really cost, and evaluate whether you achieved your initial goal of re-engineering a component at a lower price than developing it from scratch. You have to do two things:

- observe and measure

- look for a way to improve your results based on your observations

You need to measure two different things:

- the costs of reuse

- such properties of the reusable components that can be recorded, are quantifiable, are comparable, and that influence the later reuse of the component

Chapter 4 explains how you can measure the costs of reusable components in development for reuse. In the case of re-engineering for reuse, you have to modify the equations so that the costs of development for reuse are replaced by the costs of re-engineering the reusable objects, plus the costs of the adaptation. (The original development costs are not taken into account.)

Besides recording the costs of re-engineering a component, you also need to collect further information and measures about the component. It is now realized that fan-in / fan-out metrics and the conceptual distance of the parts of the component can be used to measure properties such as high internal cohesion and low coupling of reusable components. To do this, you have to collect the fan-in / fan-out values of the re-engineered components and should compare them with the values of components developed for reuse.

A long-term observation is needed to determine whether (one or more of) the following is true:

- there is a correlation between the metric values and the total number of reuses of a component

- there is a correlation between the metric values and the number of *as is* reuses of a component

- there is a correlation between the metric values and the effort needed to adapt and integrate the reusable component into a new application

High correlations might mean that bad metric values prevent *as is* reuse, and too much effort would be needed for adaptation, reducing the profits of reuse. These kinds of results are of vital interest for all kinds of reusable components, whether they are re-engineered or developed for reuse. To draw conclusions takes a long time, and requires you to collect a large amount of data.

If such correlations exist, you can use them to tune your clustering methods so that you only retrieve candidate components that fulfil the requirements of certain metric values. This should lead to fewer but better candidates, making the re-engineering process cheaper.

11.6 Related work

This section presents a very brief summary of other approaches to re-engineering, and compares our re-engineering for reuse method with them.

11.6.1 Automatic re-engineering

It is difficult to re-engineer old systems automatically. Some tools are available to translate old code into new object-oriented languages. A translator that automatically converts a FORTRAN program to a C or a C++ program is described in [Feldman90]. Unfortunately, such translators do not recognize or create objects, and therefore cannot create object-oriented code. This kind of transformation into an object-oriented language does not make a system more reusable, and is not applicable to the problem of finding objects. However, it may be useful for transforming objects already retrieved using the method we advocate.

11.6.2 Event response analysis

Trying to convert one design to another, such as an object-oriented design, is a difficult job. It is especially hard to identify parts of such a design and determine their meaning or purpose, because it is not possible to give a clear definition of what a non-object-oriented design looks like. It is therefore not possible to make the transition to object-orientation with a set of easy rules like "a component of type *xy* becomes an object of class *z*".

Different design principles provoke different ways of realizing a system or a component. If you know the principles that were used, it becomes easier to determine the purpose of an existing component, and the transition may become easier.

However, functional and object-oriented designs are not necessarily incompatible. Ward [Ward92] proposes the following method for creating a functional model that converts easily to an object-oriented model:

- Build the functional model using event-response analysis

- If a response accesses more than one type of stored data, decompose it into sub-responses that use only one type of data each

- The resulting model can be converted to an object-oriented model by grouping the lowest-level processes that access each type of data

Ward proposed the method for designing a system, but the ideas could be used as well for redesigning existing systems if you are able to extract all the information needed. You can think of it as a specialization of the *design recovery* approach, described in the next section.

11.6.3 Design recovery and re-implementation

Several papers describe design recovery subjects; for detailed information see [Bardiaux89] or [Jacobson91]. Unfortunately, most authors do not go very deeply into the problem, and propose a method that can be described roughly as follows:

1. Analyze the non-object-oriented system

2. Recover the design

3. Try to identify parts in that design which might be realized as objects

4. Re-implement the system using object-oriented techniques

This is a feasible way to make the transition to object-orientation. The smaller the system to be transformed, the better the method will work. Only a few parts of the old system will be reused, such as the design information, and the rest is lost.

Our problem is to find reusable components in existing code, rather than transforming the entire system. In this case, the strategy of recovering the entire design is very expensive. We are also trying to find a way to retrieve reusable source code objects, not object designs.

11.6.4 Strongly connected components

You can find more hints on how to handle existing systems without doing a total design recovery in [Zimmer90] and [Duntemann90]. The central idea of their approach is to find strongly-connected components that consist of data items and their accessing functions, and take these as starting points. Following this idea, it seems to be commonly accepted that retrieving objects from non-object-oriented code, or transforming a system's design into an object-oriented design, could work in the following way:

1. Find strongly-connected components

2. Turn them into objects

3. Classify the objects and group them into object classes

4. Re-implement the rest of the system in an object-oriented way

At first glance this sounds easy, but there are many problems associated with the notion of a strongly-connected component. Duntemann and Marinacci [Duntemann90] use the expression *near-objects* instead of "strongly-connected component". They describe near-objects as usually consisting of a data structure, or family of data structures, and several procedures and functions that act on those data structures.

The ideas of strongly-connected components influenced us when developing our own method. Unfortunately, we found very little support for how these strongly-connected components could be detected. As a starting point the idea does seem to be applicable for our method too, but we do not intend to transform an entire system.

11.6.5 Differences and commonalities with other approaches

The possibility of using our method in an incremental way was most important to us during its development. It is not feasible to take the entire system into account and transform it as a whole, especially when working with very large systems. There are no constraints about the size, the programming language or a special domain of the software to analyze. You are completely free to choose to which part of a program you want to apply the method, and how far you want to follow it.

Software developers are individuals, and so are their programs. A method that works perfectly on one program works badly on another. A method that is really applicable has to be flexible. The re-engineering method we proposed gives you an outline of how to proceed. The algorithms used to cluster functions or data and your interaction with the method provide freedom to tailor the method to make it suitable for different types of program and problem domain.

The methods described earlier in this section are "top-down". In contrast, REBOOT's is a type of "bottom-up" approach. We are not trying to recover the complete design of the system under investigation, at least not initially, so we need less knowledge about the system. If further information about the system (in addition to the source code) *is* available, we define where and how you can use it. Because you do not initially need an overall understanding of the system, your work can be focused on the most interesting parts, the objects to retrieve. The results you gain during the applications of our method will give you valuable input for developing a method to transform whole systems to object-orientation.

If we compare the approach proposed here to other approaches like [Jacobson91], there are a number of differences:

1. Design recovery is an important task to support understanding and reuse of existing software systems. Nevertheless, the problems involved in design recovery are not yet solved. Design recovery is therefore far from being considered an easy task. See also [Hall92b].

2. The transition from non-object-oriented design to object-oriented design requires methodological support that is still the subject of research. Ways in which this can be done have been described in [Ward92] but the quality of the results depends on the recovered functional design, and the degree to which this design meets the requirements of the method.

3. Having made the transition to an object-oriented design, it will be hard to map the retrieved object classes of the newly-generated object-oriented design to software that realizes these classes.

4. Even if it is possible to do such a mapping, the problem of functional closure of the retrieved class and its isolation remains.

Our re-engineering method does not claim to solve all the problems that occur when reusable objects are to be retrieved from existing systems, but it provides a realistic possibility.

Objects in non-object-oriented code

Retrieved objects are not only subjects of reuse in a new environment, they also can be used as "crystallization" points for existing systems. Starting from such points, an existing design could, in time, be completely converted to an object-oriented design. Work carried out to find objects in existing systems can support the maintenance of the systems. The application of the REBOOT method will not only help to harvest reusable components, but will also support maintenance and smooth the way towards object-orientation.

11.7 Tool support for re-engineering

A re-engineering method such as the one described in this chapter bases its work on a thorough understanding of the structure and behaviour of components intended to be reused, rather than on vague expectations. One of the most important preconditions for the successful adaptation of a re-engineered component, or a component retrieved from a base of reusable components, is a clear understanding of the dependencies in the component.

The method we describe, and probably all the methods that aim at reusing code, depend heavily on the quality of the source code analysis that provides the input for all follow-on activities. You need a thorough and trustworthy source code analysis that goes far beyond simple cross-referencing, and includes control-flow analysis and data-flow analysis.

A re-engineering toolset that is intended for supporting this method has been developed within the REBOOT project. This kind of support provides a powerful mechanism that may reduce a user's scepticism or mental reservations against re-engineering, and against our method. It provides a reliable data platform, and other features that are desirable for all types of re-engineering tool support, not just our method. These are summarized below:

User driven

The concept of user driven activities is one of the most important things in the REBOOT approach to re-engineering for reuse. Our methodology provides a set of guidelines on how to proceed and what to do in specific cases, but ultimately you decide what you want to do. Tools should not enforce a special way of working that must be followed. Fully automatic re-engineering is neither intended nor desirable. The tool's role should be focused on giving support to the user.

Direct access

An understanding of the program under study is most crucial to the success of all activities dealing with existing software. Graphical representations of the program, combined with direct links from the graphics to the corresponding source code and documentation, are important aids. The REBOOT toolset's internal program representation is well suited to handle all the connections needed, and graphical and textual displays provide seamless access to all parts of the code being investigated.

Proposals and transformation of source code

Different cluster techniques are available in the cluster analysis service. This proposes groups of functions and data items according to parameters you set. This gives you the opportunity to influence the cluster techniques being applied.

Source code transformation services enable easy changing of the source code of the program to match the proposals that arise from cluster analysis.

11.8 Conclusion

The re-engineering method we describe has undergone a first evaluation phase. During this phase we applied the method to software systems of a realistic size. As tool support was not available at that time, we had to do a lot of work manually or with the help of scripts. Of course, the quality of the analysis data was not as good as we would have expected with tool support, but we think the results are more reliable. During the evaluation we analyzed both C and Assembler programs with a size of up to 30 000 lines of code, and we obtained really promising results. Here are our main conclusions:

- Our method is applicable to real-world software.

- It is not dependent on the programming language used to implement the program under investigation.

- It can detect meaningful reusable parts of a reasonable size even without tool support.

- Success in extracting reusable objects depends heavily on the quality of the analyzed program. We found examples of programs that did not provide any candidates for reuse because of the poor quality of their design or implementation.

With the availability of REBOOT's re-engineering tool support, we have started a second evaluation phase of the method that will bring a much larger number of results. This will certainly lead to an evolving method that will be enriched by the experiences gained during these evaluations. We see this method just as a starting point for further work. We think our method may evolve into something that pushes the re-engineering of existing systems towards the object-oriented paradigm in the long term.

12 Cleanroom Adaptation

12.1 Introduction

This chapter describes how the development process used in Cleanroom Software Engineering [Mills87] could be adapted to development *for* and *with* reuse. Its purpose is to show by example that the general guidelines and techniques developed in Chapter 7 are adaptable to other initially non-object-oriented development processes. We believe that the Cleanroom concept has many aspects which are very well suited for reuse. We have extended the Cleanroom models to better represent *variability*, as described in Chapter 7. This has made the models more object-oriented.

The chapter is organized as follows:

- Section 12.2 gives a short overview of Cleanroom Software Engineering and summarizes the practices in Cleanroom which support reuse.

- Section 12.3 provides an overview of what we have adapted in Cleanroom to support reuse.

- Section 12.4 to Section 12.9 go into more detail about the adaptations of the different models, activities and documents in the Cleanroom process.

12.2 An overview of Cleanroom software engineering

In this section we briefly discuss the basic models and practices of the Cleanroom development process, which we will later adapt to development *for* and *with* reuse. This section is not intended as a Cleanroom tutorial, but just to give a short explanation of the models, so that the adaptations can be put in perspective. For a more thorough discussion of the Cleanroom process and concepts, refer to [Mills87].

12.2.1 Model and process overview

You use models to analyze, design and implement a software system. One of the main tasks in adapting a process to development *for* reuse is to understand the models in the process, and how to represent variability in them. The Cleanroom software development is based on the following models:

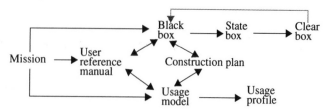

Figure 143 : The models in Cleanroom Software Engineering

The purposes of these models are as follows:

- The *mission* is a textual representation of the requirements as stated by the customer and refined by the developers. It contains both functional requirements as well as how the system is to be delivered.

- The *user reference manual* is a description of the interface of the system. If the system is to be incorporated into a larger system it is the application programmer's interface. The user reference manual is used to validate the requirements towards the customer. The user reference manual also contains information on how to configure, compose, build and install the system.

- The *black box* is the formalized specification of the system expressed as stimuli histories and responses. The *state box* is a transformation of the *black box* in which we have represented selected stimuli histories as state data. The *clear box* is a further refinement where we have identified lower level black boxes to which to propagate stimuli. The development from a top level black box to clear boxes is formalized by steps of invention, transformation and verification in the *box structure algorithm*. The black box can be considered as the system viewed from inside and out, that is, it describes the responses the system gives based on the stimuli the system can receive.

- The *usage model* represents the behaviour of the users of the system, normally expressed as a state machine. The usage model is the system seen from the outside and inside, that is, it describes a user of the system and the stimuli he provides. The *usage profile* assigns probabilities to the transitions in the usage model, providing a Markov model [Runeson92]. The Markov model is used to generate tests from which we can estimate the reliability of the system under normal operation, that is, the mean time between failures, or MTBF.

- The *construction plan* divides the development of the system into vertical increments instead of the traditional horizontal breakdown into subsystems. This gives Cleanroom a resemblance to the spiral mode for software development, as described in Section 10.6.3. In contrast to the spiral model, however, it is only the realization that is broken into increments, not the analysis. The construction plan must take into consideration the fact that it must be possible to add each increment to the previous one, and to test the sum of increments according to parts of the usage model.

A typical Cleanroom development project can be illustrated as follows:

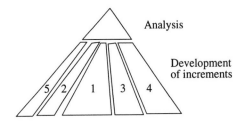

Analysis

Development
of increments

Figure 144 : Cleanroom development in increments

Here *analysis* includes all the specification models: mission, user reference manual, black box, usage model and construction plan. The remainder of the development (design, implementation and testing) can then be divided into a number of increments. These increments can be executed in serial or parallel to match the available resources and timescales. It is important to notice that the increments can be developed partly in parallel, as long as they are only dependent on finished increments. In the figure above we could envisage the following dependencies: 2 and 3 depend on 1, 5 depends on 2, and 4 on 3. Then increments 2 and 3 could be developed in parallel.

12.2.2 Sound engineering practices for supporting reuse

Most of the successes of Cleanroom techniques can be traced back to sound engineering practices that are enforced and supported by the process. This section discusses some of those we consider most important, and their connection to reuse:

- Ample time is available for analysis, and specification models are well defined. In an average Cleanroom project 50-60% of the time is used in the initial analysis, that is, in developing the specification models: the user reference manual, top level black box, usage model and construction plan. The specification models are also well defined, giving a clear medium for communication. In development for reuse it is important to collect all the requirements from all possible reusers before we make any design decisions. This is helped by the long analysis phase.

- Several independent specification models exist: the user reference manual, black box, usage model and construction plan. There are several, partly overlapping, partly complementary, specification models of the system. This improves the quality and completeness of the specification, which is important in development for reuse where the requirements must incorporate variability.

- A well-defined development algorithm exists. When development of the increments starts, Cleanroom has a well-defined box structure algorithm to transform the top level black box to code. This algorithm makes it easier to adapt the process to development for reuse, as it is clear which activities we must modify. It is also easier to verify that we are incorporating all the different requirements in our design, because we have a greater degree of intellectual control over the development process.

- Incremental development supports the development of invariant functionality in the earlier increments, which can then be reused *as is*. Later reusers can then start from these increments and add their specific functionality as additional increments.

- Roles are well defined during development. The development team is split into three subteams: specification, construction and certification. The interfaces between the teams are illustrated in the figure below:

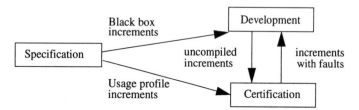

Figure 145 : Cleanroom teams and interfaces

In development for reuse, the role of the certification team may need to be extended to incorporate validation of the reusability of the components and its documentation. The separate specification team can also be a safeguard that all the reuse requirements have been realized in the development.

- Team work and frequent reviews are supported. All work is done in teams, and in the box structure algorithm there are frequent reviews and verifications that are also done in teams. The different specification models are also verified against each other before construction starts. In development for reuse frequent reviews ensure that we do not neglect some requirements, and that our solution really is reusable by all potential reusers.

- Cleanroom focuses on quality by doing it right the first time, and discovering mistakes as early as possible. This is achieved by all the previous points, and is particularly important for reusable components that are intended for reuse in several applications.

12.3 Our adaptation of the Cleanroom method

Adapting a software process to development *for* and *with* reuse means adapting the three components of the process:

- The models used to analyze the problem and express the solution have to be extended to incorporate *variability* in the problem and *generality* in the solutions.

- The activities have to be extended with specific reuse steps to take account of reuse, in development both *for* and *with* reuse.

- The documents have to be extended to record the reuse potential of the components, to enable them to be reused later. We must also support the inclusion of documentation for reused components in our design in development *with* reuse.

In our modification of Cleanroom software development, we use the following models:

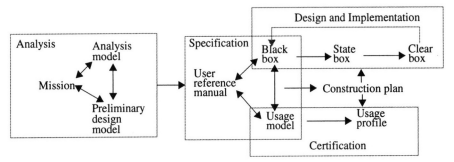

Figure 146 : Adapted Cleanroom models

We have added specific analysis and preliminary design models. This is because:

- When developing *for* reuse we need to capture different requirements from different customers (that is, potential or actual reusers). It is probably not profitable to try and incorporate all these requirements in a component. For this reason we need models to capture the requirements and examine different solution strategies.

- When developing *with* reuse we need to investigate potential components that can be reused in our system. This investigation is supported by the preliminary design model.

- In Cleanroom development, it is recommended to use 50-60% of the time in the analysis and specification phase, investigating the problem and solution domain. This will be even more important when we incorporate reuse. We have achieved this by introducing models to investigate the problem (*analysis*) and solutions (*preliminary design*).

The remaining models have the same purposes as in original Cleanroom development, but are adapted to handle variability in requirements (problems) and generality in design (solutions). The following sections describe the new analysis models and the adaptations of the existing models.

The analysis activity is an iteration between the *mission*, where the requirements are stated in written form, the *analysis model* where we use an object-oriented approach and the *preliminary design model* which is a set of collaborating black boxes.

These models are input to the specification phase where the black box, usage model and user reference manual are developed in a parallel and iterative manner until consensus about the precise specifications of the system is reached. It is important that the models correspond, since the design and implementation and the certification activities will be based on this. These two activities will be controlled by the construction plan developed by the specification team.

In the development activity, the preliminary design models are used as input to create an architectural design in which black boxes are identified. The box structure models (black, state and clear box) have also been modified to handle the variability that is necessary when developing for reuse. This is described in more detail in Section 12.7.

The *usage model* and the *usage profile* are developed in the *certification* activity in correspondence with the user reference manual. Section 12.6 describes how these models have been adapted.

12.4 The analysis phase

12.4.1 Models and reuse activities

The analysis phase is the first activity in Cleanroom development. The initial input to the analysis is a description of the requirements, in the form of a *mission* written by the customer. This describes the system to be developed in general terms, related to the customer's problem space. The analysis should clarify the specification in a form to which both the customer and the developer can agree. This is done with the help of the analysis model, which formalizes the requirements in the mission. The analysis activity has several purposes:

- To capture the customer requirements, that is, the problem domain. The information provided by the mission is usually not enough to specify the system precisely. The initial mission is detailed and clarified in the analysis activity.

- To create an understanding of the system to be developed, that is, the solution domain. This provides the opportunity to evaluate different solution strategies, and gives a better understanding of the problem. These solutions will provide input to the construction planning and development phases.

- To serve as a basis for reuse analysis. This includes development both *for* and *with* reuse.

The analysis activity incorporating reuse considerations is illustrated in Figure 147. Reuse influences the analysis process in several ways:

- New requirements from potential customers (that is, reusers) have to be considered. These new customers have a problem space different from that of the original customer, and these differences have to be identified and analyzed. We must also ensure that we can represent these differences in the preliminary design model. The identification of conflicts between the old and the new requirements can lead to a negotiation of the total set of requirements to provide the optimal solution.

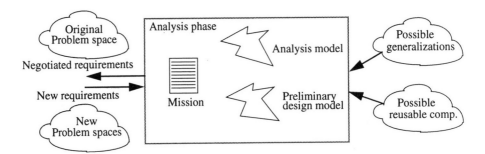

Figure 147 : The analysis phase and the factors that affect it

- When doing an analysis or a preliminary design, potential generalization opportunities will arise. These can be used to improve the reusability of the system, and can also help to bring hidden requirements to light. Reuse opportunities can be on any level of the system. For example, the entire system can be reused with some generalizations, or some of the possible subsystems might have large reuse potential. Potential generalizations are input to search for potential customers, who will in turn provide new requirements.

- The investigation of potential components that can be reused in the system under development provides opportunities either for adding new functionality, or for negotiating the original requirements so that the reusable component can be used. As stated before, it is important to start investigating potential components for reuse as early as possible in the development.

The input to the analysis is a description of the requirements in the form of a *mission* written by the customer that describes the system to be developed in general terms. This is not detailed enough to serve as a base for the development, so it is important to make an improved specification on which both the customer and the developer can agree.

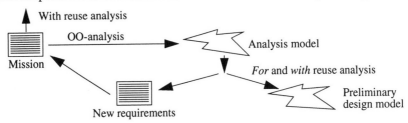

Figure 148 : The analysis process

The first step is to capture the requirements, starting with *mission*, and then collecting information from people who are or will be involved with the new system. These requirements are then incorporated into the *mission*. Based on them, it is worth searching for a reusable component that can fulfil the requirements of the entire system, or can easily be adapted to fulfil these requirements. This is the *with reuse analysis* shown in Figure 148.

If such a component does not exist, the requirements are then transformed into an analysis model. During this process new requirements might be found, for example changes to support reusability of components. The transformation is important to achieve a thorough understanding of the problem.

When an analysis model has been developed, a *for* and *with* reuse analysis is carried out, as shown in Figure 148. New requirements that improve the reusability of the system or parts of the system component can be identified. These requirements are also added to the *mission*. The *for and with reuse analysis* also serves to identify components that can be reused to fulfil parts of the analysis model, either through reuse *as is* or through reuse with adaptations. Section 12.4.3 describes the *for and with reuse analysis* further.

Analysis continues in this iterative manner until the *for* and *with* reuse analysis shows that there are no more reusable components to be found. The analysis results are then transformed into a preliminary design model. The *mission* is refined in this process, and should then be presented to the customers as a validation of correctness of their requirements.

This process of extending the requirements may seem costly, but experience has shown that it also has the advantage of stabilizing the original customer's requirements. Many unknown requirements can be uncovered when the customer sees the requirements from the potential reusers of the component, or is confronted with added functionality in reusable components. It should be a fruitful dialogue between the various potential users of the component.

Analysis might produce several different preliminary design models, depending on how reuse is taken into account, that is, including large reusable components will influence the preliminary design, as will incorporating new reuse requirements. Deciding which components to reuse and which reuse requirements to incorporate is a cost-benefit decision that is taken after the analysis phase.

The rest of this section describes techniques and processes to use in the analysis phase.

12.4.2 Object-oriented analysis

You can do object-oriented analysis in several ways:

- The most common is to let one or several analysts read the *mission* and interview the people involved in the development, including the customers and users. The analysts get an overview of the different views of the system by doing this. They then gather these views into a model that has to be accepted by all people involved. This approach can be both inefficient and time-consuming. It also demands a skilled analyst, who has to create a model that satisfies all people involved in the analysis.

- Another way to organize the analysis phase is to use a group dynamic modelling (GDM) technique [Scherlund90] to capture the requirements. This is described in Chapter 9, and summarized here. GDM is an interactive technique in which customers, future users, domain experts, designers, and others with an interest in the system gather to capture the requirements. The walls are covered with plastic sheets for drawing. The modelling language used is simple, and consists of the following:

  — Goals, subgoals and problems (the requirements)

— Concepts, relations and messages (the object model)

— Interaction scenarios (message sequence charts)

The session usually takes two consecutive half-days, and is led by a GDM expert who has studied the problem in advance. The role of the GDM expert is crucial. His mission is to keep everyone active, and to help resolve problems and inconsistencies between the participants. To ensure that everyone takes an active part in the modelling exercise, there are no chairs. The aim of GDM is to reach a consensus on what the problem is, and to agree upon terminology. GDM can be used both to capture the requirements in an analysis model as well as to define the preliminary design model. Development *for* reuse can be incorporated in this technique by including potential reusers in the modelling group. Potential for reusing existing objects (such as submodels) will also be identified, and should be noted.

12.4.3 *For* and *with* reuse analysis

When an analysis model has been developed, a *for and with reuse analysis* is performed. There are three approaches that can be used during the reuse analysis to identify potential for development both *for* and *with* reuse. These approaches must be combined to be successful:

• Finding potential customers for the system or part of the system

• Identifying reusable components through "experience"

• Identifying parts of the analysis model where a reusable component can be used to fulfil the requirements

The first point involves identifying customers that might be interested in a component. These customers could for example be found:

• Within your own organization. This will mainly be the case for smaller sized components that could be used within other development projects, such as stacks or lists.

• In the same application space. There might be other customers who could be interested in a similar product.

• Outside the application space. It might also be interesting to examine if there are other applications that have a similar structure, for example, a fire-alarm system and burglar-alarm system.

If a potential customer is found this leads to another requirements capture process. The new customer's requirements are added to the existing ones, increasing the generality of the reusable parts.

Finding reusable components through "experience" means identifying components that the analyst knows is reusable, as happens in almost all development projects. An example of this could be components for error handling. Here the analyst tries to abstract requirements that make the component as reusable as possible. This approach is probably most useful for smaller components that could be reused within the analyst's own organization. In this case the new requirements will be added directly to the existing ones.

The third approach is based on the reusable component having been developed and being available through some kind of repository. These components can then be reused if they fulfil the requirements, or can be modified to fit them.

12.4.4 Analysis techniques

There are many object-oriented analysis methods available that can be used. These methods focus on different aspects of the system and vary in usability depending on the system or the subsystem to be analyzed. Such methods all have a common goal, which is to establish an object model of the system, as shown in Figure 149.

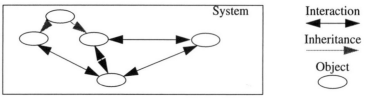

Figure 149 : System object model

Three methods we have found useful in different circumstances are:

- Object-oriented role analysis and modelling (OORAM) [Reenskaug92], which focuses on roles and their interactions. The atomic roles are composed into objects in a bottom-up manner.

- "Objectory" [Jacobson92] which focuses on *use cases*, that is, user scenarios. These use cases involve *actors* and domain objects. In the later design phase the intelligence in a use case is distributed to different kinds of objects: control objects represent the remaining functionality in the use cases, objects representing the domain objects and interface objects representing the actors.

- Object modelling technique (OMT) [Rumbaugh91] has three different models: an object model, a state model for each object and a functional model describing the function of each object.

All these methods provide different ways to attack the problem, and all should be considered.

12.5 The specification phase

The input to the specification activity is the analysis model and the selected preliminary design model. At the end of the analysis phase we decide which reuse requirements we are going to incorporate in the specification, and which reusable components we will incorporate in our design. The purpose of the specification phase is to make a precise user documentation and specification of the external properties of the system. The variability in the requirements and the analysis model must now be correctly captured and represented in the specification models.

When developing the specification it is important to consider the representation of generality. There are several ways to do this:

* *Isolation*, where we isolate the variability in a part of the specification.

* *Parametrization*, where we provide parameters to customize the specification, for example everything from binary parameters, through scalar parameters, to functional parameters.

* *Narrowing* (inheritance), where we organize the specification in an inheritance hierarchy, with the invariant parts as the abstract specification.

* *Widening* (inclusion), where we include all the functionality in one specification.

* *Configurability*, where we let the specification consist of several smaller specifications which can be composed in different ways to give variability at the system level.

* *Generators*, where we produce a dedicated language to specify systems.

The choice of how to represent variability in the requirements is a design decision that affects the specification and construction of the system. The different possibilities should be investigated in the preliminary designs that form an input to the specification phase. When you have decided how to represent variability in the top-level specification, this has to be reflected in the three specifications: user reference manual, black box and usage model, and also in the construction plan. The rest of this section discusses the influences of variability on the different specifications and the construction plan.

12.5.1 The user reference manual

The user reference manual must incorporate all the variability in the system. This includes how the system is supposed to be reused, and how someone can adapt the functionality of the system. If the "system" is not in fact one system, but instead covers a family of systems, it might not be useful to try to make a single user reference manual cover all the options, but rather provide guidelines for what a user reference manual for a single instantiation of the system should look like.

12.5.2 The black box specification

Using one top-level black box for a system with a large amount of variability might not always be cost effective or even possible, that is, the different ways of configuring the systems will change its behaviour so that the black box function will need to be different for each configuration.

To cater for this, it is possible to replace the top-level black box specification with a set of interacting black boxes that can be configured in different ways. You should keep in mind that splitting the functionality of the system into several black boxes is a design decision that should not be taken unless absolutely necessary, because the system becomes difficult to analyze due to the variability.

Sections 12.7 to 12.9 return to the representation of variability with inheritance in the box structures.

12.5.3 The usage model

The intention of making the usage model reusable is to provide support for the reuser's test and certification of the reusable component. There are several aspects you should take into account:

- If the component is reused *as is* the usage profile might change. This means that you can reuse the usage model, but you must provide new transition probabilities for the usage profile, and redo the certification.

- If the component is to be adapted, we would like to reuse as much as possible of the usage model. This means that the usage model should be adaptable in the same way as the component itself.

Section 12.6 describes the usage model further in the context of certification.

12.5.4 The construction plan

The construction plan supports developing *for* and *with* reuse in increments:

- Common invariant functionality can be allocated to earlier increments, so that reusers can start with those increments and add their particular functionality.

- It serves as a help in dividing the system into parts with reusable functionality, that is, developing reusable components in separate increments.

- It helps when developing *with* reuse, since the adaptations of the software can follow the construction plan and so ease the certification process.

- The justification, which is part of the construction plan, describes why the specific incremental division has been made.

When developing software using object-oriented methods, it is not trivial to make an incremental division of the system. A good help is the preliminary design done in the analysis phase. Sometimes the functionality gathered in an object and the functionality in an increment are partly orthogonal. This results in the object's development straddling increments, as illustrated in Figure 150.

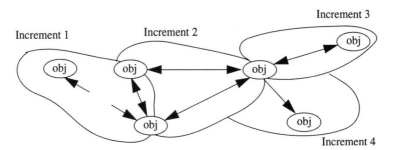

Figure 150 : Increment contents vs. object contents

This makes it harder to make an incremental division. We have found three approaches that help with this problem:

- Use subclassing as a basis for increments. The idea is to capture base functionality in a higher level object in the inheritance hierarchy. You can then add functionality in later increments using subclassing. The increments will then follow the inheritance hierarchy derived for the system.

- Isolate functionality to groups of classes. This approach is to isolate the base functionality to a number of classes. You then use these classes as the first increment in the system. You can then describe the rest of the functionality as services associated with a class or a group of classes. It is possible that part of the functionality in an increment will not be used in the present configuration, but can still be tested.

- Split classes that are on the border between increments into two.

Naturally the three approaches can be mixed. As an example, we have developed a construction plan for the fire alarm system described in Appendix A. The system is described in Figure 151.

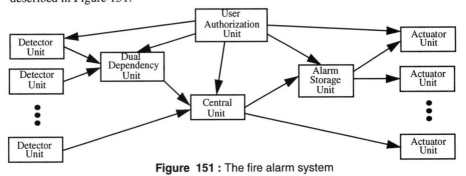

Figure 151 : The fire alarm system

The different increments are as follows:

- Increment 1 contains the Detector unit and the Actuator unit. The reason for this is that these units can be connected into a system that works and to some extent capture the base functionality of the system.

- Increment 2 contains the Central unit, which makes it possible to connect several detectors and actuators in the same system.

- Increment 3 contains the Dual dependency unit.

- Increment 4 contains the Alarm storage unit.

- Increment 5 contains the User authorization unit.

The motivation for this division is quite simple. Through it we capture the main functionality of the system and then increase the functionality by a number of added classes. It is then simple to test and certify the functionality of the system. Incremental division of the system is simple to make since the system is easily reconfigurable by virtue of its design.

12.6 The certification phase

The certification activity contains two models, a *usage model* and a *usage profile*. Usage models are intended to model the external view of the use of a component. The user behaviour should be described, and not the component's behaviour. The "users" here may be people or other software components. Modelling the use of software components has problems that do not arise when modelling the use of systems as a whole. The primary users of a component are those in its immediate vicinity, for example other components. In most cases other "users" are involved, for example end-users, which indirectly affect the use of components. The use of a component may have to be derived from an external user of the system, even if the user does not communicate directly with the component.

We assume that the usage models are created in accordance with a system structure that supports reuse. The view is still external, but the objective is to create usage model parts that conform to the structure of the system. Reusing components also means that it will be possible to reuse the usage model that describes the external usage of that particular component. The usage models of the components may combine in a way similar to the components' combination within a system, providing services to an external user. You can attach different usage profiles to one usage model.

12.6.1 The usage model

Markov chains are applied to model usage [Whittaker93]. The use of Markov chains has several advantages. The purpose of the usage model is to determine the next event to occur, based on the probabilities in the Markov chain. The chain is used to generate the next event without taking the time between events into consideration. This means that the times between events are handled separately and an arbitrary time distribution can be used.

A hierarchical Markov model, the *state hierarchy model* (SHY), has also been used [Runeson92]. The SHY model can describe different types of users, such as human users, other systems, system parts, and multiple combinations and instances of the user types.

During the development of the usage model, the user types are handled and constructed separately, and are then composed into a usage model for the system as a whole. The model, being modular, is suitable for reuse, since the objective is to ensure a conformity between the usage model and the system structure.

System configurations, such as occur in different markets, may differ in terms of user types and services available. You can construct usage models for different system configurations by combining the SHY models for the reusable components, and SHY models of the configuration-specific parts, resulting in SHY models for different system configurations. In particular, different *services* are one of the key component types to be reused. The general principles behind the SHY model are shown in Figure 152, and listed below:

• The usage is divided into a hierarchy in which each part represents an aspect of the usage

• The usage level is a state that represents the complete usage

• The user type level contains user types or categories

• The user level represents the individual users

• The service level represents the usage of the services which are available to the user. The service usage description is instantiated for different users

• The behaviour level describes the detailed usage of a single service as a normal Markov chain

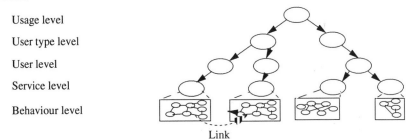

Usage level

User type level

User level

Service level

Behaviour level

Link

Figure 152 : The State Hierarchy model

The interaction between different services is modelled as *links*, implying a transition in one Markov chain on the behaviour level that causes a transition in another chain on the behaviour level. As an example, A dials B, as shown in Figure 153, where the transition from *idle* to *dial* for user A leads to a transition from *idle* to *ring* for user B. The model is discussed in more detail in [Runesson92].

Figure 153 : Link example, A dials B

12.6.2 The usage profile

The usage model is complemented with a *usage profile*, which assigns probabilities to every branch in the hierarchy, together with every transition on the behaviour level. The probabilities must be derived based on experience from earlier systems, changes expected for the actual system, or expected use of the system when it is marketed.

The probabilities in the hierarchy can be assigned static values, or be dynamically changed depending on the states of the users in the model. The latter approach is needed to enable you to model the fact that some events are more probable under certain conditions. It is, for example, more probable that a user who has recently lifted a receiver will dial a digit, than that a specific user will lift the receiver. The use of dynamic probabilities in the hierarchy is further discussed in [Runeson92].

Test cases are selected by running through the SHY model. First, a user type is selected at random, then a specific user is chosen, after which a service, available to the selected user, is selected. Finally, a transition on the behaviour level of the Markov chain for the actual service is selected. This transition corresponds to a specific stimulus that is appended to the test script, and the model is then run through again, beginning at the usage level (refer to Figure 152). Generating a specific stimulus also means generating the data put into the system as parameters to the stimulus, so the model takes data into account.

12.6.3 The usage profile and reuse

A component developed *for* reuse is certified with a particular usage profile for its initial usage, and is stored in a repository for future reuse. The component is stored together with its characteristics, usage model and usage profile.

A reliability measure is attached to the usage profile used during certification. Because the reliability measure is based on this particular usage profile, it is not valid for arbitrary use of the component. The parts of the component most frequently used in operation are those tested most frequently—this is the key objective of usage testing. These parts will have lower error rates, as failures found during certification will be corrected. A different usage profile that relates to other parts of the component may give a lower reliability measure.

When developing *with* reuse, you need to compare the certified usage profiles with the environment in which you intend to reuse the component. If you find a similar profile, the next step is to assess whether the reliability measure stored with the component is good enough for the system you are developing. If the component has not been certified for the usage profile of your new system, you must perform a new certification, using the usage model stored with the component. After certification the new profile and the new certified reliability should be stored in the repository with the component.

Objective measures of reliability for an arbitrary usage profile would be of interest in development *with* reuse. It is, however, impossible to obtain such measures, since the definition of reliability is "the probability of a device performing its purpose adequately for the period of time intended, under the operating conditions encountered". You therefore have to re-certify the component if you use it under operational conditions other than those for which it was initially profiled.

12.6.4 Reusing the usage model

You can easily reuse a usage model. The extent of model reuse and how the model is reused depends on how the system or components of the system are reused. This section presents some different reuse scenarios for component certification, together with those in a system context.

Component certification

- Reuse with the same usage model and usage profile.
  You can reuse the usage model and usage profile for a component without modification, if the component has been certified before being stored in the repository.

- Reuse of the usage model with an adjusted usage profile.
  You can reuse the usage model for a component if the component is to be certified individually with a new usage profile. Certification can be obtained with the same model by applying the new usage profile. This gives a new reliability measure of the component, based upon the new expected usage.

- Reuse with adjustments in both the usage model and the usage profile.
  You must make adjustments in the structural usage of a component if the component is changed so that it can be reused. You must therefore update the usage model accordingly and perform a new certification.

Reuse of components in a system context

- Reuse of a component without modification.
  The objective is to derive the usage model of the system from the usage models of the components when a system is composed of a set of components. This can be achieved when the structural usage of the component is unchanged, but the probabilities in the usage profile *are* changed. You should investigate further whether it is possible to derive system reliability measures from the reliability measures of the components, when the usage profiles for the components are unchanged. The main problem is that of the probable interdependence between components, which has not been assessed in component certification. This is an area for further research.

- Reuse of a component with modifications.
  The change in the usage model is a result of the change or adaptation of the component. You must therefore change the usage model of the individual component, thereby changing the usage model of the system. The system has either to be certified with the expected usage profile of the system, or the reliability of the system must be derived from the components. This problem is further addressed in [Poore93].

- Changes to the existing system.
  If you change an element of the system, for example by replacing a component with another that has different functionality, the usage of the affected component is changed in the existing usage model. You then have to carry out a new certification based on the new usage model.

Two factors concerning the SHY usage model make it suitable for reuse. First, the distinction between the usage model and the usage profile is important, since it facilitates the use of the same model, with different profiles, without changes. Secondly, the modularity of the usage model, and the traceability between the constituents in the usage model and components in the system, are essential from the reuse point of view.

12.7 The design and implementation phase

The *design and implementation* activity in Cleanroom means transforming the *black box* into code. This is achieved by a well-defined design algorithm transforming a black box through a *state box* to a *clear box*. The models developed with the box structure algorithm are illustrated in figure 154.

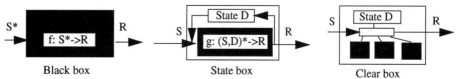

Black box   State box   Clear box

Figure 154 : Black box, State box and Clear box

The black box is an external view of a system or subsystem that accepts stimuli and produces a response for each stimulus before accepting the next stimulus. The black box omits all details of internal structure and operations and deals solely with the behaviour visible to its user in terms of stimuli and responses. Any black box response is uniquely determined by the system's stimulus history.

The *state box* gives an intermediate system view that defines an internal system state, namely the data stored from stimulus to stimulus. Mathematically it can be established that every system described by a black box can be described as a state box. One part of the state box is itself a black box that accepts both external stimuli and the internal state as stimuli. It produces as a response both the external and the new internal state, which replaces the old state. The role of the state box is to open up the black box one step at a time.

The *clear box* opens up the state box one more step in an internal view that describes the processing of the stimulus and the state. The processing is described by sequence: *alteration*, *iteration* and *concurrent*. The clear box can consist of several cooperating black boxes that accept both stimuli and state as their stimulus. They produce both a response and a new state as their response. Every system described as a state box can be described as a clear box.

Note that even if we develop a system in vertical increments according to the construction plan, there is a hierarchical decomposition into lower-level black boxes within each increment.

12.8 The box structures algorithm

In the Cleanroom process, construction is performed following the *box structures algorithm*. This is an algorithm that describes a controlled way to go from black box specification to code. The original box structures algorithm consists of a number of steps, namely:

Definition of the black box

1. Define stimuli and responses.

2. Define responses in terms of stimuli histories.

3. Validate black box.

Definition of the state box

4. Define state data to represent stimuli histories.

5. Select state data to be maintained at this level. List state data to be migrated to a lower level.

6. Modify black box to define responses in terms of stimuli and state data being maintained at this level.

7. Record type of references to state data by stimuli.

8. Verify state box.

Definition of the clear box

9. Define data abstractions for each state data. Define references to lower level boxes for migrated state data.

10. Modify state box function to represent responses in terms of stimuli, this level's state data and invocations of lower level black boxes.

11. Verify clear box.

Definition of common services

12. Recognize the opportunity to allocate processing to common service boxes. Simplify clear box using invocations to common services.

13. Verify clear box.

14. Continue until all black boxes are expanded.

Refinement of clear box

15. Select clear box.

16. Refine and/or reorganize clear box. (This step may introduce more black boxes.)

17. Verify refined/reorganized clear box.

18. Continue until all clear boxes perform as desired.

The following sections show how we modify this algorithm to handle the requirements for development *for* and *with* reuse.

12.9 Adapting the box structures

The original box structure algorithm does not incorporate any mechanism for inheritance to provide for generality. The rest of this section discusses how we enhance the box structures to include inheritance.

12.9.1 Adding inheritance to the black box

The original box structure algorithm does not incorporate any mechanism for inheritance to provide for generality. The rest of this section discusses how we enhanced the box structures to include inheritance. It uses the Fire Alarm example; you should read it in conjunction with the diagram in Section 12.5.4.

Syntax

We will use the following syntax when describing the black box:

```
Black box X
  case stimulus of
     stimulus-i:
        case stimuli-History of
           stimuli-History-i: Response;
        endcase {all stimuli histories}
  endcase {all stimuli}
```

For each black box you should list all the possible stimuli that the black box can receive. For each stimulus it is then possible that the response will differ depending on the stimulus history. Therefore it is important to make a proper description of them. Note that we have not formally defined the syntax of either stimuli histories or responses.

Example: Stimulus history

```
Black box Alarm Storage
  case stimulus of
     SCU3:Alarm-from-detector:
        case stimuli-History of
           (no RAU1:Alarm-to-Actuators since last
           (SUA10:Turn-off-Alarm or SPU1:Invocation)):
           send RAU1:Alarm-to-Actuators;
        endcase {all stimuli histories}
  endcase {all stimuli}
```

This example describes the behaviour of the Alarm Storage black box when it receives the stimulus SCU3:Alarm-from-detector. If the Alarm Storage black box has not responded with RAU1:Alarm-to-Actuator, that is, already sent an alarm to the actuators because the system was invoked or the alarm was turned off last time, then an alarm should be sent to the actuators.

Forms of variability

When entering the state box design phase of box structures, the main input is the top level black box. The black box gives the external view of the system or component, and specifies all its functionality. All possible stimuli are given, and their responses are defined using stimuli histories. We therefore represent the requirements as stimuli and responses. We can identify two major forms of variation in requirements in development *for* reuse:

- The need for additional stimuli

- The needs for "identical" stimuli, but different behaviour and/or response

Adaptations for variability

To represent these two forms of variability in the requirements, we need the ability to extend the black box syntax. We will use the well-known techniques of inheritance and virtuality from object-oriented development.

Addition of new stimuli

If the addition of new stimuli does not change the behaviour of the old stimuli, and their behaviour can be described in terms of the new stimuli and the old, we can add them:

```
X Black box Y
  case stimulus of
     stimulus-new:
        case stimuli-History of
           stimuli-History-i (X,Y): Response;
        endcase {all stimuli histories}
  endcase {new stimuli}
```

Here we have defined a subclass Y of the black box X, which adds new stimuli. Note that
this generalization hierarchy is also a good candidate for increments in the construction
plan.

Example: Additional stimuli

```
Alarm Storage Black box Alarm Storage New
   case stimulus of
      SPU9:Force-through-Alarm:
         case stimuli-History of
            (no SPU9:Force-through-Alarm
               since last SCU3:Alarm-to-Actuators)
            and (at least one SCU3:Alarm-from-detectors
            since last RAU1:Alarm-to-Actuators):
            send RAU1:Alarm-to-Actuators;
         endcase {all stimuli histories}
   endcase {all stimuli}
```

Here the new stimulus SPU9:Force-through-Alarm has been added.

Similar but slightly different stimuli

If the behaviour of a stimulus is largely the same for different customers, we can try to
isolate the invariant parts in a virtual stimulus. In the virtual stimulus we define the
common stimuli histories and responses, and leave the variations to the subclasses. The
following two black boxes illustrate the concepts:

```
Black box V
  case stimulus of
    virtual stimulus-V:
      case stimuli-History of
         stimuli-History-i (invariant): Response (invariant);
      endcase {all common stimuli histories}
  endcase {all stimuli}


V Black box W
  case stimulus of
     stimulus-V:
      case stimuli-History of
         stimuli-History-j (variant): Response (variant);
      endcase {all variant stimuli histories}
  endcase {all new or extended stimuli}
```

Here we define the common behaviour of stimulus-V in black box V, and show how this is
extended with the variant part in black box W. Note that either the stimulus history and/or
the response may vary.

Example: Virtual stimuli

```
Black box General Alarm Storage
  case stimulus of
    virtual SUA7:Turn-off-Alarm-Storage:
      case stimuli-History of
        (no SUA7:Turn-off-Alarm-Storage since last
        (SUA6:Turn-on-Alarm-Storage or SPU1:Invocation)):
          send RPU6:Alarm-Storage-turned-off;
      endcase {all stimuli histories}
  endcase {all stimuli}
```

```
General Alarm Storage Black box Special Alarm Storage
  case stimulus of
    SUA7:Turn-off-Alarm-Storage:
      case stimuli-History of
        (no SUA7:Turn-off-Alarm-Storage since last
        (SUA6:Turn-on-Alarm-Storage or SPU1:Invocation)):
          case ((no SCU3:Alarm-from-detector since last
            (SUA6:Turn-off-Alarm-Storage or SPU1:Invocation))
            and (no RAU1:Alarm-to-Actuators since last
            (SUA10:Turn-off-Alarms or SPU1:Invocation))):
              send RAU1:Alarm-to-Actuators;
          endcase;
          send RPU6:Alarm-Storage-turned-off;
      endcase {all stimuli histories}
  endcase {all stimuli}
```

We have not discussed the use of *overloading*, that is, redefinition of behaviour in sub-black boxes. We regard this as an improper use of inheritance that you should avoid, and we do not provide support for it. This means that we have to have a way to ensure that the stimulus histories are non-overlapping.

Steps in the box structure algorithm

This section describes how we modify the steps in the box structure algorithm to incorporate development for reuse:

1. Define stimuli and responses:

   — List all stimuli and responses for all the customers.

   — Identify common and specific stimuli.

   — For the common stimuli identify if the behaviour is the same.

   — Identify common parts of similar stimuli.

2. Specify a black box hierarchy with the use of additional and virtual stimuli.

3. Validate black box hierarchy with the user reference manual and usage model. Section 12.3 discussed the correspondence between the black box hierarchy, and the usage model and user reference manual.

12.9.2 Adding inheritance to the state box

Syntax

We use the following syntax for state boxes:

```
State box X
     State Data
        data
     case stimulus of
        stimulus:
           case stimuli-History and data of
              stimuli-History-i and value: Response and new value;
           endcase {all stimuli histories and data values}
     endcase {all stimuli}
```

We have represented some of the stimuli history as state data, whereas some will remain and be transformed in the clear box into stimuli to lower-level black boxes.

Example: State box

```
State box General Alarm Storage
   State Data
      Alarm-Storage-Status:
         On: (no SUA7:Turn-off-alarm-storage since last of
            (SUA6:Turn-on-alarm-storage or SPU1:Invocation))
         Off: (no SUA6:Turn-on-alarm-storage since last
            SUA7:Turn-off-alarm-storage)
   case stimulus of
      SUA7:Turn-Off-Alarm-Storage:
         case stimuli-History and data of
            (Alarm-Storage-Status = On):
            send RPU6:Alarm-Storage-turned-off;
         endcase {all stimuli histories and data-values}
   endcase {all stimuli}
```

Forms of variability

The state box is mainly a transformation step where no new variability is introduced. We must thus only preserve the variability represented in the black box hierarchy.

Adaptation for variability

It seems natural to have a one-to-one mapping between the black box and the state box hierarchy. This also means that we allocate state data as low in the inheritance hierarchy as possible.

Steps in the box structure algorithm (continued from Section 12.9.1)

Continuing the steps in the box structures algorithm described in Section 12.8:

4. List all the different stimulus histories used in black box specification and decide on state data to represent the stimuli histories.

5. Select state data to maintain at this level. We recommend that you isolate variant parts in lower-level black boxes, that is, propagate the state data while isolating the variant parts of stimulus histories to specific lower-level black boxes.

6. Specify the state box by translating stimulus histories to operations on state data maintained in the state box.

7. Record the type of reference to state data by stimuli.

8. Verify the state box. You must verify the hierarchy of boxes.

12.9.3 Adding inheritance to the clear box

Syntax

We use the following syntax for clear boxes:

```
Clear box X
  State Data
    data
  Lower level Black boxes
    boxes
  case stimulus of
    stimulus:
        case data of
          data-value: Response and new data value;
        endcase {all data values}
  endcase {all stimuli}
```

We have represented all of the stimuli history as state data, the responses being expressed by state data and calls (stimuli) to lower-level black boxes. Within the responses we also update the state data.

Forms of variability

The clear box is mainly a transformation step in which no new variability is introduced. We must therefore only preserve the variability represented in the black box and state box hierarchies.

Adaptation for variability

It seems natural to have a one-to-one mapping between the black box, state box and clear box hierarchies.

Steps in the box structure algorithm (continued from Section 12.9.2)

9. Define data abstraction for each state data at this level, and define references to lower-level black boxes for migrated stimulus histories or state data. For the sake of reusability, it is natural to isolate variability in a limited number of lower-level black boxes.

10. Allocate migrated stimuli to lower level black boxes. Modify the state box function to represent responses in terms of stimuli, state data at this level and invocations of lower-level black boxes.

11. Verify the clear box.

The remaining seven steps (12-18) listed in Section 12.8 do not change due to reuse and therefore remain the same as in the original box structures algorithm.

12.10 Conclusion

In this chapter we have shown how to adapt the Cleanroom development process to incorporate reuse. To facilitate this adaptation we have extended it with an object-oriented analysis phase for use in the initial specification process. The thorough and formalized investigation of the problem and solution spaces are important for capturing all the reuse opportunities. We have also discussed how to extend the Cleanroom models to incorporate generality, and how to adapt the activities of the development process.

Appendices

A Fire Alarm System Example

A.1 Background

At the beginning of 1992 an alarm company called "No Fire" had three fire alarm systems available on the commercial market, and was developing new systems. Its family of fire alarm systems was increasing and the company needed to reduce its lead time, or time to market, to retain its competitive edge. To achieve this, it had to reorganize its software. It also needed to establish more efficient configuration management, preferably using link-time or even run-time configuration. One way of solving such problems is to build an object-oriented framework, and this was the approach followed by "No Fire".

The fire alarm system is used as an example throughout this handbook; this appendix describes the alarm system domain, the candidate components and the fire alarm system itself (see also [R-3081]).

A.2 Strategy and plan

A.2.1 Introduction

"No Fire" develops all kinds of fire alarm systems (i.e. from fire alarms for small houses to alarms used in huge nuclear power stations). Both hardware and software are developed within "No Fire", a combination that makes development of new systems as well as maintenance of old ones easier. When developing new hardware, reuse is a natural part of the process. Unfortunately, that is not the case when it comes to software.

Today, "No Fire" has about 150 employees in seven departments. The hardware is developed and manufactured in five of those. The remaining two departments develop the software used in the fire alarm systems. So far, C and assembler language have been used for writing the applications. To raise the reusability of both design and code and also make the systems easier to maintain, TD Systems has decided to change to an object-oriented development process and use C++ for their applications.

A.2.2 Motivation for reuse

"No Fire" has realized the need to reduce the development time and cut the costs for new products to stay competitive and shorten the time to market. To meet these demands, "No Fire" has decided to introduce software reuse in their organization.

A.2.3 Reuse experiences and opportunities

There are no previous experiences with planned reuse within "No Fire". The reuse has so far been limited to the developers' ability to use parts of the source code in several systems.

A.2.4 Target reuse organization

This project is supposed to be the start of a continuing project where updates to (and development of) the framework are made iteratively.

A.2.5 Major changes needed

The organization will change from developing new systems from scratch to having a project that develops and maintains an object-oriented framework that is a base for all fire alarm applications. Since object-orientation and C++ are new concepts for the software developers within "No Fire" they will be educated by external specialists in object-orientation and software reuse.

A.2.6 Overall plan

This project consists of two phases (i.e. development *for* and *with* reuse). The results from this project will then be analyzed and evaluated.

A.3 Status at key reuse areas

This section gives a short description of the initial status for "No Fire" in each of the key reuse areas: organization, project management, repository management, metrics and development.

A.3.1 Organization of reuse

A long-term strategy for improving "No Fire" reuse capability has been developed but not yet implemented. Plans for funding reuse activities exist and will be followed up.

In this initial project, an object-oriented framework will be developed and reused in several projects in the future. The objectives are to make the new applications more profitable by cutting the costs for development and shortening the time it takes to get a new application on the market. This is possible by reusing both design and code (i.e. using a framework). The framework is seen as a product that is sold to a customer. The adaptation cost (specialization) is seen as a project but the framework as an investment paid for by the line organization.

A.3.2 Project management

A software project planning model that incorporates reuse-specific activities will be used and evaluated. This model has been developed in close cooperation with external experts on reuse. The experts will also give their support throughout this project (i.e. the ordinary development staff will work together with the REBOOT core team during the project).

Today there is no coordination between different projects and the same solutions are developed and implemented over and over again. The solution to this problem is to have a framework project that develops and maintains the framework. The framework project can then deliver specialized frameworks to the product line.

A.3.3 Management of reusable components

There is no repository management today.

A.3.4 Metrics

No metrics have been used so far, but the objective is to measure improvement when using reuse and object-orientation.

A.3.5 Development process

No development *for* or *with* reuse has been made within "No Fire" so far. The first phase in this project is development *for* reuse (i.e. development of the framework). In the next phase, development *with* reuse, an instance of the earlier produced framework will be used to build a complete application.

A.4 The alarm system domain

A.4.1 Concepts

Fire alarm systems contain the following basic components:

- *Sensor*. The sensor is a device that detects an alarm state. It returns a multi-valued signal, e.g. 1 to 255. An alarm is actuated when the value exceeds a predefined limit.

- *Detector*. The detector is a device that detects an alarm state. It returns a discrete signal (alarm/not alarm). An alarm is actuated if a signal is received from the detector.

- *Manual call point*. This is a button which can be pressed by a person. An alarm is actuated when the button is pressed.

- *Actuator*. A device for producing the alarm signal.

- *Presentation unit*. The presentation unit presents the status information and allows the system to be controlled.

A.4.2 Description

The systems in the alarm domain handle a number of sensors, detectors, alarm points, actuators and presentation units. The systems differ in the type of alarms they handle, their size, security level, cost, distribution, user interaction and so on. The common feature is that they react to signals from sensors and detectors, perform some action using different actuators, depending on the sensors or actuators that signal an alarm, and display their state using a presentation unit.

Depending on the types of sensor and detectors, actuators and presentation units used, an alarm system can be configured as a burglar alarm system, a fire alarm system, a car alarm system, and so on. Alarm systems are developed for different hardware systems using different embedded software. The fire alarm domain is a sub-domain of the alarm domain.

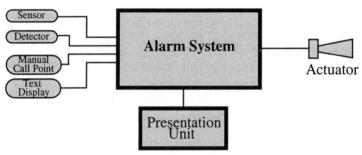

Figure 155 : A basic alarm system

A.5 Candidate components

The following sections show how to develop a framework for alarm systems that can be instantiated for different types of alarm systems. The components consist of the framework and an example of its use. Each system is described in the context of its domain analysis.

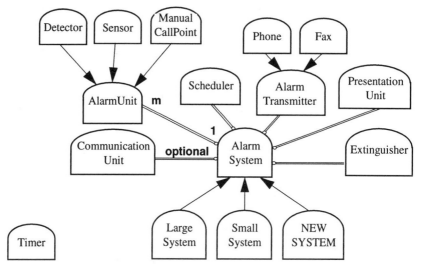

Figure 156 : An example of an architectural design of an alarm framework

A.6 The requirements for the fire alarm system

This example is throughout this handbook. The requirements for the system are as follows:

* The alarm system is a small fire alarm that can handle up to ten detectors, sensors and manual call points

* The system should be polled rather than interrupt-driven

* A fire must be detected and properly acted upon within one second

* The actuator is to be a siren

* The presentation unit is to be a display consisting of a panel of light-emitting diodes, one for each alarm unit, and a number of push-buttons to handle the alarm system

* The light-emitting diodes should, once triggered, remain lit until the corresponding alarm unit is reset, by pressing a reset button on the presentation unit

- If the alarm unit still indicates fire, the corresponding light-emitting diode should be re-illuminated

- There is to be a button for testing the alarm system. If this button is pressed, the alarm actuator is not activated, but the alarm is displayed on the presentation unit

- It should be possible to establish a dual dependency between two alarm units (that is, both must signal at the same time before the system indicates fire). It must not be possible to have dual-dependency between manual call points

- The presentation unit should display a text message and the number of the alarm unit that is indicating a fire

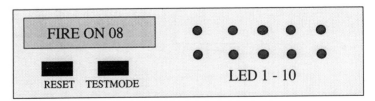

Figure 157 : The presentation unit for the example fire alarm system

The following section describes parts of the fire alarm system that is used as an example in the handbook. In the models we have used the OMT notation [Rumbaugh91]. The models show associations, aggregation, generalization, attributes and so on, that were all discovered in the analysis phase.

A.7 Models from the analysis phase

The following is part of a conceptual model of the fire alarm system:

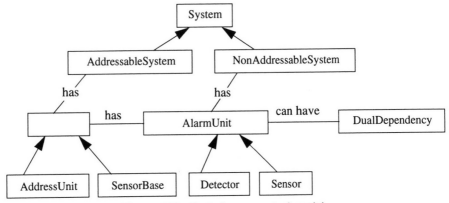

Figure 158 : Part of a conceptual model

The set of associations from the fire alarm system is shown in figure 159. In figure 160 aggregation relations are shown.

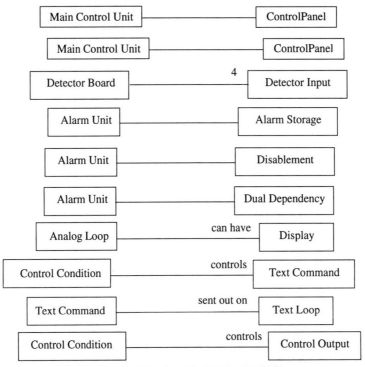

Figure 159 : Associations in the FAS

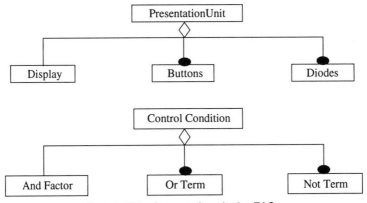

Figure 160 : Aggregations in the FAS

Figure 161 and 162 show some generalizations and abstractions.

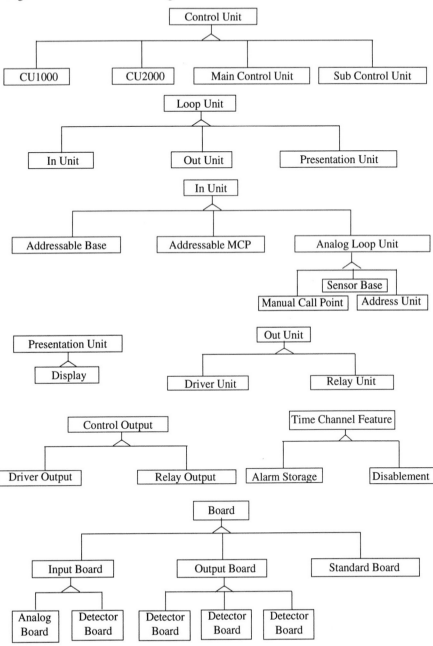

Figure 161 : Generalizations/specializations in the FAS

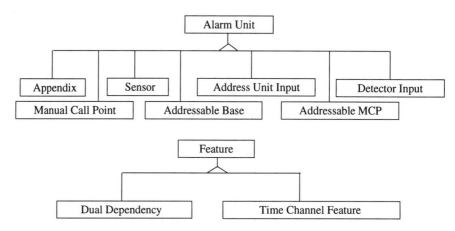

Figure 162 : Generalizations/specializations for FAS (cont)

Figure 163 shows the attributes of some of the objects from the fire alarm system.

Control Output
Control Unit #
Output Card #
Sequence #
Technical #
Presentation zone #
Presentation address
Enabled

Alarm Unit
Control Unit #
Input Card #
Sequence #
Technical #
Presentation zone #
Presentation address
Enabled
Annunciation
Disablement
Dual Dependency

Control Unit
Control Unit #
Connected
No of FBP's

Installation
No of sub control units

Sensor
Type

Analog Loop
No of displays

Text Command
Text command #

Com Loop
Loop #

Address Unit
Type

Address Unit Input
Unit #

Control Condition
No of terms

Or Term
No of factors

Figure 163 : Attributes of the FAS classes

Figures 164 and 165 show the state diagrams for some of the objects, and part of an architectural design.

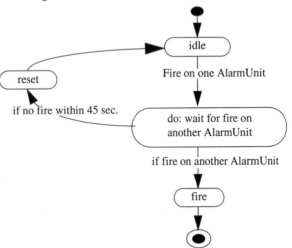

Figure 164 : State diagram for Dual Dependency

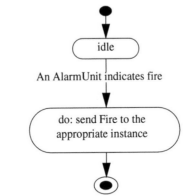

Figure 165 : State diagram for an Alarm Unit

B Documenting Reuse Implementation

B.1 Introduction

This appendix describes our recommendations for documenting a programme for the introduction of reuse.

It is acknowledged that a key factor for the success of a reuse introduction programme is good communication; this implies that any reuse initiative must be carefully described, planned and then rigorously followed-up.

This guide is intended to help you (e.g. the reuse manager) document and track progress of the reuse introduction programme and then to keep all involved people well informed of objectives and results. As a spin-off, such reports are expected to contribute to the enhancement of reuse technology and to help convince others to start reuse.

When documenting such a programme, you should take into account that it will affect a large number of people in your company, and not all of them will need the same information. The documentation will also be *living*, as it reflects an ongoing effort. We have taken this into account by indicating when the information in the different chapters should be written.

We have structured the suggested reuse introduction plan to correspond to the structure of this book. This is designed to help those familiar with the book to read and compare such plans, and to enable your company to describe its adaptations for reuse.

We believe that all the information suggested in this template is important to achieve a successful reuse implementation effort. It may be that some information does not seem relevant for some projects with a more limited scope, but in this case we recommend that a justification is given for omitting it—a detailed examination of the reasons for omission may well lead you to the discovery of further important reuse factors.

The rest of this appendix is organized as follows:

- Section B.2 describes our suggestion for the structure of a reuse introduction plan in overview.

- Section B.3 and B.3 describe the purpose and contents of parts 1 to 2 of the plan in more detail.

- Section B.5 describes how the plan is used during the different activities in the reuse implementation programme.

- Section B.3 and B.7 describe the detailed structure of the cost data and a template for evaluating reuse tools.

The suggestions given here are only guidelines, which you should adapt to the specific circumstances of your company. Our experience, however, is that initial scepticism about reuse is often overcome once a pilot application has been tried out. The suggestions in this appendix give you an overview of all aspects of reuse, and enable you to:

- define your strategy for introducing reuse,

- build a pragmatic plan for introducing and monitoring reuse,

- sustain your reuse effort by measuring and documenting progress, analyzing and overcoming problems and refining your objectives.

B.2 The overall structure

The Reuse Introduction Plan is composed of:

- a short introduction to present the purpose of the report,

- part 1 which is intended to describe the overall strategy and plan,

- part 2 which is intended to describe objectives and actions in each reuse aspect,

- part 3 which is intended to collect cost data,

- part 4 which provides a guide to evaluation of reuse tools.

The detail outline is the following:

Introduction

- Current state
  This section should contain a short description of the current state of the reuse introduction plan, including the date on which the introduction effort was started, and a summary of progress so far.

- Revision History
  This section summarizes previous issues of the plan, and the changes made in the current version.

- How this report is going to evolve
  This section summarizes the future activities that are planned for the reuse introduction exercise, and the expected contents of future releases of the plan.

Part 1: Strategy and plan

This part describes the overall objectives of the reuse implementation programme, i.e. why the company wants to improve its reuse capabilities, how it wants to achieve these objectives, and the resources allocated. This part includes a product and market reuse analysis.

Part 2: Status, objectives, actions and results

The chapters of Part 2 should describe how your company wants to improve different aspects of its reuse capabilities, document the activities to be performed, the activities actually performed, and the results obtained. This part is structured to correspond to the structure of this handbook, as follows:

- Organization of reuse (as described in Chapter 1)

- Reuse project management (as described in Chapter 2)

- Management of reusable components (as described in Chapter 3)

- Reuse metrics (as described in Chapter 4)

- Development *for* and *with* reuse (as described in Part B)

For each reuse topic covered by a section, we:

- analyze its current status with the help of the reuse assessment model

- define the improvement objectives derived from the reuse goals of the company

- determine the actions that need to be performed based on the suggested techniques in Chapters 1 to 4 and Part B, or other reuse technology

- document the results of implementing these actions

Part 3: Cost data evaluation of reuse tools

This part contains tables used to collect metrics related to reuse in specific projects.

Part 4: Evaluation of reuse tools

This part gives guidelines for evaluating the need and use of reuse tools.

B.3 Detailed structure of Part 1: Strategy and plan

This part is intended to explain the reuse initiative for the benefit of the executives of your company, linking it to the company's strategic goals.

1. Introduction

   This section briefly presents the overall reuse initiative and/or the reuse application that is being planned and/or reported on in the document, the people responsible for the reuse initiative, and how the initiative was started.

2. Motivation for reuse

   This section states the overall reuse goals and links them to your company's business goals. It lists a set of concrete reuse goals, both long and short term.

3. Reuse experiences and opportunities

   This section documents the analysis of how reuse could affect current products and the company's markets. This section also summarizes previous experiences with reuse within the company. It is important to build on any good practices that are already in place. This section can include an analysis of the reuse strategies of your competitors. It can also analyze how reuse could affect your current products and markets.

4. Target reuse organization

   This section provides a vision for how your company will appear as a mature reuse organization. It provides guidance for the reuse implementation initiative.

5. Major changes needed

   This section gives a summary of the changes needed to the five key reuse areas: *organization*, *project management*, *development process*, *component repository* and *metrics*. It also outlines the required tool support and training programmes.

6. Overall plan

   This section provides an overview of the reuse implementation plan for your company, identifying the costs and major risks.

B.4 Detailed structure of Part 2: Status, objectives, actions and results

Each section of this part corresponds to a key reuse area (KRA) and each subsection to a key reuse factor (KRF) as defined in the maturity model described in Chapter 5. This structure should help you assess your current reuse capability and then identify the most important actions needed to improve your reuse level and fulfil your objectives.

The structure allocates a subsection to each KRF. For each factor, we describe:

- the initial status within your company related to the aspect of reuse described by the KRF

- your company's objectives concerning the factor

For each KRF you decided to improve, you should also describe:

- the actions planned to reach the above objectives

- the resources allocated to reaching the objectives, where relevant

And finally document:

- the resources consumed so far, where they can be measured

- both quantitative and qualitative results obtained so far for this key reuse factor

- the problems you encountered and the decisions you made to overcome them

Therefore a completely documented KRF has the following structure (X is the number for the key reuse area, and Y for the key reuse factor):

```
X     <Key reuse area>
X.Y   <Key Reuse Factor>
X.Y.1 Initial status
X.Y.2 Objectives
X.Y.3 Planned actions and allocated resources
X.Y.4 Efforts and results so far
X.Y.5 Problems and decisions
```

The detailed structure of Part 2 of the plan can therefore be as shown below. For each key reuse factor (the second-level headings), add subsections for status, objectives, planned actions, effort and problems, as shown above:

1. Organization of reuse

   This KRA deals with the commitment of the management to reuse and with the integration of reuse into the product strategy of the company.
   1.1 Reuse strategy
       A statement of the commitment, strategy, organization, planning and funding of reuse in your company.
   1.2 Reuse assessment
       A follow-up of the ability to achieve stated reuse goals, and actions for improvement.
   1.3 Legal and contractual issues
       A section detailing the awareness and management of legal aspects.
   1.4 Costs and pricing
       A section describing reuse cost accounting procedures, funding strategy and product

pricing strategy.

1.5 Product line

A section detailing your market analysis, anticipation of customers' requirements and long-term product strategy.

2. Project management

This KRA deals with management, planning, support, and follow-up of reuse activities.

2.1 Interface management

A section describing inter-project relationships and coordination at the product line level to benefit from reuse.

2.2 Project planning

A consideration of reuse-specific activities, costs and resources in project management.

2.3 Project tracking

The measurement and analysis of reuse-specific data (efforts, time, and so on) for enhancing the reuse process.

2.4 Staffing

A section describing the reuse role assignment and allocation of adequate reuse competence to projects.

3. Management of reusable components

This KRA describes the ability to manage all parts of, and all information associated with, a reusable component, to handle relationships among components, to classify them and to manage versions and variants.

3.1 Component information

A section describing the ability to collect, store and manage information associated with a reusable component.

3.2 Component classification

A section detailing your company's efficiency of support for classification.

3.3 Change management

A section describing your ability to manage versions and variants of reusable components.

3.4 Repository maintenance

A section describing your ability and efficiency in maintaining and administering the repository.

4. Metrics

4.1 Product metrics for reuse

A section describing the maturity, usage and efficiency of the model you use to measure the quality and reusability of components.

4.2 Process metrics for reuse

A section describing the maturity, usage and efficiency of your measurement of the reuse process.

5. Development *for* and *with* reuse

This KRA defines the maturity and efficiency of your development *for* and *with* reuse processes.

5.1 Type of produced/reusable information

A definition of the types of reusable component (requirement, specification, design, code, test, documentation, and so on) with which you are concerned.

5.2 Development *for* reuse

A description of the maturity and efficiency of your *for* reuse process, handling of variability and generality, and cost-benefit evaluation.

5.3 Development *with* reuse

A description of the maturity and efficiency of your *with* reuse process. The ability to find needed components, adapt and incorporate them.

B.5 Evolution and evaluation of the plan

We recommend that you use the plan outlined in the previous sections actively throughout your reuse implementation effort. We suggest that the plan can evolve through the different phases for a given implementation effort as follows:

- *Initiate*. At this stage Part 1 of the plan is most relevant, in particular Sections 1, 2 and partly 6.

- *Reuse strategy and assessment*. At this stage the remainder of Part 1 of the plan becomes relevant, and the assessments are used to fill in the status and objectives sections in the different subsections of Part 2.

- *Implementation planning*. In this phase you describe the technical and organizational changes you need to achieve the reuse goals you selected in the previous phase. These are documented in the actions of the sections in Part 2.

- *Implement and monitor*. This phase describes your results from reuse, i.e. the results part of each section of Part 2 and the cost data in Part 3.

At the end of each phase of the implementation effort you should present the plan to the reuse board for evaluation, and present the major findings and recommendations of this phase to those involved.

B.6 Detailed structure of Part 3: Cost data

B.6.1 Introduction

This section contains the forms for collecting data for costs during development *for* and *with* software reuse. They collect data of the following types:

- Software product data, such as lines of code (LOC)

- Software project data, such as personnel capability

- Reuse data, such as the cost of extracting a reusable component from the repository

B.6.2 How to fill in the forms—and why

For all numeric data, the user enters numerical values, using the units indicated in the relevant question. The numeric value can be given in one of two ways:

- If the value is taken from a document or measured/counted directly, this value is entered as a single value, e.g. 45 person-days.

- If the value is estimated, we have to indicate how sure or unsure we are that the value is correct. This is done by entering two values that indicate the 95% interval, e.g. 30–50 person-days.

Most of the entries have a comment field, for use if there are special conditions attached to the value.

For the COCOMO cost drivers, the user inserts an "X" in the entry that describes the score level which is most relevant. If he is unsure about the correct level he may mark a maximum of two adjacent boxes.

Definitions of the terms used, such as lines of code, number of observed errors and so on are given in Section B.6.4.

The reason why we need COCOMO cost driver values is to see how much productivity variation is left when we remove the variation caused by differences in product requirements, computer resources, personnel and project type. The influence of the cost drivers will appear as the product of the corresponding scores assigned to each cost driver. The values connected to the scores "Very low", "Low", "Nominal", "High", "Very high" and "Extra high" are shown in Section B.6.4.

An example of how to use the data

The following is a small example of how the COCOMO cost drivers are used to normalize data from two projects. We assume that we have collected the following information on projects A and B:

- Project A: 10000 lines of code (LOC), high complexity and high reliability requirements. All other cost drivers are set to "nominal". This gives us a cost adjustment factor of 1.82. No reuse is done. Development cost is 67 person-months.

- Project B: 20000 lines of code, all cost drivers are set to "nominal", giving us a cost adjustment factor of 1.00. 5000 LOC are reused from previous projects and the adaptation factor (AAF) is 0.50. This gives us EQLOC = 17500. Development cost is 67 person-months.

From these data we want to compare the productivity of the projects. We do this by comparing the productivity in the two projects, defined as *delivered code* per *cost in person-months*. If we take the naive approach, we would get Productivity$_A$ = 149 LOC/person-month and Productivity$_B$ = 261 LOC/person-month. We might thus claim that project B has been 75% more productive than project A.

If, however, we take into account the differences in requirements for complexity and reliability, we find that the normalized productivity for project A is 149 * 1.82 = 271 LOC/person-month, and that it is actually more productive than project B. The reason that it looked poorer was that the complexity was higher and that it had much higher reliability requirements.

The rest of this section

The rest of this section is organized as follows:

- Section B.6.3 describes the forms used to collect data from the whole project.

- Section B.6.6 describes the forms used to collect data related to the reusable components used in the final product—development *with* reuse.

- Section B.6.7 describes the forms used to collect data about any reusable components that were produced by the project—development *for* reuse.

The forms for data collection are organized as follows:

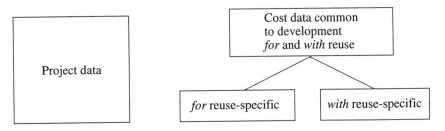

Figure 166 : Data collection form structure

Each box in the figure relates to one of the following four sections.

To arrive at sensible conclusions, we need sensible data. When using these forms, we instruct respondents to express uncertainty when they are unsure about a correct value. This allows us to incorporate these uncertainties into our analysis. We ask them to:

1. report an exact number only if it is based on written records or a real count of hours, occurrences and so on,

2. report all other numbers as intervals, for example, if confident that a value is more than 100 and less than 200, to enter 100-200.

The tables in the following sections are presented with a numbered list containing explanations of some of the entries.

B.6.3 Information on the total product and project

The information collected in this section is information concerned with a complete project. All activities, such as developing reusable components, incorporating reusable components etc. are included. Later sections will collect data that are specific to development *for* or *with* reuse..

Table 11 : Project data

Data carrier	Data value	Comments
The domain of this project [1]		
Size of system - Lines Of Code (LOC) [2]		
Total cost of development - person days (pd) [3]		
Time to develop system - calendar days [4]		
Cost of documentation - person days [5]		
Development cost spent on requirements analysis - person days [6]		
Development costs spent on design - pd		
Development costs spent on coding - pd		
Development costs spent on testing - pd		
Number of errors found in developed software during testing [7]		
Number of errors found in reused software during testing [8]		

1. The domain of the system could be, for example, "Telecommunications system" or "Factory automation" or "Banking system".

2. Lines Of Code: This includes lines with declarations and executable code, and excludes lines which are blank, contain only comments or are only used to include other files (#include....).

3. Effort: One person-day is equal to 8 person-hours of work.

4. Duration: One week equals 5 calendar days.

5. The cost of documentation should include all costs related to documentation in the following areas: user manuals, maintenance manuals and acceptance test reports.

6. This cost item includes prototyping and other activities needed to understand the customer's needs.

7. All errors found in components specifically developed for this system during integration testing, system testing and acceptance testing.
Note: If a bug X exists in a software component and test cases T1, T2 and T5 all cause a failure due to X, this should be counted as only one error.

8. All errors found in reused components during integration testing, system testing and acceptance testing.

Cost drivers (see Table 12) and lead time (Table 13) factors are collected for the project to study if and how these factors influence it. These cost drivers are also used to normalize the different projects so that they can be compared.

Table 12 : COCOMO cost drivers for the total project

Cost driver identifier	Very low	Low	Nominal	High	Very high	Extra high
Required software reliability						
Database size						
Product/component complexity						
Execution time constraints						
Main storage constraints						
Virtual machine volatility						
Computer turn-around time						
Analyst capability						
Applications experience						
Programmer capability						
Virtual machine experience						
Programming language experience						
Modern programming practices						
Use of software tools						
Required development schedule						

Table 13 : Lead time factors for the total project

Cost driver identifier	Score (in the range 0-9) [1]
Staff turnover	
Geographical distribution of participants	
Experienced time pressure	
Information flow among participants	
Experienced project priority	
Quality and commitment of management	

1. See explanations in Table 15 on page 459

B.6.4 The definition of terms used in the forms

The most important terms relating to the COCOMO cost model are listed below. The terms are listed in the same sequence as they occur in the definition table. Refer to [Boehm 81] for more detailed information.

- Reliability:
  The rating of reliability depends on the consequences of errors.

- Database:
  The rating depends on the relation between the amount of data in databases used in the system (bytes) and the system's size (LOC). Note that this cost driver is concerned with the data volume only, and not with the complexity of the database structure.

- Product or component complexity:
  This must be assessed on a subjective basis, because the notion of complexity is very company-dependent.

- Execution time:
  The score for this cost driver is based on how much of the available execution time the developed system needs. The more execution time the system needs, the more we need to do run-time optimization.

- Storage:
  The scoring is based on the percentage of the available storage needed to run the system.

- Virtual machine:
  The virtual machine is the set of software services on which the current application is built. Another term often used is *platform*. The degree of volatility is related to the volatility during development, that is, the lack of stability of the development or target environment.

- Computer turn-around time:
  The turn-around time is the time it takes to process a job on the host computer system, relative to the size of the job. This cost driver is included so that the COCOMO model can be applied to batch development environments as well.

- Analyst capability:
  The score is based on how a specific analyst is ranked compared to other analysts. If he or she is ranked among the lowest 15% the score is set to "Very low" and so on. See Figure 167, Table 13 and Table 15.

- Application experience:
  The score is based on the developer's length of experience in the application area of the product.

- Programmer capability:
  The score is based on how a specific programmer is ranked compared to other programmers. If he or she is ranked among the lowest 15% the score is set to "Very low" and so on. See Figure 167, Table 13 and Table 15.

- Virtual machine experience:
  The amount of experience a programmer has with the platform used in the project.

- Programming language experience:
  The score is based on the length of experience of the development language used.

- Modern language practices:
  The score is based on the use of structured programming, reviews of specifications, design, code and tests.

- Development schedule:
  The score is based on the relationship between the nominal schedule for the project and the schedule set by the customer or by management.

The next two tables give the definitions of the different bands for the COCOMO cost drivers and lead time factors:

Table 14 : Definition of ratings (scores) for the COCOMO cost drivers

Cost driver	Very low	Low	Nominal	High	Very high	Extra high
Reliability	slight inconvenience	easily recoverable losses	moderate, recoverable losses	high financial losses	risk to human life	NA
Database, bytes/LOC	NA	< 10	< 100	< 1000	> 1000	NA

Table 14 : Definition of ratings (scores) for the COCOMO cost drivers

Cost driver	Very low	Low	Nominal	High	Very high	Extra high
Execution time use	NA	NA	< 50% of available	< 70% of available	< 85% of available	< 95% of available
Storage utilization	NA	NA	< 50% of available	< 70% of available	< 85% of available	< 95% of available
Virtual machine major/minor change frequency	NA	12 months/ 1 month	6 months/ 2 weeks	2 months/ 1 week	2 weeks/ 2 days	NA
Computer turn-around	NA	Interactive	< 4 hours	4-12 hours	> 12 hours	NA
Analyst capability	15 percentile	35 percentile	55 percentile	75 percentile	90 percentile	NA
Application experience	< 4 months	< 1 year	< 3 years	< 6 years	< 12 years	NA
Programmer capability	15 percentile	35 percentile	55 percentile	75 percentile	90 percentile	NA
Virtual machine experience	< 1 month	4 months	1 year	3 years	NA	NA
Programming language experience	< 1 month	4 months	1 year	3 years	NA	NA
Modern programming practices	No use	beginning to use	some use	general use	routine use	NA
Software tools	basic micro-processor tools	basic mini tools	basic midi / maxi tools	strong maxi tools for programming and testing	"High" + tools for design, management and doc.	
Development schedule	75% of nominal	85% of nominal	100% of nominal	130% of nominal	160% of nominal	NA

The following table ranks lead time factors on a scale of 0–9, where 0 represents the best value and 9 the worst:

Table 15 : Definition of lead time factors

Lead time factor	Explanations
Staff turnover for the project	0 — the same people work on the project from start to end 9 — people come and go all the time. The project personnel is used as a pool for the rest of the organization.
Geographical distribution of participants	0 — all project participants have offices close to each other 9 — the project participants are in different cities, or even countries
Experienced time pressure	0 — no time pressure at all 9 — extreme time pressure, involving large amounts of overtime etc.
Information flow among participants	0 — all project participants share all relevant information 9 — no information flow. Each project participant stays mostly in his office
Experienced project priority	0 — the participants feel that everything hinges on when this particular project is finished 9 — the participants feel that nobody really cares when things are finished
Quality and commitment of management	0 — this project is the overriding concern of the best personnel in management 9 — the management involved do not appear to care

Figure 167 illustrates the concept of percentiles, as this term is used in Table 13. The figure represents a hypothetical distribution of people against a score for a selected capability. The dotted lines show how the percentage of the total area lies to the left of the line. For example, a person with a programmer capability denoted by P and an analyst capability denoted by A in the diagram will be in the 55% percentile as a programmer and in the 75% percentile as an analyst.

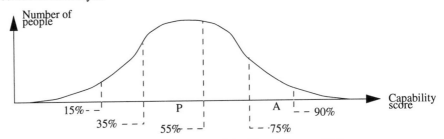

Figure 167 : Illustration of the idea of "percentile"

Numerical cost driver values

The COCOMO cost drivers show how each product, computer, personnel and project attribute influences the total project cost.

Table 16 : The COCOMO model cost drivers

	Ratings					
	Very low	Low	Nom-inal	High	Very high	Extra high
Product attributes:						
RELY Required software reliability	0.75	0.88	1.00	1.15	1.40	
DATA Database size		0.94	1.00	1.08	1.16	
CPLX Product complexity	0.70	0.85	1.00	1.15	1.30	1.65
Computer attributes:						
TIME Execution time constraints			1.00	1.11	1.30	1.68
STOR Main storage constraints			1.00	1.06	1.21	1.56
VIRT Virtual machine volatility		0.87	1.00	1.15	1.30	
TURN Computer turn-around time		0.87	1.00	1.07	1.15	
Personnel attributes:						
ACAP Analyst capability	1.46	1.19	1.00	0.86	0.71	
AEXP Applications experience	1.29	1.13	1.00	0.91	0.82	
PCAP Programmer capability	1.42	1.17	1.00	0.86	0.70	
VEXP Virtual machine experience	1.21	1.10	1.00	0.90		
LEXP Programming language experience	1.14	1.07	1.00	0.95		
Project attributes:						
MODP Modern programming practices	1.24	1.10	1.00	0.91	0.82	
TOOL Use of software tools	1.24	1.10	1.00	0.91	0.83	
SCED Required development schedule	1.23	1.08	1.00	1.04	1.10	

B.6.5 Cost data common to development *for* and *with* reuse

The costs recorded here are concerned with the general work done in the project that cannot be related to any specific reused or reusable component.

Table 17 : General information relating to reuse

Data carrier	Data value	Comments
Time spent on reuse learning—person days		
Time spent on component market analysis for potentially reusable components—person days		
Time spent looking for reusable components—person days		
Has development *for* reuse led to a better domain understanding—score 0-9		
Has development *for* reuse led to more stable requirements—score 0-9		

B.6.6 Data from developed reusable components

The following form is completed for each component the project develops for reuse.

Table 18 : Description of developed reusable component

Data carrier	Data value	Comments
Domain where the reused component was developed		
Type of component (method, class, framework, etc.)		
Size of reusable component—Lines Of Code (LOC)		
Estimated effort for making non-reusable component—pd [1]		
Actual effort for developing the reusable component—pd [2]		
Effort spent on requirements analysis—person days [3]		
Effort spent on documentation—person days [4]		
Effort spent on design—person days		
Effort spent on coding and debugging—person days		
Effort spent on testing—person days [5]		
Number of errors found during testing [6]		

1. It is an estimate of the effort (in person-days) to develop a non-reusable component offering only the functionality needed for the developed system.

2. This is the total effort for developing the reusable component. It adds up the effort spent on requirements analysis, documentation, design, coding, debugging, and testing.

3. This cost item includes prototyping and other activities needed to understand the customer's needs.

4. The cost of documentation should include all costs related to documentation in the following areas: user manuals, maintenance manuals and documentation for reuse.

5. This includes all effort spent during integration testing, system testing and acceptance testing.

6. All errors found during integration testing, system testing and acceptance testing.

B.6.7 Data from reused components

The following form is completed for each component the project has reused..

Table 19 : Description of reused component

Data carrier	Data value	Comments
Domain where the reused component was developed		
Type of component (method, class, framework, etc.)		
Size of component—Lines Of Code (LOC)		
Number of code lines changed due to reuse (LOC)		
Cost of identifying and extracting reusable component—ph [1]		
Estimated cost for developing the reused functionality from scratch—person days [2]		
Percentage of available functionality actually needed (reused)		
Cost of component adaptation—person days		
Have the changes effected the component's reusability [3]		
How satisfied are you with the reused component [4]		
Development costs spent on testing this component—pd		
Number of errors found during testing [5]		

1. Effort (in person hours). This should not include the cost of integrating the component into the new system, or any necessary changes to this system.
2. This cost item should contain the estimated cost of writing the code that is being actually needed (the reused component can contain functions which are not needed in the developed system).
3. Is the component more reusable after any changes? Score 0–9, where 0 means the same reusability as before, 9 means much more reusable than before.
4. Reuser satisfaction. Score 0–9, where 0 means very unsatisfied and 9 means very satisfied.
5. All errors found during integration testing, system testing and acceptance testing.

B.7 Detailed structure of Part 4: Reuse tools

Use the following tables to evaluate your tool support for reuse:

Table 20 : Evaluate use of tool

Data carrier	Data value	Comments
Type and version of the reuse environment used (e.g. *REBOOT V2 - dated 15 October 94*)		
Period of use (e.g. *1 June - 15 July 95*)		
Host system (e.g. Sun OS4.1)		
Context of use (e.g. *Stand alone,. Integrated into CONCERTO, etc.*)		
Local or remote access		
Number of users		
Training (*Demo, course, documentation*)		
Installation (*Easy / Normal / Difficult*)		
Creation of a new classification tree performed (*Yes / No*)		
Number and types of components entered		
Number and types of components extracted		

Table 21 : Evaluation of need and use of reuse tool support

Tool	Use level	Most activated functions	Satisfaction	Comments
Re-engineering				
Qualification				
Classification				
Navigator				
Retrieval				
Evaluation				
Adaptation				
Migration				
User Manual				
Environment				

We suggest the following codes when filling in this table:

- *Use level*: Frequent (2), moderate (1), no (0)

- *Most activated function*: One line per function if necessary

- *Satisfaction*: Good (2), sufficient (1), inadequate (0)

C Questionnaires to Support Reuse Assessment

This appendix presents a set of suggested questions which you can use in connection with the reuse maturity model presented in Section 5.4.2. Many different questionnaire formats could have been used; the one we used with the Reuse Maturity Model offers two answer possibilities: *yes* or *no*.

C.1 The reuse assessment process

Approach

The reuse assessment should be done by a team of experienced reuse professionals assisted by members of the company. The purpose of the assessment is to produce findings and recommendations which help companies set objectives and priorities for reuse improvement. Two approaches to generating recommendations are defined: question driven and model driven.

- The question-driven approach consists of developing an action plan to achieve better results in questionnaires.

- The model-driven approach consists of undertaking a coordinated set of actions to reach a level, corresponding to a set of different status values for each of the model's factors.

We used the first strategy, which has the advantage of being simple to understand and set up. The main inconvenience is that this approach can lead to a disjointed set of actions, because a questionnaire does not provide a stable basis for assessment.

The model-driven approach is more stable, as it provides a coordinated set of actions to achieve a given reuse maturity level. The difficulty is to define what such levels should be, as was mentioned in Section 5.4:2.2.

Conducting a reuse assessment

The purpose of the assessment process is to define the capacity of the company to practise reuse. External factors such as the business area potential are not taken into account. The results of this analysis, combined with a strategic analysis, are to be used in defining the company's reuse programme.

The assessment process uses the reuse maturity assessment described in Section 5.4 as input. This model defines a given number of areas that characterize a software company. In each area, specific points are defined as of prime interest, to be observed when defining and leading a reuse programme.

All assessment team members should be experienced software developers. The site where the assessment will be done should be prepared. It is important to make the company's professional staff aware of the significance and importance of the assessment, and to define the objectives, the involved people and the schedule of the assessment clearly.

C.2 Organization key reuse factors

Table 22 : Reuse strategy

Is reuse only practised in an opportunistic way, or not at all?	☐yes	☐no
Level 1: Only opportunistic reuse is practised but no reuse strategy exists		
Is the management aware of the benefits of introducing reuse?	☐yes	☐no
Is the management aware of the necessity of investment for reuse?	☐yes	☐no
Has the management invested in actions for reuse introduction on a limited scale?	☐yes	☐no
Has the company allocated a specific budget to these actions?	☐yes	☐no
Level 2: Reuse strategies are defined, budgeted and executed on a limited scale		
Has the management defined and budgeted a long-term strategy for improving the organization's reuse capability?	☐yes	☐no
Have the reuse adoption objectives been developed from the company's main strategic objectives?	☐yes	☐no
Has the reuse strategy been developed from a previous study of reuse opportunities in the company?	☐yes	☐no
Has the reuse strategy been developed from a previous study of the potential of business area(s) in which the company is involved?	☐yes	☐no
Have organizational procedures, policies, structural units been set up for supporting the introduction of reuse?	☐yes	☐no
Level 3: Management develops and implements a long-term strategy for improving the organization's reuse capability		
Are product line reuse strategies developed to maximize the benefits of reuse over sets of related products?	☐yes	☐no
Is the production activity modified in accordance with these product line reuse strategies?	☐yes	☐no
Level 4: Product line reuse strategies are developed to benefit from reuse over sets of related products. The reuse strategy is an explicit business/profit factor		

Table 23 : Reuse assessment

Are the reuse objective of projects assessed?	☐yes ☐no
Level 1: Reuse objectives are assessed	
Does senior management have a mechanism for regularly reviewing the status of development projects with respect to reuse objectives?	☐yes ☐no
Level 2: The reuse goals and resources of projects are approved by management, and the results are followed up	
Does the company have a specific unit for organizational assessment?	☐yes ☐no
Level 3: The organization has a specific group dedicated to the assessment and improvement of the reuse capabilities of the organization	
Has the company integrated reuse into its product quality assessment strategy?	☐yes ☐no
Has the company integrated reuse into its process quality assessment strategy?	☐yes ☐no
Level 4: The organization has reuse processes under quantitative control, and can assess weaknesses in the processes	
Has the company integrated reuse into its process quality assessment and overall company improvement strategy?	☐yes ☐no
Level 5: The organization continuously makes planned improvements of its reuse processes and its organizational structures	

Table 24 : Legal issues

Are any specific reuse clauses taken into account and introduced into existing legal and contractual clauses?	☐yes ☐no
Level 1: There is an awareness of legal/contractual constraints regarding reuse	
Have formal procedures been applied to review software development projects prior to the definition of legal commitments for reuse?	☐yes ☐no
Have ownership rights been defined for the customer, the developer and the future reuser?	☐yes ☐no
Has liability for reusable software been assigned?	☐yes ☐no
Has the responsibility been assigned to maintain reusable software that will be reused in future applications?	☐yes ☐no
Level 2: Main reuse legal/contractual constraints are identified and solved	
Are common standard clauses defined within the company to solve each of the previous points?	☐yes ☐no
Level 3: Specific legal and contractual clauses are standardized within the company's business processes	

Table 25 : Cost and pricing

Is reuse taken into account when setting product prices?	☐yes ☐no
Level 1: Reuse is dealt with explicitly when pricing products	
Have economic models been applied to evaluate the cost of introducing reuse?	☐yes ☐no
Have economical models been applied to evaluate the reuse introduction benefit?	☐yes ☐no
Have economic models been applied to study how the required investment to introduce and practise reuse would be covered? (return on investment)	☐yes ☐no
Have formal procedures been set up to determine the price to the reuser and end customer?	☐yes ☐no
Level 2: Reuse cost accounting procedures are determined for development of reusable components and use of reusable components respectively—who pays for what and how much?	
Has a pricing strategy been fixed, have the following questions been answered? —who pays for the development of reusable software? —who pays whom when reusable software is reused in a new development?	☐yes ☐no
Level 3: The requirements of the customers for a specific product line are anticipated in order to develop a long-term strategy	

Table 26 : Product line

Does the product strategy rely on individual experience and opportunity only?	☐yes ☐no
Level 1: The product strategy of the company only relies on the vision of individuals	
Has a study of services offered been carried out?	☐yes ☐no
Have future requirements and constraints been identified for some developments or product lines?	☐yes ☐no
Are these anticipated requirements and constraints used as input to the production process?	☐yes ☐no
Does the marketing unit take into account existing product assets to build the product line?	☐yes ☐no
Level 2: For some product lines, all the requirements of the customers are collected to develop a short-term strategy for the product's evolution and its integration into the product line	
Are all Level 2 questions true for all company product lines?	☐yes ☐no
Level 3: The requirements of the customers for each specific product line are anticipated to develop a long-term strategy	

C.3 Project management key reuse factors

Table 27 : External coordination

Is reuse only coordinated in an opportunistic way, or not at all?	☐yes	☐no
Level 1: Only opportunistic reuse. No actual coordination exists		
Is there someone specifically responsible for the reuse requirements for different product lines?	☐yes	☐no
Does the project manager negotiate reuse requirements with the person responsible for the product lines?	☐yes	☐no
Level 2: Responsibilities for reusability of product lines is defined		
Is there specific technical and methodological support from reuse experts for projects?	☐yes	☐no
Are procedures set up for the project to get support for reusing components?	☐yes	☐no
Level 3: Reuse support is defined		
Are all projects within a product line or affecting reusable components actively coordinated to achieve maximum reuse benefits?	☐yes	☐no
Level 4: Projects are coordinated with respect to reuse		

Table 28 : Project planning

Is reuse only coordinated in an opportunistic way, or not at all?	☐yes	☐no
Level 1: Project planning does not incorporate reuse		
Does the project planning model incorporate reuse-specific activities, resources and documentation?	☐yes	☐no
Level 2: Project-based reuse planning		
Are there specific cost models for reuse, or is reuse explicitly incorporated in the ordinary cost models?	☐yes	☐no
Level 3: Cost models exist for reuse		
Does project planning take the coordination of several current and future reuse projects into account?	☐yes	☐no
Level 4: Several projects are managed with respect to reuse		
Are there procedures for collecting feedback from reuse project planning, and using this feedback to improve the process?	☐yes	☐no
Level 5: Reuse project management is continuously improved		

Table 29 : Project tracking

Is tracking of reuse activities *ad hoc* or non-existent?	☐yes	☐no
Level 1: Only ad hoc tracking of reuse activities exists		
Are development *for* and *with* reuse activities well differentiated from classical development activities?	☐yes	☐no
Is effort and time tracked and compared to plans for these activities?	☐yes	☐no
Level 2: Explicit tracking of reuse activities is done		
Are data collected from reuse activities, at both a project and component level, to evaluate the effectiveness of the reuse processes?	☐yes	☐no
Level 3: Reuse activities are quantitatively evaluated		

Table 30 : Staffing

Are any actions taken to staff the project with reuse competence?	☐yes	☐no
Level 1: Some actions are taken to staff the project with reuse competence		
Is it the explicit responsibility of the project manager to obtain reuse competence for the project?	☐yes	☐no
Level 2: Project manager has explicit responsibility to acquire reuse competence for the project		
Does the company explicitly take reuse competence into account when allocating staff to projects?	☐yes	☐no
Level 3: Reuse staffing is a company responsibility		
Does a long-term plan exist to build up reuse competence, and is this plan used as a basis for allocating staff to projects?	☐yes	☐no
Level 4: Reuse competence build-up is planned		

C.4 Classification/repository key reuse factors

Table 31 : Component information

Does information supporting the reuse of components exist?	☐yes	☐no
Level 1: Information supporting the reuse of components exists		
Is the reuse information stored with the component?	☐yes	☐no
Level 2: Reuse information exists and is stored with the component		
Does information from reuse of the component exist?	☐yes	☐no
Level 3: Information from reusers exists		
Is the component information connected to the development process and used to get feedback on the development process?	☐yes	☐no
Level 4: Component information is actively used as process feedback		

Table 32 : Component classification

Are reusable components stored *ad hoc*?	☐yes	☐no
Level 1: Reusable components are stored but no storing policy exists		
Does the company systematically store all reusable components?	☐yes	☐no
Level 2: Reusable components are systematically stored		
Is there a catalogue of existing reusable components?	☐yes	☐no
Is it possible to get a list of candidate components with a given functionality?	☐yes	☐no
Level 3: A catalogue of existing reusable components is maintained and components which provide a given functionality can easily be found		
Is it possible to automatically search for components with a given functionality and other constraints?	☐yes	☐no
Level 4: Automatic retrieval of components exists		
Is information about search and use of components systematically collected and used to improve the classification and retrieval?	☐yes	☐no
Level 5: Feedback is collected and used from the retrieval		

Table 33 : Change management

Do the reusers inform the repository about reused and adapted components?	☐yes	☐no
Level 1: Use and adaptation of reusable components is recorded		
Is it possible to store adapted components as new variants in the repository?	☐yes	☐no
Level 2: Adapted components are stored as new variants in the repository		
Is it possible to be informed automatically about changes or enhancements to components in the repository?	☐yes	☐no
Level 3: Reusers are informed about updates to components		
Is information about use and changes to components collected and used to improve the components and better fit reusers' needs?	☐yes	☐no
Level 4: Feedback is used to improve the components and better fit reusers' needs		

Table 34 : Repository management

Is anyone in charge of the repository?	☐yes	☐no
Level 1: A repository exists which is not properly managed		
Does the person in charge of the repository maintain its component descriptions and approve components?	☐yes	☐no
Level 2: Repository is maintained		
Is the documentation describing the repository regularly revised, and the components inspected?	☐yes	☐no
Level 3: Repository is regularly revised		
Is quantitative feedback from search and reuse of components used to improve the repository organization?	☐yes	☐no
Level 4: Quantitative feedback is used to improve the repository organization		

C.5 Metrics key reuse factors

Table 35 : Product metrics

Are there any measurements on the quality and reusability of the reusable components?	☐yes ☐no
Level 1: Some measurements to evaluate reusable components are done	
Does the company have and use a model for measuring the quality and reusability of components?	☐yes ☐no
Are measurements on quality and reusability collected and stored with the component?	☐yes ☐no
Level 2: Reusability and quality models are defined. **Measurements are collected and stored with the components**	
Are reusability and quality also measured by the reuser (*a posteriori*)?	☐yes ☐no
Level 3: Reusability and quality are defined and measured both *a priori* and *a posteriori*	
Does a calibration routine exist to evaluate and improve the quality and reusability models?	☐yes ☐no
Level 4: The quality and reusability model is continuously improved	

Table 36 : Process metrics

Are there some metrics concerning reuse?	☐yes ☐no
Level 1: Some reuse metrics are used	
Are costs (extra efforts) and benefits (savings) of reuse activities as well as lead time systematically collected?	☐yes ☐no
Level 2: Metrics on lead time and effort exist for measuring the cost benefits of reuse	
Are improvement goals connected to, and measured based on, reuse metrics?	☐yes ☐no
Level 3: The company can set quantitative improvement goals	

C.6 Development process key reuse factors

Table 37 : Development process integration

Is reuse practised within development, but without precise guidelines and not as a specific activity?	☐yes	☐no
Level 1: Informal reuse		
Is reuse practised in a formal way?	☐yes	☐no
Is development of reusable software and its reuse identified and differentiated within the overall development process?	☐yes	☐no
Are specific activities associated with the development of reusable software and its reuse within new systems?	☐yes	☐no
Level 2: *For* and *with* reuse activities are identified and reuse is practised in a formal way.		
Are reuse specific activities defined as classical ones, that is to say described by input, output, involved roles and objective?	☐yes	☐no
Are *for* and *with* reuse specific activities integrated among classical activities within the software development process?	☐yes	☐no
Level 3: *For* or *with* reuse specific activities are well defined and integrated into the development process applied in the company		
Are *for* and *with* reuse processes assessed periodically and improved when needed?	☐yes	☐no
Level 4: *For* and *with* reuse processes are assessed periodically and improved when needed		

Table 38 : Type of produced and reused information

Does reuse of low-level information such as detailed design or code exist?	☐yes	☐no
Level 1: Reuse of detailed design information including source code with corresponding unit test information		
Does reuse of architectural information exist?	☐yes	☐no
Level 2: Reuse of architectural design information		
Does reuse of requirements, specifications, commercial proposals, communication support exist?	☐yes	☐no
Level 3: Reuse of high-level information such as requirements and specifications		

Table 39 : (For reuse) Analysis of variability

Is possible variability in requirements analyzed and documented?	☐yes ☐no
Level 1: Variability analysis exists	
Does the project follow a defined process for analyzing and documenting variability in the requirements?	☐yes ☐no
Are the goals and effort of these activities defined and followed up?	☐yes ☐no
Level 2: Variability analysis is defined in the project	
Is the process for analyzing and documenting the variability in the requirements defined at the company level?	☐yes ☐no
Level 3: Variability analysis is a company process	
Are the effort and results from variability analysis activities measured and used to estimate future needs for resources?	☐yes ☐no
Level 4: Variability analysis is under quantitative control	
Is feedback from the activities continuously collected and used to evaluate and improve the process?	☐yes ☐no
Are new techniques systematically tried out and evaluated?	☐yes ☐no
Level 5: Variability analysis is continuously improved	

Table 40 : (For reuse) Express generality

Are possible generalizations of solutions analyzed and documented?	☐yes ☐no
Level 1: Expressing generality is *ad hoc*	
Does the project follow a defined process for analyzing and documenting the generalizations of solutions?	☐yes ☐no
Are the goals and effort of these activities defined and followed up?	☐yes ☐no
Level 2: Expressing generality is defined in the project	
Is the process for analyzing and documenting the generalizations of solutions defined at the company level?	☐yes ☐no
Level 3: Expressing generality is a company process	
Are the effort and results from the activities for expressing generality measured and used to estimate future needs for resources?	☐yes ☐no
Level 4: Expressing generality is under quantitative control	
Is feedback from the activities continuously collected and used to evaluate and improve the process?	☐yes ☐no
Are new techniques systematically tried out and evaluated?	☐yes ☐no
Level 5: Expressing generality is continuously improved	

Table 41 : (For reuse) Cost-benefit analysis

Is the cost-benefit analysis of solutions analysed and documented at all or in an *ad hoc* manner?	☐yes ☐no
Level 1: Cost-benefit analysis is ad hoc	
Does the project follow a defined process for analyzing and documenting the cost-benefit analysis of solutions?	☐yes ☐no
Are the goals and efforts of these activities defined and followed up at the project level?	☐yes ☐no
Level 2: Cost-benefit analysis is defined in the project	
Is the process for analyzing and documenting the cost-benefit analysis of solutions defined at the company level?	☐yes ☐no
Are the goals and effort of these activities defined and followed up at the company level?	☐yes ☐no
Level 3: Cost-benefit analysis a company process	
Are the effort and results from the cost-benefit analysis activities measured and used to estimate future needs for resources?	☐yes ☐no
Level 4: Cost-benefit analysis is under quantitative control	
Is feedback from the activities continuously collected and used to evaluate and improve the process?	☐yes ☐no
Are new techniques systematically tried out and evaluated?	☐yes ☐no
Level 5: Cost-benefit analysis is continuously improved	

Table 42 : (With reuse) Functionality evaluation

Is there any documentation or support tools available to enable an understanding of components prior to reuse?	☐yes ☐no
Level 1: Some support is given to the user to help the understanding of components	
Have a set of general guidelines and rules been defined to guide the user in understanding a component?	☐yes ☐no
Are tools such as a browser or an analyzer available to the user?	☐yes ☐no
Level 2: Guidelines and tools are provided to help the user understand the reusable components	
Have experts been identified for consultation when a problem occurs in the understanding of a component?	☐yes ☐no
Level 3: A dedicated organizational structure has been defined to support the user in understanding a component	

Table 43 : (With reuse) Reuse cost evaluation

Is there a mean to estimate the cost of reusing and adapting a component?	☐yes ☐no
Level 1: Some information is provided to the developer to estimate the cost of reusing and adapting a component	
Are stored references to previous experience of use of the component available?	☐yes ☐no
Is quantitative information available for evaluating the costs of reusing the component based on others' experiences?	☐yes ☐no
Level 2: A collection of previous experiences has been set up, the developer can refer to these to base adaptation estimations	
Does a company standard cost estimation model exist to evaluate the reuse cost?	☐yes ☐no
Level 3: A generic costs/estimation model to estimate the adaptation costs has been defined, and validated through preliminary experiences	

Table 44 : (With reuse) Adaptation and integration

Are there some guidelines for adapting and integrating reused components in the developed system?	☐yes ☐no
Level 1: The adaptation/integration activity is made in an informal way	
Have precise guidelines and rules been defined to guide the user in adapting and integrating the component?	☐yes ☐no
Are specific programming mechanisms used to adapt the components?	☐yes ☐no
Level 2: Specific techniques and guidelines are used for adapting and integrating components	
Are high-level tools and mechanisms available to adapt and integrate reused components?	☐yes ☐no
Is a high-level and powerful development environment available to build systems from existing components?	☐yes ☐no
Level 3: The development environment used integrates automatic generation tools that are able to support adaptation	

D Glossary

This glossary provides a description of terms used throughout this book. It classifies each term by the topic area to which it belongs, as follows:

- *RS* Reuse-specific

- *OO* Object-oriented terms. These definitions are based on the IEEE standard.

- *RE* Re-engineering terms. These definitions are taken from E.J. Chikofsky and J.H. Cross II: Reverse Engineering and Design Recovery: A Taxonomy. *IEEE Software*, January 1990.

- *ME* Metrication terms

- *GE* General terms

Abstract class *(OO)*

An abstract class is an intentionally incomplete superclass (see also *Superclass (OO)* on page 497) which abstracts from method implementations. Missing method bodies are supplied only in the respective (see also subclass *Subclass (OO)* on page 497). Therefore the instantiation of abstract classes is not possible.

Abstract data type *(OO)*

An abstract data type (ADT) is the combination of data with their respective operations. The emphasis lies on the operations whose semantics are determined and described operationally or axiomatically. The concept of the ADTs allows for the specification of relevant features of data structures without the implementation aspects getting visible. One way of implementing ADTs is the class concept.

Ancestor class *(OO)*

See *Superclass (OO)* on page 497.

Attribute *(OO)*

See *Instance variable (OO)* on page 489.

Berry and Meekings style metric *(ME)*

Based on how closely a program conforms to a given set of style rules (module length, identifier length, comments, indentation, blank lines, line length, embedded spaces, constant definitions, reserved words, included files and gotos).

Black box reuse *(RS)*

Reuse of component "as is", without considering its contents. In this case, the component itself is not modified.

CASE *(GE)*

Computer-aided software engineering.

Class *(OO)*

A class describes the properties, the structure, and the behaviour of a group of similar objects. It serves as a pattern for objects of the same type. The description of a class includes:

- the name of the class

- the *protocol* of the class (see also *Member function (OO)* on page 490)

- the inheritance relations (see also *Superclass (OO)* on page 497)

- the data elements of the objects (see also *Instance variable (OO)* on page 489)

- the implementation of all operations applicable to the objects (implementation of *methods*; an exception to this is the *abstract* or deferred class)

Class library *(OO)*

"Standard" classes are managed in class libraries. These predefined "standard" classes represent universally applicable or frequently used software modules which, in addition, can be combined in any way with each other. They can either be used several times in one and the same application or be allocated to several applications. Class libraries support the reduction of implementation costs. User-specific classes are kept in user-specific class libraries.

Coarse-grained reuse*(RS)*

Refers to the reuse of large-size components, such as application subsystems, e.g. order-processing, database servers, user-interface packages, etc.

Component granularity (*RS*)

Refers to the size of manipulated components. It is mainly classified in fine-grained and coarse-grained categories.

Confidence (*ME*)

The (subjective) probability that a module, program or system performs its defined purpose satisfactorily (without failure) over a specified time in an environment other than that it was originally constructed and/or certified for.

Critical range (*ME*)

Metric values used to classify software into categories of acceptable, marginal and unacceptable.

Critical value (*ME*)

Metric value of a validated metric which is used to identify software which has unacceptable quality.

Cyclomatic number (*ME*)

Metric defined by McCabe based on graph theory to indicate the maximum number of linearly independent paths through the program. The cyclomatic number of a graph G with n vertices, e edges, and p connected components is $V(G) = e - n + p$.

Data abstraction (*OO*)

Data abstraction is a means for building abstract (high-level) primitives from data and more basic primitives. This is done by providing an abstract type and an associated set of operations. Data abstraction is generally combined with information-hiding *General reuse (RS)* on page 488. In object-oriented languages, the class concept provides data abstraction. (Note that this definition differs from the IEEE standard.)

Descendant class

See *Subclass (OO)* on page 497.

Design recovery (*RE*)

Design recovery is a subset of reverse engineering in which domain knowledge, external information, and deduction or fuzzy reasoning are added to the observations of the subject system to identify meaningful higher level abstractions beyond those obtained directly by examining the system itself.

Design recovery is distinguished by the sources and span of information it should handle. According to Ted Biggerstaff: "Design recovery recreated design abstractions from a combination of code, existing design documentation (if available), personal experience, and general knowledge about problem and application domains... Design recovery must reproduce all of the information required for a person to fully understand what a program does, how it does it, why it does it, and so forth. Thus, it deals with a far wider range of information than found in conventional software-engineering representations or code."

Difficulty *(ME)*

Halstead's software science metric, difficulty = (number of unique operators/2) * (total number of operands/number of unique operands). Reflects the effort required to understand, code, and maintain a given program or portion of code.

Direct metric *(ME)*

A metric that represents and defines a software quality factor, and which is valid by definition (e.g. mean time to software failure for the factor reliability).

Document accessibility *(ME)*

Metric that assesses the information describing, defining, specifying, reporting or certifying activities, requirements, procedures or results.

Domain *(RS)*

An application area for software products. Domains may describe *horizontal* product applications (for example, word processors, relational database managers) or *vertical* product applications (for example flight control, stock transaction processing systems, local authority tax collection systems).

Domain analysis *(RS)*

Study and formalization of domain knowledge. Specific activity of the development of reusable components.

Domain reuse *(RS)*

Reuse of components within a specific application domain (the semantics of the components is domain dependent).

Dynamic binding *(OO)*

Dynamic binding is the assignment of a method call to a method body during run-time; i.e. in this case binding does not take place during compile-time. The concept of polymorphism (see also *Polymorphism (OO)* on page 493) is implemented via this mechanism. (Note that this definition differs from the IEEE standard.)

Synonym: *late binding*

Edge weight *(RS)*

A weighting factor that relates two terms in a term space in a quantitative way.

Efficiency *(ME)*

Relative extent to which a resource is utilized (i.e. storage space, processing time, communication time).

Effort *(ME)*

Halstead's software science metric, effort = *difficulty * volume*. Represents the number of elementary mental discriminations required to understand, code, and maintain the module or program.

ELOC *(ME)*

Executable lines of code.

Encapsulation *(OO)*

Encapsulation is a means for grouping internal data or primitives and limiting external access. (Note that this definition differs from the IEEE standard.)

Entity-relationship notation *(GE)*

A diagrammatic notation used to illustrate the relationship between data items. The notation expresses relationships in the form of one-to-one, one-to-many and many-to-one connectors, which may be either mandatory (solid lines) or optional (dotted lines).

Environment independence *(ME)*

See *Hardware independence (ME)* on page 489 and *Software independence (ME)* on page 496.

Expendability *(ME)*

Criterion that recognizes those software attributes that provide for expansion of the data storage or function of the program.

Extensibility *(OO)*

Extensibility is a quality criterion of software systems. It describes how easily a software product can be adapted to changes in its specification. Extensibility is supported by subclassing.

Factor sample *(ME)*

A set of factor values which is drawn from the metrics database and used in metrics validation.

Factor value *(ME)*

A value (see also *Metric value (ME)* on page 491) of the direct metric that represents a factor.

Fan-in *(ME)*

The number of local flows into a procedure plus the number of global data structures from which a procedure retrieves information.

Fan-out *(ME)*

The number of local flows from a procedure plus the number of global data structures which the procedures updates.

Fine-grained reuse *(RS)*

Refers to the reuse of small-size components, such as I/O functions, file and database-access functions, data-structure manipulation functions; individual object classes enter in this category.

For and *With* reuse *(RS)*

Two techniques concerning reuse in a software development project:

- *for reuse* means making the extra effort to develop reusable components,

- *with reuse* means reusing existing components.

Ideally, both techniques should be used simultaneously.

Forward engineering *(RE)*

Forward engineering is the traditional process of moving from high-level abstractions and logical, implementation-independent designs to the physical implementation of a system.

While it may seem unnecessary—in view of the long-standing use of design and development terminology—to introduce a new term, the adjective "forward" has come to be used where it is necessary to distinguish this process from reverse engineering. Forward engineering follows a sequence of going from requirements through design to implementation.

Fuzzy retrieval *(RS)*

A type of retrieval that is not based on an exact match between the search condition and the classification information. This can be achieved by matching only part of the search condition, or by some other means of relaxing the search condition. Such a retrieval method will recover not only components that exactly match the search criteria, but also components that are similar. This is more useful than an exact match, because it can ensure that components are retrieved even when an exact match is impossible.

Garbage collection *(OO)*

Automatic garbage collection is—if existent—part of the run-time system of a language environment, dealing with the detection and release of memory occupied by instances which are no longer accessible.

General reuse *(RS)*

Reuse of components through different domains (the semantics of the components is domain independent). Also called *vertical reuse*.

Generality *(ME)*

Criteria that assess a component's ability to expand the usefulness of a given function beyond the existing module or program and its present scope.

Grey box reuse *(RS)*

Reuse of component by applying few changes to the component.

Halstead's software science *(ME)*

Set of metrics based on the number of unique operands and operators (see *Difficulty (ME)* on page 486, *Effort (ME)* on page 487, *Length (ME)* on page 490, *Vocabulary (ME)* on page 498 and *Volume (ME)* on page 498).

Hardware independence *(ME)*

Percentage of machine dependent code and machine dependent data representation.

Henry and Kafuras information flow *(ME)*

Metric based on the connections between a procedure and its environment (see *Fan-in (ME)* on page 487 and *Fan-out (ME)* on page 487). Cp = (fan-in * fan-out)**2.

Horizontal product *(GE)*

A product intended for use by more than one industry sector.

Hybrid metric *(ME)*

Metric composed of both code and structure information in order to capture several facets of a relationship.

Information hiding *(OO)*

Information hiding is the intentional concealing of internal data or operations. Implementation details are not visible externally. (Note that this definition differs from the IEEE standard.)

Inheritance *(OO)*

Inheritance is a structuring mechanism with respect to class development. A class can be defined by extending or modifying existing classes. The former is called a subclass and the latter a superclass. Subclasses inherit the instance variables and methods of the superclass. The differences from the superclasses are defined in the respective subclass. Inheritance results in a hierarchical order of classes that may extend over several levels. A distinction is made between single inheritance (see *Single inheritance (OO)* on page 496) and multiple inheritance (see *Multiple inheritance (OO)* on page 491).

Instance *(OO)*

The instances of a class are the objects described by the class. The different instances of a class differ only in the *values* of their instance variables, not in their operations. Instances exist during the run-time of an object-oriented system and are the interacting units of this system.

Instance variable *(OO)*

Instance variables are variables for which a local storage space is reserved in every class instance (object). The values of these variables represent the actual status of an instance and can accordingly be different for every instance. The values can be changed by the methods (some object-oriented programming languages deviate from this).

Synonym: *Attribute (OO)* on page 484.

Instantiation *(OO)*

The generation of new instances (objects) during run time of the object-oriented software system. Structure and behaviour of the instances generated are defined by their classes respectively.

Large-scale reuse *(RS)*

See *Coarse-grained reuse(RS)* on page 484.

Length *(ME)*

Halstead's software science metric, length = total number of operators + total number of operands.

LOC *(ME)*

Lines of code.

Measure *(ME)*

To ascertain or appraise by comparing to a standard; to apply a metric.

Measurement *(ME)*

1. The act or process of measuring

2. A figure, extent, or amount obtained by measuring

Member function *(OO)*

Member function is a concept specific to C++. A member function is part of a class in the same way as a *method*. A member function is part of the class protocol and can directly access the internals of the class. In C++, the opposite are "friend functions", which are not part of the class but can still access the internals of the class.

Message *(OO)*

Messages support the interaction between objects. With regard to their class definition, objects answer to incoming messages by executing one of their methods. The message specifies the receiving object, the method to be executed, and its arguments.

Synonym: *method call*

Method *(OO)*

Methods implement the operations of a class. A method is a procedure or function local to the class. The methods are authorized to access instance variables and to change their values. Methods are activated by messages.

Metric *(ME)*

Quantitative measure of a software attribute.

Metric validation *(ME)*

The act or process of ensuring that a metric correctly predicts or accesses a quality factor.

Metric value *(ME)*

An element from the range of a metric; a metric output.

Metrics framework *(ME)*

A tool used for organizing, selecting, communicating and evaluating the required quality attributes for a software system; a hierarchical breakdown of factors, subfactors and metrics for a software system.

Metrics sample *(ME)*

A set of metrics values which is drawn from the metrics database and used in metrics validation.

MTTF *(ME)*

Mean Time to Failure.

Multiple inheritance *(OO)*

With multiple inheritance, a subclass can have more than one superclass. The class typically inherits the union of the instance variables and methods of its superclasses. The classes will thus be arranged in a DAG (directed acyclic graph) structure. Many object-oriented languages do not support multiple inheritance.

Object *(OO)*

Objects describe specific and abstract phenomena of the application area. An object consists of
— instance variables
— methods (operations)

An object is a self-contained unit, which is manipulated by the operations assigned to it. Objects are described by classes. They are accordingly referred to as instances of these classes.

Object-based language *(OO)*

A programming language is said to be object based if it supports data abstraction explicitly by language constructs. However, these languages may lack the basic concepts of fully object-oriented languages, i.e. classes, class instances, inheritance, and dynamic binding.

Object-oriented design *(OO)*

Object-oriented design outlines a section of the real world. The design includes a choice of suitable objects and the specification of their communication relations. In addition, the definition of the associated classes and their hierarchical arrangement is determined by further abstraction. The classes and objects must not only meet the requirements of the application environment, but must also be structured with regard to existing class libraries as well as extensibility and reusability.

Object-oriented language *(OO)*

An object-oriented language supports at least the following four concepts by language constructs:
1) Objects as abstract units
2) The association of objects to classes
3) The organization of classes in inheritance hierarchies
4) Polymorphism by dynamic binding.

Object-oriented programming *(OO)*

Object oriented programming consists of definitions and programming, implementation of classes and arranging them within a class hierarchy. The classes result from the respective object-oriented design and are the syntactic units (system components) of the software development. The implementation of the objects as well as the sequence of object communication is determined in the class.

Object-oriented software system *(OO)*

A running system is based on instances and their communication. Communication is executed via messages to which the instances respond by executing methods. The static description of an object-oriented software system consists of a structured set of classes (modular units).

Operand *(ME)*

Common term for variables, constants and labels.

Operator *(ME)*

Arithmetical symbols (+, –, etc...), command names (WHILE, FOR, ...), and special symbols (equal, parentheses, ...). Indicate the action to be performed on operands.

Opportunistic reuse *(RS)*

Practice of reuse in an informal way without taking place in a global reuse improvement strategy.

Organized reuse *(RS)*

Practice of reuse according a long-term reuse programme plan.

Packaging *(GE)*

The additional code required to make a component into a self-contained entity that can be reused in another application.

Persistent object *(OO)*

Persistent objects are objects whose life is not limited by the run-time of an object-oriented software system. The objects are preserved over a long period of time by having them stored in a non-volatile storage medium. This is usually controlled by additional features such as a special class or an object-oriented database system.

Polymorphism *(OO)*

Polymorphism is the capability of creating references to objects whose class association is not known at first. Class association is first determined during run-time. An incoming message will cause the method of the associated class to be executed.

Predictive assessment *(ME)*

The process of using a predictor metric(s) to predict the value of another metric.

Predictive metric *(ME)*

A metric which is used to predict the values of another metric.

Process metric *(ME)*

Metric used to measure characteristics of the methods, techniques, and tools employed in acquiring, developing, verifying, operating and changing the software system.

Process step *(ME)*

Any task performed in the development, implementation or maintenance of software (e.g., identify the software components of a system as part of the design).

Product family *(RS)*

Set of products with commonalities (functionalities, architecture, ...) that are interesting to consider for their common characteristics.

Product-line reuse *(RS)*

Reuse of components within a specific application family (the semantics of the components is bound to a specific application type).

Product metric *(ME)*

Metric used to measure the characteristics of the documentation and code.

Protocol *(OO)*

The protocol is the description of the object interface within a class. It contains all messages (method names) valid for the class. (Note that this definition differs from the IEEE standard.)

Quality attribute *(ME)*

A characteristic of software; a generic term applying to factors, sub-factors, or metric values.

Quality factor *(ME)*

An attribute of software that contributes to its quality.

Quality requirement *(ME)*

A requirement that a software attribute be present in software to satisfy a contract, standard, specification, or other formally imposed document.

Quality sub-factor *(ME)*

A decomposition of a quality factor or quality sub-factor.

Readability *(ME)*

Ease of effort to read and understand a module or a text.

Re-documentation *(RE)*

Re-documentation is the creation or revision of a semantically equivalent representation within the same relative abstraction level. The resulting forms of representation are usually considered alternative views (for example, data flow, data structure, and control flow) intended for a human audience.

Re-documentation is the simplest and oldest form of reverse engineering, and many consider it to be an unintrusive, weak form of restructuring. The "re"-prefix implies that the intent is to recover documentation about the subject system that existed or should have existed.

Some common tools used to perform re-documentation are pretty printers (which display a code listing in an improved form), diagram generators (which create diagrams directly from code, reflecting control flow or code structure), and cross-reference listing generators. A key goal of these tools is to provide easier ways to visualize relationship among program components so you can recognize and follow paths clearly.

Re-engineering *(RE)*

Re-engineering, also known as both renovation and reclamation, is the examination and alteration of a subject system to reconstitute it in a new form and the subsequent implementation of the new form.

Re-engineering generally includes some form of reverse engineering (to achieve a more abstract description) followed by some form of forward engineering or restructuring. This may include modifications with respect to new requirements not met by the original system. For example, during the re-engineering of information-management systems, an organization generally reassesses how the system implements high-level business rules and makes modifications to conform to changes in the business for the future.

Repository *(RS)*

A database that allows the storage of reusable components, together with their associated documentation and classification.

Repository service *(RS)*

A tool or set of tools providing support for the management and maintenance of a *repository*.

Restructuring *(RE)*

Restructuring is the transformation from one representation to another at the same relative abstraction level, while preserving the subject system's external behavior (functionality and semantics).

A restructuring transformation is often one of appearance, such as altering code to improve its structure in the traditional sense of structured design. The term "restructuring" came into popular use from the code-to-code transform that recasts a program from an unstructured form. However, the term has a broader meaning that recognizes the application of similar transformations and recasting techniques in reshaping data models, design plans, and requirements structures. Data normalization, for example, is a data-to-data restructuring transform to improve a logical data model in the database design process.

Reusable asset/component *(RS)*

Building block that is acquired or developed for the solution of multiple problems.

Reuse introduction/adoption strategy *(RS)*

Set of policies and associated action plan to introduce and practise reuse in the most profitable way for the target company.

Reuse library *(RS)*

A repository of reusable components.

Reuse maturity assessment *(RS)*

The assessment of how well a company is able to take advantage of its reuse opportunities.

Reuse maturity model *(RS)*

A model to assess the reuse maturity of a company.

Reuse scope *(RS)*

Dimensions of the space where reuse is possible.

Reverse engineering *(RE)*

Reverse engineering is the process of analyzing a subject system to

- identify the system's components and their interrelationships, and

- create representations of the system in another form or at a higher level of abstraction.

Reverse engineering generally involves extracting design artifacts and building or synthesizing abstractions that are less implementation-dependent. While reverse engineering often involves an existing functional system as its subject, this is not a requirement. You can perform reverse engineering starting from any level of abstraction or at any stage of the life cycle.

Reverse engineering in and of itself does not involve changing the subject system or creating a new system based on the reverse-engineered subject system. It is a process of examination, not a process of change or replication.

In spanning the life cycle stages, reverse engineering covers a broad range starting from the existing implementation, recapturing or recreating the design, and deciphering the requirements actually implemented by the subject system.

There are many subareas of reverse engineering. Two subareas that are widely referred to are *Re-documentation (RE)* on page 494 and *Design recovery (RE)* on page 485.

Revision *(GE)*

A new version of a component or application that is created to allow further development.

Sample software *(ME)*

Software selected from a current or completed project from which data can be obtained for use in preliminary testing of data collection and metric computation procedures.

Saved effort *(ME)*

The difference between the effort needed to reuse a component and the effort needed to write it from scratch.

Self-descriptiveness *(ME)*

Criterion that measures how well a component explains its functions. It is provided by standard formats, prologue comments on each module, etc.

Single inheritance *(OO)*

With single inheritance a subclass has one superclass only. The classes are thus arranged in a hierarchical tree structure.

SLOC *(ME)*

Source lines of code.

Small-scale *(RS)*

See *Data abstraction (OO)* on page 485.

Software component *(ME)*

General term used to refer to a software system or an element such as module, unit, data or document.

Software independence *(ME)*

Measures the dependence of the applications on the software environment by counting the number of system references, including utilities, library routines and other operating system facilities, and the number of input/output references.

Software quality metric *(ME)*

A function whose inputs are software data and whose output is a single (numerical) value that can be interpreted as the degree to which software processes a given attribute that affects its quality.

Software reusable asset *(RS)*

Aggregate of different software life-cycle information composing a software building block.

Software reuse *(RS)*

Process of creating software systems from existing software assets rather than building software systems from scratch.

Subclass *(OO)*

A subclass is a class which inherits instance variables and methods from one or several other classes (superclasses). These inherited features can be modified or extended in the subclass.

Synonym: *descendent class*

Superclass *(OO)*

A superclass is a class within the inheritance hierarchy. It describes common characteristics of the respective subclasses which inherit instance variables and methods.

Synonym: *ancestor class*

Systematic reuse *(RS)*

See *Opportunistic reuse (RS)* on page 492 and *Organized reuse (RS)* on page 492.

Target reuser *(RS)*

Refers to the future customer of the component.

Term *(RS)*

A type of keyword used in the classification of components in a repository (see *Repository (RS)* on page 494) that is based on a controlled vocabulary and a quantitative method of relating terms one to another.

Term space *(RS)*

The combination of a set of terms and a structure that relates them.

Thesaurus *(RS)*

See *Term space (RS)* on page 497.

Understandability *(ME)*

The attribute of the software that provides explanation on its content and its possible use (see also *Self-descriptiveness (ME)* on page 496).

Usability *(ME)*

Factor that measures the effort for the training needed to operate the software (e.g. familiarization, input preparation, execution, output interpretation).

Validated metric *(ME)*

A metric whose values have been statistically associated with corresponding quality factor values.

Variability *(RS)*

The variation in requirements between different potential reusers of a component.

Verifiability *(ME)*

Effort needed to verify the specified software operation and performance relative to its specifications and requirements.

Vertical product *(GE)*

A product intended for use within a single industry sector.

Vocabulary *(ME)*

Halstead's software science metric, vocabulary = number of unique operators + number of unique operands.

Volume *(ME)*

Halstead's software science metric, volume = $length*$ $\log_2(vocabulary)$. Represents the number of bits to store the program in memory.

Weight *(term weight) (RS)*

The numerical value given to a term within a classification method.

White box reuse *(RS)*

Reuse of component by applying major changes to the component.

E References

[Albrechtsen92] H. Albrechtsen, *Software Information Systems: information retrieval techniques*, in [Hall92b].

[Arango92] Guillermo Arango, *Domain Analysis Methods*, Schlumberger Laboratory for Computer Science, Austin, Texas 78720-0015.

[Bardiaux89] Michel Bardiaux, Philippe Delhaise: *Step-by-step Transition from Dusty-deck FORTRAN to Object-Oriented Programming*; in: Proceedings to: Reuse, Maintenance and Reverse Engineering of Software 12'89.

[Barnes91] *Making Reuse Cost-Effective*, Bruce H. Barnes and Terry B. Bollinger, IEEE Software, January 1991, pp. 13-24.

[Benson91] D. Benson, *ADGE Systems Architecture Analysis*, Domain Analysis Workshop, SPC-91186-MC. Herndon, Virginia: Software Productivity Consortium, September 26-27, 1991.

[Berard93] E. V. Berard, *Essays on object-oriented software engineering*, Volume I, Prentice-Hall, 1993.

[Bieman91] J. M. Bieman: *Deriving Measures of Software Reuse in Object Oriented Systems*, Technical Report Colorado State University, CS-91-112, July 1991.

[Boehm81] B. W. Boehm: *Software Engineering Economics*, Englewood Cliffs: Prentice-Hall, 1981.

[Boehm88] B. W. Boehm: *A Spiral Model of Software Development and Enhancement*, IEEE, pp. 61-72, May 1988.

[Booch91] G. Booch, *Object-Oriented Design with Applications*, Benjamin Cummings, 1991.

[Brooks75] *The Mythical Man-Month*, Fredrick P. Brooks, Addison-Wesley, 1975.

[Brown92] Alan J. Brown: *The use of non-formal information in reverse engineering and reuse*. PhD thesis department of computer science, Brunel University 1992.

[Buschman93] Frank Buschman: *Rational Architectures for Object Oriented Software Systems*. Journal of Object Oriented Programming, September 1993.

[Campbell87] Campbell R., Johnston G., Russo V., *Choices (Class Hierarchical Open Interface for Custom Embedded Systems)*, ACM Operating Systems Review, 21(3):9-17, July, 1987.

[Campbell92] *Choices, Frameworks and Refinement*, Roy H. Campbell, Nayeem Islam, Peter Madany, Computing Systems, Vol. 5, No. 3, Summer 1992, pp. 217-257.

[Council directive] Council directive of 14 May 1991 on the legal protection of computer programs published in the Official Journal of the European Communities 17 May 1991.

[DACS79] Shirley A. Gloss-Soler, *The DACS Glossary. A Bibliography of Software Engineering Terms*. Rome Air Development Center, Griffiths Air Force Base, October, 1979.

[Dietrich89] K.W. Dietrich Jr, L.R. Nackman, and F.Gracer: *Saving a legacy with objects*, in: OOPSLA '89 Conference Proceedings, Special issue of SIGPLAN Notices 24(10):77-83, 1989.

[Duntemann90] Jeff Duntemann and Chris Marinacci: *New Objects For Old Structures*; in: Byte April 1990.

[Ellis91] C. A. Ellis et al., *Groupware - some issues and experiences*, Communications of the ACM 34(1):38-58, January 1991.

[EXPRESS92] *EXPRESS Language Reference Manual*, ISO TC184/SC4/WG1, N151, August 1992.

[Feldman90] S.I. Feldman et al: *A Fortran-to-C converter*; in: Computing Science Technical Report No. 149, AT&T Bell Laboratories, 1990.

[Gaffney92] J. E. Gaffney, Jr. and R. D. Cruickshank: *A general economics model for software reuse*, Proc. 14th Int. Conf. on Software Engineering, IEEE, Melbourne, 1992, pp 327-337.

[Gamma93] Design Patterns: *Abstraction and Reuse of Object-Oriented Design*, Erich Gamma, Richard Helm, Ralph Johnson, John Vlissides, ECOOP 93, pp. 406-431.

[Garnett90] E.S. Garnett, J.A. Mariani: *Software Reclamation*; in: Software Engineering Journal May 1990.

[Griss93] M. L. Griss / Hewlett-Packard Co.: *Software reuse: From library to factory*, IBM Systems Journal, Vol 32, No 4, 1993.

[Hall92a] P A V Hall: *Overview of reverse engineering and reuse research*, in: Information and Software Technology April 1992.

[Hall92b] P. A. V. Hall, *Software Reuse and Reverse Engineering in Practice*, Chapman & Hall 1992.

[Heard77] J. R. Herd, J. N. Postak, W. E. Russell, and K. R. Stewart, *Software cost estimation study: Study results*, Final Technical Report, RADC-TR-77-200, Doty Associated, Inc., Rockville, Md.

[IEEE83] *IEEE Standard Glossary for Software Engineering Terminology*, ANSI/IEEE Std 729-1983.

[ISO 9126] *Information technology - Software product evaluation - Quality characteristics and guidelines for their use*, Draft International Standard ISO/IEC DIS 9126, UDC 681.3.06.006.83.

[Isoda92] *Experience report on software reuse project: Its structure, activities and statistical results*, Sadahiro Isoda, In Proc. 14th Int. Conf. on Software Engineering, IEEE, Melbourne, 1992, pp 320-326.

[Jacobson91] Ivar Jacobson, F. Lindstroem: *Re-engineering of old systems to an object-oriented architecture*; in: Proceedings of OOPSLA'91 and Proceedings of TOOLS'91.

[Jacobson92] Ivar Jacobson et al., *Object-Oriented Software Engineering: A Use Case Driven Approach*, Addison Wesley, 1992.

[Karlsson92] *Weighted term spaces for relaxed search*, Even-André Karlsson, Guttorm Sindre, Sivert Sørumgård, Eirik Tryggeseth, In Proc. 1st Int'l Conf. on Information and Knowledge Management (CIKM'92), Baltimore, 5-8 Nov. 1992.

[Kotler88] Philip Kotler, *Marketing Management: analysis, planning, implementation, and control*, sixth edition, Prentice Hall, Inc., 1988.

[Krasner88] Krasner G.E., Pope S.T., *A cookbook for using the model-view-controller user interface paradigm in Smalltalk-80*, Journal of Object-Oriented Programming, 1(3):26-49, August-September, 1988.

[Krueger92] C.W. Krueger: *Software Reuse*, ACM Computing Surveys, vol. 24, No.2, June 1992.

[Larsson93] J. Larsson: *Development for reuse in the fire alarm system domain*, EP Frameworks, Jan 13, 1993, REBOOT-3083.

[MacApp89] MacApp: The Expandable Macintosh Application version 2.0B9, Apple Computers 1989, Cupertino, CA, USA.

[Martin91] Martin, Jackoway and Ranganathan: *Software Reuse Across Continents*, Proceedings of the 4th Annual Workshop on Software Reuse, Virginia Center for Innovative Technology, 1991.

[Matsumoto89] Y. Matsumoto, Y. Ohno, *Japanese Perspectives in Software Engineering*, Addison-Wesley, 1989.

[McCall80] James A. McCall and Mike T. Matsumoto, *Software Quality Assurance*, vol. II, RADC-TR-80-109, vol. II, April 1980, Griffiths AFB NY 13441-5700.

[McNicholl85] D.G. McNicholl et al., *Common Ada Missile Packages, Technical report AFATL-TR-85-17*, Eglin Air Force Base, FL, June 1985.

[Miyazaki85] Yokio Miyazaki and Kuniaki Mori, *COCOMO Evaluation and Tailoring*, CH2139-4/85/0000/0292@IEEE 1985

[Mills87] Harlan D. Mills, Michael Dyer and Richard C. Linger, *Cleanroom Software Engineering*, IEEE Software, September 1987, pp. 465-484.

[NATO91a] Nato Communications and Information Systems Committee: *Software Reuse in NATO*, 1991.

[NATO91b] Contel corporation, *Standard for Software reuse procedures*, NATO contract number 5957-ADA, 1991.

[NATO-STD] *Draft Standard for the Development of Reusable Software Components, Management of Software Reuse Library and Reuse Procedures*, Nato Unclassified, AC/317 (WG/2) N/311, November 1991.

[Ostertag92] E. Ostertag, J. Hendler, R. Prieto-Díaz, C. Braun, *Computing Similarity in a Reuse Library System*: An AI-Based Approach, ACM Transactions on Software Engineering and Methodology, July 1992.

[Pagenberg89] Pagenberg,J ,Geissler, *License Agreements*, Heymann 1989.

[Paulk91] M.C. Paulk, B. Curtis, M.B. Chrissis, et al., "Capability Maturity Model for Software", Software Engineering Institute. CMU/SEI-91-TR-24, August 1991 (updated v1.1: CMU/SEI-91-TR-25).

[Pontén91] *Overview of IT4-Reuse*, Lars Pontén, Telesoft Uppsala, Sept. 1991.

[Poore93] Poore, J. H., Mills, Harlan D., and Mutchler, David, *Planning and Certifying Software System Reliability*, IEEE Software, January 1993, pp. 88-99, 1993.

[Poulin93] J.S. Poulin, J.M.Caruso, D.R. Hancock: *The business case for software reuse*, IBM Systems Journal, Vol 32, No 4, 1993.

[Poulin94] J.S. Poulin, *Balancing the Need for Large Corporate and Small Domain-Specific Reuse Libraries*, Proc. of the 1994 ACM Symposium on Applied Computing (SAC'94).

[Prieto-Díaz85] R. Prieto-Díaz, *A Software Classification Scheme*, PhD thesis, University of California, Irvine, 1985.

[Prieto-Díaz87] *Classifying software for reusability*, R. Prieto-Díaz and Peter Freeman, IEEE Software, January 1987, pp. 6-16.

[PTO] Patent and Trademark Office, U. S. Department of Commerce. *Manual of Patent Examining Procedure*. Washington, DC. Publication 605. Section 2106.

[RAG92] *Reuse Adoption GuideBook*, Software Productivity Consortium Services Corporation, SPC -92051-CMC, version 01.00.03 November 1992.

[Ranghanathan57] S. R. Ranghanathan, *Prolegomena to Library Classification*, The Garden City Press Ltd. 1957.

[Reenskaug92] Trygve Reenskaug et al., *OORASS: Seamless support for the creation and maintenance of object oriented systems*, Journal of Object Oriented Programming, 5(6):27-41, October 1992.

[Remer82] Daniel Remer: *Legal Care for Your Software*, Addison-Wesley Publishing Company, 1982.

[Rumbaugh91] James Rumbaugh et al., *Object-Oriented Modelling and Design*, Prentice Hall 1991.

[Runeson92] Runeson, Per, and Wohlin, Claes, *Usage Modelling: The Basis for Statistical Quality Control*, Proceedings 10th Annual Software Reliability Symposium, Denver, Colorado, pp. 77–84, 1992.

[Salton89] Gerard Salton, *Automatic Text Processing: The transformation, analysis and retrieval of information by computer*, Reading, Massachusetts: Addison-Wesley, 1989

[Scherlund90] Kjell Scherlund, *Mot nya djärva språk - Modellering i gruppsamarbete med gemensam grafik*, SISU report #14/90, SISU, Box 1250, 164 28 Kista, Sweden, 1990 (In Swedish).

[Schmucker86] K.J. Schmucker: *MACAPP: An Application Framework*. Byte. Vol 11. No 8. pp.189-193, 1986.

[Schwanke89] Robert W. Schwanke and Michael A. Platoff: *Cross References Are Features*; in: Second International Workshop on Software Configuration Management. ACM Press, November, 1989. Also available as SigPlan Notices, November 1989.

[Schwanke90] Robert W. Schwanke: *An Intelligent Tool for Re-engineering Software Modularity*; internal report Siemens Corporate Research, Inc. Princeton, NJ, December 1990.

[SEL-84-101] *Manager's Handbook for Software Development*, Revision 1, Software Engineering Laboratory Series, SEL-84-101, November 1990.

[Shlaer88] Shlaer, S. L. , Mellor S. J., *Object-Oriented Systems Analysis - Modeling the world in data*, Prentice Hall, 1988.

[Shlaer89] S. Shlaer and S. J. Mellor, *An Object-Oriented Approach to Domain Analysis*, Software Engineering Notes, July 1989.

[Sindre92a] Guttorm Sindre, Even-André Karlsson, and Patricia Paul: *Heuristics for maintaining a term space structure for relaxed search*, Proc. Int'l Conf. in Database and Expert System Applications (DEXA'92), Valencia, 2-4 Sep. 1992, 6 p.

[Sindre92b] Guttorm Sindre, Even-André Karlsson, and Tor Stålhane: *Software reuse in an educational perspective*, Proc. 6th SEI Conf. on Software Engineering Education (CSEE'92), San Diego, 5-7 Oct. 1992, 14 p.

[SPC92] *Domain Engineering Guidebook*, SPC-92019-CMC version 01.00.03, Software Productivity Consortium, December 1992.

[STARS92a] *Proceedings of STARS'92*. Arlington, Virginia: STARS Technology Center.

[STARS92b] STARS *Reuse Concepts, Volume I - Conceptual Framework for reuse Processes*, February 1992. version 1.0.

[Stroustrup90] Stroustrup & Ellis, *The annotated C++ reference manual*, Addison-Wesley, 1990.

[Tichy88] W. Tichy, *Tools for Software Configuration Management*, ACM Workshop on Software Version and Configuration Management, Grassau, Jan. 27-29, 1988.

[Tracz92] W. Tracz: *Software Reuse Technical Opportunities*, Proceedings of DARPA Software Technology Conference, Los Angeles, CA, April 28-30, 1992.

[UDC79] Geoffrey Robinson, *UDC: A Brief Introduction*, International Federation for Documentation 1979.

[Verilog90] Verilog Logiscope, Technical presentation LOG/TP.A, December 1990.

[Ward92] Paul Ward: *Object Oriented Extensions of the Ward-Mellor Approach*; Software Development Concepts. In: DEC College CASE Methoden'92.

[Whittaker93] Whittaker, James A., and Poore, J. H., *Markov Analysis of Software Specifications*, ACM Transactions on Software Engineering Methodology, Vol. 2, No. 1, January 1993, pp. 93–106, 1993.

[Willars91] H. Willars, *Amplification of Business Cognition through Modelling Techniques*, Proceedings of the 11th IEA Congress, Paris, July 1991.

[Wilson90] Wilson D.A., Rosenstein L.S., Shafer D., *C++ Programming with MacApp*, Addison-Wesley, 1990.

[Wirfs90] Rebecca J. Wirfs-Brock and Ralph E. Johnson, *Surveying current research in object-oriented design*, Communication of the ACM, 33(9), pp. 104-124, September 1990, Special CACM issue on object-oriented design

[Wood88] Murray Wood, Ian Sommerville, *An information retrieval system for software components*, Software Engineering Journal, September 1988.

[Wood89] J. Wood and D. Silver, *Joint Application Design*, Wiley, 1989.

[Zimmer90] J.A. Zimmer: *Restructuring for Style*; in: Software-Practice and Experience April 1990.

Index